The Sociobiology Debate

The Sociobiology Debate

Readings on Ethical
and Scientific Issues

Edited by

Arthur L. Caplan

Harper & Row, Publishers

New York, Hagerstown, San Francisco, London

FIRST EDITION

Designed by Janice Stern

Library of Congress Cataloging in Publication Data
Main entry under title:

The Sociobiology debate.

   Includes index.
   1. Sociobiology—Addresses, essays, lectures.
I. Caplan, Arthur L.
GN365.9.S62   1978   301.2   77-3742   77-7374 pbk
ISBN 0-06-010633-6   78 79 80 81 82 10 9 8 7 6 5 4 3 2 1
ISBN 0-06-090628-6 pbk   78 79 80 81 82 10 9 8 7 6 5 4 3 2 1

Contents

PART IV. THE BIOLOGY OF SOCIOBIOLOGY

PART V. THE CONTEMPORARY DEBATE

Foreword

Arthur Caplan has performed an important service by skillfully assembling the scattered materials of the emerging debate over sociobiology. He has correctly identified the debate as the continuance of the historic conflict created in the social sciences and humanities by the mechanistic examination of human nature through the instruments of conventional biology.

I say conventional because sociobiology is a discipline, not a particular theory. By any other name—biosociology, social biology, or whatever—the systematic study of the biological basis of social behavior would now exist and be growing in substance. Its domain is the tens of thousands of social animal species, including *Homo sapiens*. Human sociobiology is only one part of this inevitable enterprise. Its findings are important but not essential to the principles of the discipline. In fact, general sociobiology allows three alternative states for our species:

1. Natural selection has exhausted the genetic variability underlying social behavior: human populations are uniform with respect to the social genotype. Furthermore, the genotype prescribes only the capacity for culture; in this sense human sociality has been freed from the genes.

2. The social genotype is uniform, but it prescribes a substantial amount of instinct-like behavior.

3. Some variability in human social behavior has a genetic basis, and, as a consequence, at least some behavior is genetically constrained.

While preparing *Sociobiology: The New Synthesis,* I was not committed to any of these alternatives by preconception. But the evidence immediately available from human genetics, psychology, and anthropology seemed to leave room only for the last conclusion, that human social behavior is to some extent genetically constrained over the entire species and furthermore subject to genetic variation within the species. This evidence is persuasively diversified in nature. For all its impressive variability, human social behavior constitutes a small subset of all of the realized patterns of behavior displayed by the tens of thousands of species of ants, termites, bees, wasps, fish, reptiles, birds, mammals and other social creatures on earth. While some of the most general human traits, including language and kinship classification, are unique and not phylogenetically traceable, those that can be compared with the repertories of animal species, including facial expressions and the most elementary forms of social play, place human beings closest to the Old World monkeys and apes. This result the zoologist should expect if monkeys and apes are our closest phylogenetic relatives (which these creatures appear to be on the basis of independent anatomical and biochemical evidence) and if human social behavior is to some extent genetically influenced.

The most emotion-laden and least rationally controlled human behaviors are generally consistent in their details with sociobiological theory. These categories include incest inhibition, bond formation, parent-offspring conflict, sex-biased infanticide, primitive warfare, territoriality, and sexual practice. They are more simply explained by the hypothesis of genetically based predisposition than by the hypothesis of purely cultural determination.

As Richard H. Wills has recently shown,* still another line of evidence may be provided by the severely mentally retarded, who have lost almost all forms of the culturally transmitted, most distinctive human forms of behavior but retain a remarkably complete repertory of mammalian behavior. This repertory comprises possessiveness, territoriality, affective bonding mediated by nonverbal signals, play, and sexual response. Finally, genetic mutants are known that affect various forms of social behavior; and the most carefully controlled of the twin studies, such as those by John C. Loehlin and Robert C. Nichols** on the 1962 National Merit Scholarship applicants, strongly indicate the existence

---

* *The Institutionalized Severely Retarded* (Springfield, Illinois: C. C. Thomas, 1973).

** *Heredity, Environment, and Personality: A Study of 850 Sets of Twins* (Austin, Texas: University of Texas Press, 1976).

of a moderate amount of heritability in a wide range of mental abilities and personality traits basic to the development of social relationships.

I believe it fair to say that those working in general sociobiology up to 1975 found none of this kind of information in the least surprising. It was my own intention in writing the final chapter of *Sociobiology* ("From Sociobiology to Sociology") to identify some of the distinctive forms of human behavior in a way that suggests their accessibility to the newer biological principles and methods. I hoped to make the connection compelling enough so that social scientists would add sociobiology to the corpus of social theory. Sociobiology and the broader evolutionary theory of which it is a part appeared to me and to others to be the most direct bridge from the natural sciences to the study of human nature and thence to the social sciences.

The critical response to human sociobiology, which is well represented in this anthology, was unexpected in two respects. The political objections forcefully made by the Sociobiology Study Group of Science for the People in particular took me by surprise. In retrospect there appear to be two levels of meaning in their protestations. The outer meaning is the literal argument they gave, that "genetic determinism" of any kind will inevitably be used to justify reactionary political doctrines, racism, sexism, aggression, and other undesirable social responses associated with acceptance of the status quo. The deeper meaning, in my opinion, was the challenge they sensed to their own authority as natural scientists devoted to the study of social problems.

The responses of many social scientists, both favorable and critical, were also initially stronger than some of my colleagues and I had expected. Our hope had been that scholars in the social sciences and humanities would acquire expertise in sociobiology and apply it to the analysis of human behavior; *then* the judgment of human sociobiology could be made. But the judgment was passed immediately by some critics, on the basis of how originally and fully other zoologists and I had been able to explain human sociality in this first amateur's approach. Thus Marshall Sahlins, in *The Use and Abuse of Biology* (1976), found kin selection theory wanting in the explanation of kinship systems and promptly rejected all of human sociobiology. This kind of overreaction is both complimentary and discouraging.

Contemporary general sociobiology might at best explain a tiny fraction of human social behavior in a novel manner. Its full applicability will be settled only by a great deal more imaginative research by both evolutionary biologists and social scientists. In this sense the true, creative debate has just begun.

EDWARD O. WILSON

Museum of Comparative Zoology
Harvard University
Cambridge, Massachusetts
November 1, 1977

Introduction

It would not be a great exaggeration to claim that sociobiology, as it has been presented in the writings of its key advocates, has been endowed with a scope and range that is beyond the capacities of specialists from any single discipline. The very boldness of the theory in attending to subjects in biology, the humanities, the social sciences, and history has elicited such a cacophony of responses from so many diverse sources that it is difficult to distinguish and understand the nature of the issues which are being discussed. The situation confronting those interested in sociobiology is made further complex by the fact that the theory has become the locus for discussion of a number of provocative questions about the nature of science, scientific expertise, and scientific responsibility.

The sheer magnitude of the number of controversial issues which are present in discussions of sociobiology poses a considerable dilemma with regard to compiling papers about the field. It is simply impossible to achieve a comprehensive review of the subject in the confines of a single volume. This is especially so since a large number of issues pertinent to sociobiology seem to merit separate book-length treatments in their own right. Readers of the selections included in this volume should thus understand that the volume is far from being a comprehensive treatment of the subject. There are a number of weighty and vital issues which have been omitted for no reasons other than the arbitrary dictates of space, the capriciousness of editorial tastes, or the limitations of editorial expertise in a wide variety of disciplines.

Given the magnitude of the subject, it seems important to say a few words about the sorts of considerations that did play a role in the selection of materials for the book.

1

First, an attempt has been made to draw together in one place a number of frequently cited papers concerned with the scientific and philosophical significance of social behavior in animals and human beings that have, until now, only been available in scattered professional journals and books.

Second, special emphasis has been placed on the inclusion of materials that seemed representative of the historical antecedents of contemporary sociobiology. There has been a tendency on the part of both advocates and critics of sociobiology to downplay or even ignore historical material as either conceptually inadequate or simply irrelevant to modern concerns. This is unfortunate since both views are simply wrong. The historical treatment of the subject of social behavior has affected the direction of argumentation concerning contemporary sociobiological accounts as much if not more than any specific model, mechanism, or conclusion of sociobiological science. This is especially true in light of previous efforts to draw ethical, political, and philosophical conclusions from biological findings. There is a good deal of value for those concerned with evaluating sociobiology that can be derived from both a careful attention to the nature of past scientific claims concerning social behavior and a thoughtful appreciation of the mistakes, misperceptions, and misunderstandings among earlier generations of scientists interested in social phenomena.

Third, the selections in the volume are intended to reflect a concern with issues that involve philosophical or conceptual puzzles rather than scientific or empirical disputes about the specific details of sociobiological theorizing. Central to this concern is the question of what is the relevance of sociobiological theory for human behavior and self-knowledge. Sociobiology is the latest and most strident of a series of efforts in the biological sciences to direct scientific and humanistic attention toward the question of what is, fundamentally, the nature of human nature. Sociobiologists believe that evolutionary inquiry into the origins and development of social behavior in organisms will shed great light on traditional philosophical puzzles concerning the ability of humans to be both influenced by and freed from the limits set by their biological constitutions.

Questions concerning the importance, validity, and feasibility of inquiring into the biological nature of the human animal become particularly vexing when they touch upon properties that are commonly thought to be distinctively human—rationality, morality, culture, mentality, linguistic ability, and intentionality or purposiveness. It is the attempt to explain properties such as these, which appear to be uniquely and quintessentially human, by means of purely biological parameters, models, and variables that has made sociobiology the subject of so much heated discussion and debate. Many of the papers included in the volume are concerned with these questions and focus on the validity of sociobiological claims concerning human nature and behavior.

Fourth, an attempt has been made to provide some record of the actual debate that surrounded the appearance of the bible of this nascent science—Edward O. Wilson's *Sociobiology: The New Synthesis.* Independent of one's personal views of the adequacy of sociobiology as a scientific theory and of the validity of claims concerning the relevance of sociobiology for the study of human behavior and human nature, it is of vital importance to realize that sociobiology stands as an instance of a rarely observed intellectual phenomenon: the attempt to produce and legitimize a new scientific discipline. The birth pangs of sociobiology provide an invaluable opportunity to study the complex variables that enter into the creation of a new scientific field and its subsequent acceptance or rejection both by other scientists and by the general public. Personalities, empirical evidence, ideologies, explanatory power, theoretical elegance, intellectual trendiness and all the other factors commonly supposed to be involved in the legitimation of theories in science are all plainly manifest in the reception which greeted the appearance of Wilson's book. Sociobiology is of interest not only for its actual claims and possible implications, but as a case study in understanding the scientific enterprise itself.

Despite the fact that a great deal of work has been conducted in evolutionary biological science on efforts to explain behavior and social behavior, it seems fair to say that the explanation of these phenomena has not until recently become a primary concern of evolutionary biologists.

Evolutionists have long concentrated on the "hard" aspects of organic properties—anatomy, physiology, and morphology—in attempting to explain the processes of organic evolution and the presence of organic diversity over time. The fact that scientists could measure, manipulate, and reconstruct these kinds of traits greatly facilitated the formulation of testable models of evolutionary mechanisms that might direct evolutionary change.

Behavioral traits in organisms have proven much less amenable to evolutionary analysis. Aside from its complexity, organic behavior is difficult to measure and particularly troublesome to reconstruct. Moreover, the obscurity of the causal genesis of behavior and social behavior has resulted in most evolutionists being quite content to assign the evolutionary study of behavior a prominent position on the back burner of theoretical concern in favor of seemingly simpler morphological and structural features.

There are a number of other factors in addition to the technical difficulties of carrying out empirical studies which may have diverted evolutionary attention away from behavior and social behavior. However, there is one additional theoretical factor that must be mentioned in attempting to explain why the evolutionary study of social behavior has only recently come into prominence as an area of legitimate biological interest. As Darwin was among the first to point out, many forms of behavior and especially social behavior in organisms seem to provide convincing empirical refutations of the validity of the whole of evolutionary theory.

Darwinian and later twentieth-century theories of biological evolution have at least this much in common. They all posit some mechanisms for producing observable organic traits from particulate sets of factors or genes. They all posit some mechanisms for producing variations in the genetic materials of organisms. They all recognize the existence of some mechanisms for transmitting genes from one generation to another. And they all recognize the existence of limitations and factors in the environment that will produce a variation in the proportion of genes successfully transmitted from one generation to the next. Thus the essential explanatory components of modern theories about organic evolutionary processes are genes, phenotypes, genetic variation, genetic transmission, and selection. The interaction of these forces is held to be adequate for explaining the origin and the presence of any and all of the persistent traits of living creatures.

Behavior and social behavior, however, seem to fly in the face of this theory. Even discounting the confusing behavioral displays and traits of humans and other mammals, a large number of relatively primitive organisms manifest complex social behaviors that are *prima facie* refutations of the adequacy of these basic mechanisms to explain evolutionary change. Many insect species possess specialized castes of workers which are completely sterile. Yet these castes appear in relatively stable proportions from one generation to the next actively performing their various tasks of defense, food gathering, nest construction, and "day care" for juveniles. The theoretical dilemma is this: how can such highly specialized groups of organisms which manifest complex and coordinated activities be explained in terms of any Darwinian evolutionary theory when they have no facility for reproduction or gene transmission? How could selection and variation combine to produce and maintain *sterile* subpopulations of organisms with highly specialized traits and behaviors? To paraphrase Darwin, no one but a fanatic could maintain the truth of a theory which presupposes the existence of gene variation and gene transmission to explain the continuous existence of sterile or neuter organisms. Not only is behavior and social behavior difficult to study for the evolutionist, but for many years it has seemed to contain the sort of evidence often demanded by critics of modern evolutionary theory—social behavior among sterile forms is an empirical example of organic diversity which appears inexplicable in terms of the mechanisms of modern evolutionary theory. Not only does such behavior provide a test of the theory's adequacy, but it would seem to show that evolutionary theory is quite false.

The difficulties posed by some forms of social behavior for evolutionary theory have fueled the analytical concerns of sociobiology. Moreover, it is the claims of sociobiologists to be able to explain these previously inexplicable behavioral phenomena within the rough framework of modern Darwinian evolutionary theory that have fueled biological interest in sociobiology.

Darwin and a number of subsequent evolutionary theorists such as J. B. S. Haldane and Sewall Wright did attempt to provide explanatory answers to the dilemmas raised by the existence of social behavior and organization in primitive but highly specialized subpopulations of species using only the standard mechanisms of evolutionary theory.

Darwin noted that while certain traits such as altruism or sterility might be disadvantageous for the particular individual who possessed them, they could be quite advantageous to families or groups in which such individuals lived. Under certain circumstances traits disadvantageous to individuals could therefore be selected for—if they could benefit groups of organisms sufficiently to allow them greater reproductive success than groups of organisms which lacked members with such traits. Darwin noted that the most extreme versions of selection in such intergroup competitions might result in the production of species or populations capable of producing highly specialized but sterile members that would prove selectively advantageous against groups which lacked such social and specializing traits.

Haldane and Wright attempted to spell out in greater detail the nature of the circumstances that might promote the formulation of highly socialized and narrowly specialized groups or subpopulations of organisms. Wright constructed models wherein various subpopulations, or what he called "demes," of a given population of organisms might, through small population sizes, high migration rates, rapidly fluctuating and isolating environmental conditions, chance fixations of genetic mutations, and various selection pressures evolve traits disadvantageous to some individuals but highly beneficial to the subgroups in which they appeared.

The difficulty with these efforts and other later models of group selection was that they seemed inadequate either because the circumstances required to selectively favor complex social organizations and arrangements containing disadvantageous individual traits were highly implausible in real world situations, or because the kind of information necessary to decide when group selection could cancel out or overpower the force of selection for advantageous traits in individuals was simply not available.

The key theoretical insight, which seems to provide the required solution to the puzzle of social organization and behavior within the confines of Darwinian evolutionary theory, was provided by W. D. Hamilton. Hamilton suggested that the problem of providing plausible circumstances under which group selection might favor social traits and behaviors against the powerful forces of selection for individual advantage in the struggle for existence could be solved if the locus of selection was broadened to include the advantages and disadvantages conferred by traits and behaviors not simply on single individuals but, rather, upon genetically similar individuals within a population. If individual organisms possessed sufficient genetic commonality, then while a particular trait or behavior might competitively disadvantage an individual, it might still be selected for in a population if the trait or behavior sufficiently benefited other individuals with similar genetic endowments. Social behaviors and specializations could be preserved over time in particular populations of organisms if the trade-off value for a given trait resulted in more overall benefit than harm to organisms with similar genetic endowments even though some individuals with such endowments might be greatly disadvantaged through lowered reproductive success, sterility, or death.

Since those organisms likely to have similar genetic endowments were siblings, parents and children, and the immediate family of a set of parents, Hamilton's models of possible group selection in organisms became dubbed "the theory of kin selection."

It is the theoretical models of kin selection, with their emphasis on coefficients of genetic relationship, population size, isolating factors, the genetic mediation of traits and behaviors, and the notion of selection acting upon sets of genetically similar subpopulations of organisms (inclusive fitness), that provided the theoretical spark for sociobiology. If it was plausible to assign key roles to genotypes in mediating some behaviors and traits, and if it was plausible to argue that selection acts to choose those organisms best endowed behaviorally to live and successfully reproduce from those present in a given population, then the answer to the dilemma that had plagued evolutionists since Darwin's day was finally at hand. The persistence of complex, peculiar, and apparently disadvantageous traits and behaviors is the end result of selection for those genotypes that could produce behaviors or traits capable of compensating for the deterimental consequences of such traits or behaviors for some individuals by benefits that accrue to other individuals with enough genetic similarity to ensure the transmission of the traits or behaviors from one generation to the next.

Hamilton's insightful recognition that genetic similarity holds the key to understanding the interaction of genetic variability and environmental constraints set off a slew of related theoretical inquiries into the phenomena of social behavior. Evolutionary biologists took a second look at group selection and posited possible scenarios under which social traits or behaviors might evolve where the degree of genetic similarity present was small or nonexistent. Simultaneously, questions were raised concerning social behavior between organisms of entirely separate species, and models of mutual benefit and cost were constructed to explain the wide range of cross-speciational social symbioses. Sexuality, sexual specializations, and sexual practices in organisms were subject to renewed evolutionary inquiry since these phenomena seemed central to understanding kin selection. Parental care, population growth rates, and reproductive strategies also became the subject of much theoretical work in evolutionary biology since genetic similarity might weigh heavily in understanding these phenomena as well. It is the total of evolutionary biological research into all these aspects of social behavior in organisms that provides the bulk of the scope and substance of sociobiological science.

One might reasonably ask, if all sociobiology amounts to is the utilization of a set of fancy population genetic and evolutionary models to explain the history of some odd behavioral phenomena in a few species of organisms, why all the fuss? How can a collection of arcane mathematical models of interest to a narrow range of scientific specialists threaten, disrupt, or confirm ideological, social, political, or economic values?

In some ways skepticism of this sort toward the dangers of biological theorizing about behavior would be justified if sociobiology were no more than its mathematical population genetic models. But it is not.

Sociobiologists have made a number of controversial claims about the scope and adequacy of their theory and its models. They have argued that sociobiological models must be utilized in any attempt to explain the presence of universal types of behavioral tendencies, trends, and patterns throughout the animal kingdom. More specifically, they have argued that insofar as humans are social animals who have also been subject to the mechanisms of evolutionary change, the biology of sociobiology has much to tell us about the origin and nature of human behavior. Most aspects of human social behavior and organization can only be understood in the light of their evolutionary history and evolutionary utility. Moreover, some sociobiologists have argued that those disciplines which are explicitly concerned with human social behavior—anthropology, economics, political science, sociology, ethics, religion, and so on—cannot hope to achieve a scientific understanding of human behavior without recognizing and incorporating the biological models of sociobiological science. Some sociobiologists have gone further and maintained that social policies, political philosophies, and normative and prescriptive ethical systems must be bounded by the findings of sociobiology concerning the evolution of human behavior and human society.

While none of these broader claims for the utility and scope of evolutionary biological science are particularly new, the claims for sociobiology have been made with a stridency and conviction that have led some to wonder whether ideological, valuational, and metaphysical presumptions are being imported into sociobiological discussions of human beings in the name of empirically valid scientific findings and methods.

If the biology underlying social behavior is to play a pivotal role in understanding and evaluating ourselves, our behaviors, our societies, and our values, then many would argue that a number of serious methodological and conceptual issues need to be resolved before credulity can be given to the models, scenarios, and findings of this eclectic new scientific enterprise. Are the models used by sociobiologists to explain social behavior plausible, testable, highly confirmed, and scientifically adequate? What is the gulf, if any, that separates human behavior from that of other creatures? Can we find universals in the domain of social behavior in the animal world? Is it at all feasible at this moment to construct theories about the evolution of social behavior given what is known and unknown about the causal determination of behavior? Why should descriptive findings about the historical evolution of human beings influence in any way the prescriptive recommendations we now make about the future course of social and behavioral evolution? And is it even wise to air broad speculative claims about the need to under stand humanity biologically in a political and ideological climate that possesses a vast potential for the misuse and misapplication of tentative scientific speculations?

It is these sorts of questions concerning the scope, validity, accuracy, and implications of sociobiological thinking for human behavior that have provoked the debate about sociobiology. While the debate touches upon a number of issues that perennially arise in trying to assess our knowledge of the biology of behavior, the theoretical power and heuristic utility of current evolutionary models for explaining organic evolution seem to demand a careful reconsideration of these fundamental issues.

Part I of this book contains a series of discussions by early evolutionary theorists of possible explanations of social behavior in lower animals and the implications of evolutionary accounts for understanding human behavior and human nature. Darwin's recognition of the problematic nature of social behavior for any evolutionary theory and his ingenious solution to the puzzle with regard to primitive insects constitutes the first selection. Brief selections from the work of the famous British sociologist Herbert Spencer and the biologist Thomas H. Huxley are next. Spencer argues that the findings of evolutionary science concerning the origin and significance of human behavior must be incorporated into any valid analysis of ethics. Ethical theory must, he says, attempt to provide a means of reconciling human evolutionary biological nature with the demands of modern social life. Huxley argues, against Spencer, that scientific analyses of social behavior in lower animals have little to offer in the way of directions for human conduct, and that human beings, unlike other animals, are social and moral as a result of conscious choice rather than inbred biological tendencies. Peter Kropotkin, a Russian intellectual and naturalist, argues that Darwin's solution for explaining social behavior is simply misconceived. Kropotkin claims that any explanation of sociality in animals via competitive advantages to individuals or groups is an ideologically inspired devaluation of the importance of cooperative behavior in nature. Social behavior defies the adequacy of any biological theory which utilizes competitive mechanisms and individual advantages as explanatory devices and, moreover, provides a biological confirmation of ethical and political philosophies that stress the desirability of altruism, sacrifice, and cooperation. While lacking in theoretical biological sophistication, the views of these early evolutionists anticipate to a remarkable degree the hopes and fears of contemporary scientists interested in the phenomena of social behavior.

In a fascinating but sadly ignored article, W. C. Allee reports on a lifetime of work during the early part of this century on social behavior in lower animals and its significance for understanding human social behavior. Allee's article is of interest not only for his claims concerning the "naturalness" of altruistic social behavior but also for his attention to the broader political and ideological issues raised by the scientific study of human behavior.

The final selection by the anthropologists Lionel Tiger and Robin Fox represents a relatively modern theoretical progenitor of sociobiology. Tiger and Fox argue that there is a good deal more animal left in the human species as a result of evolution than is commonly supposed to be there. Social scientists and humanists are urged to attend to the biologically innate programming or "biograms" of human beings if they hope to say anything useful in their respective disciplines.

Part II contains a set of discussions by contemporary biologists interested in the implications of their scientific research on social behavior for ethical theory. Konrad Lorenz, the founder of ethology, argues passionately that evolution has produced in humans some potentially nasty but highly adaptive drives and instincts. Our culture and morals can only survive, he argues, as long as they are compatible with our innate biological propensities toward competition and survival. Niko Tinbergen, also an ethologist, sounds some cautionary notes concerning Lorenzian views of the innate depravity of human nature. But he too counsels that the scientific study of the biology of behavior is an essential prerequisite for prescriptive social planning and political organization. V. C. Wynne-Edwards argues that the scientific study of human social systems reveals limits on the numbers and sizes of groups to which humans can demonstrate affinity and allegiance. He too feels that biology must serve as the ultimate arbiter of moral and social norms.

The third part contains a number of essays that are critical of attempts to draw moral lessons or conclusions from biological or evolutionary facts. Abraham Edel argues that many biological concepts are simply too vague to be useful in ethical analysis and that the analysis of the valuational import of key evolutionary concepts remains incomplete. Anthony Quinton, a philosopher, provides a comprehensive critique of crude attempts to dismiss evolution as of no relevance to morality and of Lorenzian efforts to replace morality with evolutionary facts. He argues that empirically oriented biological theories are unlikely to provide the kinds of criteria requisite for evaluating and justifying ethical theories. Anthony Flew presents a review of the traditional philosophical conundrum: the is/ought or fact/value distinction. He critically assesses some of the efforts of evolutionary biologists from Darwin to Lorenz to cross this gulf and provides some suggestions on how to avoid the naturalistic fallacy of deriving valuational conclusions from descriptive empirical observations. Leon Eisenberg argues that some biologists have, historically, utilized simplistic, crude, and even fallacious theories of the biology of human behavior to justify ethical, political, and cultural views which they found to be attractive on other grounds. All these papers reveal the complexity that awaits any scientist willing to venture into the dark domains of ethics and values.

Part IV contains a set of discussions that provide a preliminary view of the actual thinking and models of sociobiology. Wynne-Edwards's efforts to explain social behavior as a means of achieving limits on population growth are critiqued by George Williams, who argues that the real question is how social behavior of this sort can evolve in the first place. The attempts of W. D. Hamilton and Robert Trivers to give an answer to this evolutionary problem, both for genetically related and unrelated organisms, form the essential core of sociobiological thought. The central theses of these papers merit close attention. The final selection from Edward O. Wilson's *Sociobiology: The New Synthesis* is illustrative of Wilson's attempt to utilize the Hamilton and Trivers models to illuminate complex human social behaviors. The methodological assumptions presented in his selection have stimulated much comment and criticism among scientists and others concerned with the study of human behavior.

Part V attempts to trace the reaction to the theoretical efforts of Hamilton and Trivers and others as they were synthesized into a comprehensive theory by Wilson and other sociobiologists. While methodological and conceptual issues pervade the discussions of D. S. Sade, Robert Morison, C. H. Waddington, and the Sociobiology Study Group of Science for the People, a set of broader valuational, ideological, and philosophical opinions and beliefs can be seen to underlie and subtly influence their discussions. It is of particular interest to note how what began as one more version of the old nature/nurture argument between defenders and critics of sociobiology quickly evolved into a more fundamental debate about the nature of scientific theories, the scientific study of human differences, and axiomatic commitments to a set of valuational and ethical precepts.

At this juncture it seems fair to say that sociobiology has succeeded in weathering the first round of criticisms that were mounted against it. However, it may be that the deeper issues touched upon in the discussions of Stephen Gould, Joseph Alper, Stephen Emlen, and myself will prove more troublesome for devotees of an all-encompassing sociobiological theory of social behavior.

A number of these issues receive further analysis in the papers which constitute the final section of the volume. Two philosophers of science, Michael Ruse and Richard Burian, present divergent evaluations of the conceptual apparatus and methodology of sociobiology. Walter Bock and Ethel Tobach, an evolutionary biologist and comparative psychologist respectively, address themselves to a question of vital importance for evaluating sociobiological accounts of behavior: to what extent is it permissible to generalize about behavior between organisms of different species? Bock argues that social behavior can be viewed like any other organic trait and that standard comparative techniques will suffice in formulating lawful generalizations and explanations of behavior. Tobach argues that what will work for other organic traits will not work, comparatively speaking, for social behavior; thus sociobiology is doomed to failure at the outset. Marshall Sahlins and William Durham present conflicting views of the applicability and utility of biological evolutionary theories for social and cultural evolution. Ruth Mattern provides a careful critique of the sociobiological claims of Wilson and others concerning ethics. Political scientists Steven Peterson and Albert Somit maintain that, properly understood, sociobiology could have great beneficial import for large areas of political science and sociopolitical philosophy. Finally, the members of the Sociobiological Study Group, while agreeing that sociobiology has great potential for contributing to political and social policies, argue that there is nothing at all beneficial about this interaction. They argue that there is more ideology than science in sociobiology.

There has been a good deal of polarization and passion surrounding the evaluation of contemporary sociobiological theory and previous scientific efforts to study human social behavior. In such a situation it is often easy to confuse passion and emotion with sound argumentation. It is also easy in such circumstances to dismiss legitimate doubts and concerns about various aspects of the sociobiological enterprise as merely philosophical, provincial, or unscientific. It is my sincere hope that the papers and materials selected for inclusion in this volume will provide a basis for advancing rational discussion of sociobiology. Since human beings, social behavior, and scientific theories concerning behavior are likely to be with us for some time to come, it seems imperative that we learn how to talk to each other about all of them.

A. L. C.

PART I

Historical Forerunners
of Sociobiology

Neuter Insects

Charles Darwin

No doubt many instincts of very difficult explanation could be opposed
to the theory of natural selection,—cases, in which we cannot see how
an instinct could possibly have originated; cases, in which no intermediate gradations are known to exist; cases of instinct of apparently such
trifling importance, that they could hardly have been acted on by natural
selection; cases of instincts almost identically the same in animals so
remote in the scale of nature, that we cannot account for their similarity
by inheritance from a common parent, and must therefore believe that
they have been acquired by independent acts of natural selection. I
will not here enter on these several cases, but will confine myself to
one special difficulty, which at first appeared to me insuperable, and
actually fatal to my whole theory. I allude to the neuters or sterile
females in insect-communities: for these neuters often differ widely in
instinct and in structure from both the males and fertile females, and
yet, from being sterile, they cannot propagate their kind.

The subject well deserves to be discussed at great length, but I will
here take only a single case, that of working or sterile ants. How the
workers have been rendered sterile is a difficulty; but not much greater
than that of any other striking modification of structure; for it can be
shown that some insects and other articulate animals in a state of nature
occasionally become sterile; and if such insects had been social, and
it had been profitable to the community that a number should have
been annually born capable of work, but incapable of procreation, I

From Charles Darwin, *The Origin of Species by Means of Natural Selection*,
1st edition (London: J. Murray, 1859), pp. 257–262.

can see no very great difficulty in this being effected by natural selection. But I must pass over this preliminary difficulty. The great difficulty lies in the working ants differing widely from both the males and the fertile females in structure, as in the shape of the thorax and in being destitute of wings and sometimes of eyes, and in instinct. As far as instinct alone is concerned, the prodigious difference in this respect between the workers and the perfect females, would have been far better exemplified by the hive-bee. If a working ant or other neuter insect had been an animal in the ordinary state, I should have unhesitatingly assumed that all its characters had been slowly acquired through natural selection; namely, by an individual having been born with some slight profitable modification of structure, this being inherited by its offspring, which again varied and were again selected, and so onwards. But with the working ant we have an insect differing greatly from its parents, yet absolutely sterile; so that it could never have transmitted successively acquired modifications of structure or instinct to its progeny. It may well be asked how is it possible to reconcile this case with the theory of natural selection?

First, let it be remembered that we have innumerable instances, both in our domestic productions and in those in a state of nature, of all sorts of differences of structure which have become correlated to certain ages, and to either sex. We have differences correlated not only to one sex, but to that short period alone when the reproductive system is active, as in the nuptial plumage of many birds, and in the hooked jaws of the male salmon. We have even slight differences in the horns of different breeds of cattle in relation to an artificially imperfect state of the male sex; for oxen of certain breeds have longer horns than in other breeds, in comparison with the horns of the bulls or cows of these same breeds. Hence I can see no real difficulty in any character having become correlated with the sterile condition of certain members of insect-communities: the difficulty lies in understanding how such correlated modifications of structure could have been slowly accumulated by natural selection.

This difficulty, though appearing insuperable, is lessened, or, as I believe, disappears, when it is remembered that selection may be applied to the family, as well as to the individual, and may thus gain the desired end. Thus, a well-flavoured vegetable is cooked, and the individual is destroyed; but the horticulturist sows seeds of the same stock, and confidently expects to get nearly the same variety; breeders of cattle wish the flesh and fat to be well marbled together; the animal has been slaughtered, but the breeder goes with confidence to the same family. I have such faith in the powers of selection, that I do not doubt that a breed of cattle, always yielding oxen with extraordinarily long horns, could be slowly formed by carefully watching which individual bulls and cows, when matched, produced oxen with the longest horns; and yet no one ox could ever have propagated its kind. Thus I believe it has been with social insects: a slight modification of structure, or instinct, correlated with the sterile condition of certain members of the community, has been advantageous to the community: consequently the fertile males and females of the same community flourished, and transmitted to their fertile offspring a tendency to produce sterile members having the same modification. And I believe that this process has been repeated, until that prodigious amount of difference between the fertile and sterile females of the same species has been produced, which we see in many social insects.

But we have not as yet touched on the climax of the difficulty; namely, the fact that the neuters of several ants differ, not only from the fertile females and males, but from each other, sometimes to an almost incredible degree, and are thus divided into two or even three castes. The castes, moreover, do not generally graduate into each other, but are perfectly well defined; being as distinct from each other, as are any two species of the same genus, or rather as any two genera of the same family. Thus in Eciton, there are working and soldier neuters, with jaws and instincts extraordinarily different: in Cryptocerus, the workers of one caste alone carry a wonderful sort of shield on their heads, the use of which is quite unknown: in the Mexican Myrmecocystus, the workers of one caste never leave the nest; they are fed by the workers of another caste, and they have an enormously developed abdomen which secretes a sort of honey, supplying the place of that excreted by the aphides, or the domestic cattle as they may be called, which our European ants guard or imprison.

It will indeed be thought that I have an overweening confidence in the principle of natural selection, when I do not admit that such wonderful and well-established facts at once annihilate my theory. In the simpler case of neuter insects all of one caste or of the same kind, which have been rendered by natural selection, as I believe to be quite possible, different from the fertile males and females,—in this case, we may safely conclude from the analogy of ordinary variations, that each successive, slight, profitable modification did not probably at first appear in all the individual neuters in the same nest, but in a few alone; and that by the long-continued selection of the fertile parents which produced most neuters with the profitable modification, all the neuters ultimately came to have the desired character. On this view we ought occasionally to find neuter-insects of the same species, in the same nest, presenting gradations of structure; and this we do find, even often, considering how few neuter-insects out of Europe have been carefully examined. Mr F. Smith has shown how surprisingly the neuters of several British ants differ from each other in size and sometimes in colour; and that the extreme forms can sometimes be perfectly linked together by individuals taken out of the same nest: I have myself compared perfect gradations of this kind. It often happens that the larger or the smaller sized workers are the most numerous; or that both large and small are numerous, with those of an intermediate size scanty in numbers. Formica flava has larger and smaller workers, with some of intermediate size; and, in this species, as Mr F. Smith has observed, the larger workers have simple eyes (ocelli), which though small can be plainly distinguished, whereas the smaller workers have their ocelli rudimentary. Having carefully dissected several specimens of these workers, I can affirm that the eyes are far more rudimentary in the smaller workers than can be accounted for merely by their proportionally lesser size; and I fully believe, though I dare not assert so positively, that the workers of intermediate size have their ocelli in an exactly intermediate condition. So that we here have two bodies of sterile workers in the same nest, differing not only in size, but in their organs of vision, yet connected by some few members in an intermediate condition. I may digress by adding, that if the smaller workers had been the most useful to the community, and those males and females had been continually selected, which produced more and more of the smaller workers, until all the workers had come to be in this condition; we should then have had a species of ant with neuters very nearly in the same condition with those of Myrmica. For the workers of Myrmica have not even rudiments of ocelli, though the male and female ants of this genus have well-developed ocelli.

I may give one other case: so confidently did I expect to find gradations in important points of structure between the different castes of neuters in the same species, that I gladly availed myself of Mr F. Smith's offer of numerous specimens from the same nest of the driver ant (Anomma) of West Africa. The reader will perhaps best appreciate the amount of difference in these workers, by my giving not the actual measurements, but a strictly accurate illustration: the difference was the same as if we were to see a set of workmen building a house of whom many were five feet four inches high, and many sixteen feet high; but we must suppose that the larger workmen had heads four instead of three times as big as those of the smaller men, and jaws nearly five times as big. The jaws, moreover, of the working ants of the several sizes differed wonderfully in shape, and in the form and number of the teeth. But the important fact for us is, that though the workers can be grouped into castes of different sizes, yet they graduate insensibly into each other, as does the widely-different structure of their jaws. I speak confidently on this latter point, as Mr Lubbock made drawings for me with the camera lucida of the jaws which I had dissected from the workers of the several sizes.

With these facts before me, I believe that natural selection, by acting on the fertile parents, could form a species which should regularly produce neuters, either all of large size with one form of jaw, or all of small size with jaws having a widely different structure; or lastly, and this is our climax of difficulty, one set of workers of one size and structure, and simultaneously another set of workers of a different size and structure;—a graduated series having been first formed, as in the case of the driver ant, and then the extreme forms, from being the most useful to the community, having been produced in greater and greater numbers through the natural selection of the parents which generated them; until none with an intermediate structure were produced.

Thus, as I believe, the wonderful fact of two distinctly defined castes of sterile workers existing in the same nest, both widely different from each other and from their parents, has originated. We can see how useful their production may have been to a social community of insects, on the same principle that the division of labour is useful to civilised man. As ants work by inherited instincts and by inherited tools or weapons, and not by acquired knowledge and manufactured instruments, a perfect division of labour could be effected with them only by the workers being sterile; for had they been fertile, they would have intercrossed, and their instincts and structure would have become blended. And nature has, as I believe, effected this admirable division of labour in the communities of ants, by the means of natural selection. But I am bound to confess, that, with all my faith in this principle, I should never have anticipated that natural selection could have been efficient in so high a degree, had not the case of these neuter insects convinced me of the fact. I have, therefore, discussed this case, at some little but wholly insufficient length, in order to show the power of natural selection, and likewise because this is by far the most serious special difficulty, which my theory has encountered. The case, also, is very interesting, as it proves that with animals, as with plants, any amount of modification in structure can be effected by the accumulation of numerous, slight, and as we must call them accidental, variations, which are in any manner profitable, without exercise or habit having come into play. For no amount of exercise, or habit, or volition, in the utterly sterile members of a community could possibly have affected the structure or instincts of the fertile members, which alone leave descendants. I am surprised that no one has advanced this demonstrative case of neuter insects, against the well-known doctrine of Lamarck.

The Data of Ethics: The Biological View

Herbert Spencer

Here might be urged the necessity for preluding the study of moral science, by the study of biological science. Here might be dwelt on the error men make in thinking they can understand those special phenomena of human life with which Ethics deals, while paying little or no attention to the general phenomena of human life, and while utterly ignoring the phenomena of life at large. And doubtless there would be truth in the inference that such acquaintance with the world of living things as discloses the part which pleasures and pains have played in organic evolution, would help to rectify these one-sided conceptions of moralists. It cannot be held, however, that lack of this knowledge is the sole cause, or the main cause, of their one-sidedness. For facts of the kind above instanced, which, duly attended to, would prevent such distortions of moral theory, are facts which it needs no biological inquiries to learn, but which are daily thrust before the eyes of all. The truth is, rather, that the general consciousness is so possessed by sentiments and ideas at variance with the conclusions necessitated by familiar evidence, that the evidence gets no attention. These adverse sentiments and ideas have several roots.

There is the theological root. As before shown, from the worship of cannibal ancestors who delighted in witnessing tortures, there resulted the primitive conception of deities who were propitiated by the bearing of pains, and, consequently, angered by the receipt of pleasures. Through the religions of the semi-civilized, in which this conception of the divine

From Herbert Spencer, *The Principles of Ethics*, Vol. I (New York: D. Appleton and Company, 1892), pp. 95–100.

nature remains conspicuous, it has persisted, in progressively modified forms, down to our own times; and still colours the beliefs, both of those who adhere to the current creed and of those who nominally reject it. There is another root in the primitive and still-surviving militancy. While social antagonisms continue to generate war, which consists in endeavours to inflict pain and death while submitting to the risks of pain and death, and which necessarily involves great privations; it is needful that physical suffering, whether considered in itself or in the evils it bequeaths, should be thought little of, and that among pleasures recognized as most worthy should be those which victory brings. Nor does partially-developed industrialism fail to furnish a root. With social evolution, which implies transition from the life of wandering hunters to the life of settled peoples engaged in labour, and which therefore entails activities widely unlike those to which the aboriginal constitution is adapted, there comes an under-exercise of faculties for which the social state affords no scope, and an over-taxing of faculties required for the social state: the one implying denial of certain pleasures and the other submission to certain pains. Hence, along with that growth of population which makes the struggle for existence intense, bearing of pains and sacrifice of pleasures is daily necessitated.

Now always and everywhere, there arises among men a theory conforming to their practice. The savage nature, originating the conception of a savage deity, evolves a theory of supernatural control sufficiently stringent and cruel to influence his conduct. With submission to despotic government severe enough in its restraints to keep in order barbarous natures, there grows up a theory of divine right to rule, and the duty of absolute submission. Where war is made the business of life by the existence of warlike neighbours, virtues which are required for war come to be regarded as supreme virtues; while, contrariwise, when industrialism has grown predominant, the violence and the deception which warriors glory in come to be held criminal. In like manner, then, there arises a tolerable adjustment of the actually-accepted (not the nominally-accepted) theory of right living, to living as it is daily carried on. If the life is one that necessitates habitual denial of pleasures and bearing of pains, there grows up an answering ethical system under which the receipt of pleasures is tacitly disapproved and the bearing of pains avowedly approved. The mischiefs entailed by pleasures in excess are dwelt on, while the benefits which normal pleasures bring are ignored;

and the good results achieved by submission to pains are fully set forth while the evils are overlooked.

But while recognizing the desirableness of, and indeed the necessity for, systems of ethics adapted, like religious systems and political systems, to their respective times and places; we have here to regard the first as, like the others, transitional. We must infer that like a purer creed and a better government, a truer ethics belongs to a more advanced social state. Led, *à priori,* to conclude that distortions must exist, we are enabled to recognize as such, the distortions we find: answering in nature, as these do, to expectation. And there is forced on us the truth that a scientific morality arises only as fast as the one-sided conceptions adapted to transitory conditions, are developed into both-sided conceptions. The science of right living has to take account of all consequences in so far as they affect happiness, personally or socially, directly or indirectly; and by as much as it ignores any class of consequences, by so much does it fail to be science.

Like the physical view, then, the biological view corresponds with the view gained by looking at conduct in general from the stand-point of Evolution.

That which was physically defined as a moving equilibrium, we define biologically as a balance of functions. The implication of such a balance is that the several functions in their kinds, amounts, and combinations, are adjusted to the several activities which maintain and constitute complete life; and to be so adjusted is to have reached the goal towards which the evolution of conduct continually tends.

Passing to the feelings which accompany the performance of functions, we see that of necessity during the evolution of organic life, pleasures have become the concomitants of normal amounts of functions, while pains, positive and negative, have become the concomitants of excesses and defects of functions. And though in every species derangements of these relations are often caused by changes of conditions, they ever re-establish themselves: disappearance of the species being the alternative.

Mankind, inheriting from creatures of lower kinds, such adjustments between feelings and functions as concern fundamental bodily requirements; and daily forced by peremptory feelings to do the things which maintain life and avoid those which bring immediate death; has been subject to a change of conditions unusually great and involved. This has considerably deranged the guidance by sensations, and has deranged in a much greater degree the guidance by emotions. The result is that in many cases pleasures are not connected with actions which must be performed, nor pains with actions which must be avoided, but contrariwise.

Several influences have conspired to make men ignore the well-working of these relations between feelings and functions, and to observe whatever of ill-working is seen in them. Hence, while the evils which some pleasures entail are dilated upon, the benefits habitually accompanying receipt of pleasures are unnoticed; at the same time that the benefits achieved through certain pains are magnified while the immense mischiefs which pains bring are made little of.

The ethical theories characterized by these perversions, are products of, and are appropriate to, the forms of social life which the imperfectly-adapted constitutions of men produce. But with the progress of adaptation, bringing faculties and requirements into harmony, such incongruities of experience, and consequent distortions of theory, must diminish; until, along with complete adjustment of humanity to the social state, will go recognition of the truths that actions are completely right only when, besides being conducive to future happiness, special and general, they are immediately pleasurable, and that painfulness, not only ultimate but proximate, is the concomitant of actions which are wrong.

So that from the biological point of view, ethical science becomes a specification of the conduct of associated men who are severally so constituted that the various self-preserving activities, the activities required for rearing offspring, and those which social welfare demands, are fulfilled in the spontaneous exercise of duly proportioned faculties, each yielding when in action its quantum of pleasure; and who are, by consequence, so constituted that excess or defect in any one of these actions brings its quantum of pain, immediate and remote.

Evolution and Ethics

Thomas H. Huxley

I have other reasons for fearing that this logical ideal of evolutionary regimentation—this pigeon-fanciers' polity—is unattainable. In the absence of any such a severely scientific administrator as we have been dreaming of, human society is kept together by bonds of such a singular character, that the attempt to perfect society after his fashion would run serious risk of loosening them.

Social organization is not peculiar to men. Other societies, such as those constituted by bees and ants, have also arisen out of the advantage of co-operation in the struggle for existence; and their resemblances to, and their differences from, human society are alike instructive. The society formed by the hive bee fulfils the ideal of the communistic aphorism "to each according to his needs, from each according to his capacity." Within it, the struggle for existence is strictly limited. Queen, drones, and workers have each their allotted sufficiency of food; each performs the function assigned to it in the economy of the hive, and all contribute to the success of the whole co-operative society in its competition with rival collectors of nectar and pollen and with other enemies, in the state of nature without. In the same sense as the garden, or the colony, is a work of human art, the bee polity is a work of apiarian art, brought about by the cosmic process, working through the organization of the hymenopterous type.

Now this society is the direct product of an organic necessity, impelling every member of it to a course of action which tends to the good

From Thomas H. Huxley, *Evolution and Ethics* (New York: D. Appleton and Company, 1894), pp. 23–45.

of the whole. Each bee has its duty and none has any rights. Whether bees are susceptible of feeling and capable of thought is a question which cannot be dogmatically answered. As a pious opinion, I am disposed to deny them more than the merest rudiments of consciousness. But it is curious to reflect that a thoughtful drone (workers and queens would have no leisure for speculation) with a turn for ethical philosophy, must needs profess himself an intuitive moralist of the purest water. He would point out, with perfect justice, that the devotion of the workers to a life of ceaseless toil for a mere subsistence wage, cannot be accounted for either by enlightened selfishness, or by any other sort of utilitarian motives; since these bees begin to work, without experience or reflection, as they emerge from the cell in which they are hatched. Plainly, an eternal and immutable principle, innate in each bee, can alone account for the phenomena. On the other hand, the biologist, who traces out all the extant stages of gradation between solitary and hive bees, as clearly sees in the latter, simply the perfection of an automatic mechanism, hammered out by the blows of the struggle for existence upon the progeny of the former, during long ages of constant variation.

I see no reason to doubt that, at its origin, human society was as much a product of organic necessity as that of the bees. The human family, to begin with, rested upon exactly the same conditions as those which gave rise to similar associations among animals lower in the scale. Further, it is easy to see that every increase in the duration of the family ties, with the resulting co-operation of a larger and larger number of descendants for protection and defence, would give the families in which such modification took place a distinct advantage over the others. And, as in the hive, the progressive limitation of the struggle for existence between the members of the family would involve increasing efficiency as regards outside competition.

But there is this vast and fundamental difference between bee society and human society. In the former, the members of the society are each organically predestined to the performance of one particular class of functions only. If they were endowed with desires, each could desire to perform none but those offices for which its organization specially fits it; and which, in view of the good of the whole, it is proper it should do. So long as a new queen does not make her appearance, rivalries and competition are absent from the bee polity.

Among mankind, on the contrary, there is no such predestination to a sharply defined place in the social organism. However much men may differ in the quality of their intellects, the intensity of their passions, and the delicacy of their sensations, it cannot be said that one is fitted by his organization to be an agricultural labourer and nothing else, and another to be a landowner and nothing else. Moreover, with all their enormous differences in natural endowment, men agree in one thing, and that is their innate desire to enjoy the pleasures and to escape the pains of life; and, in short, to do nothing but that which it pleases them to do, without the least reference to the welfare of the society into which they are born. That is their inheritance (the reality at the bottom of the doctrine of original sin) from the long series of ancestors, human and semi-human and brutal, in whom the strength of this innate tendency to self-assertion was the condition of victory in the struggle for existence. That is the reason of the *aviditas vitae*— the insatiable hunger for enjoyment—of all mankind, which is one of the essential conditions of success in the war with the state of nature outside; and yet the sure agent of the destruction of society if allowed free play within.

The check upon this free play of self-assertion, or natural liberty, which is the necessary condition for the origin of human society, is the product of organic necessities of a different kind from those upon which the constitution of the hive depends. One of these is the mutual affection of parent and offspring, intensified by the long infancy of the human species. But the most important is the tendency, so strongly developed in man, to reproduce in himself actions and feelings similar to, or correlated with, those of other men. Man is the most consummate of all mimics in the animal world; none but himself can draw or model; none comes near him in the scope, variety, and exactness of vocal imitation; none is such a master of gesture; while he seems to be impelled thus to imitate for the pure pleasure of it. And there is no such another emotional chameleon. By a purely reflex operation of the mind, we take the hue of passion of those who are about us, or, it may be, the complementary colour. It is not by any conscious "putting one's self in the place" of a joyful or a suffering person that the state of mind we call sympathy usually arises; indeed, it is often contrary to one's sense of right, and in spite of one's will, that "fellow-feeling makes us wondrous kind," or the reverse. However complete may be the indifference to public opinion, in a cool, intellectual view, of the traditional sage, it has not yet been my fortune to meet with any actual sage who took its hostile manifestations with entire equanimity. Indeed, I doubt if the philosopher lives, or ever has lived, who could know himself to be heartily despised by a street boy without some irritation. And, though one cannot justify Haman for wishing to hang Mordecai on such a very high gibbet, yet, really, the consciousness of the Vizier of Ahasuerus, as he went in and out of the gate, that this obscure Jew had no respect for him, must have been very annoying.

It is needful only to look around us, to see that the greatest restrainer of the anti-social tendencies of men is fear, not of the law, but of the opinion of their fellows. The conventions of honour bind men who break legal, moral, and religious bonds; and, while people endure the extremity of physical pain rather than part with life, shame drives the weakest to suicide. . . .

That progressive modification of civilization which passes by the name of the "evolution of society," is, in fact, a process of an essentially different character, both from that which brings about the evolution of species, in the state of nature, and from that which gives rise to the evolution of varieties, in the state of art.

There can be no doubt that vast changes have taken place in English civilization since the reign of the Tudors. But I am not aware of a particle of evidence in favour of the conclusion that this evolutionary process has been accompanied by any modification of the physical, or the mental, characters of the men who have been the subjects of it. I have not met with any grounds for suspecting that the average Englishmen of to-day are sensibly different from those that Shakspere [sic] knew and drew. We look into his magic mirror of the Elizabethan age, and behold, nowise darkly, the presentment of ourselves.

During these three centuries, from the reign of Elizabeth to that of Victoria, the struggle for existence between man and man has been so largely restrained among the great mass of the population (except for one or two short intervals of civil war), that it can have had little, or no, selective operation. As to anything comparable to direct selection, it has been practised on so small a scale that it may also be neglected. The criminal law, in so far as by putting to death, or by subjecting to long periods of imprisonment, those who infringe its provisions, it prevents the propagation of hereditary criminal tendencies; and the poor-law, in so far as it separates married couples, whose destitution arises from hereditary defects of character, are doubtless selective agents operating in favour of the non-criminal and the more effective members of society. But the proportion of the population which they influence is very small; and, generally, the hereditary criminal and the hereditary pauper have propagated their kind before the law affects them. In a large proportion of cases, crime and pauperism have nothing to do with heredity; but are the consequence, partly, of circumstances and, partly, of the possession of qualities, which, under different conditions of life, might have excited esteem and even admiration. It was a shrewd man of the world who, in discussing sewage problems, remarked that dirt is riches in the wrong place; and that sound aphorism has moral applications. The benevolence and open-handed generosity which adorn a rich man, may make a pauper of a poor one; the energy and courage to which the successful soldier owes his rise, the cool and daring subtlety to which the great financier owes his fortune, may very easily, under unfavourable conditions, lead their possessors to the gallows, or to the hulks. Moreover, it is fairly probable that the children of a 'failure' will receive from their other parent just that little modification of character which makes all the difference. I sometimes wonder whether people, who talk so freely about extirpating the unfit, ever dispassionately consider their own history. Surely, one must be very 'fit,' indeed, not to know of an occasion, or perhaps two, in one's life, when it would have been only too easy to qualify for a place among the 'unfit.'

In my belief the innate qualities, physical, intellectual, and moral, of our nation have remained substantially the same for the last four or five centuries. If the struggle for existence has affected us to any serious extent (and I doubt it) it has been, indirectly, through our military and industrial wars with other nations.

What is often called the struggle for existence in society (I plead guilty to having used the term too loosely myself), is a contest, not for the means of existence, but for the means of enjoyment. Those who occupy the first places in this practical competitive examination are the rich and the influential; those who fail, more or less, occupy the lower places, down to the squalid obscurity of the pauper and the criminal. Upon the most liberal estimate, I suppose the former group will not amount to two percent. of the population. I doubt if the latter exceeds another two percent.; but let it be supposed, for the sake of argument, that it is as great as five percent.

As it is only in the latter group that anything comparable to the struggle for existence in the state of nature can take place; as it is only among this twentieth of the whole people that numerous men, women, and children die of rapid or slow starvation, or of the diseases incidental to permanently bad conditions of life; and as there is nothing to prevent their multiplication before they are killed off, while, in spite of greater infant mortality, they increase faster than the rich; it seems clear that the struggle for existence in this class can have no appreciable selective influence upon the other 95 percent. of the population.

What sort of a sheep breeder would he be who should content himself with picking out the worst fifty out of a thousand, leaving them on a barren common till the weakest starved, and then letting the survivors go back to mix with the rest? And the parallel is too favourable; since in a large number of cases, the actual poor and the convicted criminals are neither the weakest nor the worst.

In the struggle for the means of enjoyment, the qualities which ensure success are energy, industry, intellectual capacity, tenacity of purpose, and, at least as much sympathy as is necessary to make a man understand the feelings of his fellows. Were there none of those artificial arrrangements by which fools and knaves are kept at the top of society instead of sinking to their natural place at the bottom, the struggle for the means of enjoyment would ensure a constant circulation of the human units of the social compound, from the bottom to the top and from the top to the bottom. The survivors of the contest, those who continued to form the great bulk of the polity, would not be those 'fittest' who got to the very top, but the great body of the moderately 'fit,' whose numbers and superior propagative power, enable them always to swamp the exceptionally endowed minority.

I think it must be obvious to every one, that, whether we consider the internal or the external interest of society, it is desirable they should be in the hands of those who are endowed with the largest share of energy, of industry, of intellectual capacity, of tenacity of purpose, while they are not devoid of sympathetic humanity; and, in so far as the struggle for the means of enjoyment tends to place such men in possession of wealth and influence, it is a process which tends to the good of society. But the process, as we have seen, has no real resemblance to that which adapts living beings to current conditions in the state of nature; nor any to the artificial selection of the horticulturist.

To return, once more, to the parallel of horticulture. In the modern world, the gardening of men by themselves is practically restricted to the performance, not of selection, but of that other function of the gardener, the creation of conditions more favourable than those of the state of nature; to the end of facilitating the free expansion of the innate faculties of the citizen, so far as it is consistent with the general good. And the business of the moral and political philosopher appears to me to be the ascertainment, by the same method of observation, experiment, and ratiocination, as is practised in other kinds of scientific work, of the course of conduct which will best conduce to that end.

But, supposing this course of conduct to be scientifically determined and carefully followed out, it cannot put an end to the struggle for existence in the state of nature; and it will not so much as tend, in any way, to the adaptation of man to that state. Even should the whole human race be absorbed in one vast polity, within which 'absolute political justice' reigns, the struggle for existence with the state of nature outside it, and the tendency to the return of the struggle within, in consequence of over-multiplication, will remain; and, unless men's inheritance from the ancestors who fought a good fight in the state of nature, their dose of original sin, is rooted out by some method at present unrevealed, at any rate to disbelievers in supernaturalism, every child born into the world will still bring with him the instinct of unlimited self-assertion. He will have to learn the lesson of self-restraint and renunciation. But the practice of self-restraint and renunciation is not happiness, though it may be something much better.

That man, as a 'political animal,' is susceptible of a vast amount of improvement, by education, by instruction, and by the application of his intelligence to the adaptation of the conditions of life to his higher needs, I entertain not the slightest doubt. But, so long as he remains liable to error, intellectual or moral; so long as he is compelled to be perpetually on guard against the cosmic forces, whose ends are not his ends, without and within himself; so long as he is haunted by inexpugnable memories and hopeless aspirations; so long as the recognition of his intellectual limitations forces him to acknowledge his incapacity to penetrate the mystery of existence; the prospect of attaining untroubled happiness, or of a state which can, even remotely, deserve the title of perfection, appears to me to be as misleading an illusion as ever was dangled before the eyes of poor humanity. And there have been many of them.

That which lies before the human race is a constant struggle to maintain and improve, in opposition to the State of Nature, the State of Art of an organized polity; in which, and by which, man may develop a worthy civilization, capable of maintaining and constantly improving itself, until the evolution of our globe shall have entered so far upon its downward course that the cosmic process resumes its sway; and, once more, the State of Nature prevails over the surface of our planet.

Mutual Aid:
A Factor of Evolution

Peter Kropotkin

If we take now the teachings which can be borrowed from the analysis of modern society, in connection with the body of evidence relative to the importance of mutual aid in the evolution of the animal world and of mankind, we may sum up our inquiry as follows.

In the animal world we have seen that the vast majority of species live in societies, and that they find in association the best arms for the struggle for life: understood, of course, in its wide Darwinian sense— not as a struggle for the sheer means of existence, but as a struggle against all natural conditions unfavourable to the species. The animal species, in which individual struggle has been reduced to its narrowest limits, and the practice of mutual aid has attained the greatest development, are invariably the most numerous, the most prosperous, and the most open to further progress. The mutual protection which is obtained in this case, the possibility of attaining old age and of accumulating experience, the higher intellectual development, and the further growth of sociable habits, secure the maintenance of the species, its extension, and its further progressive evolution. The unsociable species, on the contrary, are doomed to decay.

Going next over to man, we found him living in clans and tribes at the very dawn of the stone age; we saw a wide series of social institutions developed already in the lower savage stage, in the clan and the tribe; and we found that the earliest tribal customs and habits gave to mankind the embryo of all the institutions which made later on

From Peter Kropotkin, *Mutual Aid: A Factor of Evolution* (New York: McClure Phillips & Co., 1903), pp. 293–300.

the leading aspects of further progress. Out of the savage tribe grew up the barbarian village community; and a new, still wider, circle of social customs, habits, and institutions, numbers of which are still alive among ourselves, was developed under the principles of common possession of a given territory and common defence of it, under the jurisdiction of the village folkmote, and in the federation of villages belonging, or supposed to belong, to one stem. And when new requirements induced men to make a new start, they made it in the city, which represented a double network of territorial units (village communities), connected with guilds—these latter arising out of the common prosecution of a given art or craft, or for mutual support and defence.

And finally, . . . facts were produced to show that although the growth of the State on the pattern of Imperial Rome had put a violent end to all mediaeval institutions for mutual support, this new aspect of civilization could not last. The State, based upon loose aggregations of individuals and undertaking to be their only bond of union, did not answer its purpose. The mutual-aid tendency finally broke down its iron rules; it reappeared and reasserted itself in an infinity of associations which now tend to embrace all aspects of life and to take possession of all that is required by man for life and for reproducing the waste occasioned by life.

It will probably be remarked that mutual aid, even though it may represent one of the factors of evolution, covers nevertheless one aspect only of human relations; that by the side of this current, powerful though it may be, there is, and always has been, the other current— the self-assertion of the individual, not only in its efforts to attain personal or caste superiority, economical, political, and spiritual, but also in its much more important although less evident function of breaking through the bonds, always prone to become crystallized, which the tribe, the village community, the city, and the State impose upon the individual. In other words, there is the self-assertion of the individual taken as a progressive element.

It is evident that no review of evolution can be complete, unless these two dominant currents are analyzed. However, the self-assertion of the individual or of groups of individuals, their struggles for superiority, and the conflicts which resulted therefrom, have already been analyzed, described, and glorified from time immemorial. In fact, up to the present time, this current alone has received attention from the epical poet, the annalist, the historian, and the sociologist. History, such as it has hitherto been written, is almost entirely a description of the ways and means by which theocracy, military power, autocracy, and, later on, the richer classes' rule have been promoted, established, and maintained. The struggles between these forces make, in fact, the substance of history. We may thus take the knowledge of the individual factor in human history as granted—even though there is full room for a new study of the subject on the lines just alluded to; while, on the other side, the mutual-aid factor has been hitherto totally lost sight of; it was simply denied, or even scoffed at, by the writers of the present and past generation. It was therefore necessary to show, first of all, the immense part which this factor plays in the evolution of both the animal world and human societies. Only after this has been fully recognized will it be possible to proceed to a comparison between the two factors.

To make even a rough estimate of their relative importance by any method more or less statistical, is evidently impossible. One single war—we all know—may be productive of more evil, immediate and subsequent, than hundreds of years of the unchecked action of the mutual-aid principle may be productive of good. But when we see that in the animal world, progressive development and mutual aid go hand in hand, while the inner struggle within the species is concomitant with retrogressive development; when we notice that with man, even success in struggle and war is proportionate to the development of mutual aid in each of the two conflicting nations, cities, parties, or tribes, and that in the process of evolution war itself (so far as it can go this way) has been made subservient to the ends of progress in mutual aid within the nation, the city or the clan—we already obtain a perception of the dominating influence of the mutual-aid factor as an element of progress. But we see also that the practice of mutual aid and its successive developments have created the very conditions of society life in which man was enabled to develop his arts, knowledge, and intelligence; and that the periods when institutions based on the mutual-aid tendency took their greatest development were also the periods of the greatest progress in arts, industry, and science. In fact, the study of the inner life of the mediaeval city and of the ancient Greek cities reveals the fact that the combination of mutual aid, as it was practised within the guild and the Greek clan, with a large initiative which was left to the individual and the group by means of the federative principle, gave to mankind the two greatest periods of history—the ancient Greek city and the mediaeval city periods; while the ruin of the above institutions during the State periods of history, which followed, corresponded in both cases to a rapid decay.

As to the sudden industrial progress which has been achieved during our own century, and which is usually ascribed to the triumph of individualism and competition, it certainly has a much deeper origin than that. Once the great discoveries of the fifteenth century were made, especially that of the pressure of the atmosphere, supported by a series of advances in natural philosophy—and they were made under the mediaeval city organization,—once these discoveries were made, the invention of the steam-motor, and all the revolution which the conquest of a new power implied, had necessarily to follow. If the mediaeval cities had lived to bring their discoveries to that point, the ethical consequences of the revolution effected by steam might have been different; but the same revolution in technics and science would have inevitably taken place. It remains, indeed, an open question whether the general decay of industries which followed the ruin of the free cities, and was especially noticeable in the first part of the eighteenth century, did not considerably retard the appearance of the steam-engine as well as the consequent revolution in arts. When we consider the astounding rapidity of industrial progress from the twelfth to the fifteenth centuries—in weaving, working of metals, architecture and navigation, and ponder over the scientific discoveries which that industrial progress led to at the end of the fifteenth century—we must ask ourselves whether mankind was not delayed in its taking full advantage of these conquests when a general depression of arts and industries took place in Europe after the decay of mediaeval civilization. Surely it was not the disappearance of the artist-artisan, nor the ruin of large cities and the extinction of intercourse between them, which could favour the industrial revolution; and we know indeed that James Watt spent twenty or more years of his life in order to render his invention serviceable, because he could not find in the last century what he would have readily found in mediaeval Florence or Brügge, that is, the artisans capable of realizing his devices in metal, and of giving them the artistic finish and precision which the steam-engine requires.

To attribute, therefore, the industrial progress of our century to the war of each against all which it has proclaimed, is to reason like the man who, knowing not the causes of rain, attributes it to the victim he has immolated before his clay idol. For industrial progress, as for each other conquest over nature, mutual aid and close intercourse certainly are, as they have been, much more advantageous than mutual struggle.

However, it is especially in the domain of ethics that the dominating importance of the mutual-aid principle appears in full. That mutual aid is the real foundation of our ethical conceptions seems evident enough. But whatever the opinions as to the first origin of the mutual-aid feeling or instinct may be—whether a biological or a supernatural cause is ascribed to it—we must trace its existence as far back as to the lowest stages of the animal world; and from these stages we can follow its uninterrupted evolution, in opposition to a number of contrary agencies, through all degrees of human development, up to the present times. Even the new religions which were born from time to time—always at epochs when the mutual-aid principle was falling into decay in the theocracies and despotic States of the East, or at the decline of the Roman Empire—even the new religions have only reaffirmed that same principle. They found their first supporters among the humble, in the lowest, downtrodden layers of society, where the mutual-aid principle is the necessary foundation of every-day life; and the new forms of union which were introduced in the earliest Buddhist and Christian communities, in the Moravian brotherhoods and so on, took the character of a return to the best aspects of mutual aid in early tribal life.

Each time, however, that an attempt to return to this old principle was made, its fundamental idea itself was widened. From the clan it was extended to the stem, to the federation of stems, to the nation, and finally—in ideal, at least—to the whole of mankind. It was also refined at the same time. In primitive Buddhism, in primitive Christianity, in the writings of some of the Mussulman teachers, in the early movements of the Reform, and especially in the ethical and philosophical movements of the last century and of our own times, the total abandonment of the idea of revenge, or of "due reward"—of good for good and evil for evil—is affirmed more and more vigorously. The higher conception of "no revenge for wrongs," and of freely giving more than one expects to receive from his neighbours, is proclaimed as being the real principle of morality—a principle superior to mere equivalence, equity, or justice, and more conducive to happiness. And man is appealed to to be guided in his acts, not merely by love, which is always personal, or at the best tribal, but by the perception of his oneness with each human being. In the practice of mutual aid, which we can retrace to the earliest beginnings of evolution, we thus find the positive and undoubted origin of our ethical conceptions; and we can affirm that in the ethical progress of man, mutual support—not mutual struggle—has had the leading part. In its wide extension, even at the present time, we also see the best guarantee of a still loftier evolution of our race.

Where Angels Fear to Tread: A Contribution from General Sociology to Human Ethics

W. C. Allee

Interest in the social impact of science in general and of biology in particular has been growing steadily in the last few decades. The problems imposed by the present war and by thoughts of the coming postwar world have increased this interest. My own active concern with various phases of the sub-social and social life of non-human animals has revealed enough of the complexities of these simpler social systems to make me well aware of my limitations when confronted with the modern social problems of men. It is the drive of immediate necessity rather than a feeling of competence that impels me to undertake the present discussion of the biological foundations for some fundamental phases of the social behavior of men.

I. THE BIOLOGICAL EVIDENCE

In our laboratory we are making two experimental approaches to the phenomena of biological sociology, and each yields its very different aspect of truth. On the one hand, we have been studying for over a decade the dominance-subordination relations that are characteristic of many social groups. We know from personal observations, as well as from the literature, of nip orders in fish, peck orders in flocks of several species of birds and fighting orders in mice. Usually there is one dominant animal which can bite, nip or peck others without being

From *Science* 97 (June 11, 1943), pp. 517–525. Copyright 1943 by the American Association for the Advancement of Science. Reprinted by permission of the publisher and the author.

attacked in return. Below it the others are ranked in various degrees of subservience. Similar dominance orders occur among such mammals as rats, cats, cows and men. Social organizations have also been reported with certainty for turtles and for lizards, as well as for many species of birds and mammals besides those which we have observed.

These social organizations are based immediately on fighting or bluffing ability, on individual aggressiveness or meekness, as exhibited in pair contacts between the different members of the vertebrate group in question. Usually the complete social order within a small group is determined during the first few days of contacts; often, among hens, for example, in the first series of encounters. The order, once established, is not readily upset. With fish, changes occur fairly frequently; but with hens, we have observed the same peck order to persist unchanged for as long as a year, and this is a relatively long time in the life of a hen. These social orders are a real expression of crude, person-against-person competition for social status and furnish fair illustrations of the individualistic, egocentric phase of group biology. Here is an aspect of the individual struggle for existence, and as such it illustrates an important phase of the Darwinian theory of evolution.

High position in the social peck order confers privileges. We know that top-ranking animals feed more freely; that high-ranking males of rhesus monkeys, sage grouse and the common domestic fowl have more ready access to females. Low social status may lead to semi-starvation, to psychological castration among cocks, to ejection from coveys of quail; and among many species it forces the low birds into inferior territories. In some cases, high social rank carries responsibilities for leadership or for guard duty; in other instances no correlation with social duties has been demonstrated as yet. Among others, I have published research reports and discussions of many such relationships and need not dwell on them longer.

These studies of individual aggressiveness make one experimental approach to general and comparative sociology. Our second line of attack comes from a different quarter. For more than twenty-five years we have been experimenting with group-centered tendencies which long before my time were called cooperation. Careful students nowadays point out that, among lower organisms, cooperation is entirely non-conscious. In this phase of our study we are investigating natural cooperation somewhat as many other biologists have been concerned with natural selection. Natural cooperation in its simpler forms implies merely that the interrelations between cells, for example, are more beneficial than harmful for the individual, or that the interrelations between individuals are more beneficial than harmful for the given social group.

I have added to and reviewed repeatedly the modern evidence concerning the existence of such cooperation. Mere repetition does not necessarily make for acceptance, but a good purpose may be served by summarizing in outline form the types of modern evidence that I have found compelling; the details can be filled in from the extensive literature.[1]

1. At all levels of the animal kingdom, and under a variety of conditions, there is added safety in numbers up to a given point. Animals from the protozoans to insects or man meet many adverse conditions better if optimal numbers are present rather than too few. There is danger also in overcrowding, but I am emphasizing just now the danger of the population being too sparse. For certain animals this sort of mass protection exists when the organisms are exposed to heat. Mass protection from cold is more common, as is protection from many poisons and from other harmful chemicals. Optimal numbers also protect from ultra-violet radiation, from radical changes in osmotic pressure and from many environmental deficiencies.

Macerated cells of a sponge will not regenerate if too few are present and the smallest embryonic grafts frequently fail to grow when somewhat larger ones succeed. If a natural population falls too low, it is in danger of dying out even though theoretically able to persist.

2. In keeping with the relations just outlined, many organisms, both plants and animals, are able so to condition an unfavorable medium that others following or associated with them can survive better and thrive when they could not do so in a raw, unconditioned medium.

3. Certain vital processes are adaptively retarded by increased numbers up to a given density. For example, scattered spermatozoa of many marine organisms lose fertilizing power more rapidly than they do when they are massed together.

4. Other biological processes are accelerated, perhaps beneficially, in the presence of populations of optimal size and density. Such processes are slowed down both in over-sparse populations and in those that are overcrowded. Cleavage rate in Arbacia and certain other eggs follows this rule. Various kinds of Protozoa show acceleration in rate of asexual

reproduction with medium rather than sparse population density, and similar phenomena may well have been a forerunner of

5. The evolution of the cooperative processes which are associated with sexual reproduction.

6. Colonial protozoa could hardly have evolved from solitary forms unless the simple colony of cells that remained attached after divisions had shown cooperative powers that were lacking when the cells were scattered singly. The evolution of the Metazoa from the Protozoa was probably based on similar relationships.

7. Each advance in complexity of metazoan individuals came from the natural selection of an increased ability in natural cooperation on the part of the evolving stock; the greater natural cooperation came first, and then it was selected.

8. Darwin[2] recognized that a relatively large population is a highly important factor in natural selection. Sewall Wright and others have evidence that evolution proceeds most rapidly in populations of interbreeding organisms that are intermediate in size, as compared with similar populations which are over-small or over-large.

9. The interdependence of organisms is shown by the repeated observation that all living things, from the simplest to the most complex, live in ecological communities; this is plainly seen in the many biocoenoses, such as those of the oyster bed. Further, the evolution of truly social animals has occurred independently in widely separated divisions of the animal kingdom. These could hardly have arisen so frequently and from such diverse sources if a strong substratum of generalized natural cooperation were not widespread among animals in nature. In nature no animal is solitary throughout its life history.

10. As with the individual organisms, each advance in complexity of the social life of any group of animals is based on the development of some means of closer cooperation between the individual units of the evolving group. . . .

As was shown earlier, both egoistic and group-centered forces exist in nature and both have been brought under experimentation. I had wondered for years whether we could experimentally test for possible relationships between these two basic phases of animal behavior. Might organized groups of birds, to take one possible instance, have survival values for the group in general as a result of their organization, even though there were no signs of an organized group defense? It will be remembered that such a group organization is based on individual aggressiveness and yields survival values for the high-ranking individuals in the peck order.

I have not yet been able to devise an elegant experiment to test the point. The best one I have been able to think up has been in progress for over nine months. Briefly, we have three flocks of line-bred hens which have been allowed to become organized and are kept as controls. In a similarly housed neighboring flock of the same stock, a new hen is added daily or every second day and the hen which has been longest with the flock is removed and placed in isolation for twenty-one days or more before she is again introduced into the experimental flock. By that time, apparently, she has forgotten all other hens as individuals; hence the experimental flock is in a state of continual reorganization.

I can not take time for details and without them you will be unable to make a critical judgment concerning the value of the experiment. An individual can affect the quality of the group life in these flocks; still, despite differences in individuals, the indications are that, regardless of the individuals that may be present, the organized flocks eat more, maintain weight better and spend less energy in fighting, bluffing and pecking each other than is the case with the flock that is daily subjected to reorganization. The strong suggestion is that an organized flock of hens has survival value as a flock which is lacking among an otherwise wholly similar group of hens, that is never allowed to become socially stabilized.

With all its imperfections, the experiment suggests that person to person competition, if not too severe, may lead to group organization which increases the effectiveness of the group as a cooperating social unit in competition or cooperation with other social organizations. Such a conclusion had been suggested by naturalistic evidence. Other data, certain types of which have already been summarized, indicate that cooperation at the individual level may also yield groups with increased competence in competition or cooperation at the group level. Any group organization, however achieved, may be helpful under many conditions. There is suggestive evidence that the relations between individuals which form a simple group of the first order are repeated between such groups when compounded into a unit of a higher social order. Even when society becomes still more complex, the relationships remain essentially similar. Throughout the higher social categories, there may be group-centered egoism and tendencies toward inter-group cooperation at one and the same time.

With cosmopolitan species, whether of human or of non-human animals, in last analysis, the cooperative units tend towards being worldwide in scope. If in its spread over the globe the common house sparrow becomes a new host for a virulent disease organism, the welfare of the whole species may be affected. Sessile eel grass has been devastated on the Atlantic coasts of Europe and of North America by the same mycetazoan parasite. The conclusions that I have been discussing are based primarily on objective studies with non-human animals. They are supported by much evidence from the interrelations of men; and the global scope of the cooperative interests of *Homo sapiens* are more obvious and have more possibilities for development than have those of any other species.

The picture that emerges from the cumulative studies on social biology is one in which cooperations and their opposite, disoperations, both exist. There are both egoistic and altruistic forces in nature, and both are important. The question arises insistently as to which of these is more fundamental and potent. Any such evaluation must be based on both short-run and long-run effects. After much consideration, it is my mature conclusion, contrary to Herbert Spencer, that the cooperative forces are biologically the more important and vital. The balance between the cooperative, altruistic tendencies and those which are disoperative and egoistic is relatively close. Under many conditions, the cooperative forces lose. In the long run, however, the group-centered, more altruistic drives are slightly stronger.

If cooperation had not been the stronger force, the more complicated animals, whether arthropods or vertebrates, could not have evolved from the simpler ones, and there would have been no men to worry each other with their distressing and biologically foolish wars. While I know of no laboratory experiments that make a direct test of this problem, I have come to this conclusion by studying the implications of many experiments which bear on both sides of the problem and from considering the trends of organic evolution in nature. Despite many known appearances to the contrary, human altruistic drives are as firmly based on an animal ancestry as is man himself. Our tendencies toward goodness, such as they are, are as innate as our tendencies toward intelligence; we could do well with more of both.

II. SOME IMPLICATIONS

Now I come to the more delicate part of my task. In discussing the further implications of the evidence and conclusions just presented, I am, as much as is possible, speaking in my private capacity as an American citizen with generations of American ancestors. I am both a mature biologist and a working member of a religious organization. The ideas I shall express are not necessarily those of the American Association for the Advancement of Science or of any of its sections; neither are they to be interpreted as the views of the university at which I work or of any other formal or informal organization. If at times I seem to place myself as a spokesman for all scientists or for biologists in general, please remember that I am giving my personal views and am not attempting an authoritative interpretation of the opinions of others.

As I see it, our present-day civilization is based primarily on religion, on other forms of tradition and on science. The arts furnish color and interpret the behavior and thinking of the human participants. Philosophy busies itself, or should, with trying to understand and explain the whole. The functioning of our type of civilization, if it is to be properly effective, calls for the cooperation of all these forces.

To-day, as in the past, religion wastes valuable time and energy quarrelling with science about their relative importance and over the proper division of functions, a quarrel which nowadays scientists largely ignore. Philosophy stages jurisdictional disputes with both. Too often art becomes cynical and irresponsible, and philosophy scolds all and sundry, sometimes in no friendly voice, for the general unwillingness to let philosophy direct the whole.

Philosophy insists, even yet, on its discredited age-old claim of having a special short cut to knowledge. Particularly philosophy scolds science, the most recently revitalized force in civilization; and modern religion, having attempted to use science to establish its claims, tries to carry on alone in some of the most vital activities of our times.

Here, as elsewhere in human efforts, it is easier for closely knit elements in a situation to develop and react to frictions among themselves than it is to disregard relatively petty internal troubles and make common cause against serious opposing forces. The forces in opposition to the better aspects of our none-too-perfect civilization are strong enough to demand united efforts from the arts, philosophy, science and religion if they are to be properly met. Perhaps plain speaking from a somewhat unorthodox friend of all these elements of civilization may be helpful.

Religion has much to learn from science in objectivity, in willingness and courage to follow evidence fearlessly and even in judging what constitutes valid evidence. Particularly religion can learn from science the advantage of giving up the thundering "thus saith the Lord" in favor of the more humble and essentially more effective summary of "this appears to be the evidence." In short, religion can profit by becoming intellectually more sound without losing for a moment its proper emphasis on the deep emotions of man.

And science has much to learn from religion. I mean from real religion, not from the pseudo-science of theology which, too often, consists mainly of expert verbal manipulations, related to scholasticism rather than to science.

Apparently I must take time to suggest what I mean by religion. Religion is ill-served by past and present emphasis on mystical and supernatural improbabilities. To me "God" is a possibly permissible name for the personification of all the best that the human race has been able to think and do and of all the beauty we have created, together with all the natural beauty we can appreciate. Such a conception transcends tradition and mere emotion and has both power, and dignity. While by no means final, this is as close an approach to the truth as real evidence permits at present.

Science has much to learn from such a religion as I have just outlined, a religion characterized by unselfish living and honest thinking combined with propaganda of the deed. More specifically, scientific men can profit by greater humbleness in the face of our immense ignorance about matters well within our several fields of professed competence. We can also dispense with excessive pride in the usually small discoveries we are able to make.

We scientists can profit by a frank admission of our awe and admiration for the pervading beauty of the phenomena we study, the charm of which often escapes us because of our preoccupation with details. We will profit by being less certain that the more unpalatable the interpretation, the closer the approach to truth. We will gain in the long run by working in our chosen fields more inconspicuously and quietly. Science, and mankind too, will profit by scientists who live closer to the ideals expressed and practised by the more devoted men of science or of religion.

I could make these suggestions in stronger language were it not for the fact that from a fairly wide and close acquaintanceship with many kinds of people, individual exceptions aside, scientists in general and biologists in particular seem the best people I know. This may be an expression of prejudice based on congeniality of temperament. I am inclined, however, to regard the difference between my scientific and my other friends as real and to attribute it to the training furnished by scientific practises.

The biological sciences impose an especially effective discipline in that they combine an impressive amount of precision in detail with a large content of imponderables. The combination is the more effective in that a mistake in judgment concerning the imponderables is usually exposed relatively soon by some precision measurement. The continuous checking of ideas against evidence does something to make conscientious followers of the scientific method essentially more honest and less given to the self-deception which is one of the weaknesses among those skilled primarily in the manipulation of ideas or of words.

As with followers of other disciplines, we scientists are very human. Our frequent preoccupation with "my status," "my experiment," "my theory," "my priority" and even with "my little bug" is a source of weakness for which correction can be found in a closer approach to the ideals of science or of religion.

Despite my firm belief in the essential goodness of my biological colleagues, I must admit that advanced laboratory study and the introduction to research does not automatically produce some of the higher types of altruism. When recurrent opportunities come to recommend some one to teach biology in a deserving though struggling Negro college, or in remote, ill-equipped, much-needed Chinese or Hindu laboratories, I have learned to turn to students with a strong religious background for men with vision enough to see that the opportunities may, in the long run, repay the sacrifices.

Let us take another approach. No one of us passes much time without being reminded that we are living in a world at war and in a country that is closely engaged in that war. We went into this present conflict with, on the whole, commendable calm, and the war is being prosecuted more efficiently because wartime emotions are at a minimum as yet. It is questionable how long this frame of mind will continue. Our sons and friends and students are engaged on many fighting fronts and tension mounts as the casualty lists trickle through. We need to examine frequently our responsibilities as biologists in our world to-day, for, like other animals, biologists do not live in a vacuum insulated from the impacts of their time.

It has come as a shock to many that their hard-won biological skills are of so little direct use in the war. The closer the approach to preventative or curative medicine, the greater the immediate applicability of our biological training. It is true that in the war effort there have been some fairly amusing practical applications of highly impractical phases of biology, for it is impossible to predict what bit of pure science of to-day will be the basis for the applied science of to-morrow.

For most, particularly for those of us in the upper-age brackets, we must continue for the foreseeable future at our present jobs or at something closely approximating them. We may need to shift teaching and research somewhat; many have already done so. Primarily, however, our main job must be to remain steadfastly at our usual, routine tasks. These are by no means unimportant even for a world at war. The younger generation needs as many steady points of reference as possible in their rapidly shifting world. This need is tacitly admitted when they come, as they do, to talk themselves quiet in the presence of a sympathetic, calm, older person in whom they place some confidence.

We have a heavy responsibility to our younger friends and students in the armed forces of the world, in the civilian public service camps, in concentration camps or in prisons, so to act that they have a recognizable world to which to return. We, as well as they, have our responsibilities to defend and later to rebuild our civilization, using the techniques we know best. Our phase of the task is as important as it is undramatic.

In the present and immediate future we have the task of helping maintain our forms of government both locally and nationally. Closer home, we have the pressing work of maintaining academic standards and the honesty of academic credits, certificates, fellowship and other awards and even of academic degrees.

In addition to attempting to maintain present levels of competence in intellectual training, we need to give full play to all usable forces that make for emotional stability. Admittedly we are highly ignorant concerning methods for the education of the emotions at the college or graduate level. Mainly we trust to the added stability that comes with maturity. We need to pool our ignorance and attempt positive steps towards training emotion as well as intellect. We have some hints on which to work. Project methods of laboratory study can be helpful as can volunteer summer work camps, honest competitive group sports and many kinds of informal group living. The difficulty of the task and ignorance of how to educate the emotions does not warrant us in continued neglect of this important phase of education.

For the somewhat more remote future, there is an obligation that rests with especial weight on biologists to attempt to make sure that mankind does not lose the peace that will follow this war. We have less hope of winning the peace if all of us become emotionally engulfed in the war. Among other consequences of this duty not to lose the peace, we have an obligation to keep fundamental research projects going even in wartime. I am fully convinced that those nations will have the best opportunity to win the peace who emerge from the present conflict with their program of basic research most nearly intact. This includes the necessity for maintaining a supply of trained research workers in the basic disciplines and the retention of enough of the brilliant younger men to ensure a steady trickle of researches in a great variety of academic fields, many of which are far removed from the immediate war.

Biologists, as their part of the war effort, are searching with almost frantic haste for new techniques for patching up men's bodies and for solving problems of adequate nutrition for ourselves and our associates. This introduces another phase of the relation of science to war that must be faced honestly. Science is the maker and user of gadgets as well as the discoverer of the shadowy outlines of the tools of the future. Science is fighting this war in laboratories all over the world that were built to search impartially for basic evidence, for the truth, as we naively used to say, and for all people, not for one group or another.

The success of scientists in helping to win the war will be used to blame science itself later. When the war is over, the scientists who are now so praised and courted on almost all sides will be told in no uncertain terms, as we have been in the past, that the war itself was all our doing. And there will be insistent calls from many whose motives are not altogether disinterested, for a moratorium on scientific research lest bigger and more destructive wars have to be fought in the future. Such anti-scientists will forget the long series of vicious wars that were fought before science became a major force in our civilization. There will be some truth in the accusation, for biological science is not wholly free from war guilt. This is not only because we have been the inventors of tools for mass destruction but because we have been responsible for giving interpretations to some aspects of Darwinian theories of evolution that provide a convenient, plausible explanation and justification for all the aggressive, selfish behavior of which man is capable.

Herbert Spencer in 1901 in his "Principles of Ethics" gave a mild statement of this doctrine (p. 189): "But to say that each individual shall reap the benefits brought to him by his own powers, inherited and acquired, is to enumerate egoism as an ultimate principle of biological conduct. . . . Under its biological aspect this proposition can not be contested by those who agree in the doctrine of evolution."

T. H. Huxley[3] asserts the same principle and characteristically steps up the emphasis. In speaking about primitive men and "their less erect and more hairy compatriots," Huxley's statement was: "As among these, so among primitive men, the weakest and stupidest went to the wall, while the toughest and shrewdest, those best fitted to cope with their circumstances, but not the best in any other sense, survived. Life was a continual free fight and beyond the limited and temporary relations of the family, the Hobbesian war of each against all was the normal state of existence." Huxley's general position was that amelioration of this egoistic struggle was a contribution made by "ethical man" despite his animal ancestry. Ernst Haeckel[4] took a wholly similar point of view.

According to this interpretation, the altruistic drives of man are primarily human attributes that arise from the development of sympathies at the human level and are connected with the mass of animal behavior by a very slender stalk. We know, for example, that the aggression of hens high in the peck order may be modified by individual tolerances towards certain of their subordinates in a manner that strongly suggests human personal preferences. Also it appears that male chimpanzees show a chivalry pattern towards females that are in oestrus. Such modifications of aggressiveness are weak foundations on which to base the idea of a natural drive toward altruism among men. In fact, it is a fairly common interpretation that such altruistic drives as exist are based primarily on some sort of enlightened selfishness.

It is not to be wondered that apologists for human behavior seized on the doctrine so authoritatively set forth, as a proof that man, having descended from other animals, had inherited fighting tendencies which it was almost useless to resist. The natural fate of all was to engage in a physical struggle for existence softened only by slight checks imposed by more or less artificial rules for human conduct.

The biological support for this fatalistic view regarding, among other things, the inevitableness of intra-species human conflict, is now opposed by strong evidence which indicates that the idea of a ruthless struggle for existence is not the whole, or even the major contribution of current biology to social philosophy and social ethics. This newer evidence, which was outlined earlier, does not cast doubt on the existence of the human vices of pride, covetousness, lust, anger, gluttony, envy and sloth and it does not remove indications that they find natural roots in infra-human behavior. The newer findings do strengthen decidedly the older evidence for a biological basis for the human virtues of faith, hope and love and supply renewed indications that men inherited these tendencies too. This strongly suggests that the present high state of development of the seven capital sins just named is mainly a result of man's learned devilishness rather than his inevitable response to inherited nature. On the other hand, we know too that man has been able to enlarge greatly his natural drives toward being godlike.

From such considerations, I insist again that the data of biology, if properly understood, do not furnish sound support for a social philosophy based primarily on the idea that might makes right in interpersonal contacts or in international relations. Those who assert that the whole trend of science is to lend support to the present war system in settling international disagreements are relying on a mistaken, outmoded phase of biological thought to bolster up a much older and unreasoned drive toward conflict. The philosophy that condones war is not based on all the biological evidence or on recent interpretations made in the light of that evidence. Science is indeed largely responsible for designing the tools with which men fight and for undue emphasis even in the recent past on some of the implications of the Darwinian doctrine.

Otherwise scientists as such bear only their proportionate share of the responsibility for the misuse man is making of the powers we have discovered and placed in his hands.

When this war does end, the intelligent public should have much to say about the terms of a just and workable peace. Happily there is interest in this subject among responsible biologists and I want to encourage continued consideration of all its complicated ramifications. Such a study will emphasize again the unity of all the forces that make for civilization. For example, certain phases of modern biology furnish a basis of objective evidence for the age-old religious insight that the fundamentals of a just and enduring peace are to be found in a positive application of the rule: behave towards all others as you would have all others behave towards you.

Speaking for the moment as a humanist, rather than primarily as a biologist (the two points of view are not unduly dissimilar) there are some implications of this ethical rule as applied to the coming peace which I shall outline. It should be understood that the biological drives toward natural cooperation support the general tenor of the following program without favoring this or any other precise formulation of proposed social action.

1. We are not to look forward to punishment for defeated *peoples* at the close of the present war.

2. In under-nourished Europe and elsewhere as needed, administer relief according to ability to furnish it and to need only, not according to politics or boundaries.

3. Set up a world organization which will, in principle from the start, and in detail as much as possible, treat victors and vanquished alike. This implies similar treatment of all peoples with regard to:

    a. Disarmament; if we disarm other nations, we must be willing similarly to disarm ourselves.

    b. International police; if we subject any major portion of the world to the control of an international police force, we, ourselves, should accept a similar control on the same general principles.

    c. Curtailment of sovereignty; national governments of powerful, along with those of weak peoples, must discontinue the present policy of determining their own actions in all matters deemed by themselves to lie within the limits of their own national interests.

d. Educate all alike for the processes that make for change by the use of peaceful, non-violent techniques. All nations and many classes within nations do and will continue to need such education for a long time to come.

e. Behave towards the defeated peoples from the outset more as the English treated the Boers or the United States treated the Filipinos at the turn of the century rather than as our carpet-bag governments coerced the South after 1865 or as England governs troublesome India; and by all means not as Nazi Germany has treated her victims.

We should not overlook the existence of strong, competitive, egoistic drives among all animals, ourselves included. These might be duly considered in any workable plan for a world order. Our job is to keep them in their true place, somewhat subservient to the even more fundamental cooperative, altruistic forces of human nature. They should not again be allowed to steal the international show. These competitive urges can serve mankind well if turned to their original function of driving man in his struggle against his enemies among other species of living things. This struggle is on a global scale, and the members of all countries and races can unite in it. Each can compete against the others for racial, national or personal preeminence in this common task. Competitive drives for worthy ends have real strength. I have only to mention the word priority to a biological audience to make the point.

Consideration of these egoistic drives brings us back again to the hen coops from which we started. Man, like so many of his fellow vertebrates, has a strong tendency to set up social orders among individuals and between groups. In the past, man has made repeated trials of informal and finally of a more formal world organization based on dominance and subordination. There have been the hen-like peck orders of the early world empires to which the atavistic Nazi system is an attempted return. Until recently these rigid peck orders were being replaced by the more democratic dovelike give and take of territorial orders, in which, certain empires aside, each nation had the peck-right over all comers in its home territory. With nations, as with many territorial birds, when space became crowded, the dove-like peck dominance changed to the more despotic peck right.

To-day, a major biological contribution to the discussion of a postwar world is that, solidly as the peck-right system is grounded in animal behavior, it is not the only pattern for human action that biology has to offer. Other animals show a somewhat stronger tendency toward essential cooperations than they do toward struggles for egoistic power. Man can, if he chooses, focus on his innate drives toward cooperation and attempt to set up a new order based primarily on some altruistic pattern such as I have outlined. The task will be easier since modern biological teachings in these matters resemble many of the social doctrines of the ethical religions.

The difficulties in the transition from the power politics of the international peck order to a system based on international cooperation are impressive. The change is possible. If the attempt is deferred for the present, it will most certainly come in the future and I prefer to start toward the future now. If we again turn toward the solutions of the past, we face the disheartening certainty that power politics have never avoided war for more than a few decades and will not avoid war again. We are aided in working toward a more rational goal by the fact that, one or two nations aside, there is a general and strong mind-set toward peace throughout the peoples of the world. Our task as biologists, and as citizens of a civilized country, is a practical engineering job. We need to help arrange so that the existing trend toward a workable world organization will be guided along practical lines which accord with sound biological theory. And we must remember always that in such matters the idealist with the long-range view is frequently the true realist.

NOTES

1. W. C. Allee, *The Social Life of Animals* (New York: Norton, 1938).
2. Charles Darwin, *Origin of Species* (London: Murray's Library Edition, 1859), p. 74.
3. *Evolution and Ethics and Other Essays* (London: Macmillan, 1894), pp. 203–204.
4. *Freie Wissenschaft und Freie Lehre* (Stuttgart, 1878), p. 73.

The Human Biogram

Lionel Tiger and Robin Fox

We have confidently asserted that identifiable propensities for behavior are in the wiring. Unless we look to divine intervention, these got there by the same route as they got into the wiring of any other animal: by mutation and natural selection. One of the sturdiest theories in science, widely and agreeably accepted, is that animals vary along a normal curve in a number of respects, and that selection occurs in terms of this curve. Taller giraffes could secure more food and consequently reproduce more and better offspring—which is why they developed long necks. Early turtles with hard backs could survive their enemies by withdrawing behind a shelter of their own; they lived to endow their successors with this specialized characteristic. The broad outlines of the theory, and the process, are clear and indisputable: biological change results from a knowable and known procedure.

This is easily seen when physical characteristics change through selection. More subtle and more exciting is the matter of behavioral evolution, which the science of ethology has forced us to recognize as a central issue. We can readily see that species can be defined physically, but as we get better information about how they behave in natural settings, we begin to see how they can be classified behaviorally. The implication here is important: regularities of behavior are as predictable and discernible as the color of plumage and the shape of eggs. But how is this

From Lionel Tiger and Robin Fox, *The Imperial Animal* (New York: Holt, Rinehart and Winston, 1971), pp. 17–23. Copyright © 1971 by Lionel Tiger and Robin Fox. Reprinted by permission of Holt, Rinehart and Winston, Publishers, and Martin Secher & Warburg Limited. [Footnotes omitted. Ed.]

regularity controlled? Why is it that, while almost anything can happen in principle, only a limited and specialized set of actions occurs in practice?

Back to the wiring, and back to the new data we have about genetics and the control of living systems. Though we have known for many years how genetic systems worked, breaking the genetic code—the structure of the DNA molecule—allowed a rather hard-headed species to see with its own eyes how the life of an animal was controlled by facts of nature as comprehensible as a computer program. The genetic code *is* a program, and it *is* a way of transmitting a program from generation to generation. DNA is immensely complex in itself and in what it does, but its overriding work is carrying from the parents to the offspring a program that includes behavior as well as body shape, color, and sense of smell. The most obvious program is the life cycle itself, which is both profoundly physical and profoundly behavioral at the same time. The caterpillar turns into a butterfly in an astonishing display of life-cycling. The human infant begins to smile at a predictable time, and the boy soon loses his shrillness and darting lightness and becomes a character more uncertain, more portentous, more annoying to his elders. He is, without doubt, a different creature, and all at once subject to forces even free will and the force of government cannot hold back. His behavior changes as it is programmed to do. He is wired so that this will happen, and indeed not only human boys but also young males in many other primate groups suffer the scorn of their elders and the uncertainty of a transition from one difficult role to another. It is as much a behavior as dying. The geneticist J. Z. Young once defined death as "what happens when there is no longer a program to repair the program to repair the program to repair the program . . . etc., etc." It is unnecessary to labor the point that living involves successful programs and that successful behavioral programs are as much a result of natural selection as the opposable thumb and the reproductive differences between men and women.

The unique outcome of the human wiring is human cultural behavior, with its rich symbolic content, its complex social traditions, and its nongenetic mode of transferring information from one generation to another. But how did the human animal get wired for culture in the first place? The theory used to be that, for some reason or other, at some time or other, the human brain expanded to the point where it was capable of producing first symbols and then culture. This no longer seems plausible. Our little-brained ape-man ancestors of two million years ago—with skull spaces no larger than a gorilla's—were doing cultural things. For a start, they were making tools of bone and stone. At first glance this may not seem a great leap forward (after all, the rudiments of toolmaking occur in chimpanzees), but it implies that these creatures were organizing their experience in a manner that was already typically human. They had diverged from the rest of the primates as surely in this respect as in the upright stance and the splayed big toe, and this divergence was a consequence of the momentous transition from vegetarianism to systematic hunting. It was *after* they started doing cultural things that the brain grew in size and complexity—for the making of butchering tools to deal with the proceeds of cooperative hunting implies foresight and planning, a complex system of cooperation, and a division of labor that in turn presupposes some fairly advanced form of communication. Obviously there was a selective advantage to cultural behavior, as in the clear cases of the hard shell of the turtle and the neck of the giraffe. There was a premium on an animal which could learn a lot and learn it quickly and which did not depend too heavily on direct instructions from the genes for each item of behavior. Selection favored the smarter animals, and they in turn bred smarter ones still, whose skills and cunning enabled them to survive and flourish. But this process constantly created a new environment for the human animal—an environment of its own making. Once the animal became dependent for survival on speech, for example, selection would favor whatever mutations produced some improvement in the speech organs; if the variable were imagination, selection would operate in the same way. The genetic qualities that favored scientific activity or associative learning, "general intelligence" or the ability to inhibit present gratification in anticipation of future wants, or the propensity to obey rules, would be subject to selection as much as the muscular qualities that facilitated the striding walk.

Obeying rules is important: the animal had not only to do things, but *not* to do them as well. It was beginning to shed its dependency on the precarious certainty of instinct, but it still had to get done—somehow—the jobs that instinct did for other animals. It substituted customs and habits, but these had nonetheless to be obeyed like instincts, and they had to be almost semiautomatic to be successful. Selection, then, clearly favored those creatures with a propensity to obey rules, to feel guilty about breaking them, and, generally, to control their sexual and aggressive tendencies enough to let otherwise recalcitrant individuals form a working society. In a real sense, this yielded citizens more effective for the evolving human social group and its evolving cultural patterns. Selection put into the actual wiring those qualities and propensities that made for a successful social and cultural animal. It left a lot of variety, of course—that is nature's way.

What happened was that culture itself became a selection pressure that favored animals with attributes which served a culture-bearing creature. Man became dependent on cultural modes of surviving: the more capable of cultural behavior he was, the more he prospered. And the result was an animal that is not only the producer of culture but its product as well. It is not surprising that man is driven to produce that which produced him.

In sum: we behave culturally because it is in our nature to behave culturally, because natural selection has produced an animal that has to behave culturally, that has to invent rules, make myths, speak languages, and form men's clubs, in the same way that the hamadryas baboon has to form harems, adopt infants, and bite its wives on the neck.

We fail to appreciate this infrastructure of our cultural behavior because our perspective on ourselves as a species is chronically limited. To most of us a generation is a long time. How many people can grasp with any constructive imagination the period of a life span? To all of us the period of known history is a very long time and fades into indistinction with the advent of civilization. But that five thousand years which is civilization is, in evolutionary terms, as but an evening gone. From the perspective of the evolution of the species, nothing much has happened in that period except an unprecedented rise in population. It is just an episode. Given the right perspective, everything is just an episode. The order of Primates, our order, is a seventy-million-year-old episode in the history of the mammals—itself an episode in the history of the vertebrates, itself an episode in the history of organic life. The line leading to man probably broke off from the other primates more than twenty million years ago, while indisputable remains of our ape-man ancestor—*Australopithecus*—date back some five and one-half million years. The first upright and big-brained human—*Homo erectus*—is usually credited with about one million years of history. *Homo sapiens* is half a million years old, while the appearance of truly modern man—*Cro-Magnon*—dates from forty or fifty thousand years ago.

This is our time scale for the evolution not only of physique but also of social behavior, emotions, patterns of learning, loving, and hating. Stored in the older parts of the brain are all those codes and messages held over from that ancient time—the heat of the jungle past and the long drag on the Pliocene savannas. Surrounding and coming to terms with this old brain is a new brain forged mostly in the cool-to-icy environment of the Pleistocene and the touch-and-go battle with the snaking ice. And since then? Fire is maybe half a million years old; agriculture at least ten thousand years; large settlements five thousand; elaborate cities three thousand; steam power and industrial explosion a mere two hundred. Nuclear man appeared yesterday.

If we made an hour-long film to represent the history of tool-making man, industrial man would flash by in a few seconds at the end—he would barely be seen. Yet it is only the flashy and tortured complexity of industrial man that is so often taken to be truly human. Or, at best, we use civilized man as our model. But civilized man is an evolutionary afterthought. We remain Upper Paleolithic hunters, fine-honed machines designed for the efficient pursuit of game. Nothing worth noting has happened in our evolutionary history since we left off hunting and took to the fields and the towns—nothing except perhaps a little selection for immunity to epidemics, and probably not even that. "Man the hunter" is not an episode in our distant past: we are still man the hunter, incarcerated, domesticated, polluted, crowded, and bemused.

We have overtaken ourselves with those fantasy structures called civilizations, and with the sheer overpowering growth of our numbers. For most of our hunting past—for ninety-nine percent of our history—the population of the species stayed steady at about one million. With the dawn of agriculture it leaped to one hundred million. Since the advent of industry it has reached 3,700 million, and by the year 2000 it will be 7,000 million. A creature evolved for living in bands of 50 or so cannot but have problems with such a series of population explosions and their organizational consequences. Most of what we take for granted in human nature is in fact an end product of the pathological events attendant on the incarceration of our hunting selves. We are all in this together, treading on one another's toes.

Without a grasp of this perspective we will never understand ourselves or our societies or the sustaining and yet undermining role of our culture-producing brains. We have to make the imaginative and unsettling leap into understanding that *agricultural and industrial civilizations have put nothing into the basic wiring of the human animal.* We are wired for hunting—for the emotions, the excitements, the curiosities, the regularities, the fears, and the social relationships that were needed to survive in the hunting way of life. And we are wired basically on a primate model. This primate wiring was adjusted and readjusted for over seventy million years before we emerged as distinct from the rest of our order. In this perspective even the forebrain is an afterthought. The cerebral cortex struggles with a heritage it did not ask for and has frequently wished aloud it did not have. "What art thou, O Man, when thou art full of lust?" said an anguished prophet. What, when thou art full of compassion, or ambition, or the urge to exchange, or the pleasure in taking risks, or the skill in dealing with associates, or the compulsion to explore, or the need to be talked to?

Ours is a heritage stretching over millions of years of the primate hunting past and capped by a recently acquired symbolizing brain. Yet we are still living inside our own skulls and feeding on our fantasies. When we see how helpless we are to prevent war and civil violence, when we rail against the pollution of our air and rivers, when we find ourselves unable to bridge the gap of understanding between old and young, when we watch our cities fall into greater and grimier decay, when we come up against the seemingly inexorable nature of racial conflict and religious prejudice—when, in short, we look at or hide from the progressively awful spectacle we present to ourselves, we can react only in terms of what our intellect offers us as alibis. We blame the decline of monopoly capitalism, the communist conspiracy, the military-industrial complex, the corruption of the powerful, the permissiveness of parents, the viciousness of the right or the subversiveness of the left, the falling away from God, affluence, imperialism, racism, Marxism, the cult of youth, overpopulation, the shadow of the bomb, and the innate brutality of man.

But in the cold eye of nature we are just another species in trouble.

This has happened before, and there were no conspirators to blame then. If a species fails to adapt, it does not survive. It is finally as simple as that. It did the tyrannosaurs no good to blame one another for their failure. They could not adapt to reality, and they became extinct. If and when we are gone, our quarrels about which of us was to blame will merely seem funny—except that there will be nobody there to laugh. We are the first species to hold in its own hands the power to affect consciously its own survival. But this can be achieved only if we know ourselves as a species, and, more important, *sense* ourselves as a species, and, in the last resort, *act* as a species in the interests of the species as a whole.

PART II

Animal Behavior
and Morality

The Functional Limits
of Morality

Konrad Lorenz

In order correctly to appreciate how indispensable cultural rites and social norms really are, one must keep in mind that, as Arnold Gehlen has put it, man is by nature a being of culture. In other words, man's whole system of innate activities and reactions is phylogenetically so constructed, so "calculated" by evolution, as to *need* to be complemented by cultural tradition. For instance, all the tremendous neurosensory apparatus of human speech is phylogenetically evolved, but so constructed that its function presupposes the existence of a culturally developed language which the infant has to learn. The greater part of all phylogenetically evolved patterns of human social behavior is interrelated with cultural tradition in an analogous way. The urge to become a member of a group, for instance, is certainly something that has been programmed in the pre-human phylogeny of man, but the distinctive properties of any group which make it coherent and exclusive are norms of behavior ritualized in cultural development. . . . Without traditional rites and customs representing a common property valued and defended by all members of the group, human beings would be quite unable to form social units exceeding in size that of the primal family group which can be held together by the instinctive bond of personal friendship. . . .

The equipment of man with phylogenetically programmed norms of behavior is just as dependent on cultural tradition and rational respon-

From *On Aggression* by Konrad Lorenz. Copyright © 1963 by Dr. G. Borotha-Schoeler Verlag, Wien; English translation copyright © 1966 by Konrad Lorenz, pp. 264–274. Reprinted by permission of Harcourt Brace Jovanovich, Inc.

sibility as, conversely, the function of both the latter is dependent on instinctual motivation. Were it possible to rear a human being of normal genetic constitution under circumstances depriving it of all cultural tradition—which is impossible not only for ethical but also for biological reasons—the subject of the cruel experiment would be very far from representing a reconstruction of a pre-human ancestor, as yet devoid of culture. It would be a poor cripple, deficient in higher functions in a way comparable to that in which idiots who have suffered encephalitis during infantile or fetal life lack the higher functions of the cerebral cortex. No man, not even the greatest genius, could invent, all by himself, a system of social norms and rites forming a substitute for cultural tradition.

In our time, one has plenty of unwelcome opportunity to observe the consequences which even a partial deficiency of cultural tradition has on social behavior. The human beings thus affected range from young people advocating necessary if dangerous abrogations of customs that have become obsolete, through angry young men and rebellious gangs of juveniles, to the appearance of a certain well-defined type of juvenile delinquent which is the same all over the world. Blind to all values, these unfortunates are the victims of infinite boredom.

The means by which an expedient compromise between the rigidity of social norms and the necessity of adaptive change can be effected is prescribed by biological laws of the widest range of application. No organic system can attain to any higher degree of differentiation without firm and cohesive structures supporting it and holding it together. Such a structure and its support can, in principle, only be gained by the sacrifice of certain degrees of freedom that existed before. A worm can bend all over, an arthropod only where its cuticular skeleton is provided with joints for that purpose.

Changes in outer or inner environment may demand degrees of freedom not permitted by the existing structure and therefore may necessitate its partial and/or temporary disintegration, in the same way that growth necessitates the periodic shedding of the shell in crustacea and other arthropods. This act of demolishing carefully erected structures, though indispensable if better adapted ones are to arise, is always followed by a period of dangerous vulnerability, as is impressively illustrated by the defenseless situation of the newly molted soft-shelled crab.

All this applies unrestrictedly to the "solidified," that is to say institutionalized, system of social norms and rites which function very much like a supporting skeleton in human cultures. In the growth of human cultures, as in that of arthropods, there is a built-in mechanism providing for graduated change. During and shortly after puberty human beings have an indubitable tendency to loosen their allegiance to all traditional rites and social norms of their culture, allowing conceptual thought to cast doubt on their value, and to look around for new and perhaps more worthy ideals. There probably is, at that time of life, a definite sensitive period for a new object-fixation, such as in the case of the object-fixation found in animals and called imprinting. If at that critical time of life old ideals prove fallacious under critical scrutiny and new ones fail to appear, the result is complete aimlessness, the utter boredom which characterizes the young delinquent. If, on the other hand, the clever demagogue, well versed in the dangerous art of producing supranormal stimulus situations, gets hold of young people at the susceptible age, he finds it easy to guide their object-fixation in a direction subservient to his political aims. At the postpuberal age some human beings seem to be driven by an overpowering urge to espouse a cause and failing to find a worthy one may become fixated on astonishingly inferior substitutes. The instinctive need to be the member of a closely knit group fighting for common ideals may grow so strong that it becomes inessential what these ideals are and whether they possess any intrinsic value. This, I believe, explains the formation of juvenile gangs whose social structure is very probably a rather close reconstruction of that prevailing in primitive human society.

Apparently this process of object-fixation can take its full effect only once in an individual's life. Once the valuation of certain social norms or the allegiance to a certain cause is fully established, it cannot be erased again, at least not to the extent of making room for a new, equally strong one. Also it would seem that once the sensitive period has elapsed, a man's ability to embrace ideals at all is considerably reduced. All this helps to explain the hackneyed truth that human beings have to live through a rather dangerous period at, and shortly after, puberty. The tragic paradox is that the danger is greatest for those who are by nature best fitted to serve the noble cause of humanity.

The process of object-fixation has consequences of an importance that can hardly be overestimated. It determines neither more nor less than that which a man will live for, struggle for, and, under certain circumstances, blindly go to war for. It determines the conditioned stimulus situation releasing a powerful phylogenetically evolved behavior which I propose to call that of militant enthusiasm.

Militant enthusiasm is particularly suited for the paradigmatic illustration of the manner in which a phylogenetically evolved pattern of behavior interacts with culturally ritualized social norms and rites, and in which, though absolutely indispensable to the function of the compound system, it is prone to miscarry most tragically if not strictly controlled by rational responsibility based on causal insight. The Greek word *enthousiasmos* implies that a person is possessed by a god; the German *Begeisterung* means that he is controlled by a spirit, a *Geist,* more or less holy.

In reality, militant enthusiasm is a specialized form of communal aggression, clearly distinct from and yet functionally related to the more primitive forms of petty individual aggression. Every man of normally strong emotions knows, from his own experience, the subjective phenomena that go hand in hand with the response of militant enthusiasm. A shiver runs down the back and, as more exact observation shows, along the outside of both arms. One soars elated, above all the ties of everyday life, one is ready to abandon all for the call of what, in the moment of this specific emotion, seems to be a sacred duty. All obstacles in its path become unimportant; the instinctive inhibitions against hurting or killing one's fellows lose, unfortunately, much of their power. Rational considerations, criticism, and all reasonable arguments against the behavior dictated by militant enthusiasm are silenced by an amazing reversal of all values, making them appear not only untenable but base and dishonorable. Men may enjoy the feeling of absolute righteousness even while they commit atrocities. Conceptual thought and moral responsibility are at their lowest ebb. As a Ukrainian proverb says: "When the banner is unfurled, all reason is in the trumpet."

The subjective experiences just described are correlated with the following, objectively demonstrable phenomena. The tone of the entire striated musculature is raised, the carriage is stiffened, the arms are raised from the sides and slightly rotated inward so that the elbows point outward. The head is proudly raised, the chin stuck out, and the facial muscles mime the "hero face," familiar from the films. On the back and along the outer surface of the arms the hair stands on end. This is the objectively observed aspect of the shiver!

Anybody who has ever seen the corresponding behavior of the male chimpanzee defending his band or family with self-sacrificing courage will doubt the purely spiritual character of human enthusiasm. The chimp, too, sticks out his chin, stiffens his body, and raises his elbows; his hair stands on end, producing a terrifying magnification of his body contours as seen from the front. The inward rotation of his arms obviously has the purpose of turning the longest-haired side outward to enhance the effect. The whole combination of body attitude and hair-raising constitutes a bluff. This is also seen when a cat humps its back, and is calculated to make the animal appear bigger and more dangerous than it really is. Our shiver, which in German poetry is called a *"heiliger Schauer,"* a "holy" shiver, turns out to be the vestige of a pre-human vegetative response of making a fur bristle which we no longer have.

To the humble seeker of biological truth there cannot be the slightest doubt that human militant enthusiasm evolved out of a communal defense response of our pre-human ancestors. The unthinking single-mindedness of the response must have been of high survival value even in a tribe of fully evolved human beings. It was necessary for the individual male to forget all his other allegiances in order to be able to dedicate himself, body and soul, to the cause of the communal battle. *"Was schert mich Weib, was schert mich Kind"*—"What do I care for wife or child," says the Napoleonic soldier in a famous poem by Heinrich Heine, and it is highly characteristic of the reaction that this poet, otherwise a caustic critic of emotional romanticism, was so unreservedly enraptured by his enthusiasm for the "great" conqueror as to find this supremely apt expression.

The object which militant enthusiasm tends to defend has changed with cultural development. Originally it was certainly the community of concrete, individually known members of a group, held together by the bond of personal love and friendship. With the growth of the social unit, the social norms and rites held in common by all its members became the main factor holding it together as an entity, and therewith they became automatically the symbol of the unit. By a process of true Pavlovian conditioning plus a certain amount of irreversible imprinting these rather abstract values have in every human culture been substituted for the primal, concrete object of the communal defense reaction.

This traditionally conditioned substitution of object has important consequences for the function of militant enthusiasm. On the one hand, the abstract nature of its object can give it a definitely inhuman aspect and make it positively dangerous—what do I care for wife or child; on the other hand it makes it possible to recruit militant enthusiasm in the service of really ethical values. Without the concentrated dedication of militant enthusiasm neither art, nor science, nor indeed any of the great endeavors of humanity would ever have come into being. Whether enthusiasm is made to serve these endeavors, or whether man's most powerfully motivating instinct makes him go to war in some abjectly silly cause, depends almost entirely on the conditioning and/or imprinting he has undergone during certain susceptible periods of his life. There is reasonable hope that our moral responsibility may gain control over the primeval drive, but our only hope of its ever doing so rests on the humble recognition of the fact that militant enthusiasm is an instinctive response with a phylogenetically determined releasing mechanism and that the only point at which intelligent and responsible supervision can get control is in the conditioning of the response to an object which proves to be a genuine value under the scrutiny of the categorical question.

Like the triumph ceremony of the greylag goose, militant enthusiasm in man is a true autonomous instinct: It has its own appetitive behavior, its own releasing mechanisms, and, like the sexual urge or any other strong instinct, it engenders a specific feeling of intense satisfaction. The strength of its seductive lure explains why intelligent men may behave as irrationally and immorally in their political as in their sexual lives. Like the triumph ceremony, it has an essential influence on the social structure of the species. Humanity is not enthusiastically combative because it is split into political parties, but it is divided into opposing camps because this is the adequate stimulus situation to arouse militant enthusiasm in a satisfying manner. "If ever a doctrine of universal salvation should gain ascendancy over the whole earth to the exclusion of all others," writes Erich von Holst, "it would at once divide into two strongly opposing factions (one's own true one and the other heretical one) and hostility and war would thrive as before, mankind being—unfortunately—what it is!"

The first prerequisite for rational control of an instinctive behavior pattern is the knowledge of the stimulus situation which releases it.

Militant enthusiasm can be elicited with the predictability of a reflex when the following environmental situations arise. First of all, a social unit with which the subject identifies himself must appear to be threatened by some danger from outside. That which is threatened may be a concrete group of people, the family or a little community of close friends, or else it may be a larger social unit held together and symbolized by its own specific social norms and rites. As the latter assume the character of autonomous values . . . they can, quite by themselves, represent the object in whose defense militant enthusiasm can be elicited. From all this it follows that this response can be brought into play in the service of extremely different objects, ranging from the sports club to the nation, or from the most obsolete mannerisms or ceremonials to the ideal of scientific truth or of the incorruptibility of justice.

A second key stimulus which contributes enormously to the releasing of intense militant enthusiasm is the presence of a hated enemy from whom the threat to the above "values" emanates. This enemy, too, can be of a concrete or of an abstract nature. It can be "the" Jews, Huns, Boches, tyrants, etc., or abstract concepts like world capitalism, Bolshevism, fascism, and any other kind of ism; it can be heresy, dogmatism, scientific fallacy, or what not. Just as in the case of the object to be defended, the enemy against whom to defend it is extremely variable, and demagogues are well versed in the dangerous art of producing supranormal dummies to release a very dangerous form of militant enthusiasm.

A third factor contributing to the environmental situation eliciting the response is an inspiring leader figure. Even the most emphatically anti-fascistic ideologies apparently cannot do without it, as the giant pictures of leaders displayed by all kinds of political parties prove clearly enough. Again the unselectivity of the phylogenetically programmed response allows for a wide variation in the conditioning to a leader figure. Napoleon, about whom so critical a man as Heinrich Heine became so enthusiastic, does not inspire me in the least; Charles Darwin does.

A fourth, and perhaps the most important, prerequisite for the full eliciting of militant enthusiasm is the presence of many other individuals, all agitated by the same emotion. Their absolute number has a certain influence on the quality of the response. Smaller numbers at issue with a large majority tend to obstinate defense with the emotional value of "making a last stand," while very large numbers inspired by the same enthusiasm feel the urge to conquer the whole world in the name of their sacred cause. Here the laws of mass enthusiasm are strictly analogous to those of flock formation . . . here, too, the excitation grows in proportion, perhaps even in geometrical progression, with the increasing number of individuals. This is exactly what makes militant mass enthusiasm so dangerous.

I have tried to describe, with as little emotional bias as possible, the human response of enthusiasm, its phylogenetic origin, its instructive as well as its traditionally handed-down components and prerequisites. I hope I have made the reader realize, without actually saying so, what a jumble our philosophy of values is. What is a culture? A system of historically developed social norms and rites which are passed on from generation to generation because emotionally they are felt to be values. What is a value? Obviously, normal and healthy people are able to appreciate something as a high value for which to live and, if necessary, to die, for no other reason than that it was evolved in cultural ritualization and handed down to them by a revered elder. Is, then, a value only defined as the object on which our instinctive urge to preserve and defend traditional social norms has become fixated? Primarily and in the early stages of cultural development this indubitably was the case. The obvious advantages of loyal adherence to tradition must have exerted a considerable selection pressure. However, the greatest loyalty and obedience to culturally ritualized norms of behavior must not be mistaken for responsible morality. Even at their best, they are only functionally analogous to behavior controlled by rational responsibility. In this respect, they are no whit different from the instinctive patterns of social behavior. . . . Also they are just as prone to miscarry under circumstances for which they have not been "programmed" by the great constructor, natural selection.

In other words, the need to control, by wise national responsibility, all our emotional allegiances to cultural values is as great as, if not greater than, the necessity to keep in check our other instincts. None of them can ever have such devastating effects as unbridled militant enthusiasm when it infects great masses and overrides all other considerations by its single-mindedness and its specious nobility. It is not enthusiasm in itself that is in any way noble, but humanity's great goals which it can be called upon to defend. That indeed is the Janus head of man:

The only being capable of dedicating himself to the very highest moral and ethical values requires for this purpose a phylogenetically adapted mechanism of behavior whose animal properties bring with them the danger that he will kill his brother, convinced that he is doing so in the interests of these very same high values. *Ecce homo!*

On War and Peace in Animals and Man

Niko Tinbergen

In 1935 Alexis Carrel published a best seller, *Man—The Unknown.*[1] Today, more than 30 years later, we biologists have once more the duty to remind our fellowmen that in many respects we are still, to ourselves, unknown. It is true that we now understand a great deal of the way our bodies function. With this understanding came control: medicine.

The ignorance of ourselves which needs to be stressed today is ignorance about our behavior—lack of understanding of the causes and effects of the function of our brains. A scientific understanding of our behavior, leading to its control, may well be the most urgent task that faces mankind today. It is the effects of our behavior that begin to endanger the very survival of our species and, worse, of all life on earth. By our technological achievements we have attained a mastery of our environment that is without precedent in the history of life. But these achievements are rapidly getting out of hand. The consequences of our "rape of the earth" are now assuming critical proportions. With shortsighted recklessness we deplete the limited natural resources, including even the oxygen and nitrogen of our atmosphere.[2] And Rachel Carson's warning[3] is now being followed by those of scientists, who give us an even gloomier picture of the general pollution of air, soil, and water. This pollution is seriously threatening our health and our food supply. Refusal to curb our reproductive behavior has led to the population explosion. And, as if all this were not enough, we are waging

From *Science* 160 (June 28, 1968): pp. 1411–1418. Copyright 1968 by the American Association for the Advancement of Science. Reprinted by permission of the publisher, and the author.

war on each other—men are fighting and killing men on a massive scale. It is because the effects of these behavior patterns, and of attitudes that determine our behavior, have now acquired such truly lethal potentialities that I have chosen man's ignorance about his own behavior as the subject of this paper.

I am an ethologist, a zoologist studying animal behavior. What gives a student of animal behavior the temerity to speak about problems of human behavior? Of course the history of medicine provides the answer. We all know that medical research uses animals on a large scale. This makes sense because animals, particularly vertebrates, are, in spite of all differences, so similar to us; they are our blood relations, however distant.

But this use of zoological research for a better understanding of ourselves is, to most people, acceptable only when we have to do with those bodily functions that we look upon as parts of our physiological machinery—the functions, for instance, of our kidneys, our liver, our hormone-producing glands. The majority of people bridle as soon as it is even suggested that studies of animal behavior could be useful for an understanding, let alone for the control, of our own behavior. They do not want to have their own behavior subjected to scientific scrutiny; they certainly resent being compared with animals, and these rejecting attitudes are both deep-rooted and of complex origin.

But now we are witnessing a turn in this tide of human thought. On the one hand the resistances are weakening, and on the other, a positive awareness is growing of the potentialities of a biology of behavior. This has become quite clear from the great interest aroused by several recent books that are trying, by comparative studies of animals and man, to trace what we could call "the animal roots of human behavior." As examples I select Konrad Lorenz's book On Aggression[4] and The Naked Ape by Desmond Morris.[5] Both books were best sellers from the start. We ethologists are naturally delighted by this sign of rapid growth of interest in our science (even though the growing pains are at times a little hard to endure). But at the same time we are apprehensive, or at least I am.

We are delighted because, from the enormous sales of these and other such books, it is evident that the mental block against self-scrutiny is weakening—that there are masses of people who, so to speak, want to be shaken up.

But I am apprehensive because these books, each admirable in its own way, are being misread. Very few readers give the authors the benefit of the doubt. Far too many either accept uncritically all that the authors say, or (equally uncritically) reject it all. I believe that this is because both Lorenz and Morris emphasize our knowledge rather than our ignorance (and, in addition, present as knowledge a set of statements which are after all no more than likely guesses). In themselves brilliant, these books could stiffen, at a new level, the attitude of certainty, while what we need is a sense of doubt and wonder, and an urge to investigate, to inquire.

POTENTIAL USEFULNESS
OF ETHOLOGICAL STUDIES

Now, in a way, I am going to be just as assertative as Lorenz and Morris, but what I am going to stress is how much we do not know. I shall argue that we shall have to make a major research effort. I am of course fully aware of the fact that much research is already being devoted to problems of human, and even of animal, behavior. I know, for instance, that anthropologists, psychologists, psychiatrists, and others are approaching these problems from many angles. But I shall try to show that the research effort has so far made insufficient use of the potential of ethology. Anthropologists, for instance, are beginning to look at animals, but they restrict their work almost entirely to our nearest relatives, the apes and monkeys. Psychologists do study a larger variety of animals, but even they select mainly higher species. They also ignore certain major problems that we biologists think have to be studied. Psychiatrists, at least many of them, show a disturbing tendency to apply the *results* rather than the *methods* of ethology to man.

None of these sciences, not even their combined efforts, are as yet parts of one coherent science of behavior. Since behavior is a life process, its study ought to be part of the mainstream of biological research. That is why we zoologists ought to "join the fray." As an ethologist, I am going to try to sketch how my science could assist its sister sciences in their attempts, already well on their way, to make a united, broad-fronted, truly biological attack on the problems of behavior.

I feel that I can cooperate best by discussing what it is in ethology that could be of use to the other behavioral sciences. What we ethologists do not want, what we consider definitely wrong, is uncritical application of our results to man. Instead, I myself at least feel that it is our method of approach, our rationale, that we can offer,[6] and also a little simple common sense, and discipline.

The potential usefulness of ethology lies in the fact that, unlike other sciences of behavior, it applies the method or "approach" of biology to the phenomenon behavior. It has developed a set of concepts and terms that allow us to ask:

1. In what ways does this phenomenon (behavior) influence the survival, the success of the animal?
2. What makes behavior happen at any given moment? How does its "machinery" work?
3. How does the behavior machinery develop as the individual grows up?
4. How have the behavior systems of each species evolved until they became what they are now?

The first question, that of survival value, has to do with the effects of behavior; the other three are, each on a different time scale, concerned with its causes.

These four questions are, as many of my fellow biologists will recognize, the major questions that biology has been pursuing for a long time. What ethology is doing could be simply described by saying that, just as biology investigates the functioning of the organs responsible for digestion, respiration, circulation, and so forth, so ethology begins now to do the same with respect to behavior; it investigates the functioning of organs responsible for movement.

I have to make clear that in my opinion it is the comprehensive, integrated attack on all four problems that characterizes ethology. I shall try to show that to ignore the questions of survival value and evolution—as, for instance, most psychologists do—is not only short-sighted but makes it impossible to arrive at an understanding of behavioral problems. Here ethology can make, in fact is already making, positive contributions.

Having stated my case for animal ethology as an essential part of the science of behavior, I will now have to sketch how this could be done. For this I shall have to consider one concrete example, and I select aggression, the most directly lethal of our behaviors. And, for reasons that will become clear, I shall also make a short excursion into problems of education.

Let me first try to define what I mean by aggression. We all understand the term in a vague, general way, but it is, after all, no more than a catchword. In terms of actual behavior, aggression involves approaching an opponent, and, when within reach, pushing him away, inflicting damage of some kind, or at least forcing stimuli upon him that subdue him. In this description the effect is already implicit: such behavior tends to remove the opponent, or at least to make him change his behavior in such a way that he no longer interferes with the attacker. The methods of attack differ from one species to another, and so do the weapons that are used, the structures that contribute to the effect.

Since I am concentrating on men fighting men, I shall confine myself to intraspecific fighting, and ignore, for instance, fighting between predators and prey. Intraspecific fighting is very common among animals. Many of them fight in two different contexts, which we can call "offensive" and "defensive." Defensive fighting is often shown as a last resort by an animal that, instead of attacking, has been fleeing from an attacker. If it is cornered, it may suddenly turn round upon its enemy and "fight with the courage of despair."

Of the four questions I mentioned before, I shall consider that of the survival value first. Here comparison faces us right at the start with a striking paradox. On the one hand, man is akin to many species of animals in that he fights his own species. But on the other hand he is, among the thousands of species that fight, the only one in which fighting is disruptive.

In animals, intraspecific fighting is usually of distinctive advantage. In addition, all species manage as a rule to settle their disputes without killing one another; in fact, even bloodshed is rare. Man is the only species that is a mass murderer, the only misfit in his own society.

Why should this be so? For an answer, we shall have to turn to the question of causation: What makes animals and man fight their own species? And why is our species "the odd man out"?

CAUSATION OF AGGRESSION

For a fruitful discussion of this question of causation I shall first have to discuss what exactly we mean when we ask it.

I have already indicated that when thinking of causation we have to distinguish between three subquestions, and that these three differ from one another in the stretch of time that is considered. We ask, first: Given an adult animal that fights now and then, what makes each outburst of fighting happen? The time scale in which we consider these recurrent events is usually one of seconds, or minutes. To use an analogy, this subquestion compares with asking what makes a car start or stop each time we use it.

But in asking this same general question of causation ("What makes an animal fight?") we may also be referring to a longer period of time; we may mean "How has the animal, as it grew up, developed this behavior?" This compares roughly with asking how a car has been constructed in the factory. The distinction between these two subquestions remains useful even though we know that many animals continue their development (much slowed down) even after they have attained adulthood. For instance, they may still continue to learn.

Finally, in biology, as in technology, we can extend this time scale even more, and ask: How have the animal species which we observe today—and which we know have evolved from ancestors that were different—how have they acquired their particular behavior systems during this evolution? Unfortunately, while we know the evolution of cars because they evolved so quickly and have been so fully recorded, the behavior of extinct animals cannot be observed, and has to be reconstructed by indirect methods.

I shall try to justify the claim I made earlier, and show how all these four questions—that of behavior's survival value and the three subquestions of causation—have to enter into the argument if we are to understand the biology of aggression.

Let us first consider the short-term causation; the mechanism of fighting. What makes us fight at any one moment? Lorenz argues in his book that, in animals and in man, there is an internal urge to attack. An individual does not simply wait to be provoked, but, if actual attack has not been possible for some time, this urge to fight builds up until the individual actively seeks the opportunity to indulge in fighting. Aggression, Lorenz claims, can be spontaneous.

But this view has not gone unchallenged. For instance, R. A. Hinde has written a thorough criticism,[7] based on recent work on aggression in animals, in which he writes that Lorenz's "arguments for the spontaneity of aggression do not bear examination" and that "the contrary view, expressed in nearly every textbook of comparative psychology . . ." is that fighting "derives principally from the situation"; and even more explicitly: "There is no need to postulate causes that are purely internal to the aggressor." At first glance it would seem as if Lorenz and Hinde disagree profoundly. I have read and reread both authors, and it is to me perfectly clear that loose statements and misunderstandings on both sides have made it appear that there is disagreement where in fact there is something very near to a common opinion. It seems to me that the differences between the two authors lie mainly in the different ways they look at internal and external variables. This in turn seems due to differences of a semantic nature. Lorenz uses the unfortunate term "the spontaneity of aggression." Hinde takes this to mean that external stimuli are in Lorenz's view not necessary at all to make an animal fight. But here he misrepresents Lorenz, for nowhere does Lorenz claim that the internal urge ever makes an animal fight "in vacuo"; somebody or something is attacked. This misunderstanding makes Hinde feel that he has refuted Lorenz's views by saying that "fighting derives principally from the situation." But both authors are fully aware of the fact that fighting is started by a number of variables, of which some are internal and some external. What both authors know, and what cannot be doubted, is that fighting behavior is not like the simple slot machine that produces one platform ticket every time one threepenny bit is inserted. To mention one animal example: a male stickleback does not always show the full fighting behavior in response to an approaching standard opponent; its response varies from none at all to the optimal stimulus on some occasions, to full attack on even a crude dummy at other times. This means that its internal state varies, and in this particular case we know from the work of Hoar[8] that the level of the male sex hormone is an important variable.

Another source of misunderstanding seems to have to do with the stretch of time that the two authors are taking into account. Lorenz undoubtedly thinks of the causes of an outburst of fighting in terms of seconds, or hours—perhaps days. Hinde seems to think of events which may have happened further back in time; an event which is at any particular moment "internal" may well in its turn have been influenced previously by external agents. In our stickleback example, the level of male sex hormone is influenced by external agents such as the length of the daily exposure to light over a period of a month or so.[9] Or, less far back in time, its readiness to attack may have been influenced by some experience gained, say, half an hour before the fight.

I admit that I have now been spending a great deal of time on what would seem to be a perfectly simple issue: the very first step in the analysis of the short-term causation, which is to distinguish at any given moment between variables within the animal and variables in the environment. It is of course important for our further understanding to unravel the complex interactions between these two worlds, and in particular the physiology of aggressive behavior. A great deal is being discovered about this, but for my present issue there is no use discussing it as long as even the first step in the analysis has not led to a clearly expressed and generally accepted conclusion. We must remember that we are at the moment concerned with the human problem: "What makes men attack each other?" And for this problem the answer to the first stage of our question is of prime importance: Is our readiness to start an attack constant or not? If it were—if our aggressive behavior were the outcome of an apparatus with the properties of the slot machine—all we would have to do would be to control the external situation: to stop providing threepenny bits. But since our readiness to start an attack is variable, further studies of both the external and the internal variables are vital to such issues as: Can we reduce fighting by lowering the population density, or by withholding provocative stimuli? Can we do so by changing the hormone balance or other physiological variables? Can we perhaps in addition control our development in such a way as to change the dependence on internal and external factors in adult man? However, before discussing development, I must first return to the fact that I have mentioned before, namely, that man is, among the thousands of other species that fight, the only mass murderer. How do animals in their intraspecific disputes avoid bloodshed?

THE IMPORTANCE OF "FEAR"

The clue to this problem is to recognize the simple fact that aggression in animals rarely occurs in pure form; it is only one of two components of an adaptive system. This is most clearly seen in territorial behavior, although it is also true of most other types of hostile behavior. Members of territorial species divide, among themselves, the available living space and opportunities by each individual defending its home range against competitors. Now in this system of parceling our living space, avoidance plays as important a part as attack. Put very briefly, animals of territorial species, once they have settled on a territory, attack intruders, but an animal that is still searching for a suitable territory or finds itself outside its home range withdraws when it meets with an already established owner. In terms of function, once you have taken possession of a territory, it pays to drive off competitors; but when you are still looking for a territory (or meet your neighbor at your common boundary), your chances of success are improved by avoiding such established owners. The ruthless fighter who "knows no fear" does not get very far. For an understanding of what follows, this fact, that hostile clashes are controlled by what we could call the "attack-avoidance system," is essential.

When neighboring territory owners meet near their common boundary, both attack behavior and withdrawal behavior are elicited in both animals; each of the two is in a state of motivational conflict. We know a great deal about the variety of movements that appear when these two conflicting, incompatible behaviors are elicited. Many of these expressions of a motivational conflict have, in the course of evolution, acquired signal function; in colloquial language, they signal "Keep out!" We deduce this from the fact that opponents respond to them in an appropriate way: instead of proceeding to intrude, which would require the use of force, trespassers withdraw, and neighbors are contained by each other. This is how such animals have managed to have all the advantages of their hostile behavior without the disadvantages: they divide their living space in a bloodless way by using as distance-keeping devices these conflict movements ("threat") rather than actual fighting.

GROUP TERRITORIES

In order to see our wars in their correct biological perspective one more comparison with animals is useful. So far I have discussed animal species that defend individual or at best pair territories. But there are also animals which possess and defend territories belonging to a group, or a clan.[10]

Now it is an essential aspect of group territorialism that the members of a group unite when in hostile confrontation with another group that approaches, or crosses into their feeding territory. The uniting and the aggression are equally important. It is essential to realize that group territorialism does not exclude hostile relations on lower levels when the group is on its own. For instance, within a group there is often a peck order. And within the group there may be individual or pair territories. But frictions due to these relationships fade away during a clash between groups. This temporary elimination is done by means of so-called appeasement and reassurance signals. They indicate "I am a friend," and so diminish the risk that, in the general flare-up of anger, any animal "takes it out" on a fellow member of the same group.[11] Clans meet clans as units, and each individual in an intergroup clash, while united with its fellow members, is (as in interindividual clashes) torn between attack and withdrawal, and postures and shouts rather than attacks.

We must now examine the hypothesis (which I consider the most likely one) that man still carries with him the animal heritage of group territoriality. This is a question concerning man's evolutionary origin, and here we are, by the very nature of the subject, forced to speculate. Because I am going to say something about the behavior of our ancestors of, say, 100,000 years ago, I have to discuss briefly a matter of methodology. It is known to all biologists (but unfortunately unknown to most psychologists) that comparison of present-day species can give us a deep insight, with a probability closely approaching certainty, into the evolutionary history of animal species. Even where fossil evidence is lacking, this comparative method alone can do this. It has to be stressed that this comparison is a highly sophisticated method, and not merely a matter of saying that species A is different from species B.[12] The basic procedure is this. We interpret differences between really allied species as the result of adaptive divergent evolution from common stock, and we interpret similarities between nonallied species as adaptive convergencies to similar ways of life. By studying the adaptive functions of species characteristics we understand how natural selection can have produced both these divergencies and convergencies. To mention one striking example: even if we had no fossil evidence, we could, by this method alone, recognize whales for what they are—mammals that have returned to the water, and, in doing so, have developed some similarities to fish. This special type of comparison, which has been applied so successfully by students of the structure of animals, has now also been used, and with equal success, in several studies of animal behavior. Two approaches have been applied. One is to see in what respects species of very different origin have convergently adapted to a similar way of life. Von Haartman[13] has applied this to a study of birds of many types that nest in holes—an anti-predator safety device. All such hole-nesters center their territorial fighting on a suitable nest hole. Their courtship consists of luring a female to this hole (often with the use of bright color patterns). Their young gape when a general darkening signals the arrival of the parent. All but the most recently adapted species lay uniformly colored, white or light blue eggs that can easily be seen by the parent.

An example of adaptive divergence has been studied by Cullen.[14] Among all the gulls, the kittiwake is unique in that it nests on very narrow ledges on sheer cliffs. Over 20 peculiarities of this species have been recognized by Mrs. Cullen as vital adaptations to this particular habitat.

These and several similar studies[15] demonstrate how comparison reveals, in each species, systems of interrelated, and very intricate adaptive features. In this work, speculation is now being followed by careful experimental checking. It would be tempting to elaborate on this, but I must return to our own unfortunate species.

Now, when we include the "Naked Ape" in our comparative studies, it becomes likely (as has been recently worked out in great detail by Morris) that man is a "social Ape who has turned carnivore."[16] On the one hand he is a social primate; on the other, he has developed similarities to wolves, lions and hyenas. In our present context one thing seems to stand out clearly, a conclusion that seems to me of paramount importance to all of us, and yet has not yet been fully accepted as such. As a social, hunting primate, man must originally have been organized on the principle of group territories.

Ethologists tend to believe that we still carry with us a number of behavioral characteristics of our animal ancestors, which cannot be eliminated by different ways of upbringing, and that our group territorialism is one of those ancestral characters. I shall discuss the problem of the modifiability of our behavior later, but it is useful to point out here that even if our behavior were much more modifiable than Lorenz maintains, our cultural evolution, which resulted in the parceling-out of our living space on lines of tribal, national, and now even "bloc" areas, would, if anything, have tended to enhance group territorialism.

GROUP TERRITORIALISM IN MAN?

I put so much emphasis on this issue of group territorialism because most writers who have tried to apply ethology to man have done this in the wrong way. They have made the mistake, to which I objected before, of uncritically extrapolating the results of animal studies to man. They try to explain man's behavior by using facts that are valid only of some of the animals we studied. And, as ethologists keep stressing, no two species behave alike. Therefore, instead of taking this easy way out, we ought to study man in his own right. And I repeat that the message of the ethologists is that the methods, rather than the results, of ethology should be used for such a study.

Now, the notion of territory was developed by zoologists (to be precise, by ornithologists),[17] and because individual and pair territories are found in so many more species than group territories (which are particularly rare among birds), most animal studies were concerned with such individual and pair territories. Now such low-level territories do occur in man, as does another form of hostile behavior, the peck order. But the problems created by such low-level frictions are not serious; they can, within a community, be kept in check by the apparatus of law and order; peace within national boundaries can be enforced. In order to understand what makes us go to war, we have to recognize that man behaves very much like a group-territorial species. We too unite in the face of an outside danger to the group; we "forget our differences." We too have threat gestures, for instance, angry facial expressions. And all of us use reassurance and appeasement signals, such as a friendly smile. And (unlike speech) these are universally understood; they are cross-cultural; they are species-specific. And, incidentally, even within a group sharing a common language, they are often more reliable guides to a man's intentions than speech, for speech (as we know now) rarely reflects our true motives, but our facial expressions often "give us away."

If I may digress for a moment: it is humiliating to us ethologists that many nonscientists, particularly novelists and actors, intuitively understand our sign language much better than we scientists ourselves do. Worse, there is a category of human beings who understand intuitively more about the causation of our aggressive behavior: the great demagogues. They have applied this knowledge in order to control our behavior in the most clever ways, and often for the most evil purposes. For instance, Hitler (who had modern mass communication at his disposal, which allowed him to inflame a whole nation) played on both fighting tendencies. The "defensive" fighting was whipped up by his passionate statements about "living space," "encirclement," Jewry, and Freemasonry as threatening powers which made the Germans feel "cornered." The "attack fighting" was similarly set ablaze by playing the myth of the Herrenvolk. We must make sure that mankind has learned its lesson and will never forget how disastrous the joint effects have been—if only one of the major nations were led now by a man like Hitler, life on earth would be wiped out.

I have argued my case for concentrating on studies of group territoriality rather than on other types of aggression. I must now return, in this context, to the problem of man the mass murderer. Why don't we settle even our international disputes by the relatively harmless, animal method of threat? Why have we become unhinged so that so often our attack erupts without being kept in check by fear? It is not that we have no fear, nor that we have no other inhibitions against killing. This problem has to be considered first of all in the general context of the consequences of man having embarked on a new type of evolution.

CULTURAL EVOLUTION

Man has the ability, unparalleled in scale in the animal kingdom, of passing on his experiences from one generation to the next. By this accumulative and exponentially growing process, which we call cultural evolution, he has been able to change his environment progressively out of all recognition. And this includes the social environment. This new type of evolution proceeds at an incomparably faster pace than genetic evolution. Genetically we have not evolved very strikingly since Cro-Magnon man, but culturally we have changed beyond recognition, and are changing at an ever-increasing rate. It is of course true that we are highly adjustable individually, and so could hope to keep pace with these changes. But I am not alone in believing that this behavioral adjustability, like all types of modifiability, has its limits. These limits are imposed upon us by our hereditary constitution, a constitution which can only change with the far slower speed of genetic evolution. There are good grounds for the conclusion that man's limited behavioral adjustability has been outpaced by the culturally determined changes in his social environment, and that this is why man is now a misfit in his own society.

We can now, at last, return to the problem of war, of uninhibited mass killing. It seems quite clear that our cultural evolution is at the root of the trouble. It is our cultural evolution that has caused the population explosion. In a nutshell, medical science, aiming at the reduction of suffering, has, in doing so, prolonged life for many individuals as well—prolonged it to well beyond the point at which they produce offspring. Unlike the situation in any wild species, recruitment to the human population consistently surpasses losses through mortality. Agricultural and technical know-how have enabled us to grow food and to exploit other natural resources to such an extent that we can still feed (though only just) the enormous numbers of human beings on our crowded planet. The result is that we now live at a far higher density than that in which genetic evolution has molded our species. This, together with long-distance communication, leads to far more frequent, in fact to continuous, intergroup contacts, and so to continuous external provocation of aggression. Yet this alone would not explain our increased tendency to kill each other; it would merely lead to continuous threat behavior.

The upsetting of the balance between aggression and fear (and this is what causes war) is due to at least three other consequences of cultural evolution. It is an old cultural phenomenon that warriors are both brainwashed and bullied into all-out fighting. They are brainwashed into believing that fleeing—originally, as we have seen, an adaptive type of behavior—is despicable, "cowardly." This seems to me due to the fact that man, accepting that in moral issues death might be preferable to fleeing, has falsely applied the moral concept of "cowardice" to matters of mere practical importance—to the dividing of living space. The fact that our soldiers are also bullied into all-out fighting (by penalizing fleeing in battle) is too well known to deserve elaboration.

Another cultural excess is our ability to make and use killing tools, especially long-range weapons. These make killing easy, not only because a spear or a club inflicts, with the same effort, so much more damage than a fist, but also, and mainly, because the use of long-range weapons prevents the victim from reaching his attacker with his appeasement, reassurance, and distress signals. Very few aircrews who are willing, indeed eager, to drop their bombs "on target" would be willing to strangle, stab, or burn children (or, for that matter, adults) with their own hands; they would stop short of killing, in response to the appeasement and distress signals of their opponents.

These three factors alone would be sufficient to explain how we have become such unhinged killers. But I have to stress once more that all this, however convincing it may seem, must still be studied more thoroughly.

There is a frightening, and ironical paradox in this conclusion: that the human brain, the finest life-preserving device created by evolution, has made our species so successful in mastering the outside world that it suddenly finds itself taken off guard. One could say that our cortex and our brainstem (our "reason" and our "instincts") are at loggerheads. Together they have created a new social environment in which, rather than ensuring our survival, they are about to do the opposite. The brain finds itself seriously threatened by an enemy of its own making. It is its own enemy. We simply have to understand this enemy.

THE DEVELOPMENT OF BEHAVIOR

I must now leave the question of the moment-to-moment control of fighting, and, looking further back in time, turn to the development of aggressive behavior in the growing individual. Again we will start from the human problem. This, in the present context, is whether it is within our power to control development in such a way that we reduce or eliminate fighting among adults. Can or cannot education in the widest sense produce nonaggressive men?

The first step in the consideration of this problem is again to distinguish between external and internal influences, but now we must apply this to the growth, the changing, of the behavioral machinery during the individual's development. Here again the way in which we phrase our questions and our conclusions is of the utmost importance.

In order to discuss this issue fruitfully, I have to start once more by considering it in a wider context, which is now that of the "nature-nurture" problem with respect to behavior in general. This has been discussed more fully by Lorenz in his book *Evolution and Modification of Behaviour;*[18] for a discussion of the environmentalist point of view I refer to the various works of Schneirla.[19]

Lorenz tends to classify behavior types into innate and acquired or learned behavior. Schneirla rejects this dichotomy into two classes of behavior. He stresses that the developmental process, of behavior as well as of other functions, should be considered, and also that this development forms a highly complicated series of interactions between the growing organism and its environment. I have gradually become convinced that the clue to this difference in approach is to be found in a difference in aims between the two authors. Lorenz claims that "we are justified in leaving, at least for the time being, to the care of the experimental embryologists all those questions which are concerned with the chains of physiological causation leading from the genome to the development of . . . neurosensory structures." In other words, he deliberately refrains from starting his analysis of development prior to the stage at which a fully coordinated behavior is performed for the first time. If one in this way restricts one's studies to the later stages of development, then a classification in "innate" and "learned" behavior, or behavior components, can be considered quite justified. And there was a time, some 30 years ago, when the almost grotesquely environmentalist bias of psychology made it imperative for ethologists to stress the extent to which behavior patterns could appear in perfect or near-perfect form without the aid of anything that could be properly called learning. But I now agree (however belatedly) with Schneirla that we must extend our interest to earlier stages of development and embark on a full program of experimental embryology of behavior. When we do this, we discover that interactions with the environment can indeed occur at early stages. These interactions may concern small components of the total machinery of a fully functional behavior pattern, and many of them cannot possibly be called learning. But they are interactions with the environment, and must be taken into account if we follow in the footsteps of the experimental embryologists, and extend our field of interest to the entire sequence of events which lead from the blueprints contained in the zygote to the fully functioning, behaving animal. We simply have to do this if we want an answer to the question to what extent the development of behavior can be influenced from the outside.

When we follow this procedure the rigid distinction between "innate" or unmodifiable and "acquired" or modifiable behavior patterns becomes far less sharp. This is owing to the discovery, on the one hand, that "innate" patterns may contain elements that at an early stage developed in interaction with the environment, and, on the other hand, that learning is, from step to step, limited by internally imposed restrictions.

To illustrate the first point, I take the development of the sensory cells in the retina of the eye. Knoll has shown[20] that the rods in the eyes of tadpoles cannot function properly unless they have first been exposed to light. This means that, although any visually guided response of a tadpole may well, in its integrated form, be "innate" in Lorenz's sense, it is so only in the sense of "nonlearned," not in that of "having grown without interaction with the environment." Now it has been shown by Cullen[21] that male sticklebacks reared from the egg in complete isolation from other animals will, when adult, show full fighting behavior to other males and courtship behavior to females when faced with them for the first time in their lives. This is admittedly an important fact, demonstrating that the various recognized forms of learning do not enter into the programing of these integrated patterns. This is a demonstration of what Lorenz calls an "innate response." But it does not exclude the possibility that parts of the machinery so employed may, at an earlier stage, have been influenced by the environment, as in the case of the tadpoles.

Second, there are also behavior patterns which do appear in the inexperienced animal, but in an incomplete form, and which require additional development through learning. Thorpe has analyzed a clear example of this: when young male chaffinches reared alone begin to produce their song for the first time, they utter a very imperfect warble; this develops into the full song only if, at a certain sensitive stage, the young birds have heard the full song of an adult male.[22]

By far the most interesting aspect of such intermediates between innate and acquired behavior is the fact that learning is not indiscriminate, but is guided by a certain selectiveness on the part of the animal. This fact has been dimly recognized long ago; the early ethologists have often pointed out that different, even closely related, species learn different things even when developing the same behavior patterns. This has been emphasized by Lorenz's use of the term "innate teaching mechanism." Other authors use the word "template" in the same context. The best example I know is once more taken from the development of song in certain birds. As I have mentioned, the males of some birds acquire their full song by changing their basic repertoire to resemble the song of adults, which they have to hear during a special sensitive period some months before they sing themselves. It is in this sensitive period that they acquire, without as yet producing the song, the knowledge of "what the song ought to be like." In technical terms, the bird formed a *Sollwert*[23] (literally, "should-value," an ideal) for the feedback they receive when they hear their own first attempts. Experiments have shown[24] that such birds, when they start to sing, do three things: they listen to what they produce; they notice the difference between this feedback and the ideal song; and they correct their next performance.

This example, while demonstrating an internal teaching mechanism, shows, at the same time, that Lorenz made his concept too narrow when he coined the term "innate teaching mechanism." The birds have developed a teaching mechanism, but while it is true that it is internal, it is not innate; the birds have acquired it by listening to their father's song.

These examples show that if behavior studies are to catch up with experimental embryology our aims, our concepts, and our terms must be continually revised.

Before returning to aggression, I should like to elaborate a little further on general aspects of behavior development, because this will enable me to show the value of animal studies in another context, that of education.

Comparative studies, of different animal species, of different behavior patterns, and of different stages of development, begin to suggest that wherever learning takes a hand in development, it is guided by such *Sollwerte* or templates for the proper feedback, the feedback that reinforces. And it becomes clear that these various *Sollwerte* are of a bewildering variety. In human education one aspect of this has been emphasized in particular, and even applied in the use of teaching machines: the requirement that the reward, in order to have maximum effect, must be immediate. Skinner has stressed this so much because in our own teaching we have imposed an unnatural delay between, say, taking in homework, and giving the pupil his reward in the form of a mark. But we can learn more from animal studies than the need for immediacy of reward. The type of reward is also of great importance, and this may vary from task to task, from stage to stage, from occasion to occasion; the awards may be of almost infinite variety.

Here I have to discuss briefly a behavior of which I have so far been unable to find the equivalent in the development of structure. This is exploratory behavior. By this we mean a kind of behavior in which the animal sets out to acquire as much information about an object or a situation as it can possibly get. The behavior is intricately adapted to this end, and it terminates when the information has been stored, when the animal has incorporated it in its learned knowledge. This exploration (subjectively we speak of "curiosity") is not confined to the acquisition of information about the external world alone; at least mammals explore their own movements a great deal, and in this way "master new skills." Again, in this exploratory behavior, *Sollwerte* of expected, "hoped-for" feedbacks play their part.

Without going into more detail, we can characterize the picture we begin to get of the development of behavior as a series, or rather a web, of events, starting with innate programing instructions contained in the zygote, which straightaway begin to interact with the environment; this interaction may be discontinuous, in that periods of predominantly internal development alternate with periods of interaction, or sensitive periods. The interaction is enhanced by active exploration; it is steered by selective *Sollwerte* of great variety; and stage by stage this process ramifies; level upon level of ever-increasing complexity is being incorporated into the programing.

Apply what we have heard for a moment to playing children (I do not, of course, distinguish sharply between "play" and "learning"). At a certain age a child begins to use, say, building blocks. It will at first manipulate them in various ways, one at a time. Each way of manipulating acts as exploratory behavior: the child learns what a block looks, feels, tastes like, and so forth, and also how to put it down so that it stands stably.

Each of these stages "peters out" when the child knows what it wanted to find out. But as the development proceeds, a new level of exploration is added: the child discovers that it can put one block on top of the other; it constructs. The new discovery leads to repetition and variation, for each child develops, at some stage, a desire and a set of *Sollwerte* for such effects of construction, and acts out to the full this new level of exploratory behavior. In addition, already at this stage the *Sollwert* or ideal does not merely contain what the blocks do, but also what, for instance, the mother does; her approval, her shared enjoyment, is also of great importance. Just as an exploring animal, the child builds a kind of inverted pyramid of experience, built of layers, each set off by a new wave of exploration and each directed by new sets of *Sollwerte,* and so its development "snowballs." All these phases may well have more or less limited sensitive periods, which determine when the fullest effect can be obtained, and when the child is ready for the next step. More important still, if the opportunity for the next stage is offered either too early or too late, development may be damaged, including the development of motivational and emotional attitudes.

Of course gifted teachers of many generations have known all these things[25] or some of them, but the glimpses of insight have not been fully and scientifically systematized. In human education, this would of course involve experimentation. This need not worry us too much, because in our search for better educational procedures we are in effect experimenting on our children all the time. Also, children are fortunately incredibly resilient, and most grow up into pretty viable adults in spite of our fumbling educational efforts. Yet there is, of course, a limit to what we will allow ourselves, and this, I should like to emphasize, is where animal studies may well become even more important than they are already.

CAN EDUCATION END AGGRESSION?

Returning now to the development of animal and human aggression, I hope to have made at least several things clear: that behavior development is a very complex phenomenon indeed; that we have only begun to analyze it in animals; that with respect to man we are, if anything, behind in comparison with animal studies; and that I cannot do otherwise than repeat what I said in the beginning: we must make a major research effort. In this effort animal studies can help, but we are still very far from drawing very definite conclusions with regard to our question: To what extent shall we be able to render man less aggressive through manipulation of the environment, that is, by educational measures?

In such a situation personal opinions naturally vary a great deal. I do not hesitate to give as my personal opinion that Lorenz's book *On Aggression*, in spite of its assertativeness, in spite of factual mistakes, and in spite of the many possibilities of misunderstandings that are due to the lack of a common language among students of behavior—that this work must be taken more seriously as a positive contribution to our problem than many critics have done. Lorenz is, in my opinion, right in claiming that elimination, through education, of the internal urge to fight will turn out to be very difficult, if not impossible.

Everything I have said so far seems to me to allow for only one conclusion. Apart from doing our utmost to return to a reasonable population density, apart from stopping the progressive depletion and pollution of our habitat, we must pursue the biological study of animal behavior for clarifying problems of human behavior of such magnitude as that of our aggression, and of education.

But research takes a long time, and we must remember that there are experts who forecast worldwide famine 10 to 20 years from now; and that we have enough weapons to wipe out all human life on earth. Whatever the causation of our aggression, the simple fact is that for the time being we are saddled with it. This means that there is a crying need for a crash program, for finding ways and means for keeping our intergroup aggression in check. This is of course in practice infinitely more difficult than controlling our intranational frictions; we have as yet not got a truly international police force. But there is hope for avoiding all-out war because, for the first time in history, we are afraid of killing ourselves by the lethal radiation effects even of bombs that we could drop in the enemy's territory. Our politicians know this. And as long as there is this hope, there is every reason to try and learn what we can from animal studies. Here again they can be of help. We have already seen that animal opponents meeting in a hostile clash avoid bloodshed by using the expressions of their motivational conflicts as intimidating signals. Ethologists have studied such conflict movements in some detail,[26] and have found that they are of a variety of types. The most instructive of these is the redirected attack; instead of attacking the provoking, yet dreaded, opponent, animals often attack something else, often even an inanimate object. We ourselves bang the table with our fists. Redirection includes something like sublimation, a term attaching a value judgment to the redirection. As a species with group territories, humans, like hyenas, unite when meeting a common enemy. We do already sublimate our group aggression. The Dutch feel united in their fight against the sea. Scientists do attack their problems together. The space program—surely a mainly military effort—is an up-to-date example. I would not like to claim, as Lorenz does, that redirected attack exhausts the aggressive urge. We know from soccer matches and from animal work how aggressive behavior has two simultaneous, but opposite effects: a waning effect, and one of self-inflammation, of mass hysteria, such as recently seen in Cairo. Of these two the inflammatory effect often wins. But if aggression were used successfully as the motive force behind nonkilling and even useful activities, self-stimulation need not be a danger; in our short-term cure we are not aiming at the elimination of aggressiveness, but at "taking the sting out of it."

Of all sublimated activities, scientific research would seem to offer the best opportunities for deflecting and sublimating our aggression. And, once we recognize that it is the disrupted relation between our own behavior and our environment that forms our most deadly enemy, what could be better than uniting, at the front or behind the lines, in the scientific attack on our own behavioral problems?

I stress "behind the lines." The whole population should be made to feel that it participates in the struggle. This is why scientists will always have the duty to inform their fellowmen of what they are doing, of the relevance and the importance of their work. And this is not only a duty, it can give intense satisfaction.

I have come full circle. For both the long-term and the short-term remedies at least we scientists will have to sublimate our aggression into an all-out attack on the enemy within. For this the enemy must be recognized for what it is: our unknown selves, or, deeper down, our refusal to admit that man is, to himself, unknown.

I should like to conclude by saying a few words to my colleagues of the younger generation. Of course we all hope that, by muddling along until we have acquired better understanding, self-annihilation either by the "whimper of famine" or by the "bang of war" can be avoided. For this, we must on the one hand trust, on the other hand help (and urge) our politicians. But it is no use denying that the chances of designing the necessary preventive measures are small, let alone the chances of carrying them out. Even birth control still offers a major problem.

It is difficult for my generation to know how seriously you take the danger of mankind destroying his own species. But those who share the apprehension of my generation might perhaps, with us, derive strength from keeping alive the thought that has helped so many of us in the past when faced with the possibility of imminent death. Scientific research is one of the finest occupations of our mind. It is, with art and religion, one of the uniquely human ways of meeting nature, in fact, the most active way. If we are to succumb, and even if this were to be ultimately due to our own stupidity, we could still, so to speak, redeem our species. We could at least go down with some dignity, by using our brain for one of its supreme tasks, by exploring to the end.

NOTES

1. A. Carrel, *L'Homme, cet Inconnu* (Librairie Plon, Paris, 1935).
2. AAAS Annual Meeting, 1967 [see *New Scientist* 37, 5 (1968)].
3. R. Carson, *Silent Spring* (Houghton Mifflin, Boston, 1962).
4. K. Lorenz, *On Aggression* (Methuen, London, 1966).
5. D. Morris, *The Naked Ape* (Jonathan Cape, London, 1967).
6. N. Tinbergen, *Z. Tierpsychol.* 20, 410 (1964).
7. R. A. Hinde, *New Society* 9, 302 (1967).
8. W. S. Hoar, *Animal Behaviour* 10, 247 (1962).
9. B. Baggerman, in *Symp. Soc. Exp. Biol.* 20, 427 (1965).
10. H. Kruuk, *New Scientist* 30, 849 (1966).
11. N. Tinbergen, *Z. Tierpsychol.* 16, 651 (1959); *Zool. Mededelingen* 39, 209 (1964).
12. _____, *Behaviour* 15, 1–70 (1959).
13. L. von Haartman, *Evolution* 11, 339 (1957).
14. E. Cullen, *Ibis* 99, 275 (1957).
15. J. H. Crook, *Symp. Zool. Soc. London* 14, 181 (1965).
16. D. Freeman, *Inst. Biol. Symp.* 13, 109 (1964); D. Morris, ed., *Primate Ethology* (Weidenfeld and Nicolson, London, 1967).
17. H. E. Howard, *Territory in Bird Life* (Murray, London, 1920); R. A. Hinde et al., *Ibis* 98, 340–530 (1956).
18. K. Lorenz, *Evolution and Modification of Behaviour* (Methuen, London, 1966).
19. T. C. Schneirla, *Quart. Rev. Biol.* 41, 283 (1966).
20. M. D. Knoll, *Z. Vergleich. Physiol.* 38, 219 (1956).

21. E. Cullen, *Final Rept. Contr. AF 61 (052)-29,* USAFRDC, 1–23 (1961).
22. W. H. Thorpe, *Bird-Song* (Cambridge Univ. Press, New York, 1961).
23. E. von Holst and H. Mittelstaedt, *Naturwissenschaften* 37, 464 (1950).
24. M. Konishi, *Z. Tierpsychol.* 22, 770 (1965): F. Nottebohm, *Proc. 14th Intern. Ornithol. Congr.* 265–80 (1967).
25. E. M. Standing, *Maria Montessori* (New American Library, New York, 1962).
26. N. Tinbergen, in *The Pathology and Treatment of Sexual Deviation,* I. Rosen, ed. (Oxford Univ. Press, London, 1964), pp. 3–23, N. B. Jones, *Wildfowl Trust 11th Ann. Rept.,* 46–52 (1960); P. Sevenster, *Behaviour, Suppl.* 9, 1–170 (1961); F. Rowell, *Animal Behaviour* 9, 38 (1961).

Ecology and the Evolution
of Social Ethics

V. C. Wynne-Edwards

ALTRUISM IN ANIMALS

Some forty years ago, in a short but well-known passage, Haldane (1932, pp. 207–10) examined the logical possibilities of evolving altruistic behaviour through natural selection in man. He said that, 'if any genes are common in mankind which promote conduct biologically disadvantageous to the individual in all types of society, but yet advantageous to society, they must have spread when man was divided into small endogenous groups. As many eugenists have pointed out, selection in large societies operates in the reverse direction.' Even so, such conditions appeared to him to be far from sufficient for the spread of inborn altruism, because self-sacrifice is bound to come off second best and the genes responsible for it consequently to diminish, in proportion to alternative alleles. He concluded with the comment that 'I find it difficult to suppose that many genes for absolute altruism are common to man.'

But our knowledge of social behaviour, in non-human animals at least, has advanced since that was written. We know, for example, that there are many species of birds in which the breeding pairs receive assistance from other members of the colony or social group, either in nest-building, feeding the parent on duty at the nest, or caring for the young. These are socially valuable adaptations of no immediate or certain advantage to the helpers who sacrifice their energies for the common good. A different kind of illustration can be seen in the mass emigration of Scandinavian lemmings from regions where population density is high, removing an expendable surplus of which few if any members survive. Though nothing is known about the genetical transmission of adaptations like these it must in every case be safeguarded so that they cannot be abolished by a mutation at a single locus, which would allow its bearers to evade the obligation of accepting personal risks in the interest of the survival of the stock.

In most of the higher animals, in addition to the hereditary transmission of information by genes, there is important social information that is transmitted from one generation to another by tradition. It includes all the information pertaining to special localities, for instance those where breeding, feeding, or wintering take place. Vertebrates in particular often tend to confine their breeding to traditionally-identified places, and there are certain instances where we can tell these have been in use for more than a thousand years. In some species an individual has first got to succeed in claiming a site within the traditional area before it can attempt to breed; and though there may be many unsuccessful candidates they are strongly inhibited from going off to a new locality and setting up on their own.

There is no critical demarcation between this kind of tradition and the more elaborate body of learning that constitutes a culture: the one expands to produce the other. But both demand an underlying gene-determined ability to learn, and an impulse to obey, the dictates of traditional codes.

THE EMERGENCE OF RATIONAL BEHAVIOUR

The contributions that genes and traditions make to the inheritance of the information necessary for population control no doubt vary in proportion from one type of animal to another. In the traditional breeding colonies I have just mentioned, such as those of sea-birds and seals, adults that are candidates for status as breeders have to compete for individual sites which they hold and defend as mating or nesting territories. The sites are small ones, so small in a gannet colony, for instance, that the owner standing on its nest can reach and defend with its biting bill every point in the territory. The perimeter of the colony itself is established by use, and if the gannet fails to acquire a site within the socially acceptable area it cannot nest at all. Inhibition against the nesting of pairs in isolation appears to be virtually complete. Even the pairs situated round the boundary have been shown in another sea-bird, the kittiwake, to have a lower level of breeding success than the ones in the middle of the colony (Coulson 1968). And just as with grouse on the moor, there is not usually enough room to accommodate all the adults that attempt to gain admission, and the quota of breeders is consequently limited in an analogous way.

In early man the traditional or customary element in achieving population homeostasis had mushroomed at the expense of automatic, innate controls. Social competition ceased to have a direct physiological effect on fertility, and in the place of automatic mechanisms primitive man had developed traditional codes of behaviour to take care of population control. Local tribes had their own hunting territories, and corresponding systems of land tenure were developed by pastoral and later by agricultural peoples, down to historic times. Customary restrictions were placed on fertility in the place of physiological ones, and so far as we know all primitive peoples practised family limitation in some form. The four commonest methods were by the deferment of marriage for ten years or more beyond puberty, by compulsory abstention from intercourse which resulted in births being widely spaced, by abortion, and by infanticide. One or more of these was found in every stone-age race that survived into modern times. In addition some tribes, at initiation ceremonies marking the admission of recruits into the breeding caste, performed mutilations of the genitalia which diminished the ease of sexual consummation.

The rise of civilization opened up an outlet for the surplus population produced in agricultural areas, by off-loading them into villages and towns where they could take up useful trades. Civilized communities have never had to impose family limitations by social and legal codes, as their stone-age forbears did, because their evergrowing skills enabled them to keep the production of food and other staples rising ahead of demand, and a growing population could produce more labourers, traders, and soldiers and increased security and prosperity. Family limitation, being voluntary and against the public interest, ceased to be practised on the scale required to prevent the population's growth. It is of course this atrophy of homeostatic control within historic times, coupled with the very recent growth of preventive medicine, that has led us now to a population crisis.

There must have been a long span of pre-human evolution during which the importance of traditional and legal methods of population control were growing and the physiological components were being allowed to lapse. The change was basically a genetic one, requiring not only the suppression of physiological control mechanisms but equally the strengthening of the innate mental predisposition, on which obedience to traditional social custom depends. And although in the last few thousand years the civilized world has allowed the homeostatic function of sociality to wither away, human laws governing other forms of social conduct have never been more comprehensive and complex than they are today. The innate genetical foundations on which our social conduct is built remain to all intents the same as they were in palaeolithic times. We are still deeply motivated to be parochial and insular, to be intolerant of strangers and particularly of races that are physically or culturally different from our own, and to join with the rest of our community in promoting our own collective good. We are strongly predisposed to love the land of our childhood, and can readily be taught to respect persons, institutions, and superstitions, and to abide by the law; but we should notice too that remaining faithful to these principles depends now, as formerly, very much on continual reinforcement by our associates, which contemporary society may or may not be moved to give.

I am concerned in this lecture especially with the conflict between the individual and society, which for man has become transformed into a question of morality, or social ethics. Morality for present purposes is the same as altruism; as I have said, it means putting the welfare of the group first and subordinating personal advantage to it. But in man and to a minor extent in other mammals, altruistic conduct has come to rely on a different material basis from the one found in the lower animals.

These lower animals, as we saw, obey the social code because they are rigidly bound to do so: for them the 'ten commandments' are genetically fixed and the instinctive drive to comply with them is mandatory. In many other spheres, however, these animals are free to alter and adapt their behaviour in the light of experience or insight.

In man the freedom to choose the most appropriate course of action is enormously developed. Our instinctive urges, though still varied and strong, can generally be overruled by persuasion and reason. Our capacity for rational behaviour, based on insight into the probable consequences of alternative courses of action, benefits the social group just as much as it does our own individual welfare. Our use of spoken language allows people to take counsel together and pool their collective experience and ingenuity, and in doing this their differences of opinion and independence of mind contribute very greatly towards reaching wise decisions. Individual freedom of ideas leads similarly to practical originality and inventiveness. But at the same time it lays society open to the danger that free will may be turned towards crime and subversion, and for that reason a massive and highly necessary part of our social code is concerned with directing free action into socially acceptable channels.

Man's intellectual emancipation has of course arisen through the processes of natural selection. His cerebral cortex has become so powerful a tool that within less than a million years he has been able to dominate all other forms of life. But simply because intellectual freedom can bring such great advantages to society and yet is so dangerous and double-edged, it is clear that it could not have evolved except in parallel with safeguards strong enough to curb the abuse of personal freedom, for purposes that threatened the safety of the group.

The safeguards appear still to belong to the same two kinds as we have already repeatedly met. The first kind are built into the social code, handed down through custom and tradition, and learnt by each new generation from its predecessors. Traditions have become vastly more complex and voluminous in man than they are in any other species. They prescribe, often in detail, what activities are right and praiseworthy and what are wrong and forbidden. They set up respected legal authorities to judge, commend, or punish in the society's name.

The second kind of safeguard appears to have a genetic basis, and to be a typical piece of evolutionary compromise. As children we learn the elements of morality from our elders, among much else that is needed to equip us for adult life, and we accept what they tell us very largely on trust. Children have no reason to question what they are taught about the existence of a supernatural world, and the inculcation of moral principles and codes of conduct has traditionally been reinforced by fostering at the same time a belief in divine powers, which are beyond challenge and bid us to regard morality as sacred; together these form the foundation for religion. But there is a third ingredient of moral persuasion that seems not to be learnt like the other two, but instead to be emotional and inborn. It is conscience, the *alter ego* which resides in us and constrains us to do what is right in conformity with moral law. It is conscience that stirs us, for instance, to acts of personal sacrifice, acts whose performance nevertheless needs to be tempered with practical judgment: conscience does not bind us too tightly therefore. Presumably its character and strength varies genetically from one person to another; without doubt it is influenced by habit and association and by the moral climate in which we live. Part of its emotional effect is to impose on ostensibly free and rational men a predisposition to cling to supernatural beliefs, even in the face of continual challenge from the world of experience and objective perception.

In his classic work *The Elementary Forms of the Religious Life*, Durkheim (1915) showed with extraordinary clarity that religion is an eminently social, collective phenomenon. It is an attribute of the group as a kind of super-organism rather than of the members as separate individuals. It divides all things into sacred and profane categories, and its principal object, Durkheim concluded (p. 420), is to act on moral life. It gives people aspirations towards an ideal society. Secondly its object is to explain the world and satisfy thinking, questioning mortals, whose knowledge of real science is small and leaves many mysteries unsolved. The first function is directed towards action, the second towards thought. Religion gives man a realization of the nature of society; and it helps him too to rise above the miseries of the world, to enjoy and not be oppressed by the apparent futility of mortal life; to identify himself, through a sense of the world to come, with the immortality of his group.

Science has latterly made enormous strides towards solving the mysteries of the universe, formerly held within the sacred province of religious teaching; and religious belief has had to make huge concessions to real truth in consequence, losing credibility and influence in the process. Our contemporary loss of religious reinforcement has serious repercussions on social conduct, so serious that it could eventually undermine the authority on which the survival of existing societies depends.

The difficulty is partly that it is not equally easy to persuade all men to act for the social good, purely on rational grounds. The innate conscience is stronger in some and weaker in others; some receive better social reinforcement than others, depending on their companions and their information media, and the morality that prevails among them. Nor is it possible to compel moral behaviour entirely by a system of codified laws, because they rely on enforcement by the police or other appointed agents, and the difficulties inherent in this preclude any significant extension of the influence of the law. Over a vast area of behaviour, conformity with the social code depends on self-discipline; and in the absence of religious reinforcement, especially the fear of a divine all-seeing eye and retribution from heaven, self-discipline is enforced rather weakly, or not at all, by the common desire to conform with public opinion and avoid incurring censure.

A second difficulty, which may have existed from early times but has grown enormously in the modern world, is that individuals do not manage to see themselves unequivocally as members of a main social group to which they owe their primary allegiance. The geographical structure of populations has partly broken down, and the clear and simple hierarchy of loyalties it provided, to the family, the local community united by mutual acquaintance, and to the larger tribal society, has become far more complex. Our primary geographical units are sovereign nations, numbering millions of subjects; but intermarriage, emigration, travel, intellectual pursuits, and common international problems allow us to identify ourselves with still larger groups, for example with the Commonwealth, the Western Bloc, and sometimes with the whole of mankind. Within our own nation, in the other direction, we may develop strong and special loyalties towards our particular ethnic or religious group, trade union, and so on.

Social codes normally forbid the individual to take the law into his own hands, and do certain things that are permitted only in the society's name, for example taking human life or inflicting retribution for wrongs done to himself or to others. But society collectively is so empowered to take these measures when its own rights or those of its members are endangered, not only by wrong-doers from within but by other societies that threaten it from without. What is wrongful in the context of the individual can become righteous in that of the group.

Moreover, what properly constitutes a society in that context depends on how the individuals concerned divide their loyalties. Loyalties are at bottom instinctive and emotional and can sometimes be very blindly and irrationally bestowed. A threat to the welfare of any group to which we are prepared to give sufficient allegiance can incite righteous militance, followed by collective and perhaps violent action, notwithstanding that this action is inimical to the national interest or to that of the world as a whole.

Granted that there is a formidable and conflicting hierarchy of social groupings that are effective at different levels, ranging at the bottom from that of a few individuals temporarily banded together for a mutual end, right up to the human species as a single whole, are there any criteria that a biologist can give, by which the individual can be guided in dividing his loyalties? From the biological point of view, his overriding duty should be to ensure the survival of the stock to which he belongs and whose torch he temporarily bears. This is the primary purpose towards which his moral or altruistic behaviour ought therefore to be directed. Theoretically each smaller social grouping should be subordinate to the larger one of which it forms a part, whenever the welfare of the larger group is threatened. Ultimately it is the species itself whose existence ought to be assured.

In a world where the global environment is under threat from pollution, the population explosion, and the possibility of nuclear war, should one on these grounds be prepared always to submerge community and even national interests in favour of supra-national ones?

It seems to me that for the present the answer must be No, for two reasons. First, though all mankind is one in the face of common threats, we nevertheless comprise among us a wealth of genetically and culturally differing peoples, and this still remains a source of resilience, multiplying the chances of finding ways of overcoming regional dangers, or at worst of allowing some sections of the human species to survive even if others perish.

The second is perhaps more practically important. It is that for human groupings above a certain level of size, especially at supra-national levels, the allegiance that individuals are capable of feeling towards them weakens. Great concessions ought to be made to international organizations seeking to obtain agreement on concerted action, by which alone the global dangers can be overcome. But one must recognize that a society is held intact by the loyalty it can inspire in its members and by the effectiveness of its legislature and legal system; and there is no doubt, judged on these criteria, that sovereign nations continue to be the most effective and dependable social units in the contemporary world. It would appear therefore that on biological as well as traditional grounds, it is to his sovereign state that the individual's first loyalty should continue to be given.

REFERENCES

Coulson, J. C. (1968). "Differences in the Quality of Birds Nesting in the Centre and on the Edges of a Colony." *Nature, Lond.* 217, pp. 478–9.

Darwin, C. (1859). *The Origin of Species* (6th edn. 1872) (London: John Murray).

Durkheim, E. (1915). *The Elementary Forms of the Religious Life*, transl. J. W. Swain (London: Allen and Unwin).

Haldane, J. B. S. (1932). *The Causes of Evolution* (London: Longmans).

Jenkins, D., Watson, A., and Miller, G. R. (1963). "Population studies on Red Grouse, *Lagopus lagopus scoticus* (Lath.) in North-east Scotland." *J. anim. Ecol.* 32, pp. 317–76.

Lack, D. (1966). *Population Studies of Birds* (Oxford: Clarendon Press).

Miller, G. R., Watson, A., and Jenkins, D. (1970). "Responses of Red Grouse Populations to Experimental Improvement of Their Foods." In *Animal Populations in Relation to their Food Resources* (ed. A. Watson) (Oxford and Edinburgh: Blackwell Scientific Publications).

Moss, R. (1967). "Probable Limiting Nutrients in the Main Food of Red Grouse *(Lagopus lagopus scoticus)*." In *Secondary Productivity of Terrestrial Ecosystems* (ed. K. Petrusewicz) (Warsaw and Crakow: Panstowowe Wydawnicto Naukowe).

Watson, A. (1970). "Territorial and Reproductive Behaviour of Red Grouse." *J. Reprod. Fert.* suppl. 11, pp. 3–14.

————— and Jenkins, D. (1968). "Experiments on Population Control by Territorial Behaviour in Red Grouse." *J. Anim. Ecol.* 37, pp 595–614.

Wynne-Edwards, V. C. (1959). "The Control of Population Density through Social Behaviour: a Hypothesis." *Ibis.* 101, pp. 436–41.

————— (1962). *Animal Dispersion in Relation to Social Behaviour* (Edinburgh and London: Oliver and Boyd).

Part III

Biology, Human Nature, and Ethical Theory

Attempts to Derive Definitive Moral Patterns from Biology

Abraham Edel

MAJOR DIRECTIONS

It is fairly evident by now that biology has been overworked, especially during the past century, in the attempts to provide a "scientific ethics." In fact some of the disrepute into which this concept has fallen in many quarters stems from the haste with which whole moralities were erected on general biological theories.

The most prominent and spectacular of these moralities were evolutionary, rising to a crest with the popularity of Darwinism. There seems little or no limit to the variety of moral lessons that men have read on the basis of the sober facts of biological evolution. In addition, many have looked to biology for an account of the "ultimate" nature of man, seeking a set of fixed characteristics on which to build a determinate morality. Biology has also provided perennial models, such as the organism concept, on which ethical theories have been patterned.

EVOLUTIONARY MORAL ORDERS

The mainstream of 19th and early 20th century ethical interpretations of evolution sang the praises of struggle as the instrument of upward movement. Herbert Spencer's *Social Statics* which (as Spencer pointed out later) actually antedated Darwin's *The Origin of Species,* launched

From Abraham Edel, *Ethical Judgment: The Use of Science in Ethics* (New York: Macmillan, 1955), pp. 115–121. Copyright 1955 by The Free Press, a Corporation. Reprinted by permission of Macmillan Publishing Co., Inc.

an era in which the *struggle for existence* and the *survival of the fittest* were to become major slogans of a predatory business ethics. The sufferings of the poor and the miseries of the oppressed were seen as by-products of a beneficent evolutionary process in which the able came to the top and the unfit were wiped out. Any interference with this self-propelling upward and onward system of struggle and competition was evil, an absolute violation of nature's moral law. The influence of this whole constellation of ethical justification in American life may be judged from Holmes's dissenting opinion in the Lochner case, in which he opposed this outlook, stating bluntly that the 14th Amendment was not intended to enact Herbert Spencer's *Social Statics* into American law.[1] The law which the Supreme Court struck down as unconstitutional had simply attempted to limit the working hours of bakers in New York as a public health measure.

Competing patterns of interpretation for nature's moral order have taken many different paths. Kropotkin marshalled impressive data for the role of cooperation in survival and development, and tried to see the whole of human history in terms of a rising tide of mutual aid.[2] Many, seeing the growth of larger and larger cohesive human social groups, have read evolution as justifying a coming universalism. Others see the perennial conflict of in-group and out-group and draw moral lessons of the need for group independence through strength and readiness for war.[3] Others search for persistent evolutionary trends such as increased range and variety of adjustments of organism to environment,[4] and are ready to equate the more evolved with the humanly better.

SEARCH FOR "ULTIMATE" INSTINCTS

Those who look to biological accounts of the organism and its make-up for a moral ground-plan often come to rest on some fact of fundamental drives or instincts as the ultimate nature of man. The underlying assumption is that an ethics has to take man for what he is. To be rooted in a biological mechanism serving a biological need seems to many to be all the justification human behavior can ultimately ask. In this way, eating and drinking and sexual activity are obviously sanctioned. A variety of other invariant human tendencies, it is believed, will be found similarly to rest on more subtle biological mechanisms and thus prove their merit. Any institution claiming roots in instinct can thus clothe itself with the moral authority of absolute fixity. The history of social psychology is strewn with the wreckage of instincts intended to support prevalent institutional forms, such as pugnacity instincts to prop up war, acquisitive instincts to reinforce private property, and a variety of specific instincts to support the family.[5]

USE OF BIOLOGICAL MODELS

Some attempts to give determinate shape to ethical theory employ organic processes as *models*. Most common has been the treatment of society as a kind of organism, followed by elaboration of a concept of social health and a set of moral precepts required for maintaining this health and well-being. Leslie Stephen, for example, in his *The Science of Ethics* (1882) uses the language of social tissue and its vitality. The most influential recent model is Cannon's concept of *homeostasis*.[6] Primarily, it refers to the maintenance of a steady state—for example, in temperature or in sugar concentration of the blood. Regulatory processes come into action to preserve the state as it reaches one or another extreme. There has been some tendency to apply this concept in social theory; thus the maintenance of a social order or a cultural pattern can be seen as a kind of social homeostasis. Rights and duties can be defined in such a conception by seeing the regulations functioning to maintain the steady state.

GENERAL EVALUATION

These various attempts to derive absolute or determinate moral patterns from biology in the form of evolutionary orders, instinctual constitutions or process models, raise serious problems of evaluation. They may be estimated briefly along three main lines—the clarity of their concepts, the factual truth of their assertions, and the desirability of their implicit valuations.

Many of the concepts employed in the several accounts are not as clear as they seem on the surface. Darwin himself had some qualms about the meaning of the term "struggle for existence." It clearly assumes a quite different character where it refers to a plant struggling against drought, men struggling against disease, individuals competing with one another in a socially structured set of activities, different human groups making war against one another, or one species using another for food. Similar issues arise in the meaning of "cooperation," "adaptation," etc. And further complications of meaning arise when it is asserted that struggle or cooperation have been "primary" in the evolutionary process. Nor have the criteria of what rates as "instinctive" nor what constitutes an "organism" or "organic whole" been elaborated with the precision that would warrant their ethical application.

Examination is also required of factual assumptions. There have been numerous controversies about the descriptive picture of evolutionary processes, mechanisms of transmission, conditions of group or type stability and change, and so on, whose answers would have a quite varying ethical potential. Moreover, it will be found that on the whole ethical conclusions in the apparently biological ethics use anthropological and historical as well as biological premises,[7] and these too would have to be scrutinized for their accuracy.

Beyond the conceptual and factual issues lie the problems of implicit valuation in the several forms of biological ethics. To what extent can the basic activities focused upon in the various conceptions—life, struggle, cooperation, individual or group expression, themselves be regarded as good rather than as neutral or in some cases evil? Many volumes of criticisms in recent decades have made clear the distinction between finding an evolutionary order and going on to declare it a moral order or a progressive order—obviously the world may be going downhill. These criticisms have, it is true, sometimes overlooked the complexity of the theories which at their best were not just tracing an order of events but describing the evolution of valuations themselves within the order. Nonetheless, especially in the light of all this criticism, an evolutionary ethics does require an explicit account of its value components. Similarly, the call for instinctual expression, maintenance of a steady state or adaptation to a given set of conditions must show the grounds for assuming the goodness of the activity, state, or results. Why not call instead for repression, change of state, change of conditions?

Now the mere multiplication of issues is not itself fatal to the hope of a self-sufficient biological basis for a determinate morality. The vague concepts might be clarified, the factual issues might be further explored and adjudicated, the valuational standpoint stabilized. And the past excesses might be seen as ideological use of biological data constituting distorted interpretation. But these possibilities do not seem enough. In fact the more biological materials are developed, the clearer it becomes that ethical judgment is dependent on the coupling of biological data with that furnished by the other human sciences. We shall see even in this chapter that the simplest values propounded on biological grounds require justification in part in at least psychological terms. This suggests that we should no longer look to the biological perspective for an independent ethics but rather for foundations and at most a partial framework.

FUNDAMENTAL CONTRIBUTIONS TO THE PROBLEM OF ETHICAL RELATIVITY

Once the search is narrowed down in this way, we find that a biological perspective has made and can make a vast contribution to our subject. For if man, in the old Aristotelian definition, is a rational animal, biology has given the picture of his animality on a wider canvas than any other branch of human knowledge. Briefly then, I should like to consider the following contributions of the biological perspective to analyzing ethical relativity. It exhibits man as part of nature, made of the same common clay as other living beings, and points to the animal basis underlying the human spirit. It thereby imposes on us the task of carrying out a fuller "naturalization" of moral phenomena themselves. Second, it lays foundations, together with psychology, for a scientific evaluation of life, pleasure and pain, as basic referents in ethical judgment of variable forms of human activity. Third, it brings into the center of ethical attention man's biological impulses and drives and, by applying to these its evolutionary theory, furnishes a mode of evaluating their role. Fourth, as a consequence, it makes possible the adoption of health as an evaluative criterion, and provides a groundwork for a general evaluation of frustration. In addition, it lays the foundation for two important analytical tools in the whole range of the human sciences which are central to ethical evaluation. In the first place, it develops and sustains the insight that moral phenomena always served some *functional* role, an insight which has been confirmed and extended by the psychological, social and historical sciences. Secondly, by its very long-time perspective, looking at the struggle of populations for survival, it emphasizes a group orientation in formulating ethical issues. This proves a helpful corrective to some of the individualist formulations that have dominated the modern scene.

NOTES

1. *Lochner* v. *New York* 198 U.S. 45 (1905). For a study of the manifold impact of the evolutionary modes of thought in American social theory, see Richard Hofstadter, *Social Darwinism in American Thought 1860–1915* (Philadelphia: University of Pennsylvania Press, 1945).
2. Peter Kropotkin, *Mutual Aid* (London: Penguin Books, 1902). Darwin had himself, in *The Descent of Man,* underscored the values of sympathetic feelings in human society as major survival aids; he even regarded these bases of the moral sense as instinctive.
3. E.g., Sir Arthur Keith, *Evolution and Ethics* (New York: Putnam's, 1946), pp. 145–147, 192–193.
4. For a brief study of such interpretations, see G. Gaylord Simpson, *The Meaning of Evolution* (New York: Mentor Book, 1951), chs. 7, 10.
5. Compare the way in which instincts are treated in William McDougall, *An Introduction to Social Psychology* (Boston: J. W. Luce, 1908), and Otto Klineberg, *Social Psychology* (New York: Holt, 1940).
6. W. B. Cannon, *The Wisdom of the Body* (New York: Norton, 1932).
7. This is explicit in Spencer. Recent discussions such as Julian Huxley's in *Touchstone for Ethics* (New York: Harper, 1947), or Ashley Montagu's in *On Being Human* (New York: Schuman, 1950) make considerable use of contemporary psychological materials.

Ethics and the Theory
of Evolution

Anthony Quinton

Soon after the publication of *The Origin of Species* it was seen that
the theory of evolution might have an important bearing on ethics.
Large-scale ethical systems were constructed on an evolutionary basis
by Herbert Spencer and Leslie Stephen and interesting suggestions were
put forward in essays by T. H. Huxley and W. K. Clifford. More recently, however, evolutionary ethics has fallen into something very like
oblivion. The attempts of Julian Huxley and C. H. Waddington to
reopen the qeustion have evoked little attention from moral philosophers. The reason for this is the extraordinary authority and influence
of G. E. Moore's refutation of ethical naturalism. First presented to
the world in his *Principia Ethica* in 1903 it has dominated philosophical
inquiry into morals in Great Britain ever since. Moore's way of showing
that the concepts and propositions of morality were radically distinct
in logical character from those of natural science has been amended
and improved but the thesis itself remains an almost unquestioned point
of departure for philosophical ethics. One reason why I believe that
evolutionary ethics should be considered afresh is that I do not find
the doctrine of anti-naturalism, in any of its forms, to be even plausible,
let alone convincing. But even if it were correct the issue of the relevance
of evolution to ethics would not be closed. As well as his anti-naturalism,
Moore has imposed on subsequent ethical inquiry an extraordinarily
contracted view of the scope of the subject. As he has practised it, it
is little more than a general logical characterization of the nature of

From I. T. Ramsey, ed., *Biology and Personality* (Oxford: Basil Blackwell,
1966), pp. 107–130. Reprinted by permission of the publisher and the author.

moral discourse. He has had little to say about the internal relations of moral concepts, about the relations of moral to other forms of practical thinking, about the place of moral agency in human nature or about the character of morality as a social institution. He has encouraged in this way an abstract and profoundly unrealistic approach by philosophers to the problems of morality.

I. A PRELIMINARY OBSTACLE: ANTI-NATURALISM

There are a number of different but approximately coincident ways of formulating the anti-naturalist principle. One is to say that moral and natural properties are utterly distinct. Another is to say that there can be no valid inference from scientific or factual premises to moral conclusions. A third is to assert the radical difference of function, and so of kind of meaning, of descriptive and evaluative discourse. In any of its forms the principle regards evolutionary ethics as naturalistic and so mistaken since it attempts to make a scientifically establishable matter of fact, the general trend of the evolutionary process, into the rational criterion for the validity of moral propositions.

Moore's own technique for proving the anti-naturalist principle was crude and unsatisfactory. His successors have discreetly drawn a veil over it and replaced it with something much more persuasive. Moore held that the distinction of moral and natural properties could be discerned, first of all, by simple inspection. Take a moral and a natural term, 'good' and 'pleasant' let us say, attend closely to them so that their meanings, the properties they express, are present to your mind and just see if they are not quite different. The belief that any such procedure could possibly prove the point at issue rests on the exploded psychologistic view that concepts, the meanings of words, are mental entities, susceptible of direct inspection. In fact the meaning of a term is an abstract and more or less complicated social practice, the established way of using the word in question. It cannot be fully and finally articulated by any method as simple as Moore's. If it could the making of dictionaries would be a great deal easier than it is.

A second, slightly more sophisticated, argument says that if any moral term M and any natural term N were identical in meaning the question 'Is this N thing M?' would be insignificant since it would mean no more than 'Is this N thing N?'. The relevant consideration is that if

M and N were identical in meaning the statement that this N thing is M would be analytic and the statement that this N thing is not M would be self-contradictory. But this again is not a matter that can generally be decided by inspection, though it can be sometimes. It is possible and indeed common for people to understand the statements that there is not and that there is a largest prime number without knowing that either, let alone which, is analytic or contradictory.

Two further objections to both of Moore's arguments are that his general conclusion rests on an induction from particular cases and that he gives no clear account of the distinction between moral and natural terms. In philosophy inductions are out of place. At best they can suggest hypotheses which must then be proved. Furthermore it is a condition of the acceptability of an inductive conclusion that the general terms which occur in it should be clearly understood so that the relevance of the supposed particular instances on which it rests is beyond question. Without a better interpretation than Moore provides for 'moral' and 'natural' we cannot tell what ethical theories his principle rules out or even attach any definite sense to it.

All these objections are circumvented by the method of arriving at Moore's general conclusion about the logical uniqueness of moral concepts which his successors have devised. This method distinguishes two broad classes of concepts in the light of their respective functions in discourse. There are the theoretical concepts which describe and the practical concepts which prescribe or evaluate. Since the functions of the two are quite different there can be no logical connection between them. In this mode of argument particular cases are used to illustrate, not to support, the thesis. The two sorts of term are clearly distinguished from the start and in such a way that their logical distinctness necessarily follows.

The simplest version of this argument says that the propositions of science are indicative while those of morals are imperative. As Poincaré puts it: 'There can be no such thing as a scientific morality. It is for a reason, how shall I put it, of a purely grammatical kind.' Popper says: 'It is impossible to derive norms or decisions or proposals from facts.' Ayer concludes: 'Ethical statements are not really statements at all, . . . they are not descriptive of anything . . . they cannot be either true or false.'

The first objection to this theory is that not only are moral utterances not literally imperative but that they do not even behave like imperatives. Moral judgements can be expressed in the past tense; imperatives cannot be. We can say 'you ought not to have done that' but not 'don't have done that'. Furthermore we can speak of knowledge, belief and doubt, of truth, probability and falsehood, just as properly in connection with the moral as with the merely descriptive features of actions and their agents. These objections will be resisted. It will be argued that a moral judgement in the past tense somehow embodies a general imperative in the timeless present ('you ought not to have done that' implies 'don't anyone ever do what you did') and that the epistemic terms have a different sense when they occur in moral judgements, that of signifying the nature and degree of the speaker's subjective commitment to the policy he is prescribing. The point of this resistance is the belief that judgements of value have an intimate relation to conduct which is not possessed by ordinary, straightforward descriptions of matters of fact. 'This is green', as theoretical, is used to get one's hearers to think in a certain way about the thing described: 'this is bad' is used to get them to avoid it.

There is an initial difficulty here in the indefiniteness of the distinction between the influencing of beliefs and the influencing of actions. Even if we are unwilling to define belief, with Bain, as a propensity to act in certain ways it does seem that the connection between holding a belief and acting appropriately is more than contingent. More fundamental, perhaps, is the difficulty of stating just what the special relations to belief and to action in the two cases actually are. We cannot define an utterance as practical, with Stevenson, as one that can or does cause action since any utterance can and utterances of all possible sorts do. Nor does it help to say that utterances are practical if they are *intended* to cause action. Plain statements of fact like 'the building is on fire' can and do cause action and can be intended to do so. Moral judgements like 'Genghis Khan was a bad man' can fail to cause action and can be used without the intention of affecting it, when, for example, I do not suppose my hearer to have either the desire or the opportunity to imitate him.

A more promising account of practicality, provided by Hare, attaches it to any utterance whose sincere acceptance commits the acceptor to acting in a certain way. On this criterion both 'shut the door' and 'you ought to shut the door' are practical but 'the door is open' is not. In general it brings together as practical all those utterances which are direct responses, making no presumptions about the wishes of the inquirer, to requests for advice, to the question 'what shall I do?' But to establish this much logical affinity between judgements of value and imperatives does not establish, though it may suggest, a more comprehensive identity of logical character. Since imperatives are practical some practical utterances are not statements. But this does not prove that moral utterances, being practical, are not statements either. If there were some practical utterances which plainly were statements the suggestion that moral utterances were not statements, which already has all the grammatical and logical appearances against it, would have hardly anything left to recommend it.

But in fact there is such a class of unquestionably descriptive practical statements, namely what I shall call 'appetitive utterances' which indicate the objects or states of affairs that the person addressed will most enjoy or like or will get most satisfaction from. 'You will most like or enjoy the Red Lion' is as good, sufficient and direct an answer to the question 'which hotel shall I stay at?' as 'stay at the Red Lion' or 'the Red Lion is the best hotel'. It is like them and different from 'the Red Lion is the smartest or largest or quietest hotel' in that no contingent presumption needs to be made about the special tastes or requirements of the questioner in order to predict the action that will follow on his sincere acceptance of the advice or, at any rate, to be assured of its relevance to his inquiry. Of course he can accept the statement as correct and still not act on it. The Red Lion may be too expensive for him. But just the same situation can arise compatibly with his sincere acceptance of the judgement that the Red Lion is the best hotel. This is an important point since it distinguishes value-judgements and appetitive utterances, which are defeasible in this way, from straight imperatives, which are not. There can be no serious question that appetitive utterances are both practical, in the way that judgements of value and imperatives are, and factual, capable of being established as true or false. If a man accepts an appetitive utterance addressed to him and fails to act accordingly it must either be that his acceptance is insincere or that he is somehow prevented from following it up or that there is some stronger practical claim on him. The capacity of a thing to give satisfaction, like its excellence or its moral obligatoriness, cannot, without some kind of absurdity, be taken as a reason against choosing it, but its smartness or its largeness or its quietness perfectly well can.

The acceptable residue of anti-naturalism is the important point that there is an intimate relation between judgements of value and conduct; such judgements are logically, and not just contingently, good reasons for conduct of the recommended kind. It follows that there is a logical distinction between judgements of value and neutral, strictly theoretical, statements of fact. But there is no conflict between the practical character of an utterance and its being a statement of fact. Ironically the most persistent and familiar type of naturalist ethical theory, Moore's principal target, the type of theory which interprets moral concepts in appetitive terms, is what derives most support from a reconstructed version of his arguments while his own brand of intuitionism, which takes judgements of value to report the incidence of non-natural properties, is clearly refuted by it.

A satisfactory ethical theory, then, must interpret judgements of value in practical terms. But to say this is not to rule out all attempts to derive judgements of value from factual premises. Provided that the premises are practical as well as factual there is no logical objection to the procedure.

II. ARE STATEMENTS ABOUT EVOLUTION PRACTICAL?

If my partial demolition of anti-naturalism is to be of any help to the project of finding in evolutionary theory the fundamental ethical criterion, we must see if the relevant assertions of evolutionary theory can be understood as practical in nature. They are not, prima facie, appetitive. To describe some state of affairs or course of conduct as adaptive or biologically efficient is not the same as to say that it will give enjoyment or satisfaction to the person addressed. But I do not pretend to have shown that appetitive statements are the only practical utterances apart from imperatives and judgements of value. To show that these three kinds of utterance are all species of the practical genus is not to show that there are not other species as well.

I believe, in fact, that there is a class of practical concepts, distinct from those of general evaluation such as 'good' and those of the appetitive domain such as 'satisfying', which constitute a further species of the genus and amongst which the relevant evolutionary concepts can be found. These concepts are those of what I shall call, in a broad sense, 'technical evaluation'. A body of scientific knowledge consists of general statements, systematically articulated into theories, which enable us to predict and explain natural occurrences. In most but not all cases a system of technological prescriptions can be derived from scientific theories which tell us what to do if we want to achieve certain results. Consider the case of medicine. Anatomy provides us with a theoretical account of the structure, and physiology of the working, of the human body. Pathology provides us with an account of the nature and causes of diseased or abnormal conditions of the body. From these departments of medical science we can derive the two great branches of medical technology, in other words, of applied medical science or clinical medicine; namely therapeutics, concerned with the cure of disease, and hygiene, concerned with its prevention. The concepts of technical evaluation in use here are, of course, the concepts of health and disease. To characterize a condition of the human organism as diseased is to make a practical statement. It is to recommend that the condition be removed or avoided. One cannot sincerely accept that a condition or course of conduct is healthier than another and fail to pursue it unless prevented from doing so or unless there is some stronger countervailing practical consideration. Furthermore it is absurd to choose a course of conduct just because it is unhealthy and for no other reason, such as a desire to avoid military service.

Health is one of the most obvious concepts of technical evaluation but there are many others. Technology, in a fairly narrow sense, employs the concept of efficiency, perhaps the most general and inclusive concept of this kind. From economics we derive the concept of the economical. Sociology, of a rough and ready descriptive kind, allows the derivation of that technology of conventional social behaviour we call etiquette, with its governing notion of the polite, that is to say the done or expected thing.

Statements in which these technical values are ascribed to objects or policies seem flatly to contravene the conventional dichotomy of the evaluative and the descriptive. On the one hand they are unquestionably practical, in that they are good, sufficient and direct reasons for action and in that there is an absurdity involved in taking them to be reasons against acting in the naturally indicated way; on the other hand they are unquestionably statements of fact, capable of being empirically established as true or false and, furthermore, in the most favoured way, namely by means of scientific investigation. It is really very peculiar that the defenders of the dichotomy should have failed to notice their existence.

In works of evolutionary biology there is a collection of terms which appear to stand for technical values of this kind. Examples are 'adaptive,' 'progressive,' 'genetically or biologically efficient' and 'anagenetic.' It is not clear to me that these are all different ways of saying the same thing. It would seem natural to call a particular favourable variation adaptive but to describe the present condition of a species or the structure of an organ as biologically efficient. However these biological valuations appear to be logically interconnected—a variation is adaptive, for example, if it contributes to the biological efficiency of the organ or species involved—and the same ultimate evidence is appealed to for the ascription of any of them. Species, organs and variations are not the only things that can be intelligibly evaluated in these terms. The ends which they serve can equally be served by the modes of behaviour, policies and social institutions which are the subject-matter, in a broad sense, of ethics. Waddington's notion of 'biological wisdom' is simply their application in this field as a criterion for the adequacy of received ethical ideas and practices.

There are two general remarks to be made about this whole class of technical values. In the first place these values are plural, in the sense that they can come into competition with one another, and in consequence they are subordinate and not final. They may, when they come into conflict, require us to adjudicate between them by reference to some overriding principles of value. The most efficient cook or electric fire or garage or electoral system or raincoat is not always the most economical one. Again, the suggestions of economy may be countered by the requirements of health and efficiency; economy and health may all come into conflict with morality. But the fact that technical values of this kind are not final or absolute values does not mean that they are not values at all.

Secondly, these technical values all have some implicit appetitive element. They are ascribed to things in virtue of the contribution of those things to some end and these ends will be ones that are generally desired by men and are generally satisfying to them. Thus the healthy is that which contributes to long and painless life; the efficient is that which produces a given result with the least outlay of time, attention and scarce materials; the economical is that which produces a given result with the minimum cost. That there should be such concepts of technical evaluation requires that there should be certain things which men generally agree in wanting to achieve or avoid. This dependence of technical value on the appetitive is brought out most clearly perhaps by the utilitarian foundations of classical economics. Here certain assumptions are made about human preferences and behaviour which are sufficiently obvious to be regarded as giving a definition of economic rationality. An allocation of resources or of factors of production generally is regarded as economical to the extent that it yields more total utility than any alternative allocation.

In the evolutionary case the relevant, generally desired, end is the effective survival of the human species, its continuation despite the dangers of the physical environment, the hostility of other species and the increasingly perilous character of its internal dissensions. Now if the survival of the human species is a technical end the biological efficiency of some policy or institution is certainly a good and sufficient reason for choice *other things being equal,* just as its efficiency or economy or healthiness are, but it is not a final or overriding reason for choice in all circumstances. Furthermore that biological efficiency is a technical value at all requires that the survival of the species is something that men generally desire. No one would seriously question that in some sense they do but the notion of survival is a highly flexible one and can take many different forms which will evoke rather varying degrees of appetite.

There is a further consideration about the technical values of evolutionary biology which marks them off from some of the others though it applies to some small extent to the value of health. They have a certain ambiguity which is also shown by those puzzlingly sinuous concepts the natural and the normal. To speak of some sequence of changes as an evolution or a progress may be simply to describe it as a change. In the same way the natural or the normal may be simply that which ordinarily or on the average or on the whole does occur. But more usually an evolution or a progress is a sequence of changes in an upward direction, an improvement. Similarly to describe something as natural or normal is usually to imply that it is what ought to happen rather than that it is just what generally does. The point is that it is conceivable that the most biologically efficient condition of the human species at a certain stage of its development might be an entirely nonprogressive one. This would be the case if all possible variations were unfavourable. In other words the mere fact of change is of no more value than mere averageness. If we are to derive from the general course of the evolutionary process so far a criterion for the comparison of alternative futures it can only be to the extent that we can regard its present phase as an improvement on its starting-point and not simply as different from it. Text-books of pathology are extremely cautious about definitions and prefer to start off right away with the examination in detail of particular forms of disease. When they do define disease it is often in terms of the barely statistical concept of normality. This is all right in practice since by and large people feel better and manage their lives more effectively if their kidneys are in the same condition as most other people's are for most of the time. But if I feel better, think more clearly and work more efficiently when my temperature is 100 degrees F. than when it is at any other figure it would be thoroughly odd to say that I was permanently ill, and positively undesirable to keep my temperature down to the conventional 98.6. Just as the statistical definition of disease rests on the extra-statistical reinforcement of absence of pain and discomfort and of efficient functioning so the use of the actual evolutionary process as a criterion of progress requires reinforcement from outside.

III. THE EARLIER FORMS OF EVOLUTIONARY ETHICS

So far we have been concerned with the rather abstract question of the possibility in principle that a contribution should be made to the central problem of ethics by evolutionary biology. I have argued that since the anti-naturalist argument is invalid this possibility cannot be ruled out in advance. Secondly I have suggested that there are some valuations which evolutionary considerations can directly establish. These, however, are not final but subordinate valuations, and are themselves dependent on the appetitive value, the general satisfyingness, of the end of survival to which they relate. It is now time to turn to the positive theories of evolutionary ethics in order to see whether any stronger claim for the ethical relevance of evolution can be justified.

Admittedly the survival of the human species is a generally accepted end along with health, economy and efficiency. The question remains—can it be shown to have some more fundamental significance than these other ends? The first clearly evolutionary system of ethics was Herbert Spencer's. His final criterion of value was 'quantity of life in breadth and depth.' The qualification about breadth and depth shows that he was not taking increase in the sheer bulk of living matter as the ultimate good. But just what else he did mean is not very clear. The words 'breadth' and 'depth' in this connection have an obvious evaluative implication though what it is is not very definite. It would seem to involve multiplicity of species and complexity in the organization of these species. In fact, it is not necessary to go into the matter of his precise intentions here since Spencer clearly recognized the insufficiency of his formula however it was to be interpreted. For he reinforced it with the palpably appetitive notion of 'surplus of agreeable feeling.' He would appear to have realized that quantity of life could increase 'in breadth and depth' with undesirable results.

The most notorious consequence that Spencer drew from his rather diaphanous axiom was that society should not interfere with the workings of natural selection. In practice this involved strenuous opposition to the welfare activities of the state, to the public relief and support of the destitute, the insane, the chronically sick. Spencer even objected to public support of education. In his view society, by attempting to remedy these misfortunes, was interfering with the beneficent workings of natural selection in its weeding out of unsatisfactory human stocks. The trouble with this argument is not so much its conflict with conventional moral responses but its weakness from an evolutionary point of view. A society run on Spencer's lines, with its members pursuing their own interests in a ruthlessly competitive way, would not indeed be a very pleasant one to belong to. It would be full of aggression, cold-heartedness and anxiety. But more to the point, it would be poorly situated vis-à-vis other, less unamiable societies since it would lack internal harmony and thus be weakened in its competition with them. A further consideration, of course, is that Spencer's aim, the elimination of undesirable stocks, of the stupid, the lazy, the feckless, the diseased and so on, is one that can be much more economically attained than by the very blunt instrument of natural selection. Always supposing that broad agreement can be obtained as to which traits are both undesirable and inheritable, it would be much more efficient, as well as much more contributory to Spencer's 'surplus of agreeable feeling,' to eliminate them by the methods of artificial selection proposed by the supporters of eugenics.

A social morality directly opposed to Spencer's was derived from the theory of evolution by W. K. Clifford. In his view the essential condition for the evolutionary success of a society was social harmony, a state of affairs in which the individual subjected his own interests to the demands of the 'tribal self.' Much the same point was made by T. H. Huxley when he said that 'social disorganization follows on immorality.' Man cannot survive on his own but only as a member of a society and the effective persistence of a society requires that its members should rate the claims of its welfare above their own advantage. Huxley went on to say that it might well be that the self-assertiveness which had been of evolutionary value in the primitive, more or less pre-social, conditions of human life had become a great danger to man as a fully social being.

In its earliest phase, then, evolutionary ethics took the form of 'the gladiatorial theory of existence,' in which it was used to recommend the unwavering pursuit of individual interest, and also of the doctrine of the tribal self, in which it was brought to the aid of an, at any rate local, variety of altruism. With apparent inconsistency Huxley went on in another lecture to argue that the main task of morality was not to foster but positively to counteract the cosmic process of evolution with all its injustices. At this stage of his thought Huxley took the view that evolutionary ethics made an illicit play on the word 'fittest.' Those best equipped to survive were not necessarily those who really ought to survive. Spencer's gladiatorial theory was, then, subjected to two, apparently inconsistent lines of attack. On the one hand uncontrolled competition was held to be inefficient from an evolutionary point of view; on the other, the evolutionary process itself was morally condemned. In fact the inconsistency can be removed without difficulty. Huxley's two doctrines can be reconciled by taking him to say that the socially uncontrolled process of evolution has produced a good result by means on which we are now in a position to improve.

IV. THE CENTRAL PROBLEM: C. H. WADDINGTON AND J. S. HUXLEY

Two main points emerge from this discussion of the earlier forms of evolutionary ethics. First, an evolutionary criterion of ethical value seems insufficient by itself and must be reinforced by some further principle for selecting between different possible directions of evolution. Even the most resolute supporter of evolutionary ethics, Herbert Spencer, had to appeal to the extra-biological concept of 'surplus of agreeable feeling.' Secondly, even if the basic evolutionary principle is accepted there is considerable doubt as to just what sort of moral system it endorses. Both of these weaknesses are present in the most recent presentations of evolutionary ethics. Waddington is more resolute than Huxley in excluding extra-biological considerations from the formulation of his fundamental criterion of value but neither of them gives an at all clear or convincing account of the connection between the evolutionary principle of value and concrete moral convictions. Waddington discourses in a confident but uninformative way about 'the discoverable general trend of evolution' while Huxley, though he is copious enough in stating his pacific, liberal, internationalist ideals, does nothing very much to establish their support by the evolutionary principle.

In his book *The Ethical Animal* Waddington puts forward as the fundamental criterion of value what evolutionary biology shows to be most efficient. This is a strong theory since it makes no appeal to extra-biological considerations. He identifies the biologically efficient with what is favoured by the discoverable general trend of the evolutionary process. There is a difficulty here which he does not face. Biological efficiency is a local or relative notion, conformity with the general trend of evolution is not. Thus a particular adaptive variation may in fact contribute to the ultimate extinction of a species. For example, the more perfectly adapted a species is to its existing physical environment the more vulnerable it is to large changes in that environment. The trouble is that the general trend takes place against a background of many more variables than a particular increase in biological efficiency. So a change that increases adaptation to a certain stable context may be a reduction of efficiency when viewed in relation to changes in that environment. A commonsensical social analogue of this situation is provided by the process of industrialization. A community of highly specialized industrial workers is, in a sense, better adapted to its environment than a community of pioneers but a major disaster of flood and earthquake is more likely to be effectively surmounted by the more primitive community. Waddington's criterion, then, although purely biological, is nevertheless somewhat ambiguous. And the ambiguity is important since the general trend provides the criterion he really wants but only the more local facts about biological efficiency are likely to be at all precisely available. However the problem of specifying the criterion can be deferred for the moment. What matters here is that Waddington's criterion is an exclusively biological one.

Huxley starts from the point that ethics, as a part of the evolutionary process, itself evolves. Evolution has a direction—towards a higher degree of organization—and this is a movement that the deliberate control of human society should seek to foster. At first it seems that the objective standard which Huxley claims to have found is the simple imperative: keep evolution going. But this soon becomes encrusted with various extra-biological impurities. Human action, he says, should be directed towards the realization of new *evolutionary possibilities*, it should assist individual *development*, it should further *social evolution*, it should promote *higher values*, the *welfare* and *dignity* of the individual. The italicized expressions are all intended in a non-biologically evaluative sense as becomes clear when he goes on to describe his criterion as that of the *desirable* direction of evolution. Huxley realizes that there are many possible lines of future evolutionary development. Unless there were, indeed, it is hard to see how evolution could be relevant to choice. But which of these are we to select as the criterion of value? The one that will occur if we leave things to go on as they are? The one that is most directly continuous with the course of evolution hitherto? Huxley makes his selection by reference to 'higher values' of a wholly extra-biological kind. An ethical theory that requires this sort of reinforcement, however much evolutionary material it makes use of, is not really an evolutionary ethics at all. It is just another teleological system, defining the rightness of actions in terms of their contribution to ends of assumed value, which emphasizes that if this contribution is to be correctly worked out attention must be paid to the facts revealed by evolutionary biology about the effects of policies and institutions.

We must return, then, to the type of strong theory, as I have called it, proposed by Waddington. This holds that the general trend of evolution is discoverable and that the ultimate justification of moral beliefs is to be found in the extent to which they further this trend. Waddington does not say what the trend of evolution is in any but the most formal way. His confidence that it can be discovered seems to be based on the general agreement amongst biologists about the ordering of the evolutionary hierarchy. He does offer three indications of biological progress which might be taken as a general account of the trend: increase in independence of the environment, in complexity of relations with environmental variables and in power to control the environment. But he makes no very serious attempt to show how these general criteria of evolutionary progress are to be applied to the actual situations of human choice. One feature of the general agreement about the ordering of the evolutionary hierarchy which might be used is the unanimous opinion that man is the most evolved species, the one that shows the highest degree of biological progress. He has certainly won the contest between animal species in that it is only on his sufferance that any other species exist at all, amongst species large enough to be seen at any rate. In the light of this fact the survival of the human species can be made into a minimal criterion.

There are two possibilities to be considered here. First, we may be confronted by alternative roads to survival, one of which is less efficient or guaranteed of success than the other. Is it really inconceivable that a higher degree of biological security or efficiency might cost more than it is rational to pay? In other words would it be reasonable always to sacrifice Huxley's 'higher values' for an increased chance for the survival of the human species? The danger of being run over can be avoided by spending the whole of one's life indoors but the consequent impoverishment of life is too high a price to pay.

The second and more poignant possibility is one of a choice between survival and elimination. It is, in fact, a somewhat implausible situation since neither outcome is anything like guaranteed for any of the actual choices with which the human species is confronted. But, ignoring this, is it self-evident that we should prefer a continued and miserable life for the species to a short and gay one? The problem of nuclear disarmament is often presented in these terms as a plain choice between the destruction of the human species and communist domination. Now, whatever communist domination might actually turn out to be like, is it not perfectly conceivable that for the human species, as for Victorian young ladies, there can be fates worse than death?

Of course the evolutionary argument is a strong one here. As long as the species keeps going, on whatever terms, there is hope of an improvement in the long run. But some of its apparent force may be derived from the same insecure foundation as Hobbes's view that the right to life was so overridingly important that all other rights should be sacrificed for its sake if necessary. Merely being alive is of no value in itself. If one's right to live is infringed, of course, one has no rights at all but this does not make it of any value by itself. Salt is essential in our diet but it cannot be a staple nourishment on its own.

The same line of argument is applicable to Waddington's criterion of 'anagenesis.' It is no doubt broadly desirable that we should increase our independence of, the complexity of our relations with and our control over our environment. But if such an increase can only be secured by means which involve a considerable deterioration in the experienced quality of life it is not irrational to do without it.

Waddington has an argument to show that an evolutionary criterion is fundamental to ethics which should be briefly considered. The function of systems of moral beliefs, he says, is the mediation of the progress of human evolution. No doubt moral convictions have been an important causal factor in the social development of mankind. But to say this is not to say that the promotion of evolution was the intended purpose of these moral beliefs, nor, more importantly, is it to say that the promotion of evolution is what morality is really and fundamentally for, in the sense that this is the purpose that it ought to serve and by reference to which it should be judged. It is not indeed even true to say that it is *the* function of morality to promote evolution, any more than it would be to say that the function of cars is to eliminate accident-prone strains in the population, of secondary modern schools to keep adolescents off the streets or of the monarchy to provide a focus of social aspiration.

I conclude that the case for the primacy of biological efficiency amongst the set of technical values has not been made out. That it is *a* good cannot seriously be questioned. What has not been shown is that it is *the* good.

V. PROBLEMS OF PREDICTION AND APPLICATION

At various points in the discussion so far the difficulty has emerged of formulating a general evolutionary principle that is sufficiently definite to be effectively applied to the task of judging between conflicting moral beliefs. First of all there are three issues to be considered about the general trend of evolution if its character is to be taken as a criterion of value. (1) Suppose that it is both discoverable and inevitable as, in the eyes of Marxists, the smaller-scale evolutionary movement towards the classless society is. It does not follow that its continuation should be accelerated or assisted. It is perfectly possible to be a Marxist theoretically but an anti-Marxist practically, to believe that the course of history is inevitably towards the formation of proletarianized mass societies and also to believe that one should struggle against this process. One can strive to delay or complicate the birth-pangs of the new order in much the same way as one might strive to resist the onset of senility with tennis, brightly coloured clothing, and vigorous participation in youthful amusements. There will naturally be a certain pathos about this but it may be preferred to gloomy resignation. (2) Even if we allow that the general trend is good and should be fostered there is the problem of determining precisely what social policies and practices are calculated to encourage it on its way. The disagreement mentioned earlier between Spencer and Clifford shows how firm commitment to the beneficence of the general trend can issue in directly opposed views about the right course of action to adopt. We hardly need evolutionary theory to tell us that nuclear warfare should be avoided or the geometrical progression of population increase be controlled. No doubt there is a good evolutionary justification for our instinctive condemnation of incest but what has evolutionary theory to say about divorce, variations of income, urban styles of living, the allocation of decisions as between society and the individual or the desirable limits of conformity? In short, there are certain rather general ends which have the support of the general trend of evolution but do not need it since they are broadly agreed upon already while as far as more particular and intermediate purposes are concerned, and it is these that are the matters of serious controversy, the general trend of evolution does not come down clearly on the side of either party to the dispute. (3) An explanation of this indeterminacy of guidance is afforded by the consideration, advanced by Professor Popper in his *Poverty of Historicism,* that trends are not extrapolable and do not provide a rationally well-founded basis for prediction. As he rightly insists there is no 'law of evolution' but only a broadly characterized trend towards greater complexity and flexibility vis-à-vis the environment. What evolutionary theory fundamentally consists of are the genetic theories of inheritable characteristics and chance variation and the theory of natural selection. This entails the important but nonetheless tautological conclusion that if adaptive variations occur within a given population these will come to characterize the whole population in a space of time inversely proportionate to the degree of the variations' adaptiveness. The trouble is that there is no sure way of telling in advance which variations are adaptive; that is a judgement we can only make *ex post facto* in order to explain the actual changes in the characteristics of a given population. Popper does not deny that a trend may suggest a *law,* namely a universal statement which, applied to the conditions of a population at any given stage of the trend, may permit the derivation of the later stages. What makes this a somewhat Utopian hope as far as the process of biological evolution is concerned is that the occurrence of variations still appears to be a matter of chance and that the set of environmental variables in their relation to which the adaptiveness of variations consists is exceedingly large, very heterogeneous and contains elements which are themselves of a very low degree of predictability, such as major climatic changes, and also beyond the competence of biology to pronounce upon.

These final considerations bear as well on the possibility of making well-founded judgements in advance about biological efficiency of a less comprehensive kind than those which define it in terms of contribution to the general trend. Even if we wish to judge some variation to be biologically efficient locally rather than comprehensively, to be efficient in relation to an environment which in its broad outlines is presumed to be stable, the outcomes of encouraging or stifling it by deliberate social action will be so complicatedly different that they will be hard to predict and, when predicted, hard to adjudicate between. And although this type of prediction of efficiency does seem possible in principle the artificial assumption of stability on which it rests makes it that much more hypothetical and so unreliable as a guide to action.

VI. FROM BIOLOGICAL TO SOCIAL EVOLUTION

A further limitation on the relevance of biology to even the broadest kind of ethical problem is imposed by the fact that the sort of evolution that is of ethical interest is social rather than biological. There are two independent ways of making this point. It is suggested by some biologists that in fact biological evolution, or, at any rate, the biological evolution of the human species, is at an end. This is a curious and, in its more general form, implausible assertion. More to the point is the fact that the time-scale of biological change is incommensurable with that of social policy. Where biologists think in terms of millions of years the framer of social policies thinks in decades. However it might be argued that the rough and ready processes of natural selection can be very greatly speeded up by deliberate human interference. The stock-breeder's activities have none of the laborious prevarication of nature's. It remains true, all the same, that it is the socially acquired rather than the genetically inherited characteristics of men which have been responsible for the conspicuous changes in the nature of human life in the historical period, and indeed for much longer than that. Furthermore it is to these socially acquired characteristics that the moral innovator or framer of social policy must primarily address himself. He is concerned with the dispositions, habits and modes of behaviour of men which have been imposed by society in the course of the post-natal process of learning and not with those received through ante-natal genetic inheritance. These social characteristics can be altered from one generation to the next by simply varying the environment in which the learning process takes place.

It is, of course, perfectly all right to talk of the evolution and of the natural selection of these social characteristics. But the limits of their analogy with genetically inherited characteristics should not be forgotten. In the first place our social or cultural inheritance is not biparental: in this respect we are the direct heirs of all the ages. We can acquire knowledge, techniques, values and institutions from anyone, anywhere, at any time by the simple act of verbal communication. The result of an effective system of verbal communication in which it is possible to get words from one place to another and to present them in an intelligible form is an immensely rapid diffusion of social characteristics. The most striking instance of this is naturally the diffusion of industrial skill, nationalist ideology and the technique of urban living from Europe to the non-European world in this century. In the second place social characteristics can be acquired at any age but our genetic outfit is determined by the condition of our parents at the moment of our conception and we shall only pass on anything new to our offspring if the variations occur before we beget or conceive them. Social evolution, then, is certainly a field in which natural selection occurs; unfavourable variations are eliminated by a large variety of failures to communicate them, if their possessors have no offspring to teach them to or no desire to teach them or no success in getting them accepted. But the social law of inheritance is a very much more complicated and amorphous affair than its biological counterpart.

There remains, nevertheless, one sphere in which our genetic inheritance is strictly relevant to ethics and social policy, that of eugenics. There is a number of generally desired or favoured characteristics—intelligence, immunity to some forms of disease, sanity—which there is reason to believe are to a preponderant extent matters of genetic inheritance and whose diffusion through the human population is therefore capable of being brought about by the control of reproduction. T. H. Huxley argued against eugenics that we do not really know what characteristics we ought to breed for. Even if this were true it would not undermine the eugenist's programme. Though we may not be very clear about the properties of the superman we can at least identify various types of subman without much difficulty or dispute. The real obstacle here, as Sir C. G. Darwin has pointed out, is that man is a wild species and so not amenable to any large-scale experiments in controlled breeding. The dilemma is a practical one. Devices for bringing about differential fertility seem to be either ineffective (e.g. family allowances proportionate to income) or socially dangerous and disruptive (e.g. surgical sterilization).

VII. SOME CONCLUDING CONSIDERATIONS

Despite my rejection of anti-naturalism, then, I conclude that evolutionary biology does not have much to contribute to the solution of the central problem of ethics: the discovery of a criterion for the justification of judgements of value. Although evolutionary knowledge can give rise to value-judgements these are of a subordinate and defeasible nature. Secondly, these judgements of biological value are inevitably of an *ex post facto* character, since the evolutionary process is a trend not a law and one that depends on a unpredictably numerous and variegated set of variables. Finally the evolving and naturally selected human characteristics which are principally relevant to ethics and social policy are socially acquired and not genetically inherited. I agree with the anti-naturalists, then, that there can be no well-founded evolutionary ethics as traditionally understood. It remains to be considered whether our knowledge about evolution can be of use to ethics in any other way. I believe that there are, in fact, two spheres in which it can make a contribution.

1. *The evolution of moral agency.* Both Waddington and J. S. Huxley lay a good deal of emphasis on the fact that just as morality as a social institution is an evolutionary phenomenon so the moral capacity of the individual, his possession of moral beliefs and their tendency to influence his actions, is something that has evolved. They connect this, furthermore, with the Freudian theory of the formation of the conscience or super-ego. The strictly ethical conclusion they then draw is that since moral agency or the moral sense is not innate the theory of moral intuitionism, which holds that the fundamental propositions, at any rate, of a system of moral beliefs must be directly apprehended, is false. In fact these three considerations—that morality has evolved, that conscience is not innate, and that intuitionism is false—are not logically connected in the way that they suppose. To start with it is perfectly consistent, and for a biologist, one would have thought, rather natural, to assert both that morality has evolved and that conscience is innate. Suppose an initial population whose members' behaviour is dominated by impulses of Hobbesian and amoral egoism. Suppose further that a variation occurs in one or several members of the population, one that equips them with altruistic or public-spirited or self-sacrificing impulses. If Clifford and T. H. Huxley are right the offspring of these emotional mutants will have an evolutionary advantage since they will be able to form a mutual protection society. In due course the egoistic stocks will be eliminated and innate, inheritable altruism will come to characterize the whole population. I am not suggesting that this supposition is in fact correct, though it strikes me as being not utterly implausi-

ble if taken in a very broad sense. My only purpose is to point out that to say that morality has evolved is not to say that it has evolved socially rather than genetically. A further point to notice is that the evolution of morality can be understood in two different ways, an external and an internal, so to speak. By the external evolution of morality I mean the movement from premoral egoism to some sort of altruism or social-mindedness. By its internal evolution I mean the movement from concern for the tribe to concern for humanity or the whole sentient creation, from parochial to cosmopolitan morality in other words, or, again, from a crude morality of overt acts to a morality which concerns itself with motivation, or yet again, from a morality which demands rigorously conceived forms of conduct to one that prescribes the pursuit, by any of a range of critically selected means, of certain broad general ends. It would seem reasonable to suppose that the external evolution of morality is genetic even if its internal evolution is social. However, there may be something wrong with the initial assumption of the theory of external evolution, for it supposes, with Hobbes, that the natural condition of men is exclusively self-regarding. But it might well be argued that the initial human population is not like that since it is equipped with an inheritance of social-mindedness from its ancestors among the higher animals. On the whole, then, it seems reasonable enough to suppose that the internal details of individual moral capacity are acquired by a process of social evolution, and so are amenable to the type of explanation offered by Freud's super-ego theory, but that if the broad instinctive substructure of men has evolved at all within the life-span of the species and is not part of the initial genetic equipment of *homo sapiens* it may well have done so genetically.

We may now turn to the supposed incompatibility between the idea that our fundamental moral convictions are acquired and not innate and the intuitionist theory of morals. The source of this belief seems to be the traditional identification of necessary with innate knowledge. Ethical intuitionism, in one of its prevalent forms, has compared moral beliefs to the propositions of logic and mathematics as being unconditionally necessary and, in some crucial cases, self-evident. Plato's doctrine of *anamnesis* sought to explain necessary knowledge in this way and it was against this inference from necessary to innate knowledge that the first book of Locke's *Essay* was directed. The Platonic theory was revived by Herbert Spencer who held that the important discoveries of ancestors were inherited as self-evident certainties by descendants. The point to notice is that even if their innateness is an adequate *explanation* of our possession of beliefs in self-evident and necessary propositions it does not *follow logically* from their self-evidence and necessity. The Plato-Spencer theory, in holding some of our beliefs to be necessary because they are innate, implies that if a belief is not necessary it cannot be innate. This is not to say that if a belief is not innate it cannot be necessary. To show this it would have to be proved that a belief cannot be necessary unless it is innate.

The other main form of ethical intuitionism compares fundamental moral judgements to judgements of sense-perception, arguing that these moral judgements, like the deliverances of the senses, are objective and yet directly apprehended, by a special faculty of some sort, and not inferred. But evolutionary considerations do not rule out a moral sense theory which conceives the moral sense in rather close analogy to the physical senses. The objective and uninferred character of judgements of colour is not undermined by the fact that the eye has evolved or even by the fact that an element of socially enforced convention enters into our actual colour-discriminations.

There is a sense, however, in which evolution does tend to undermine intuitionist ethics. For by treating morality and moral agency as natural phenomena, by considering morality as a functioning social institution, and so firmly connecting it to our desires and satisfactions it repudiates the essentially other-worldly conception of morality which is characteristic of intuitionism. Intuitionist ethics is a kind of secularized version of the ethics of divine command in which the supernatural law-giver is internalized and placed, rather incongruously, alongside our natural inclinations. On this view man is understood to be moved by two radically different and entirely discontinuous sorts of motivation. The evolutionary way of thinking asserts the continuity between the traditionally separated sides of human nature, the ape and the angel, just as it asserts the continuity between man and the rest of the animal world.

2. *Evolutionary knowledge of means to moral ends.* It would be widely agreed that evolutionary biology, by contributing to our knowledge about the consequences of action, can have an important subsidiary place in the rational formation of moral convictions. This would not be accepted by those deontologists, like Kant and, even more conspicuously, Prichard, who contend that the rightness and wrongness of actions

is an intrinsic property of them and in no way dependent on the consequences that accrue to them. But this rather foolish opinion is more an intellectual curiosity than a serious challenge. Allowing, as even most professed deontologists do in practice, for example Ross, that the consequences of an action are relevant to its moral quality, we may admit that evolutionary knowledge, by giving us a new idea of the results to which conventionally approved lines of conduct will lead, may require the critical revision or development of these conventional approvals. The difficulty here . . . is to determine just what consequences evolutionary theory does or can predict.

Despite this sceptical reservation there are two reasons for thinking that evolutionary theory is particularly relevant to the ethical problems of our age. The first of these is the very much increased rate of change of the human environment due to the accelerating increase of population and of the technological complexity of our mode of life. In changing circumstances what may be called the derivative moral principles, those which ascribe rightness and wrongness to particular lines of conduct, tend to become rapidly out of date. For with the change of circumstances lines of conduct come to have quite different consequences from those in the light of which rightness or wrongness was originally ascribed to them. Secondly, the nature of the change reinforces the effect of change itself. In a densely populated and technologically complex society forms of action have many more humanly relevant consequences and so acts which were once harmless and neutral come to be maleficent in their effects. To take a very simple example: the first European inhabitants of Australia could afford to be careless about the conservation of natural resources, the disposal of refuse and even the making of noise in a way that the inhabitants of a modern industrial city can not.

This leads on to a further point. By a series of accidents the morality which ethical philosophers study has come to be understood in an absurdly contracted way at a time when it crucially needs to be enlarged. What Aristotle meant by ethics was a rational inquiry into the whole management of human life. A contemporary moral philosopher and partly in consequence, most people who think at all generally about problems of conduct, understands by ethics the study of immediate, inter-personal obligation. The currently conventional, narrow conception of ethics is limited in two ways. On the one side it leaves out in its obsessive Protestant concentration on the compulsory, the whole business of rational choice between different styles of life, the topic of the great tradition of *moralistes*. This is an impoverishment of ethical thinking, but not, perhaps, a very disastrous one. What is left out on the other side is more vital and indispensable, namely ideology, conceived not as a collection of more or less fanatically held dogmas but as a rational concern with the fundamental principles of social policy. Morality as conventionally understood deals with the rather short-run effects of individual action; what I have called ideology deals with the longer-run effects of collective action. As the world becomes more technologically complex it is the latter type of effects that have an increasing importance for the life of the individual. This is not due simply to the fact that social action is more effective and known to be so but also because large areas of what were once personal responsibility have been handed over to society at large from the family, for example education and the care of the old and ill. The great virtue of the evolutionary moralists is that they are adept in a style of practical thinking which is of a scope appropriate to the problems of our time and set an example which should be more widely followed. Critics often complain about the triviality of contemporary moral philosophy. Their protest is just enough in outline but misplaced in detail. It is not so much that we should turn from the rights and wrongs of returning borrowed books by post to those of suicide but rather that we should enlarge our perspective to take in the problems of society as a whole and not those of such an artificial, transitory and fundamentally unimportant group as that of the two parties to an obligation.

From Is to Ought

Anthony Flew

The panorama presented by evolutionary biology is, though often terrible, magnificent; and to have brought the development of all living things within the scope of a single theory constitutes one of the greatest achievements of the human mind. 'Thus,' in the concluding words of the *Origin*, 'from the war of nature, from famine and death, the most exalted object which we are capable of conceiving, namely, the production of the higher animals, directly follows. There is grandeur in this view of life, with its several powers originally breathed by its Creator into a few forms or into one; and that, whilst this planet has gone cycling on according to the fixed law of gravity, from so simple a beginning endless forms most beautiful and most wonderful have been, and are being evolved.'[1] There is indeed.

It is, therefore, as we insisted at the very beginning, neither surprising nor discreditable that people should want to adjust their ideas to this vision, and to seek possible wider applications for the concepts of evolutionary theory. In the previous section we considered one kind of suggestion about 'the philosophical implications of Darwinism.' In the present section we shall run through some major variations on the theme of the Naturalistic Fallacy. This has certainly been central in much which has been called evolutionary ethics; so much so that it has often, but wrongly, been thought to be the essential and polymorphous error which must both constitute and vitiate everything so labelled.

From Anthony Flew, "Evolutionary Ethics," in *New Studies in Ethics,* W. Hudson, ed. (London and Basingstoke: Macmillan & Co., Ltd.; New York: St. Martin's Press, Inc., 1967), pp. 31–51. Reprinted by permission of the publishers.

142

I. A SPECIAL CASE

The first move is to distinguish what is peculiar to one special case from what is common to all such attempted deductions. Their general character, as has been indicated already, is determined by the fact that all the premises are, or should be, purely descriptive; whereas the conclusions obtained are to be taken as prescriptive. The peculiarity of the special case is that here the premises are universal propositions the truth of which is dependent upon their being consistent with the facts that we do do whatever it may be that we do actually do. But it must be radically preposterous, not but what it has been and is common, to try to generate some mandate to do this rather than that from propositions which, to be truly what they pretend to be, must either be equally consistent with the choice of either alternative or be wholly inconsistent with our having any alternatives at all. It would be idle and absurd to seek prescriptions for our behaviour where we are not confronted with options for choice, and unless the prescriptions sought are to require some of these and to forbid others.

We have already noticed one instance of the special case. . . . We also . . . approached from a rather different direction the presently crucial point. D. G. Ritchie was there quoted as trying to rebut the policy of prudential restraint urged by Malthus, by urging that this must lead to 'the survival of the unfittest.' Yet this is a conclusion which must be, in Darwinian terms, contradictory. For survival, or—strictly—survival to reproduce, is not the reward but the criterion of biological fitness. But, of course, in so far as we maintain—and rightly—some standard of human excellence other than mere reproduction or multiplication, there may indeed be all too much reason for us to fear and deplore the present and likely future outcome of high reproductive rates among the backward, the improvident, and the fanatical.

Further examples of what we are distinguishing as the special case can be generated wherever we have what is supposed to be a law of nature including human action within its scope. For if it really is a law of nature, then it follows that nothing which has happened, is happening, or will happen can be inconsistent with it; any occurrence inconsistent with it constitutes a sufficient reason for disallowing its claim to express a law of nature. There is, therefore, a further special absurdity—over and above whatever general fallacy may be involved in any attempt to deduce normative conclusions from neutrally descriptive premises—in appealing to a premise of this sort as if, simultaneously, it could both express such a law of nature and constitute a reason for acting in one way rather than another.

The crux can be illustrated, light-heartedly but very aptly, by referring to a crisp exchange recorded in Mr. Raymond Chandler's *Farewell, My Lovely.* Philip Marlowe is conversing with Anne Riordan: "You take awful chances, Miss Riordan." "I think I said the same about you. I had a gun. I wasn't afraid. There's no law against going down there." "Uh-huh. Only the law of self-preservation." With his accustomed acuteness Marlowe, returning the gun, corrects himself: "Here. It's not my night to be clever."[2] Certainly, interpreted as other than a wisecrack, his remark would be foolish. For, precisely in so far as there were a psychological law of self-preservation under which all our actual actions could be subsumed, there could be no point in appealing to this law as a reason for acting not in one way but another; while if after all no such law holds, then it cannot provide any reasonable ground for anything. All those who in martyrdom witness to their conviction that survival can sometimes be too dearly bought do not thereby rebel against Nature's law of self-preservation. Rather they demonstrate that no such law obtains; or, at any rate, that if it does, the human animal does not fall within its scope.

Various misunderstandings of and ambiguities in the key terms and expressions have in the Darwinian context helped to conceal this absurdity; notwithstanding that . . . the great diversity and the frequent mutual inconsistency of the practical morals actually drawn ought surely to have made the supposed method of derivation suspect. Since the major misunderstandings and ambiguities have been noticed already in passing, we need here only to review them and to provide further illustrations.

First, and certainly not confined to our present biological context, is the failure to distinguish two kinds of law of nature—or, better, two senses of 'law of nature': the descriptive, in which such a law cannot have any genuine exceptions, since the occurrence of any event inconsistent with the truth of a proposed law constitutes a sufficient reason for failing the candidate; and the prescriptive, in which the occurrence of violations constitutes no reason at all for maintaining that the law originally propounded does not really obtain. The point of the passage just quoted from *Farewell, My Lovely* lies in its wisecracking exploitation of this ambiguity. But, as is shown by other examples which we have given and shall give, the fact that one can draw an illustration from such a source must be interpreted not as evidence of the universal obviousness of the crucial distinction but as one more indication of the quality of Chandler.

Second, the expression 'natural selection' seems to be used in two crucially different senses: both, more narrowly, in an incompatible contrast with '(artificial) selection' and, comprehensively, in such a way that the latter is just a special case of the former. It becomes absolutely essential to make this distinction the moment we wish to take account of the actual or possible impact of human choice upon the course of biological evolution. We have already tried . . . to show how the past, present, and potential impact of our own species upon and within this development rules out any possibility of discovering at the sub-human levels some comfortably reassuring substitute for Divine Providence. We can now appreciate, in the light of everything which has been said in this present subsection, why it is even more fundamentally misguided to hope to make a law of natural selection into the arbiter or the scapegoat on to which we can shuffle off the burdens of human decision and human responsibility. For in so far as the law applies to us at all it can only be because 'natural selection' is being construed in the comprehensive second sense in which there can be no antithesis between natural and artificial selection, because whatever we do in fact select is by that token shown to have been selected naturally.

With all the advantages of hindsight we may well regret that Darwin himself did not in the *Origin* explicitly make, and make much of, this distinction between a narrower and a wider sense of 'natural selection.' But it is much more regrettable, and far less excusable, that a writer on *Darwin and the Darwinian Revolution* now, a full century later, should still fail altogether to seize the points involved. Thus we read that: 'Francis Galton, Darwin's cousin and great champion, who made it his mission, as he thought, to give practical content to Darwin's theory, was by this very enterprise denying that theory. The science of eugenics, devoted to the improvement of the human stock, was designed "to further the ends of evolution more rapidly and with less distress than if events were left to their own course." ' Darwin's own sympathetic yet pessimistic reactions to one of Galton's eugenic proposals are then mentioned, and the occasion grasped to rebuke poor Darwin because 'It did not seem to have occurred to him that it vitiated his essential principle, making survival independent of the natural struggle for existence.'[3] On this scandalous bit of commentary we may comment in turn, equally superciliously but with justification, that it does not seem to have occurred to the authoress that a programme for the improvement—by reference, presumably, to some human standards of excellence and fitness—of our own human stock could be no more and no less inconsistent with Darwin's theory than are the activities of those throughout the centuries who have selected for desired varieties of plants and animals and against others—activities to which he himself gave the most careful attention in the first chapter of the *Origin*, and elsewhere.

Third, the two logically connected expressions 'natural selection' and 'survival of the fittest' are within the theory implicitly so defined that whatever is in fact 'selected' and survives must necessarily be the fittest, regardless of all other merits or demerits, and notwithstanding that both expressions contain terms which are often or always elsewhere employed for commendation. Granted this Darwinian criterion of fitness it becomes a necessary truth that whatever survives to reproduce is fit, and must have been naturally selected; although this, it is just worth reiterating, does not imply, what is not true, that to say that natural selection occurs is to utter a tautology.[4] When a failure to take account of the difference between the Darwinian and other more ordinary criteria of fitness for selection is combined with a blindness to the equivocation between two senses of 'law,' it becomes easy, first to misplace the idea of necessity, and then to misconstrue it. A logical necessity is thus unwittingly transmogrified into, and hence appears to reinforce, a moral necessity: compare the way in which . . . the logical necessity of an implication may be alchemically transmuted into the practical inevitability of an event. To say within the terms of Darwinian theory that in natural selection the fittest must survive is to utter only a tautology. But this can be mistaken to be an urgent practical imperative, categorically demanding that we make every sacrifice to ensure that they in fact do.

Thus—to go straight to the bottom—consider the savage 'Social Darwinism' which Adolf Hitler assimilated in the Vienna of his youth: 'If we did not respect the law of nature, imposing our will by the right of the stronger, a day would come when the wild animals would again devour us—then the insects would eat the wild animals, and finally nothing would exist on earth except the microbes'; or again, 'By means of the struggle the élites are continually renewed. The law of selection justifies this incessant struggle by allowing the survival of the fittest. Christianity is a rebellion against natural law, a protest against nature. Taken to its logical extreme Christianity would mean the systematic cult of human failure.'[5]

These passages from an outrageous source very effectively underline the present point: actual survival to reproduce is itself within Darwin's theory the sole and sufficient criterion of fitness thus to survive; and the mere capacity to survive and to reproduce is the only and often humanly very questionable merit for which natural selection necessarily selects. An 'élite' selected simply on this basis could be, literally as well as metaphorically, the scum which rises to the top. But the same passages also illustrate the crucial confusions between the two senses of 'law' and the two senses of 'natural selection.' The anti-Christian moral which Hitler draws may be salutarily compared with Rockefeller's Sunday-school claim, quoted already in our Introduction: 'The growth of a large business is merely a survival of the fittest. . . . This is not an evil tendency in business. It is merely the working out of a law of nature and a law of God.'

We end this subsection with two further illustrations: one to show that the same misconceptions have been accepted by more disinterested protagonists, the other to reveal that a first-rate philosopher is not necessarily immune. First, from the founder and first General of the Salvation Army: 'In the struggle of life the weakest will go to the wall and there are so many weak. The fittest, in tooth and claw, will survive. All we can do is to soften the lot of the unfit and make their sufferings less horrible than at present.'[6] Although we have provided already all the instruments required for the dissection, it is perhaps just worth adding that many of those who, by Booth's human and humane criteria, scored as the weakest who went to the wall would, by the biological criterion of mere survival to multiply, not have counted as weak at all. For in Booth's day as today high fertility was often both a cause and a consequence of poverty.

Second, from C. S. Peirce: '*The Origin of Species* of Darwin merely extends politico-economical views of progress to the entire realm of animal and vegetable life. . . . As Darwin puts it on his title page, it is the struggle for existence; and he should have added for his motto: "Every individual for himself, and the Devil take the hindmost!" Jesus, in his Sermon on the Mount, expressed a different opinion.' Peirce goes on to tell us that 'The Gospel of Christ says that progress comes from every individual merging his individuality in sympathy with his neighbours,' and Peirce contrasts this with what 'may accurately be called the Gospel of Greed.' It was not one of Peirce's good days, for only a page or two later, in the same article, on 'Evolutionary Love,' he says: 'Another thing: anaesthetics had been [in 1859] in use for thirteen years. Already, people's acquaintance with suffering had dropped off very much; and, as a consequence, that unlovely hardness, by which our times are so contrasted with those that immediately preceded them, had already set in and inclined people to relish a ruthless theory.'[7]

II. THE NATURALISTIC FALLACY AS SUCH

In (I) above, although most of our distinctions and arguments had some wider application, we were primarily concerned with one special case of the attempt to deduce normative conclusions from the purely descriptive premises provided by evolutionary theory. We now proceed to consider the Naturalistic Fallacy in general, although always of course with special reference to its application in our context. The label 'Naturalistic Fallacy' derives from G. E. Moore's *Principia Ethica* (1903). It is an apt label, since one very typical way of committing this fallacy is by offering some supposedly neutral descriptive statement about what is allegedly natural as if it could by itself entail some conclusion about what is in some way commendable. Yet Moore's own account is so wrapped up in various unfortunate assumptions that—all other reasons apart—it is wise to begin from the now much-quoted passage from Hume, noting by the way that *Principia Ethica* neither quotes nor mentions this earlier classical authority.

Hume presents his remarks as an important afterthought to the first Section of Book iii of his *Treatise of Human Nature* (1740), under the section title 'Moral Distinctions not Derived from Reason': 'In every system of morality which I have hitherto met with I have always remarked that the author proceeds for some time in the ordinary way of reasoning, and establishes the being of a God, or make observations concerning human affairs; when of a sudden I am surprised to find, that instead of the usual copulations of propositions, *is* and *is not,* I meet with no proposition that is not connected with an *ought* or *ought not.* This change is imperceptible; but is, however, of the last consequence. For as this *ought* or *ought not* expresses some new relation or affirmation, it is necessary that it should be observed and explained; and at the same time a reason should be given, for what seems altogether inconceivable, how this new relation can be a deduction from others, which are entirely different from it.'

This observation is so important—and one is tempted to add, mischievously, so clear and so clearly sound—that there is now no lack of well-girded champions eager to contest both its accepted interpretation and its truth. We can here eschew most of the details of Hume scholarship, doing so the less reluctantly for having ourselves participated vigorously in the recent discussion in the journals.[8] Yet it is relevant to our present purposes to warn the unwary not to be misled by Hume's irony. It would be completely wrong to take him absolutely literally, as if he were modestly claiming only to have noticed, and to have become seized of the vast importance of, a distinction which, however unwittingly, everyone was always and systematically making already. If that really had been Hume's contention it would, of course, have been quite obviously false, and could have been disposed of even more briskly than some of his most impatient critics have thought to be rid of it.[9]

However, Hume was not that—or any—sort of a fool. His immediate thesis was not that a distinction always is made, and that it is invariably marked by those different copulations of propositions, *ought* and *is;* but rather that it always ought to be made, because it is 'of the last consequence.' And why it is of the last consequence is, in Hume's view, that it is an expression and an implication of what he thought to be the great fundamental truth—and one of his own prime insights in philosophy—that values are not any sort of property of things in themselves, but that they are in some way a projection out on to the things around us of human needs and human desires. (One resulting problem, more obvious perhaps to us than to Hume, is that of explaining how values can be in some such fundamental way dependent on, and some sort of function of, human needs and human desires, without its thereby becoming the case that some purely descriptive statements about what people do want or would want must entail consequences about what ought to be. It is more than enough here for us simply to notice this problem, and to remark that it is at least not obvious that Hume completely forgot his point of the last consequence when he came to give his positive accounts of morals and aesthetics.)

Once Hume's ostensibly afterthought observation is understood, the first question is whether such a distinction, with a logical Grand Canyon between its terms, really can be made and maintained. It must be entirely beside the point to preen oneself—as some have done—upon having rustled up a herd of words which combine elements of both sorts in their meanings, or of expressions which can be ambiguous as between one and the other. For what has to be shown is not that this basic distinction is not in fact always made, but that in principle it cannot be.

Another recent approach calls attention to a 'class of unquestionably descriptive practical statements, namely what I shall call *appetitive utterances,* which indicate the objects or states of affairs that the person addressed will most enjoy or like or will get most satisfaction from. "You will most like or enjoy the Red Lion" is as good, sufficient and direct an answer to the question "Which hotel shall I stay at?" as "Stay at the Red Lion" or "The Red Lion is the best hotel." It is like them and different from "The Red Lion is the smartest or largest or quietest hotel" in that no contingent presumption needs to be made about the special tastes or requirements of the questioner in order to predict the action that will follow on his sincere acceptance of the advice, or at any rate to be assured of its relevance to his enquiry."[10]

Yet neither that you would most enjoy the Red Lion, nor that it is the best hotel, constitutes an indefeasibly good reason for your staying there. You may, for instance, not be able or willing to afford the best, just as you may have some special reason, moral or other, which forbids indulgence on this (or any other) occasion. What is special about these appetitive utterances is, not that they make no contingent presumption about the requirements of the person addressed, but that the presumption involved is in fact almost always correct. But even if it were correct, not just usually but absolutely invariably, the conclusion to be derived from any appetitive premise would still be purely factual: if it is enjoyment you are after—as in fact, like everybody else, you are—then this is what in this particular case will serve your turn. So the subsistence of appetitive truths seems to have in itself no tendency to show that an *ought* can, after all, be deduced from an *is*.

A third and very plausible approach . . . urges that at least part of what distinguishes moral ideals and moral values from ideals and values of other sorts is that morality is always supposed to be directed towards the welfare of those concerned. Now if this is indeed so, and assuming that no one's welfare could be consistent with the wholesale frustration of all his desires, it might seem that one should be able to deduce some moral conclusions from some collections of flawlessly factual premises about what is or would be desired. Certainly from premises about what people want we can hope to deduce conclusions about what would satisfy or frustrate them; while equally certainly we can, if we like, characterise the promotion of their satisfaction as moral. Such a characterisation can probably be justified both by an appeal to (much of) the common usage of the term 'moral' and its associates, and also by reference to the point and purpose of moral discourse. Yet no such attempt, however successful, to construe 'moral' in terms of what is or would be desired by any individual or group could even begin to show that we can validly deduce, from the proposition that something is in this way and by these persons desired, the totally different conclusion that it is indeed desirable (in the sense of being what ought to be desired). For the crucial difference will still warrant the crucial distinction: between, on the one hand, simply stating quite neutrally that these are the things which would satisfy such and such desires; and, on the other hand, going on to prescribe that these particular desires are desires which ought to be satisfied.

However, the present occasion no more demands an exhaustive defence of Hume's thesis in its accepted interpretation than it calls for an attempt to show that that interpretation embodies the correct reading of Hume; and here again we can disclaim the task with a better conscience for having already taken a part in discussion in the journals. The main reason for making those remarks which we have made is further to clarify what the Naturalistic Fallacy is supposed to be, before proceeding to examine some particular moves—moves which can be seen to be fallacious without the support of any fully worked-out and impregnably defended general characterisation; and yet moves the unsoundness of which will need somehow to be taken into account by those philosophers who propose to deny that the Naturalistic Fallacy is a fallacy. The need to allow for this should give pause; as, in another way, should the recognition that though the label was a philosopher's coinage the idea itself is not peculiar to our notoriously fallible and perverse profession. Einstein, for instance, took it as obvious that 'As long as we remain within the realm of science proper, we can never meet with a sentence of the type "Thou shalt not" . . . Scientific statements of facts and relations . . . cannot produce ethical directives.'[11]

When we come to particular cases the most notable thing is precisely the lack of precision as to what the connection between the biological facts and the ethical directives is supposed to be. For instance, Julian Huxley tells us that 'in the broadest possible terms evolutionary ethics must be based on a combination of a few main principles: that it is right to realise ever new possibilities in evolution, notably those which are valued for their own sake; that it is right both to respect human individuality and to encourage its fullest development; that it is right to construct a mechanism for further social evolution which shall satisfy these prior conditions as fully, efficiently, and rapidly as possible.'[12]

It would be hard to dispute either that this is a statement 'in the broadest possible terms,' or—as he goes on to say—that 'to translate these arid-sounding generalities into concrete terms and satisfying forms is beyond the scope of a lecture.' Again, after our earlier stress on the enormous difference between saying that something is desired and saying that it is desirable, we are bound to notice the tendency to equate the valuable with what is in fact valued: 'that it is right to realise ever new possibilities in evolution, notably those which are valued for their own sake.' But it is not necessarily an objection, although it is no doubt true, to say that the directives indicated seem in no way distinctively evolutionary. Certainly they might have been—indeed they often were and are—accepted without benefit of Darwin. Yet the claim to be propounding an evolutionary ethics might still have been abundantly vindicated if only Huxley had spelt out, as he never did, the steps of the logical deduction which, as 'the evolutionary moralist,' he maintained was possible: 'He [the evolutionary moralist] can tell us that the facts of nature, as demonstrated in evolution, give us the assurance that knowledge, love, beauty, selfless morality, and firm purpose are ethically good.'[13] Well, no doubt he can tell us. But that, in default of any less elliptical exposition, is no sufficient reason for agreeing that what he tells us is true.

Again, if we turn to Spencer we find a similar indeterminacy about precisely what supposed evolutionary facts are to be connected with the desired ethical directives, and how; an indeterminacy which, in his case, cannot plausibly be excused by reference to any restriction of space. It is significant that in the Preface to the second heavy volume of *The Principles of Ethics* he is ready to concede that, in the last two parts, 'the Doctrine of Evolution . . . helps us in general ways though not in special ways.' But, even in a part to which this is supposed not to apply, a section which begins with the bold promise that 'Acceptance of the doctrine of organic evolution determines certain ethical conceptions' ends with only the unshattering and uncommunicative conclusion that it is 'an inevitable inference from the doctrine of organic evolution, that the highest type of living being, no less than all lower types, must go on moulding itself to those requirements which circumstances impose.'[14] One may perhaps recall here the statement which once introduced the lead story in an international news magazine notorious for the breathless urgency of its house style: 'Last week, as in every week in human history, in the best of times and in the worst of times, the leaders of the world's nations played out their separate parts.'

The proper objection to this is that it suffers not so much from a surfeit of generality as from a deficiency of substance. But there are other claims against which the same charge could not be laid. Consider three: first, 'that the conduct to which we apply the name *good,* is the relatively more evolved conduct; and *the bad* is the name which we apply to conduct which is relatively less evolved'; second, that 'no school can avoid taking for the ultimate moral aim a desirable state of feeling . . . gratification, enjoyment, happiness. Pleasure somewhere, at some time, to some being or beings, is an inexpugnable element of the conception'; and third, that 'the process of evolution must inevitably favour all changes of nature which increase life and augment happiness: especially such as do this at small cost.'[15] . . .

Darwin's theory provides no basis for concluding that there is any such law of progress as Spencer seems to be proclaiming in the third of these passages. Nor will it do to say, what the first passage seems to be suggesting, that moral behaviour is somehow more sophisticated biologically, or more a product of evolution, than immoral. For even if we allow 'the origin of the moral sentiments, in the same way as other natural phenomena, by a process of evolution,' still 'as the immoral sentiments have no less been evolved, there is, so far, as much natural sanction for the one as for the other.'[16] The temptation, compounded by the strong suggestion of ordinary usage that any evolution must be from the inferior to the superior, is to mistake it that evolution in the Darwinian context must be ever towards more and better. Then, conjoining this misconception with the second less exceptionable claim, we bring forth the comfortable conclusion that the process of biological evolution must be a progress towards the supreme good of the classical Utilitarians, the greatest happiness of the greatest number.

In this argument, which can at best be a reconstruction of only one strand of Spencer's thinking, the conclusion is mediated by an ambiguity in 'evolution': between, on the one hand, the neutral scientific sense, and, on the other hand, a sense in which any evolution necessarily tends in a direction which must be rated as good. Even supposing, what we earlier urged is not and cannot be the case, that there really were some immanent guarantee that as a matter of contingent fact evolution in the former sense does produce these good results, still it must be quite wrong to try to equate the evolved with the good or the good with the evolved. The crucial point was made forcefully by Russell over fifty years ago, in words which read piquantly today: 'If evolutionary ethics were sound, we ought to be entirely indifferent as to what the course of evolution may be, since whatever it is is thereby proved to be the best. Yet if it should turn out that the Negro or the Chinaman was able to oust the European, we should cease to have any admiration for evolution; for as a matter of fact our preference of the European to the Negro is wholly independent of the European's great prowess with the Maxim gun.'[17] And, it is fair to add, the same could with the appropriate alterations be said of Russell's own present preference for the Chinese and the Vietcong.

Russell's argument is decisive against any attempt to define the ideas of right and wrong, good and evil, in terms of a neutrally scientific notion of evolution. It can, as we shall see, be equally effective against the rather different suggestion that Darwin's theory can supply us with a, or even with the, satisfactory moral criterion. But before moving on to that we must break a lance with the shrewd and scholarly author of *The Moral Theory of Evolutionary Naturalism*. For, notwithstanding that he himself notices and cites earlier and better formulations by Hume and others, what seems to be the main thesis of his book constitutes an instructive example of an ideologically important misconception encouraged by one of the peculiarities of Moore's treatment. This thesis is that 'in so far as the evolutionary moralists' treatment of ethical questions is naturalistic, it is not normative; and that in so far as normative considerations are introduced it is not naturalistic.' He refers, approvingly, to Guyau: 'Most Evolutionary Naturalists, he declares, have made the great mistake of giving a naturalistic account and "also pretending to have rendered it . . . imperative in its precepts." ' [18] Quillian's conclusion is that by introducing the normative the evolutionary naturalists have tacitly acknowledged the inadequacy of a naturalistic world-view.[19]

To understand both why this should be thought and why it is mistaken it is necessary to go back first to Moore and then to Hume. Moore, as we have said, introduced the label 'Naturalistic Fallacy,' but, as we also mentioned, he characterised the mistake in a most unfortunate manner (a way, incidentally, which would make it a mistake in introspective psychology and not in logic—and hence not, strictly speaking, a fallacy at all). It was for him the error of believing 'that when we think "This is good," what we are thinking is that the thing in question bears a definite relation to some one other thing.' But then immediately, and without perhaps fully appreciating the possibilities of confusion opened up by thus using the word 'naturalistic' both in a peculiar and also in a less peculiar sense, he goes on to distinguish two sorts of view: on the one hand, 'Naturalistic Ethics'; and, on the other, 'Metaphysical Ethics.' In Moore both equally are taken to involve the Naturalistic Fallacy. The former is distinguished by the fact that here the value words are implicitly or explicitly defined in terms of something natural. This too is duly explained: 'By "nature" . . . I mean . . . that which is the subject-matter of the natural sciences and also of psychology.'[20]

So far it might seem that Quillian had simply misread his Moore, however excusably. But Moore straightway proceeds to introduce a distinction between natural and non-natural properties, and asks: 'Which among the properties of natural objects are natural properties and which are not?' He insists that goodness—for Moore *good* is always the key term in ethics—is just such a non-natural characteristic: 'For I do not deny that good is a property of certain natural objects: certain of them, I think, *are* good.'[21] Now if this were all right, then there would be certain things in the universe possessing properties which must necessarily be beyond the range of 'the natural sciences and of psychology.' And if to introduce the normative is, as this suggests, tacitly to recognise the subsistence of such non-natural properties, then indeed the evolutionary naturalists—and everyone else too who does the same—is thereby implicitly acknowledging the inadequacy of a naturalistic worldview.

This shows how Quillian, by following Moore, could be led to think what he did. To appreciate why this thought is mistaken it is helpful to go back further still, to Hume. As everyone must know, it was Hume's ambition 'to introduce the experimental method of reasoning into moral subjects,'[22] and thereby to effect a sort of Copernican revolution in reverse. For Hume the paradigm for this exercise was the achievement of the new optics, construed as showing that colours are not truly qualities of the things which we uninstructedly describe as coloured. Rather they are somehow projections from our own 'sensoria.'[23] It was in these terms that Hume would have us see 'that morality is nothing in the abstract nature of things, but is entirely relative to the sentiment or mental taste of each particular being, in the same manner as the distinctions of sweet and bitter, hot and cold arise from the particular feeling of each sense or organ.'[24]

But now if, as Hume suggests, putting a value on something or commending some course of action neither is nor presupposes the ascription of any supposed non-natural characteristics to anything, then there is no longer any reason for thinking that anyone who—as we all must—values, commends, recommends, prescribes, and so on, must thereby be—however unwittingly—acknowledging the existence of some reality of which a naturalistic world-outlook cannot take account. For except in so far as some Moorean account is correct, none of these proceedings seems to present any insuperable obstacle to tough-mindedly naturalistic description. Certainly many spokesmen of a naturalistic world-outlook, including most of Quillian's Evolutionary Naturalists, have also been, like many of their opponents, committers of the Naturalistic Fallacy. But there is no necessary connection between naturalism, in the sense in which the word refers to a sort of world-view, and naturalism, in the rather artificial sense in which a naturalist would be one who tried to deduce *oughts* from *ises*. Hume, for instance, and in this he was not inconsistent, was as surely a naturalist in the first sense as he was committed to rejecting naturalism in the second.

III. NOT THE MEANING BUT THE CRITERION?

In the previous subsection we considered the possibility of deducing ethical conclusions directly from premises supplied by evolutionary biology. For any such move to be sound the prescription in the conclusion must be somehow incapsulated in the premises; for, by definition, a valid deduction is one in which you could not assert the premises and deny the conclusion without thereby contradicting yourself. A more modest suggestion, not always properly distinguished as such, is that, although the present meanings of our moral words cannot be explicated either wholly or partly in evolutionary terms, still evolution somehow supplies a necessary criterion. This seems to be the view of, for instance, Needham. For he welcomes the 'expulsion of ethics from biology and embryology' and notes: 'That *good* and *bad, noble* and *ignoble, beautiful* and *ugly, honourable* and *dishonourable,* are not terms with a biological meaning is a proposition which it has taken many centuries for biologists to realize.' Nevertheless, elsewhere he urges: 'The evolutionary process itself supplies us with a criterion of the good.'[25]

Now, assuming that our reading is correct, this move involves no crude attempt to deduce a moral *ought* from an evolutionary *is*. But Needham is still exposed to Russell's objection: 'If evolutionary ethics were sound, we ought to be entirely indifferent as to what the course of evolution may be, since whatever it is it is thereby proved to be the best.' The decisiveness of this objection was no doubt concealed from Needham by two things: first, the by now familiar ambiguity in the word 'evolution'; and second, his own conviction that, as a matter of contingent fact, biological evolution has a direction which he was prepared to rate as progressive. The shift from the neutral to a commendatory sense of 'evolution' is well illustrated in the paragraph from which our second quotation is taken: in that particular sentence the sense must be the former. But two or three sentences further on it is equally clearly the latter: 'The kind of behaviour which has furthered man's social evolution in the past can be seen very well by viewing human history; and the great ethical teachers, from Confucius onwards, have shown us . . . how men may live together in harmony, employing their several talents to the general good.'[26]

It might perhaps be suggested that Russell's point really would lose its force if once it were to be conceded that, as a matter of contingent fact, evolution is tending to move, and is perhaps actually moving, in a commendable direction. If only, it might be urged, this were to be conceded, then there could be no objection to adopting some evolutionary criterion of the good; and we might proceed to argue that 'when we have found our Ten Commandments in general evolution' we can go on to 'discover our *Deuteronomy* in political analysis.'[27]

The one grain of truth in the main suggestion is that anyone equipped with such a mixed factual-cum-evaluative premise would be in a position to make valid inferences from purely factual evolutionary premises to evaluative conclusions. But, precisely because of the mixed character of this second premise, this must be without prejudice to anything so far said about inferences from purely factual premises to evaluative conclusions. What is not true in this suggestion is the heart of the matter, the idea that Russell's objection can be escaped by appealing to such a mixed premise. It cannot. For consider how the exchanges must go. The protagonist says that his criterion of the right is found in the actual direction of evolution. The deuteragonist replies that in that case the protagonist is committed to approving the direction of evolution quite regardless of what it may turn out to be. The latter then triumphantly appeals to his happy discovery that, as a matter of fact, the direction of evolution is as it ought to be. But now, on the protagonist's own chosen terms, this discovery must be wholly lacking in factual content. For, in so far as his criterion of the right lies in the actual direction of evolution, it becomes necessarily true that the actual direction is as it ought to be. The contingent fact to which the protagonist appealed thus disappears; but not before the very making of any such appeal has tacitly conceded Russell's point.

Waddington's striking employment of Biblical terms may usefully provoke the reflection that all the moves and counter-moves which we have been discussing here can be paralleled in discussion as to whether moral ideas can be defined in terms of the will of God, or whether—failing that—God's will could serve as an acceptable criterion of the right and the good. It might indeed even be urged that a main justification for going through all these moves and counter-moves at length here is as a training for recognising and dealing with mistakes of the same form made in other contexts.

Be that as it may, there certainly are some remarkable formal analogies between evolutionary ethics as expounded by Waddington and the arguments of those moral theologians who have tried to derive their often peculiarly clerical norms from the supposed intentions of nature: for instance, the argument—rather less frequently heard in the last year or two—that all 'artificial' contraception must be wrong because it involves a frustration of the natural function of sex, and so on.

Such comparisons will no doubt be disconcerting to both parties, but they surely ought to be more embarrassing to the secular. For if you are, however mistakenly, committed to the belief that the whole universe is an expression of the intentions of an omnipotent and righteous author, then this belief provides you with a positive reason both for accounting nature good and for speaking of intentions in this connection. But, for anyone who disowns such beliefs, to look to nature as his moral arbiter must be as incongruous and gratuitous as it is for the same person to hope to find some natural law of progress to do substitute duty for Providence. T. H. Huxley in his famous Romanes Lecture on 'Evolution and Ethics' may well have gone too far, particularly in replacing a positive connection by a negative rather than by no connection at all. But for an atheist or an agnostic his sort of approach is, surely, more appropriate: 'Let us understand, once for all, that the ethical progress of society depends, not on imitating the cosmic process, still less in running away from it, but in combating it.'[28]

Waddington has made several essays towards an evolutionary ethics. Indeed he was largely responsible for a revival of interest in the possibilities in Britain during the early 1940s: first by provoking a discussion in *Nature;* and then by editing a consequent book on *Science and Ethics.* We have noticed, and shall notice, his contributions to that book only incidentally: partly because Professor D. D. Raphael has already dealt very faithfully with them as part of his philosopher's contribution to a commemorative volume of *A Century of Darwin;* but mainly because Waddington has since made it clear that he would prefer to be judged by his later work on *The Ethical Animal.* In his contributions to *Science and Ethics* he seemed to be wanting to read norms off immediately from biological descriptions: 'It is a complicated matter to describe what is normal, as opposed to abnormal growth, but it can be done; and, once it is done there is a generally valid criterion of goodness in food. . . .'[29] But in the latter he advocates a rather more sophisticated operation: 'If we investigate by normal scientific methods the way in which the existence of ethical beliefs is involved in the causal nexus of the world's happenings, we shall be forced to conclude that the function of ethicising is to mediate the progress of human evolution. . . . We shall also find that this progress, in the world as a whole, exhibits a direction. . . . Putting these two points together we can define a criterion which does not depend for its validity on any pre-existing ethical belief,' and he is most insistent that what is distinctive about his view is that this criterion is 'a criterion for deciding between alternative systems of belief.'[30]

It is hard to determine whether one ought to be more surprised or more distressed that Waddington should think that, by thus making his evolutionary criterion not directly a criterion of the right but rather a criterion for judging which is the best among rival systems of belief about what is right, he escapes objections of the kind we have been deploying. But, once the key passages have been picked out for attention, it is surely obvious that it does not. For what is a criterion for deciding which is best among rival systems of belief about what is right if it is not a means of deciding which set of beliefs is, on balance, the most correct (which exercise obviously necessitates some prior criterion of what is right)? If in reply it is suggested that Waddington's criterion is intended only as a criterion of the efficiency or otherwise of different systems of ethicising [sic] in their supposed biological function, 'to mediate the progress of human evolution,' then the further question arises, whether the putative direction of human evolution is being taken to be commendable as such, or only in so far as the actual direction satisfies some other standards. If the former, then—in a catch-phrase of the old pre-television era—this is where we came in. If the latter, then, as far as our present sort of evolutionary ethics is concerned, that's that.

NOTES

1. Darwin, p. 429.
2. Chandler, p. 46.
3. Himmelfarb, p. 351.

4. See Manser; and cf. Flew (2).
5. Trevor-Roper, pp. 39, 51; and cf., perhaps more accessibly, Bullock, pp. 36, 89, 398–9, 672, 693.
6. Booth, p. 44; T. H. Huxley, perhaps a trifle unfairly, drew attention to this passage in a letter to *The Times* on 29 December 1890.
7. Peirce, vol. vi, pp. 293, 298.
8. See MacIntyre, Atkinson, Hunter, and Flew and Hunter; the whole controversy is now conveniently collected in Chappell, pp. 240–307.
9. See Searle; and cf. Flew (1).
10. Quinton, pp. 110–11; punctuation made to conform.
11. Einstein, p. 114.
12. J. S. Huxley, p. 124.
13. Ibid., pp. 125, 214.
14. Spender, vol. ii, pp. vi, 25, 260.
15. Ibid., vol. i, pp. 25 (italics supplied), 46; vol. ii, p. 432.
16. T. H. Huxley, p. 80.
17. Russell, p. 24.
18. Quillian, pp. 78, 95.
19. See especially ibid., p. 137; and cf. p. 109.
20. Moore, pp. 38, 39–40.
21. Ibid., p. 41; italics in original.
22. Hume (1), title page.
23. Newton, especially pp. 124–5; the same, idea is, of course, found earlier—in Galileo, for instance, and among the Greek atomists.
24. Hume (2), p. 23 n.
25. Needham, pp. 151 (italics supplied), 56.
26. Ibid., p. 56.
27. Waddington (1), p. 125. Entirely by the way: if we are going to bring in pre-Columbian Mexico—or anything else—let us get it right. The author on the previous page conjures up "an Aztec of Chicken [*sic*] Itza,' whereas in fact Chichen Itza was founded by the Maya, was later taken over by the Toltecs, but was never Aztec.
28. T. H. Huxley, p. 82.
29. Waddington (1), p. 41.
30. Waddington (2), pp. 59, 173.

REFERENCES

Atkinson, R. F. (1961). " 'Hume on *Is* and *Ought*': A Reply to Mr. MacIntyre." *Philosophical Review* 70.
Booth, W. (1890). *In Darkest England, and the Way Out* (London: Salvation Army).
Bullock, A. (1962). *Hitler: A Study in Tyranny* (Harmondsworth: Penguin Books).
Chandler, R. (1949). *Farewell, My Lovely* (Harmondsworth: Penguin Books).

Chappell, V. C., ed. (1966). *Hume: A Collection of Critical Essays* (New York: Doubleday-Anchor).

Darwin, C. (1872). *The Origin of Species,* 6th ed. (London: J. Murray).

Einstein, A. (1950). *Out of My Later Years* (London: Thames & Hudson).

Flew, A. G. N. (1) (1964–5). "On Not Deriving *Ought* from *Is.*" *Analysis* 25.

———. (2) (1966). " 'The Concept of Evolution': A Comment." *Philosophy* 41, no. 155.

———, and Hunter, G. (1963). " 'The Interpretion of Hume' and a Rejoinder to the Same." *Philosophy* 38.

Himmelfarb, G. (1959). *Darwin and the Darwinian Revolution* (London: Chatto & Windus).

Hofstadter, R. (1944). *Social Darwinism in American Thought (1860–1915)* (Philadelphia: University Of Pennsylvania Press).

Hume, D. (1) (1896). *A Treatise of Human Nature,* ed. L. A. Selby-Bigge (London: Oxford University Press).

———. (2) (1955). *An Inquiry Concerning Human Understanding,* ed. C. W. Hendel (New York: Liberal Arts Press). The passage quoted is a note to section 1, found only in the first and second editions published in Hume's lifetime.

Hunter, G. (1962). "Hume on *Is* and *Ought.*" *Philosophy* 37, no. 140.

Huxley, J. S. (1947). Contributions to J. S. and T. H. Huxley, *Evolution and Ethics* (London: Pilot Press).

Huxley, T. H. (1947). "Evolution and Ethics." In J. S. and T. H. Huxley, *Evolution and Ethics* (London: Pilot Press).

MacIntyre, A. C. (1959). "Hume on *Is* and *Ought.*" *Philosophical Review* 68.

Manser, A. R. (1965). "The Concept of Evolution." *Philosophy* 40, no. 151.

Moore, G. E. (1903). *Principia Ethica* (Cambridge: Cambridge University Press).

Needham, J. (1943). *Time: The Refreshing River* (London: Allen & Unwin).

Newton, I. (1952). *Opticks,* pbk. ed. (New York: Dover).

Peirce, C. S. (1931–5). *Collected Papers,* ed. C. Hartshorne and P. Weiss (Cambridge, Mass.: Harvard University Press).

Quillian, W. F. (1945). *The Moral Theory of Evolutionary Naturalism* (New Haven: Yale University Press).

Quinton, A. M. (1966). "Ethics and the Theory of Evolution." In *Biology and Personality,* ed. I. T. Ramsey (Oxford: Blackwell).

Russell, B. A. W. (1966). *Philosophical Essays,* rev. ed. (London: Allen & Unwin).

Searle, J. R. (1964). "How to Derive *Ought* from *Is.*" *Philosophical Review* 73.

Spender, J., and Lehmann, J., eds. (1939). *Poems for Spain* (London: Hogarth Press).

Trevor-Roper, H. R., ed. ((1953). *Hitler's Table Talk* (London: Weidenfeld & Nicolson).

Waddington, C. H., ed. (1) (1942). *Science and Ethics* (London: Allen & Unwin).

———. (2) (1960). *The Ethical Animal* (London: Allen & Unwin).

The "Human" Nature of Human Nature

Leon Eisenberg

Understanding the nature of man and his works has become a precondition for the survival of our species, as well as for the enhancement of the flowering of human individuality. The search for that understanding is the central purpose of the university and the source of its relevance to society. After a period of public worship that verged on idolatry, universities have become the target of sustained and bitter attack. Yesterday's idolatry may have been a worship of false gods: credentials to an affluent life, technological virtuosity with little concern for its ends, and a meritocracy that excluded ethnic and linguistic minorities. But today's exorcism is aimed at false devils: the freedom to explore unpopular ideas, the transmission of our cultural heritage, and the support of fundamental research. The young excoriate universities for their corruption by the Establishment, the Establishment for their receptivity to the new, and governments for their failure to guarantee docile citizens.

The criticism, if indiscriminate and shrill, is not without substance; it must be heeded if the universities are to excise the accretions of age. Like others, those connected with the university find it easiest to do what they have done before. Yet, if there is a single leitmotiv of our time, it is a constantly accelerating rate of change. With each decade, scientific findings translated into technology radically reshape the way we live. Technical capacity has been the ruling imperative, with no reckoning of cost, either ecological or personal. If it could be done, it

From *Science* 176 (April 14, 1972): pp. 123–128. Copyright © 1972 by the American Association for the Advancement of Science. Reprinted by permission of the publisher and the author.

has been done. Foresight has lagged far behind craftsmanship. At long last we are beginning to ask, not *can* it be done, but *should* it be done? The challenge is to our ability to anticipate the second- and third-order consequences of interventions in the ecosystem before the event, not merely to rue them afterward. The power of our technology so foreshortens the time between its application and the possibility of its correction that we must learn to think through before we act out.[1]

If we were to understand each other even half as well as we comprehend the energy of the stars, we might yet spare ourselves the horrors we face from traducing those energies into weapons that endanger all life. If psychiatry cannot yet provide a firm basis for that understanding, it may nonetheless be of service if it dispels the myths and the pseudo-knowledge that obscure the search for truth.

SELF-FULFILLING PROPHECIES

The title of this article implies its conclusion: that there is to human nature a nature that is other than naked ape, actuated by territorial imperatives and impelled by aggressive instincts. Such a conclusion must seem outrageously optimistic in an era in which Americans "waste" Vietnamese, in which West Pakistani massacre their countrymen to the East—but there is no need to retell the litany of violence. How, in the teeth of this "evidence," can we disbelieve Morris, Ardrey, or Lorenz?[2] How can we challenge Freud, his illusions of civilization shattered by the barbarities of World War I when he wrote:[3] "The very emphasis of the Commandment: Thou shalt not kill, makes it certain that we are descended from an endlessly long chain of generations of murderers whose love of murder was in their blood as it is perhaps also in our own . . ."? Or again:[4] "The tendency to aggression is an innate, independent, instinctual disposition in man . . ."? How, indeed?

This is no mere academic exercise, of concern only to students of behavior. The planets will move as they always have, whether we adopt a geocentric or a heliocentric view of the heavens. It is only the equations we generate to account for those motions that will be more or less complex; the motions of the planets are sublimely indifferent to our earthbound astronomy. But the behavior of men is not independent of the theories of human behavior that men adopt. One example may serve to explicate this thesis.

So long as the "nature" of insanity was thought to be violent, and so long as the insane were chained, beaten, and locked in cells, madmen raged and fumed. With the introduction of the "moral treatment" of the insane at the beginning of the 19th century, violence in mental asylums markedly abated.[5] A century later, the "nature" of insanity was perceived as social incompetence; the sick were "protected" from stress, and the institution assumed responsibility for all decision-making. Misguided benevolence stripped the patient of adult status and generated automaton-like compliance; the result was the chronicity of the back wards of our state hospitals. A generation ago, the concept of the therapeutic environment, with its rediscovery of self-government and personal responsibility as the bases for attaining competence, began to reverse the cycle of self-perpetuating hospitalization. This led to a decline in what had been a steadily rising population in U.S. mental hospitals, a decline that began before the era of psychotropic drugs.[6] Do not mistake me. Psychosis is no mere social convention; it has a psychobiological existence independent of systems of belief. But its manifestations and its course are profoundly influenced by the social field in which the patient and his caretakers operate. Belief systems act no less profoundly on the remainder of mankind. The doctor's very presence relieves pain. Teachers' expectations govern pupils' performance. The citizens' confidence in the benevolence of the social order maintains its stability.

What we believe of man affects the behavior of men, for it determines what each expects of the other. Theories of education, of political science, of economics, and the very policies of governments are based on implicit concepts of the nature of man. Is he educable? Is he actuated only by self-interest? Is he a creature of such dark lusts that only submission to sovereign authority can save him from himself?

What we choose to believe about the nature of man has social consequences. Those consequences should be weighed in assessing the belief we choose to hold, even provisionally, given the lack of compelling proof for any of the currently fashionable theories. In insisting on an assessment of potential outputs in addition to a critique of inputs, I do *not* suggest that we ignore scientific evidence when it does not suit our fond wishes. Any hope of building a better world must begin with a tough-minded appraisal of the facts that are to be had. The thrust of my argument is that there is no solid foundation to the theoretical extrapolation of the instinctivists, the ethologists, the behaviorists, *or* the psychoanalysts, despite the special pleading that often is so seductive to those eager for a "real science" of behavior. Further to the point, belief helps shape actuality because of the self-fulfilling character of social prophecy. To believe that man's aggressiveness or territoriality is in the nature of the beast is to mistake some men for all men, contemporary society for all possible societies, and, by a remarkable transformation, to justify what is as what needs must be; social repression becomes a response to, rather than a cause of, human violence. Pessimism about man serves to maintain the status quo. It is a luxury for the affluent, a sop to the guilt of the politically inactive, a comfort to those who continue to enjoy the amenities of privilege. Pessimism is too costly for the disenfranchised; they give way to it at the price of their salvation. No less clearly, the false "optimism" of the unsubstantiated claims made for behavioral engineering, claims that ignore biological variation and individual creativity, foreclose man's humanity.

What is known about the power of the social-psychological determinants of human behavior compels the conclusion that the set of axioms for a theory of human nature must include a Kantian categorical imperative: men and women must believe that mankind can become fully human in order for our species to attain its humanity. Restated, a soberly optimistic view of man's potential (based on recognition of mankind's attainments, but tempered by knowledge of its frailties) is a precondition for social action to make actual that which is possible.

INNATE SCHEMATA AND RACIAL PURITY

Some readers may object to "politicizing" what should be a "scientific" discussion. My contention is that it is necessary to make overt what is latent in treatises on the "innate" nature of man. Consider, for example, Lorenz. Surely, those who have been charmed by his film of himself leading, like a mother goose, a brood of greylag geese about the farmyard will recoil from identifying his works as political. What is political about inborn schemata, innate releasing mechanisms, species-specific mating patterns, and the like? A great deal, as his own writings make clear, when such concepts, of dubious applicability to animal behavior itself,[7] are transposed directly to man without attending to species differences and to phyletic levels. Lorenz found it possible to write, in 1940, that the effects of civilization on human beings parallel those of domestication in animals.[8] In domesticated animals, he argued, degenerative mutations result in the loss of species-specific releaser mechanisms responding to innate schemata that govern mating patterns and that serve in nature to maintain the purity of the stock. Similar phenomena are said to be an inevitable by-product of civilization unless the state is vigilant (8, pp. 56–75).

The only resistance which mankind of healthy stock can offer . . . against being penetrated by symptoms of degeneracy is based on the existence of certain innate schemata. . . . Our species-specific sensitivity to the beauty and ugliness of members of our species is intimately connected with the symptoms of degeneration, caused by domestication, which threaten our race. . . . Usually, a man of high value is disgusted with special intensity by slight symptoms of degeneracy in men of the other race. . . . In certain instances, however, we find not only a lack of this selectivity . . . but even a reversal to being attracted by symptoms of degeneracy. . . . Decadent art provides many examples of such a change of signs. . . . The immensely high reproduction rate in the moral imbecile has long been established. . . . This phenomenon leads everywhere . . . to the fact that socially inferior human material is enabled . . . to penetrate and finally to annihilate the healthy nation. The selection for toughness, heroism, social utility . . . must be accomplished by some human institution if mankind, in default of selective factors, is not to be ruined by domestication-induced degeneracy. *The racial idea as the basis of our state has already accomplished much in this respect.* The most effective race-preserving measure is . . . the greatest support of the natural defenses. . . . We must—and should—rely on the healthy feelings of our Best and charge them with the selection which will determine the prosperity or the decay of our people . . . [italics added].

Thus, it would appear, science warrants society's erecting social prohibitions in order to replace the degenerated innate schemata for racial purity. Lorenz's "scientific" logic justified Nazi legal restrictions against intermarriage with non-Aryans. The wild extrapolations from domestication to civilization, from ritualized animal courtship patterns to human behavior, from species to races, are so gross and unscientific, the conclusions so redolent of concentration camps, that further commentary should be superfluous. Perhaps it is impolite to recall in 1972 what was written in 1940, but I, at least, find 1940 difficult to forget; indeed, I believe it should not be forgotten, lest we find ourselves in Orwell's *1984* for the very best of "scientific" reasons.

My position should not be misconstrued as condemning the study of comparative psychology or the search for biological determinants of human behavior as though such efforts were inherently fascist. What I do inveigh against is the formulation of pseudoscientific support for a priori social ideologies that are projected onto, not "found" in, nature. Such pseudoscience ignores species differences and phyletic levels and misrepresents analogy as homology. For example, attack behavior can be observed in organisms as varied as insect, bird, carnivore, ape, and man. In the first, it may be triggered by trace chemicals; in the second, by territorial defense, but only during the breeding season; in the third, by prey, but only if the appropriate internal state of arousal is present; in the fourth, by the appearance of a predator, if escape routes are unavailable and if the troop is threatened; and in man, by a mere verbal slur, if the social context and prior individual experience indicate attack as the socially appropriate response. The mere observation in divergent species of similar behavioral outcomes that fit the generic label "attack" justifies no conclusion about an underlying aggressive instinct, without detailed study of the conditions evoking, and the mechanisms governing, the behavior of each. Such "explanations" reify a descriptive label that has been indiscriminately applied to markedly different levels of behavioral organization, as though naming were the same as explaining.

TELEOLOGY OR ONTOGENESIS

Indeed, reports on animal behavior[9] fail to support the concept of an aggressive instinct as an independent motivational force analogous to hunger. That is, there is no predictable periodicity, no measurable change in internal parameters (such as glucose concentrations in the blood), and no evidence of a "need" to attack in the absence of provocative stimuli. This is not to deny that the ease with which, and the circumstances under which, attack is elicited differs among species, nor that hormones, notably androgens, may have a profound impact on the probability of a fight rather than a flight response in higher organisms.[10] The characteristics of the species, the genetic endowment of the individual organism, its prior experience, and the immediate stimuli interact to produce the behavioral outcome. Similar outcomes may result from quite different underlying mechanisms; meaningful comparisons become possible only when the mechanisms have been identified.

Examples could be multiplied. At the most general level, the problem stems from a telic orientation: behavior is "explained" by its outcome, rather than by an analysis of its ontogenesis. The cause is assumed to exist preformed in the organism as an "instinct" or innate pattern of behavior. The Platonic ideal is immanent in the organism. But where is it, when does it appear, and how does it come into being? Not even the most ardent instinctivist would any longer argue that the "instinct" for aggression or courtship rituals or nest building is *in* the fertilized egg. Yet it is confidently asserted that it must have been precoded and ready to go because it appears without any apparent requirement for prior learning.

Let us agree: behavior, like structure, is under genetic control. Animals of two species, reared in an identical environment, will nonetheless behave differently. The argument for innateness—in the sense of an inherited component—is compelling when the distribution of a given characteristic in an offspring generation can be predicted from knowledge of its distribution in the parent generation and the pattern of mating in that generation. However, the genetic evidence does not warrant the other sense in which innate is used—that is, developmental fixity, an imperviousness to environmental influences. Environment influences development by mechanisms that need have nothing to do with learning. For example, certain mutations in wing and eye structure of drosophila are temperature sensitive; if the eggs are maintained at 18°C, the wing or eye develops normally, despite the presence of the mutant gene. This is hardly "learning," but it is evidence that expressivity depends on the environment. It does not make the characteristic any less genetic that its phenotypic expression is modified by temperature. But, by having discovered an array of such factors, the investigator has made a start at identifying the biochemical mechanisms underlying the action of genes. The central issue in the study of development is the problem of the interactions among the programmed but modifiable unfolding of the genome, its cellular envelope, and the surround. If the nucleus of a frog's intestinal cell transplanted into an enucleated frog's egg gives rise to a normal animal,[11] then for all of the phenotypic differences between cell types, they share, as we knew they must, the same genetic apparatus, but an apparatus whose expressivity is under cytoplasmic as well as nuclear control.

Even in closely related species, differences are more revealing than similarities in elucidating the principles that govern behavior. Consider the study of bird vocalization, which, beyond its intrinsic fascination, may yet provide important clues to the understanding of sound imitation in man.[12] It is a graphic example of a behavioral characteristic that displays remarkable ontogenetic differences in closely related species. Song sparrows, isolated from conspecifics and foster-reared by canaries, nonetheless acquire their own song. Yet meadowlarks, similarly isolated as fledglings, acquire the song of the particular foster species: wood pewees, yellowthroats, or red-winged blackbirds.[13] Still different is the white-crowned sparrow, which must hear the adult model of its song during a "sensitive period" of development in order to acquire it; nonetheless, if the fledgling white-crowned sparrow is simultaneously exposed to conspecifics and to two sympatric species, it "learns" only its own song. Once learned, the song persists, even if the adult is isolated. In the case of the goldfinch, the adult bird is able to learn new flight songs from other species.[14] These few examples merely hint at the complexity of a growing field of inquiry. Precise attention to differences among species, the interrelationship of those differences with the ecology of the species, and the ultimate identification of the underlying neuro-mechanisms are what we will require for models that may have heuristic value in studying imitation behavior in man.

LANGUAGE: A UNIVERSAL HUMAN TRAIT

Man's biological equipment is now, if ever, an essential topic of study. That equipment evolved over the 5 million years which elapsed between the australopithecine homonids and *Homo sapiens;* it provided the means for survival in an environment not yet altered by artifacts. The spread of our species and the rapid multiplication of our numbers in the past five millennia attest to the adaptability of that biological equipment to circumstances that did not exist when it was elaborated. It is becoming painfully evident that the changes we have wrought in the past five decades threaten our continuing survival under conditions of an exponential rate of population growth. It now becomes necessary to ask: How adaptable is man? Is mere perpetuation of the species, without concern for the quality of life, a sufficient criterion for man, even if it has been so for nature? Man's intelligence permits him the conscious choice of goals and so differentiates him from the rest of animate existence.

How, then, to discern the nature of man? Two general approaches suggest themselves—the comparative and the developmental. In the first, we compare and contrast the characteristics of men and women in the diverse societies that people this planet in the hope of extracting common denominators that express man's "essential nature"; in the second, we study the interaction between the infant and his social and biological environment as he grows to adulthood.

One trait common to man everywhere is language; in the sense that only the human species displays it, the capacity to acquire language must be genetic. As Chomsky has pointed out,[15] among the unique aspects of human language learning are the child's ability to infer syntactical rules from a limited set of input samples and, in consequence, his extraordinary capacity to generate grammatical sentences that he has never heard. The language he speaks is determined by the language he hears, but the capacity for language must be a consequence of the genetic programming of brain networks as these respond to maturation and experience. Languages, insofar as they have been studied, appear to share fundamental structural characteristics, a universality that argues for an as-yet-to-be-identified basis in common structures in the central nervous system. Recall the example of the white-crowned sparrow, which, though it must learn its song, is structured in such a way that its neural networks resonate only to a restricted set of external harmonic sequences. The data of linguistics suggest the possibility of a similar restriction on the form of language and the nature of grammatical structures; they imply limited variability in the neural schemata underlying language structures. Further refinement in our knowledge of these cognitive universals may yet enable us to propose models of neural mechanisms, which must then be sought experimentally.

Benzer[16] has brought the tools of genetic analysis to bear on behavioral mutants in drosophila. By the ingenious use of mosaics with phenotypic characteristics that permit the morphological identification of individual cells that carry or lack the mutant gene for phototaxis, he has found the source of the behavioral deviation to be structural abnormalities in the affected eye. In flies in which mosaicism is present within a single eye, histological techniques and single cell recordings can specify the deficit even more precisely. Cellular markers "provide powerful techniques for tracing the details of cell lineage during development, as well as genetic dissection of the functioning nervous system."[17]

Even the limited complexity of the drosophila's central nervous system defies analysis by current techniques, but an important beginning has been made in relating genetically determined behavioral differences to underlying physiological mechanisms.

THE DIVERSITY OF HUMAN CULTURE

If language be one of the common features of human culture, even more remarkable are the diverse behaviors that cultures shape and are shaped by. What is labeled "masculine" in one culture and ascribed to the nature of maleness is regarded as "feminine" in another. Children are permitted uninhibited sexual expression and yet become monogamous adults in one culture; in another, preadult sexuality is heavily censored, whereas adult monogamy is privately violated while it is publicly proclaimed. Child care may be the responsibility of the nuclear family or of the group. The same Netsilik Eskimos who are loving and devoted parents can allow a female infant who is not "spoken for" in a prearranged marriage to die unattended and ignored if she is not given a name and is thus, by definition, not yet human. The phenomenon of war is unknown to one society, appears in a second only under environmental stress, but is a lethal "game" without apparent material benefit in a third. Indeed, if we were to permit ourselves the argument that the more "primitive" the society, the more true to man's original nature the behavior displayed therein, we should have to conclude, as did Sahlins,[18] that "war increases in intensity, bloodiness and duration . . . through the evolution of culture, reaching its culmination in modern civilization." However agreeable, the argument for the pacific character of natural man, uncorrupted by the social order, is inadmissible; culture is as complete and complex in contemporary hunting and gathering tribes, despite their primitive technology, as it is in our own— man is man only in society.

What is striking in this very partial inventory is the remarkable diversity of the human behaviors evoked by various but viable cultures. If we explain the murderous raids of Brazilian Indians on the basis of an innate aggressive instinct, we shall have to invent an involved theory of repression, reaction formation, and sublimation to account for the peacefulness of the Eskimo. Would it not be far more parsimonious to begin with the assumption that men are by nature neither aggressive nor peaceful, but rather are fashioned into one or another as the result of a complex interaction between a widely, but not infinitely, modifiable set of biological givens and the shaping influences of the biological environment, the cultural envelope, and individual experience?

The very ubiquity of violence in Western society, however we explain its genesis historically, guarantees that children are surfeited with opportunities to learn violent behavior. The child sees that violence pays off; he is provided with adult models of violent behavior with whom to identify (television pales beside real life). Violence as an appropriate response to the resolution of intergroup conflict is sanctioned by national leaders. Reflect: the President of the United States intervened to prevent the immediate imprisonment of Calley, an officer convicted of mass murder in Vietnam by a jury of combat veterans. Consider: the Attorney General of the United States declined to press charges in the Kent State student murders. What are the ethical values these actions by national leaders convey? When violence is sanctioned, it will increase. It can be expected to generalize to situations not "intended" to come within official pardon. Learning may not account completely for human aggression, but the social forces in contemporary society that encourage its development are so evident[19] that preoccupation with hypothesized biological factors is almost quixotic.

Emphasis on the very marked differences among cultures may obscure what has been, until recently, a conservative tradition within each. Children reared within a particular value system could expect to complete their days within that system. Values now change so rapidly that what a child is taught by his parents may no longer be functional when that child becomes an adolescent, let alone an adult. However wide the range of behaviors man can exhibit—evidenced by the comparison of one society with another—the task of developing adaptive attributes is very different when radically changed behaviors are required within an *individual's* lifetime rather than over the history of a people. The question now becomes, not how malleable is man, but how much change can a man undergo and still maintain his psychic integration?

Here we lack empirical data; there is no precedent for such rapid change. We confront the fundamental relevance of studies of child development. In a stable society, the price demanded by acculturation may or may not have been burdensome, but clearly it was bearable, or else that society would not have perpetuated itself. Studies of child development were important even then, if only to learn how to mitigate those burdens. But if we are to enable our children to cope with a world whose present shape we barely comprehend and whose future configurations we can only guess at dimly, then we are embarked on an enterprise that is the very keystone of the sciences of survival.

MAN AS HIS OWN CHIEF PRODUCT

I will forego detailing what we already know and ignore at the peril of the next generation: that the rapidly growing brain of fetus and infant is excruciatingly dependent on the adequacy of its nutrition;[20] surely, no further amassing of scientific facts is needed to justify international commitment to the protection of the unborn and the newly born. What has become equally evident is that the nutriment the growing brain requires is affective and cognitive as well as alimentary. The extraordinary dependence of the human young upon adult care and caring provides both an unparalleled opportunity for mental and emotional development and a period of vulnerability to profound distortion by neglect.[21] Infants in orphanages lag markedly in development, despite normal food intake, if denied a responsive human environment. There are indeed gaps in our knowledge of this early developmental sequence: just how much stimulation is optimal, just what balance is to be struck between gratification and denial, just what is the best mix between social interaction and time to be alone? Yet the outlines are clear enough to allow no excuse for what we permit to befall defenseless children, who suffer from the contumely we visit on their parents. Each infant differs from the others: no two, except for identical twins, share a common genome, and even identical twins may differ phenotypically because of gestational inequalities. We do not understand individual variability sufficiently well to fashion optimal environments for each child, but surely this does not mitigate our failure to provide at least those general requirements shared by all children.[22]

Ignorance, as well as lack of commitment, becomes a limiting factor when children reach the years of formal education. The shortcomings of available theories of learning constrain our ability to respond to individual differences in the way children fashion their personalities and cognitive styles.[23] There may be much to be gained from comparative studies of animal learning—to be sure, we are primates ourselves, but primates of a very special sort. We are no less subject to classical and operant conditioning, to trial and error learning, and the like, but only we have the capacity for superordinate modes of verbal learning, and these require much deeper study than has been devoted to them. Our challenge is no longer transmitting solutions that have been successful in the past, but helping our children to acquire attitudes and sets for problem-solving that will enable them to meet undreamed-of challenges to their capacities.

We have done least well at the task of encouraging the development of humane values based upon the recognition that we are a single species. The idea of brotherhood is not new, but what is special to our times is that brotherhood has become the precondition for survival. It may have sufficed in the past to spur a child to learn for the sheer satisfaction of his own success. If we have listened to what our students are telling us, learning for personal embellishment or for the acquisition of virtuosity no longer satisfies a generation intensely aware of injustice and impermanence. Learning must become a social enterprise, informed by concern for others.[24]

This it can become. Man is his own chief product. The infant who discovers that he can control the movements of his own fingers transforms himself from observer into actor. The child who masters reading unlocks the treasury of the world's heritage. The adolescent who insists upon a critical reexamination of conventional wisdom is making himself into an adult. And the adult whose concerns extend beyond family and beyond nation to mankind has become fully human.

By acting on behalf of our species we become men and women. In a world in which wars rage, in which repressive governments subjugate their peoples, in which the pursuit of personal affluence ravages an environment that must be shared by all, there can be no neutrality. Members of the university community carry a heavy measure of responsibility for the privilege accorded them; that responsibility is to pledge themselves to the service of man if knowledge is to be transformed into wisdom.

The study of man takes its meaning from involvement in the struggle for human betterment. Struggle it is and will be: privilege does not surrender easily; false belief is not readily dispelled. The optimism about man's potential I urge upon you is not the self-comfort of reading history as a saga of progressive liberation which will one day be complete. It matters, and matters dearly, to Vietnamese and to Pakistani, to Americans and to Canadians, whether that day comes sooner or later; whether it comes at all is not determined by history but by the men and the women who make history. This has been eloquently stated by the Cuban poet Padilla, who has recently been released from prison in his own country. The final lines of his poem "Important Occasions" read:[25]

> History's going to save us—we were
>   thinking.
> Going to save us—were we dreaming?
> It wasn't all just uprisings, barricades,
>   bonfires:
> in our heads it was a dress of bubbling
>   foam, a
> Rhine maiden with clear eyes, smiling,
>   standing
> at the door, hand outstretched
> toward a hungry and waiting people.
>   But there was no one in the door-
>   way. Nor in the house.
>   Instead we stumbled. They shoved
>   us inside. We broke our teeth
>   going in, got our jaw smashed.
> We found tools and weapons and we
> fought, we struggled, we worked and
>   continued
> fighting. But it's true, old Marx,
> that History is not enough.
>   Important occasions,
>   man makes them.
>   It's a real, live man who does it,
> who masters it, who will fight.
> History by itself does
>   nothing, dear friends.
>   It does absolutely nothing.

NOTES

1. N. Wiener, *Science* 131, 1355 (1960).
2. D. Morris, *The Naked Ape* (McGraw-Hill: New York, 1967); R. Ardrey, *African Genesis* (Dell: New York, 1961); *The Territorial Imperative* (Dell: New York, 1966); K. Lorenz, *On Aggression* (Harcourt, Brace & World, New York, 1966).
3. S. Freud, *Reflections on War and Death* (Moffat, Yard, New York, 1918), p. 60.
4. S. Freud, *Civilization and Its Discontents* (Hogarth, London, 1930), p. 102.

5. P. Pinel, *A Treatise on Insanity,* D. D. Davis, transl. (Hafner, New York, 1962); G. Rosen, *Madness in Society* (Univ. of Chicago Press, Chicago, 1968); A. Deutsch, *The Mentally Ill in America* (Columbia Univ. Press, New York, ed. 2, 1949).

6. E. M. Gruenberg, *Amer. J. Orthopsychiat.* 37, 645 (1967).

7. D. S. Lehrman, in *Development and Evolution of Behavior,* L. R. Aronson, E. Tobach, D. S. Lehrman, J. S. Rosenblatt, eds. (Freeman, San Francisco, 1970); E. Tobach, L. R. Aronson, E. Shaw, eds. *The Biopsychology of Development* (Academic Press, New York, 1971); L. R. Aronson, E. Tobach, D. S. Lehrman, J. S. Rosenblatt, eds., *Selected Writings of T. C. Schneirla* (Freeman, San Francisco, 1972).

8. K. Lorenz, *Z. Angew. Psychol. Charakterkunde* 59, 2 (1940).

9. J. P. Scott, *Aggression* (Univ. of Chicago Press, Chicago, 1958).

10. _____, *Amer. J. Orthopsychiat.* 40, 568 (1970).

11. J. B. Gurdon, *Sci. Amer.* 219, 24 (Sept. 1968); _____ and H. R. Woodland, *Biol. Rev.* 43, 233 (1968).

12. R. A. Hinde, ed., *Bird Vocalizations* (Cambridge Univ. Press, London, 1969).

13. M. Konishi and F. Nottebohm, in *Bird Vocalizations,* R. A. Hinde, ed. (Cambridge Univ. Press, London, 1969), pp. 29–48.

14. P. C. Mundinger, *Science* 168, 480 (1970).

15. N. Chomsky, *Language* 35, 26 (1959); *Language and Mind* (Harcourt, Brace & World, New York, 1968); J. Lyons, *Noam Chomsky* (Viking, New York, 1970).

16. S. Benzer, *Proc. Nat. Acad. Sci. U.S.* 58, 1112 (1967); *J. Amer. Med. Ass.* 218, 1015 (1971); R. J. Konopka and S. Benzer, *Proc. Nat. Acad. Sci. U.S.* 68, 2112 (1971).

17. Y. Hotta and S. Benzer, *Proc. Nat. Acad. Sci. U.S.* 67, 1156 (1970).

18. M. D. Sahlins, *Sci. Amer.* 203, 76 (Sept. 1960).

19. J. L. Singer, ed., *The Control of Aggression and Violence* (Academic Press, New York, 1971).

20. M. Winick, *Pediatrics* 47, 969 (1971); H. G. Birch and J. D. Gussow, *Disadvantaged Children: Health, Nutrition and School Failure* (Harcourt Brace Jovanovich, New York, 1970); H. G. Birch, C. Pineiro, E. Alcade, T. Toga, J. Cravioto, *Pediat. Res.* 5, 579 (1971).

21. L. Eisenberg, in *The Social Responsibility of Gynecology and Obstetrics,* A. C. Barnes, ed. (Johns Hopkins Press, Baltimore, 1965), pp. 53–79.

22. B. M. Caldwell, *Amer. J. Orthopsychiat.* 37, 8 (1967); L. Eisenberg, *ibid.* 39, 389 (1969).

23. S. H. White and H. D. Fishbein, in *Behavioral Science in Pediatric Medicine,* M. Talbot, J. Kagan, L. Eisenberg, eds. (Saunders, Philadelphia, 1971), pp. 188–227.

24. L. Eisenberg, *Science* 167, 1688 (1970); K. Kenniston, *Amer. J. Orthopsychiat.* 40, 577 (1970); S. E. Luria and Z. Luria, *Daedalus* 99, 75 (1970).

25. H. Padilla, "Important Occasions," P. Blackburn, transl., *New York Review of Books* (3 June 1971), p. 5.

PART IV

The Biology
of Sociobiology

Intergroup Selection in the Evolution of Social Systems

V. C. Wynne-Edwards

In a recent book I advanced a general proposition which may be summarized in the following way: (1) Animals, especially in the higher phyla, are variously adapted to control their own population densities. (2) The mechanisms involved work homeostatically, adjusting the population density in relation to fluctuating levels of resources; where the limiting resource is food, as it most frequently is, the homeostatic system prevents the population from increasing to densities that would cause overexploitation and the depletion of future yields. (3) The mechanisms depend in part on the substitution of conventional prizes—namely, the possession of territories, homes, living space and similar real property, or of social status as the proximate objects of competition among the members of the group concerned, in place of the actual food itself. (4) Any group of individuals engaged together in such conventional competition automatically constitutes a society, all social behavior having sprung originally from this source.

In developing the theme it soon became apparent that the greatest benefits of sociality arise from its capacity to override the advantage of the individual members in the interests of the survival of the group as a whole. The kind of adaptations which make this possible, as explained more fully here, belong to and characterize social groups as entities, rather than their members individually. This in turn seems to entail that natural selection has occurred between social groups as evolutionary units in their own right, favoring the more efficient variants

---

From *Nature* 200 (1963), pp. 623–626. Reprinted by permission of Macmillan Journals Limited.

among social systems wherever they have appeared, and furthering their progressive development and adaptation.

The general concept of intergroup selection is not new. It has been widely accepted in the field of evolutionary genetics, largely as a result of the classical analysis of Sewall Wright. He has expressed the view that "selection between the genetic systems of local populations of a species . . . has been perhaps the greatest creative factor of all in making possible selection of genetic systems as wholes in place of mere selection according to the net effects of alleles." Intergroup selection has been invoked also to explain the special case of colonial evolution in the social insects.

In the context of the social group a difficulty appears, with selection acting simultaneously at the two levels of the group and the individual. It is that the homeostatic control of population density frequently demands sacrifices of the individual; and while population control is essential to the long-term survival of the group, the sacrifices impair fertility and survivorship in the individual. One may legitimately ask how two kinds of selection can act simultaneously when on fundamental issues they are working at cross purposes. At first sight there seems to be no easy way of reconciling this clash of interests; and to some people consequently the whole idea of intergroup selection is unacceptable.

Before attempting to resolve the problem it is necessary to fill in some of the background and give it clearer definition. The survival of a local group or population naturally depends among other things on the continuing annual yield of its food resources. Typically, where the tissues of animals or plants are consumed as food, persistent excessive pressure of exploitation can rather quickly overtax the resource and reduce its productivity, with the result that yields are diminished in subsequent years. This effect can be seen in the overfishing of commercial fisheries which is occurring now in different parts of the world, and in the overgrazing of pastoral land, which in dry climates can eventually turn good grassland into desert. Damage to the crop precedes the onset and spread of starvation in the exploiting population, and may be further aggravated by it. The general net effect of overpopulation is thus to diminish the carrying-capacity of the habitat.

In natural environments undisturbed by man this kind of degradation is rare and exceptional: the normal evolutionary trend is in the other direction, toward building up and sustaining the productivity of the habitat at the highest attainable level. Predatory animals do not in these conditions chronically depress their stocks of prey, nor do herbivores impair the regeneration of their food-plants. Many animals, especially among the larger vertebrates (including man), have themselves virtually no predators or parasites automatically capable of disposing of a population surplus if it arises.

It is the absence or undependability of external destructive agencies that makes it valuable, if not in some cases mandatory, that animals should be adapted to regulate their own numbers. By so doing, the population density can be balanced around the optimum level, at which the highest sustainable use is made of food resources.

Only an extraordinary circumstance could have concealed this elementary conclusion and prevented our taking it immediately for granted. Some eight or more thousand years ago, as neolithic man began to achieve new and greatly enhanced levels of production from the land through the agricultural revolution, the homeostatic conventions of his hunting ancestors, developed there as in other primates to keep population density in balance with carrying capacity, were slowly and imperceptibly allowed to decay. We can tell this from the centrally important place always occupied by fertility-limiting and functionally similar conventions in the numerous stone-age cultures which persisted into modern times. Since these conventions disappeared nothing has been acquired in their place: growing skills in resource development have, except momentarily, always outstripped the demands of a progressively increasing population; there has consequently been no effective natural selection against a freely expanding economy. So far as the regulation of numbers is concerned, the human race provides a spectacular exception to the general rule.

A secondary factor, tending to obscure the almost universal powers possessed by animals for controlling their numbers, is our everyday familiarity with insect and other pests which appear to undergo uncontrolled and sometimes violent fluctuations in abundance. In fact, human land-use practices seldom leave natural processes alone for any length of time: vegetation is gathered, the ground is tilled, treated, or irrigated, single-species crops are planted and rotated, predators and competitors are destroyed, and the animals' regulating mechanisms are thereby, understandably, often defeated. In the comparably drastic environmental fluctuations of the polar and desert regions, similar population fluctuations occur without human intervention.

The methods by which natural animal populations curb their own increase and promote the efficient exploitation of food resources include the control of recruitment and, when necessary, the expulsion and elimination of unwanted surpluses. The individual member has to be governed by the homeostatic system even when, as commonly happens, this means his exclusion from food in the midst of apparent plenty, or detention from reproduction when others are breeding. The recruitment rate must be determined by the contemporary relation between population density and resources; under average conditions, therefore, only part of the potential fecundity of the group needs to be realized in a given year or generation.

This is a conclusion amply supported by the results of experiments on fecundity versus density in laboratory populations, in a wide variety of animals including Crustacea, insects, fish, and mammals; and also by field data from natural populations. But it conflicts with the assumption, still rather widely made, that under natural selection there can be no alternative to promoting the fecundity of the individual, provided this results in his leaving a larger contribution of surviving progeny to posterity. This assumption is the chief obstacle to accepting the principle of intergroup selection.

One of the most important premises of intergroup selection is that animal populations are typically self-perpetuating, tending to be strongly localized and persistent on the same ground. This is illustrated by the widespread use of traditional breeding sites by birds, fishes, and animals of many other kinds; and by the subsequent return of the great majority of experimentally marked young to breed in their native neighborhood. It is true of nonmigratory species, for example the more primitive communities of man; and all the long-distance two-way migrants that have so far been experimentally tagged, whether they are birds, bats, seals, or salmon, have developed parallel and equally remarkable navigating powers that enable them to return precisely to the same point, and consequently preserve the integrity of their particular local stock. Isolation is normally not quite complete, however. Provision is made for an element of pioneering, and infiltration into other areas; but the gene-flow that results is not commonly fast enough to prevent the population from accumulating heritable characteristics of its own. Partly genetic and partly traditional, these differentiate it from other similar groups. Local groups are the smallest racial units capable of continuous existence for long enough to undergo evolutionary differentiation. In the course of generations some die out; others survive, and have the opportunity to spread into new or vacated ground as it becomes available, themselves subdividing as they grow. In so far as the successful ones take over the habitat left vacant by the unsuccessful, the groups are in a relation of passive competition. Their survival or extinction is partly a matter of chance, arising from various forms of *force majeure*, including secular changes in the environment; for the rest it is determined, in general terms, by heritable qualities of fitness.

Gene-frequencies within the group may alter as time passes, through gene-flow, drift (the Sewall Wright effect), and selection at the individual level. Through the latter, adaptations to local conditions may accumulate. Population fitness, however, depends on something over and above the heritable basis that determines the success as individuals of a continuing stream of independent members. It becomes particularly clear in relation to population homeostasis that social groups have highly important adaptive characteristics in their own right.

When the balance of a self-regulating population is disturbed, for example by heavy accidental mortality, or by a change in food-resource yields, a restorative reaction is set in motion. If the density has dropped below the optimum, the recruitment rate may be increased in a variety of ways, most simply by drawing on the reserve of potential fecundity referred to earlier, and so raising the reproductive output. Immigrants appearing from surrounding areas can be allowed to remain as recruits also. If the density has risen too high, aggression between individuals may build up to the point of expelling the surplus as emigrants; the reproductive rate may drop; and mortality due to social stress (and in some species cannibalism) may rise. These are typical examples of density-dependent homeostatic responses.

Seven years of investigation of the population ecology of the red grouse *(Lagopus scoticus)* near Aberdeen, by the Nature Conservancy Unit of Grouse and Moorland Ecology, have revealed many of these processes at work. Their operation in this case depends to a great extent on the fact that individual members of a grouse population living together on a moor, even of the same sex, are not equal in social status.

Some of the cock birds are sufficiently dominant to establish themselves as territory owners, parceling out the ground among them and holding sway over it, with a varying intensity of possessiveness, almost the whole year round. During February–June their mates enjoy the same established status.

In the early dawn of August and September mornings, after a short and almost complete recess, the shape of a new territorial pattern begins to be hammered out. In most years this quickly identifies a large surplus of males, old and young, which are not successful in securing any part of the ground, and consequently assume a socially inferior status. They are grouped with the hens at this stage as unestablished birds; and day by day their security is so disturbed by the dawn aggressive stress that almost at once some begin to get forced out, never to return. By about 8 A.M. each day the passion subsides in all but the most refractory territorial cocks, after which the moor reverts to communal ground on which the whole population can feed freely for the rest of the day. As autumn wears on and turns to winter, the daily period of aggression becomes fiercer and lasts longer; birds with no property rights have to feed at least part of the time on territorial ground defended by owners that may at any moment chase them off. More and more are driven out altogether; and since they can rarely find a safe nook to occupy elsewhere in the neighborhood, they become outcasts, and are easily picked up by hawks and foxes, or succumb to malnutrition. Females are included among those expelled; but about February the remaining ones begin to establish marital attachments; and at the same time, quite suddenly, territories are vigorously defended all day. Of the unestablished birds still present in late winter, some achieve promotion by filling the gaps caused by casualties in the establishment. Some may persist occasionally until spring; but unless a cock holds a territory exceeding a minimum threshold capacity, or a hen becomes accepted by a territorially qualified mate, breeding is inhibited.

Territories are not all of uniform size, and on average the largest are held by the most dominating cocks. More important still, the average territory size changes from year to year, thus varying the basic population density, apparently in direct response to changes in productivity of the staple food-plant, heather *(Calluna vulgaris)*. As yet this productivity has been estimated only by subjective methods; but significant mutual correlations have been established between annual average values for body-weight of adults, adult survival, clutch-size, hatching success, survival of young, and, finally, breeding density the following year. As would be expected with changing densities, the size of the autumn surplus, measured by the proportions of unestablished to established birds, also varies from year to year.

There are increasing grounds for concluding that this is quite a typical organization, so far as birds are concerned, and that social stratification into established and unestablished members, particularly in the breeding season, is common to many other species, and other classes of animals. In different circumstances the social hierarchy may take the form of a more or less linear series or peck-order. Hierarchies commonly play a leading part in regulating animal populations; not only can they be made to cut off any required proportion of the population from breeding, but also they have exactly the same effect in respect of food when it is in short supply. According to circumstances, the surplus tail of the hierarchy may either be disposed of or retained as a nonparticipating reserve if resources permit.

It is not necessary here to explore in detail the elaborate patterns of behavior by which the social hierarchy takes effect. The processes are infinitely varied and complex, though the results are simple and functionally always the same. The hierarchy is essentially an overflow mechanism, continuously variable in terms of population pressure on one hand, and habitat capacity on the other. In operation it is purely conventional, prescribing a code of behavior. When a more dominant individual exerts sufficient aggressive pressure, usually expressed as threat although frequently in some more subtle and sophisticated form, his subordinates yield, characteristically without physical resistance or even demur. It may cost them their sole chance of reproduction to do so, if not their lives. The survival of the group depends on their compliance.

This has been taken as an example to illustrate one type of adaptation possessed by the group, transcending the individuality of its members. It subordinates the advantage of particular members to the advantage of the group; its survival value to the latter is clearly very great. The hierarchy as a system of behavior has innumerable variants in different species and different phyla, analogous to those of a somatic unit like the nervous or vascular system. Like them, it must have been subject to adaptive evolutionary change through natural selection; yet it is essentially an "organ" of a social group, and has no existence if the members are segregated.

A simple analogy may possibly help to bring out the significance of this point. A football team is made up of players individually selected for such qualities as skill, quickness, and stamina, material to their success as members of the team. The survival of the team to win the championship, however, is determined by entirely distinct criteria, namely, the tactics and ability it displays in competition with other teams, under a particular code of conventions laid down for the game. There is no difficulty in distinguishing two levels of selection here, although the analogy is otherwise very imperfect.

The hierarchy is not the only characteristic of this kind. There are genetic mechanisms, such as those that govern the optimum balance between recombination and linkage, in which the benefit is equally clearly with the group rather than the individual. Without leaving the sphere of population regulation, however, we can find a wide range of vital parameters, the optima of which must similarly be determined by intergroup selection. Among those discussed at length in the book already cited are (1) the potential life-span of individuals and, coupled with it, the generation turnover rate; (2) the relative proportions of life spent in juvenile or nonsexual condition (including diapause) and in reproduction; (3) monotely (breeding only for a single season) versus polytely; (4) the basal fecundity-level, including, in any one season, the question of one brood versus more than one.

These and similar parameters, differing from one species or class to another, are interconnected. Their combined effects are being summed over the whole population at any one time and over many generations in any given area. It is the scale of the operation in time and space that precludes an immediate experimental test of group selection. An inference that may justifiably be drawn, however, is that maladjustment sufficient to interfere persistently with the homeostatic mechanism must either cause a progressive decline in the population or, alternatively, a chronic overexploitation and depletion of food resources; in the end either will depopulate the locality.

There still remains the central question as to how an immediate advantage to the individual can be suppressed or overridden when it conflicts with the interests of the group. What would be the effect of selection, for example, on individuals the abnormal and socially undesirable fertility of which enabled them and their hereditary successors to contribute an ever increasing share to future generations?

Initially, groups containing individuals like this that reproduced too fast, so that the over-all recruitment rate persistently tended to exceed the death-rate, must have repeatedly exterminated themselves in the manner just indicated, by overtaxing and progressively destroying their food resources. The earliest adaptations capable of protecting the group against such recurrent disasters must necessarily have been very ancient; they may even have been acquired only once in the whole of animal phylogeny, and in this respect be comparable with such basic morphological elements as the mesoderm, or, perhaps, the coelom. Once acquired, the protective adaptations could be endlessly varied and elaborated. It is inherently difficult to reconstruct the origin of systems of this kind; but genetic mechanisms exist which could give individual breeding success a low heritability, or, in other words, make it resistant to selection. This could be relatively simply achieved, for example, if the greatest success normally attached to heterozygotes for the alleles concerned, creating the stable situation characteristic of genetic homeostasis.

A more complex system can be discerned, as it has developed in many of the higher vertebrates where the breeding success of individuals is very closely connected with social status. This connection must necessarily divert an enormous additional force of selection into promoting social dominance, and penalizing the less fortunate subordinates in the population that are prevented from breeding or feeding, or get squeezed out of the habitat. Yet it is self-evident that the conventional codes under which social competition is conducted are in practice not jeopardized from this cause: selection pressure, however great, does not succeed in promoting a general recourse to deadly combat or treachery between rivals, nor does it, in the course of generations, extinguish the patient compliance of subordinates with their lot.

The reason appears to be that social status depends on a summation of diverse traits, including virtually all the hereditary and environmental factors that predicate health, vigor, and survivorship in the individual. While this is favorable to the maintenance of a high-grade breeding stock, and can result in the enhancement through selection of the weapons and conventional adornments by which social dominance is secured, dominance itself is again characterized by a low heritability, as experiments have shown. In many birds and mammals, moreover, individual status, quite apart from its genetic basis, advances progressively with the individual's age. Not only are the factors that determine social and breeding success numerous and involved, therefore, but the ingredients can vary from one successful individual to the next. A substantial part of the gene pool of the population is likely to be involved and selection for social dominance or fertility at the individual level correspondingly dissipated and ineffective, except in eliminating the substandard fringe.

Such methods as these which protect group adaptations, including both population parameters and social structures, from short-term changes, seem capable of preventing the rise of any hereditary tendency toward antisocial self-interest among the members of a social group. Compliance with the social code can be made obligatory and automatic, and it probably is so in almost all animals that possess social homeostatic systems at all. In at least some of the mammals, on the contrary, the individual has been released from this rigid compulsion, probably because a certain amount of intelligent individual enterprise has proved advantageous to the group. In man, as we know, compliance with the social code is by no means automatic, and is reinforced by conscience and the law, both of them relatively flexible adaptations.

There appears therefore to be no great difficulty in resolving the initial problem as to how intergroup selection can override the concurrent process of selection for individual advantage. Relatively simple genetic mechanisms can be evolved whereby the door is shut to one form of selection and open to the other, securing without conflict the maximum advantage from each; and since neighboring populations differ not only in genetic system but in population parameters (for example, mean fecundity) and in social practices (for example, local differences in migratory behavior in birds, or in tribal conventions among primitive men), there is no lack of variation on which intergroup selection can work.

The Genetical Evolution
of Social Behavior

W. D. Hamilton

I. INTRODUCTION

With very few exceptions, the only parts of the theory of natural selection which have been supported by mathematical models admit no possibility of the evolution of any characters which are on average to the disadvantage of the individuals possessing them. If natural selection followed the classical models exclusively, species would not show any behavior more positively social than the coming together of the sexes and parental care.

Sacrifices involved in parental care are a possibility implicit in any model in which the definition of fitness is based, as it should be, on the number of adult offspring. In certain circumstances an individual may leave more adult offspring by expending care and materials on its offspring already born than by reserving them for its own survival and further fecundity. A gene causing its possessor to give parental care will then leave more replica genes in the next generation than an allele having the opposite tendency. The selective advantage may be seen to lie through benefits conferred indifferently on a set of relatives each of which has a half chance of carrying the gene in question.

From this point of view it is also seen, however, that there is nothing special about the parent-offspring relationship except its close degree and a certain fundamental asymmetry. The full-sib relationship is just as close. If an individual carries a certain gene the expectation that a

From *The Journal of Theoretical Biology* 7 (1964), pp. 1–16. Reprinted by permission of Academic Press, Inc. (London), Limited.

random sib will carry a replica of it is again one-half. Similarly, the half-sib relationship is equivalent to that of grandparent and grandchild with the expectation of replica genes, or genes "identical by descent" as they are usually called, standing at one quarter; and so on.

Although it does not seem to have received very detailed attention the possibility of the evolution of characters benefiting descendants more remote than immediate offspring has often been noticed. Opportunities for benefiting relatives, remote or not, in the same or an adjacent generation (i.e., relatives like cousins and nephews) must be much more common than opportunities for benefiting grandchildren and further descendants. As a first step toward a general theory that would take into account all kinds of relatives this paper will describe a model which is particularly adapted to deal with interactions between relatives of the same generation. The model includes the classical model for "nonoverlapping generations" as a special case. An excellent summary of the general properties of this classical model has been given by Kingman. It is quite beyond the author's power to give an equally extensive survey of the properties of the present model but certain approximate deterministic implications of biological interest will be pointed out.

As is already evident the essential idea which the model is going to use is quite simple. Thus although the following account is necessarily somewhat mathematical it is not surprising that eventually, allowing certain lapses from mathematical rigor, we are able to arrive at approximate principles which can also be expressed quite simply and in nonmathematical form. The most important principle, as it arises directly from the model, is outlined in the last section of this paper, but a fuller discussion together with some attempt to evaluate the theory as a whole in the light of biological evidence will be given in the sequel.

II. THE MODEL

The model is restricted to the case of an organism which reproduces once and for all at the end of a fixed period. Survivorship and reproduction can both vary but it is only the consequent variations in their product, net reproduction, that are of concern here. All genotypic effects are conceived as increments and decrements to a basic unit of reproduction which, if possessed by all the individuals alike, would render the population both stationary and nonevolutionary. Thus the fitness a^*

of an individual is treated as the sum of his basic unit, the effect δa of his personal genotype and the total e° of effects on him due to his neighbors which will depend on their genotypes:

$$a^\bullet = 1 + \delta a + e^\bullet. \tag{1}$$

The index symbol $\bullet$ in contrast to $\circ$ will be used consistently to denote the inclusion of the personal effect δa in the aggregate in question. Thus equation (1) could be rewritten

$$a^\bullet = 1 + e^\bullet.$$

In equation (1), however, the symbol $\bullet$ also serves to distinguish this neighbor modulated kind of fitness from the part of it

$$a = 1 + \delta a$$

which is equivalent to fitness in the classical sense of individual fitness.

The symbol δ preceding a letter will be used to indicate an effect or total of effects due to an individual treated as an addition to the basic unit, as typified in

$$a = 1 + \delta a.$$

The neighbors of an individual are considered to be affected differently according to their relationship with him.

Genetically two related persons differ from two unrelated members of the population in their tendency to carry replica genes which they have both inherited from the one or more ancestors they have in common. If we consider an autosomal locus, not subject to selection, in relative B with respect to the same locus in the other relative A, it is apparent that there are just three possible conditions of this locus in B, namely that both, one only, or neither of his genes are identical by descent with genes in A. We denote the respective probabilities of these conditions by c_2, c_1 and c_0. They are independent of the locus considered; and since

$$c_2 + c_1 + c_0 = 1,$$

the relationship is completely specified by giving any two of them. Li and Sacks have described methods of calculating these probabilities adequate for any relationship that does not involve inbreeding. The mean number of genes per locus i.b.d. (as from now on we abbreviate the phrase "identical by descent") with genes at the same locus in A for a hypothetical population of relatives like B is clearly $2c_2 + c_1$. One half of this number, $c_2 + \frac{1}{2}c_1$, may therefore be called the expected fraction of genes i.b.d. in a relative. It can be shown that it is equal to Sewall Wright's Coefficient of Relationship r (in a non-inbred population). The standard methods of calculating r without obtaining the complete distribution can be found in Kempthorne. Tables of

$$f = \tfrac{1}{2}r = \tfrac{1}{2}(c_2 + \tfrac{1}{2}c_1) \text{ and } F = c_2$$

for a large class of relationships can be found in Haldane and Jayakar.

Strictly, a more complicated metric of relationship taking into account the parameters of selection is necessary for a locus undergoing selection, but the following account based on use of the above coefficients must give a good approximation to the truth when selection is slow and may be hoped to give some guidance even when it is not.

Consider now how the effects which an arbitrary individual distributes to the population can be summarized. For convenience and generality we will include at this stage certain effects (such as effects on parents' fitness) which must be zero under the restrictions of this particular model, and also others (such as effects on offspring) which although not necessarily zero we will not attempt to treat accurately in the subsequent analysis.

The effect of A on specified B can be a variate. In the present deterministic treatment, however, we are concerned only with the means of such variates. Thus the effect which we may write $(\delta a_{\text{father}})_A$ is really the expectation of the effect of A upon his father but for brevity we will refer to it as the effect on the father.

The full array of effects like $(\delta a_{\text{father}})_A$, $(\delta a_{\text{specified sister}})_A$, etc., we will denote

$$\{\delta a_{\text{rel.}}\}_A.$$

From this array we can construct the simpler array

$$\{\delta a_{r,c_2}\}_A$$

by adding together all effects to relatives who have the same values for the pair of coefficients (r, c_2). For example, the combined effect $\delta a_{\frac{1}{4},0}$ might contain effects actually occurring to grandparents, grandchildren, uncles, nephews and half-brothers. From what has been said above it is clear that as regards changes in autosomal gene-frequency by natural selection all the consequences of the full array are implied by this reduced array—at least, provided we ignore (a) the effect of previous generations of selection on the expected constitution of relatives, and (b) the one or more generations that must really occur before effects to children, nephews, grandchildren, etc., are manifested. From this array we can construct a yet simpler array, or vector,

$$\{\delta a_r\}_A,$$

by adding together all effects with common r. Thus $\delta a_{1/4}$ would bring together effects to the above-mentioned set of relatives and effects to double-first cousins, for whom the pair of coefficients is $(\frac{1}{4}, \frac{1}{16})$.

Corresponding to the effect which A causes to B there will be an effect of similar type on A. This will either come from B himself or from a person who stands to A in the same relationship as A stands to B. Thus corresponding to an effect by A on his nephew there will be an effect on A by his uncle. The similarity between the effect which A dispenses and that which he receives is clearly an aspect of the problem of the correlation between relatives. Thus the term e^o in equation (1) is not a constant for any given genotype of A since it will depend on the genotypes of neighbors and therefore on the gene-frequencies and the mating system.

Consider a single locus. Let the series of allelomorphs be G_1, G_2, G_3, . . . , G_n, and their gene-frequencies p_1, p_2, p_3, . . . , p_n. With the genotype G_iG_j associate the array $\{\delta a_{rel.}\}_{ij}$; within the limits of the above-mentioned approximations natural selection in the model is then defined.

If we were to follow the usual approach to the formulation of the progress due to natural selection in a generation, we should attempt to give formulae for the neighbor modulated fitnesses a_{ij}^*. In order to formulate the expectation of that element of e_{ij}^o which was due to the return effect of a relative B we would need to know the distribution of possible genotypes of B, and to obtain this we must use the double measure of B's relationship and the gene-frequencies just as in the problem of the correlation between relatives. Thus the formula for e_{ij}^o will involve all the arrays $\{\delta a_{..,c_2}\}_{ij}$ and will be rather unwieldy (see Section 4).

An alternative approach, however, shows that the arrays $\{\delta a_r\}_{ij}$ are sufficient to define the selective effects. Every effect on reproduction which is due to A can be thought of as made up of two parts: an effect on the reproduction of genes i.b.d. with genes in A, and an effect on the reproduction of unrelated genes. Since the coefficient r measures the expected fraction of genes i.b.d. in a relative, for any particular degree of relationship this breakdown may be written quantitatively:

$$(\delta a_{\text{rel.}})_A = r(\delta a_{\text{rel.}})_A + (1 - r)(\delta a_{\text{rel.}})_A.$$

The total of effects on reproduction which are due to A may be treated similarly:

$$\sum_{\text{rel.}} (\delta a_{\text{rel.}})_A = \sum_{\text{rel.}} r(\delta a_{\text{rel.}})_A + \sum_{\text{rel.}} (1 - r)(\delta a_{\text{rel.}})_A,$$

or

$$\sum_{r} (\delta a_r)_A = \sum_{r} r(\delta a_r)_A + \sum_{r} (1 - r)(\delta a_r)_A,$$

which we rewrite briefly as

$$\delta T_A^* = \delta R_A^* + \delta S_A,$$

where δR_A^* is accordingly the total effect on genes i.b.d. in relatives of A, and δS_A is the total effect on their other genes. The reason for the omission of an index symbol from the last term is that here there is, in effect, no question of whether or not the self-effect is to be in the summation, for if it is included it has to be multiplied by zero. If index symbols were used we should have $\delta S_A^* = \delta S_A^*$, whatever the subscript; it therefore seems more explicit to omit them throughout.

If, therefore, all effects are accounted to the individuals that cause them, of the total effect δT_{ij}^* due to an individual of genotype $G_i G_j$ a part δR_{ij}^* will involve a specific contribution to the gene-pool by this genotype, while the remaining part δS_{ij} will involve an unspecific contribution consisting of genes in the ratio in which the gene-pool already possesses them. It is clear that it is the matrix of effects δR_{ij}^* which determines the direction of selection progress in gene-frequencies; δS_{ij} only influences its magnitude. In view of this importance of the δR_{ij}^* it is convenient to give some name to the concept with which they are associated.

In accordance with our convention let

$$R_{ij}^* = 1 + \delta R_{ij}^*;$$

then R_{ij}^* will be called the *inclusive fitness*, δR_{ij}^* the *inclusive fitness effect* and δS_{ij} the *diluting effect*, of the genotype G_iG_j. Let

$$T_{ij}^* = 1 + \delta T_{ij}^*.$$

So far our discussion is valid for nonrandom mating but from now on for simplicity we assume that it is random. Using a prime to distinguish the new gene-frequencies after one generation of selection we have

$$p_i' = \frac{\sum_j p_i p_j R_{ij}^* = p_i \sum_{j,k} p_j p_k \delta S_{jk}}{\sum_{j,k} p_j p_k T_{jk}^*} = p_i \frac{\sum_j p_j R_{ij}^* + \sum_{j,k} p_j p_k \delta S_{jk}}{\sum_{j,k} p_j p_k T_{jk}^*}$$

The terms of this expression are clearly of the nature of averages over a part (genotypes containing G_i, homozygotes G_iG_i counted twice) and the whole of the existing set of genotypes in the population. Thus using a well-known subscript notation we may rewrite the equation term by term as

$$p_i' = p_i \frac{R_{i.}^* + \delta S_{..}}{T_{..}^*}$$

$$\therefore p_i' - p_i = \Delta p_i = \frac{p_i}{T_{..}^*}(R_{i.}^* + \delta S_{..} - T_{..}^*)$$

or

$$\Delta p_i = \frac{p_i}{R_{..}^* + \delta S_{..}}(R_{i.}^* - R_{..}^*). \tag{2}$$

This form clearly differentiates the roles of the R_{ij}^* and δS_{ij} in selective progress and shows the appropriateness of calling the latter diluting effects.

For comparison with the account of the classical case given by Moran, equation (2) may be put in the form

$$\Delta p_i = \frac{p_i}{T_{..}^*}\left(\frac{1}{2}\frac{\partial R_{..}^*}{\partial p_i} - R_{..}^*\right)$$

where $\partial/\partial p_i$ denotes the usual partial derivative, written d/dp_i by Moran.

Whether the selective effect is reckoned by means of the a_{ij} or according to the method above, the denominator expression must take in all effects occurring during the generation. Hence $a\overset{..}{.} = T\overset{..}{.}.$.

As might be expected from the greater generality of the present model the extension of the theorem of the increase of mean fitness presents certain difficulties. However, from the above equations it is clear that the quantity that will tend to maximize, if any, is $R\overset{.}{.}.$, the mean inclusive fitness. The following brief discussion uses Kingman's approach.

The mean inclusive fitness in the succeeding generation is given by

$$R\overset{.}{.}.' = \sum_{i,j} p_i' p_j' R_{ij}^* = \frac{1}{T\overset{.}{.}^2} \sum_{i,j} p_i p_j R_{ij}^* (R_i^* + \delta S\overset{.}{.})(R_{.j}^* + \delta S\overset{.}{.}).$$

$$\therefore R\overset{.}{.}.' - R\overset{.}{.}. = \Delta R\overset{.}{.}. = \frac{1}{T\overset{.}{.}^2} \left\{ \sum_{i,j} p_i p_j R_{ij}^* R_i^* . R_{.j}^* + \right.$$

$$\left. + 2\delta S\overset{.}{.} \sum_{i,j} p_i p_j R_{ij}^* R_i^* . + R\overset{.}{.}.\delta S\overset{.}{.}^2 - R\overset{.}{.}. T\overset{.}{.}^2 \right\}.$$

Substituting $R\overset{.}{.}. + \delta S\overset{.}{.}$ for $T\overset{.}{.}.$ in the numerator expression, expanding and rearranging:

$$\Delta R\overset{.}{.} = \frac{1}{T\overset{.}{.}^2} \left\{ \left(\sum_{i,j} p_i p_j R_{ij}^* R_i^* R_j^* - R\overset{.}{.}.^3 \right) + \right.$$

$$\left. + 2\delta S\overset{.}{.} \left(\sum_{i,j} p_i p_j R_{ij}^* R_i^* . - R\overset{.}{.}.^2 \right) \right\}.$$

We have $(\ ) \geq 0$ in both cases. The first is the proven inequality of the classical model. The second follows from

$$\sum_{i,j} p_i p_j R_{ij} R_i^* . = \sum_i p_i R_i^* .^2 \geq \left(\sum_i p_i R_{.}^* \right)^2 = R\overset{.}{.}.^2.$$

Thus a sufficient condition for $\Delta R\overset{.}{.}. \geq 0$ is $\delta S.. \geq 0$. That $\Delta R\overset{.}{.}. \geq 0$ for positive dilution is almost obvious if we compare the actual selective changes with those which would occur if $\{R_{ij}^*\}$ were the fitness matrix in the classical model.

It follows that $R\overset{.}{.}.$ certainly maximizes (in the sense of reaching a local maximum of R ∴) if it never occurs in the course of selective changes that δS .. < 0. Thus R ∴ certainly maximizes if all $\delta S_{ij} \geq 0$ and therefore also if all $(\delta a_{rel.})_{ij} \geq 0$. It still does so even if some or all δa_{ij} are negative, for, as we have seen δS_{ij} is independent of δa_{ij}.

Here then we have discovered a quantity, inclusive fitness, which under the conditions of the model tends to maximize in much the same way that fitness tends to maximize in the simpler classical model. For an important class of genetic effects where the individual is supposed to dispense benefits to his neighbors, we have formally proved that the average inclusive fitness in the population will always increase. For cases where individuals may dispense harm to their neighbors we merely know, roughly speaking, that the change in gene frequency in each generation is aimed somwhere in the direction of a local maximum of average inclusive fitness, but may, for all the present analysis has told us, overshoot it in such a way as to produce a lower value.

As to the nature of inclusive fitness it may perhaps help to clarify the notion if we now give a slightly different verbal presentation. Inclusive fitness may be imagined as the personal fitness which an individual actually expresses in its production of adult offspring as it becomes after it has been first stripped and then augmented in a certain way. It is stripped of all components which can be considered as due to the individual's social environment, leaving the fitness which he would express if not exposed to any of the harms or benefits of that environment. This quantity is then augmented by certain fractions of the quantities of harm and benefit which the individual himself causes to the fitnesses of his neighbors. The fractions in question are simply the coefficients of relationship appropriate to the neighbors whom he affects: unity for clonal individuals, one-half for sibs, one-quarter for half-sibs, one-eighth for cousins, . . . and finally zero for all neighbors whose relationship can be considered negligibly small.

Actually, in the preceding mathematical account we were not concerned with the inclusive fitness of individuals as described here but rather with certain averages of them which we call the inclusive fitnesses of types. But the idea of the inclusive fitness of an individual is nevertheless a useful one. Just as in the sense of classical selection we may consider whether a given character expressed in an individual is adaptive in the sense of being in the interest of his personal fitness or not, so in the present sense of selection we may consider whether the character or trait of behavior is or is not adaptive in the sense of being in the interest of his inclusive fitness.

III. THREE SPECIAL CASES

Equation (2) may be written

$$\Delta p_i = p_i \frac{\delta R_{i.} - \delta R^{\bullet}_{..}}{1 + \delta T^{\bullet}_{..}}.$$ (3)

Now $\delta T^{\bullet}_{ij} = \sum_r = (\delta a_r)_{ij}$ is the sum and $\delta R^{\bullet} = \sum_r r(\delta a_r)_{ij}$ is the first moment about $r = 0$ of the array of effects $\{\delta a_{rel}\}_{ij}$ cause by the genotype G_iG_j; it appears that these two parameters are sufficient to fix the progress of the system under natural selection within our general approximation.

Let

$$r^{\bullet}_{ij} = \frac{\delta R_{ij}}{\delta T^{\bullet}_{ij}}, \quad (\delta T^{\bullet}_{ij} \neq 0);$$ (4)

and let

$$r^{3}_{ij} = \frac{\delta R^{3}_{ij}}{\delta T^{3}_{ij}}, \quad (\delta T^{3}_{ij} \neq 0).$$ (5)

These quantities can be regarded as average relationships or as the first moments of reduced arrays, similar to the first moments of probability distributions.

We now consider three special cases which serve to bring out certain important features of selection in the model.

(a) The sums $\delta T^{\bullet}_{ij}$ differ between genotypes, the reduced first moment $r^{\bullet}$ being common to all. If all higher moments are equal between genotypes, that is, if all arrays are of the same "shape," this corresponds to the case where a stereotyped social action is performed with differing intensity or frequency according to genotype.

Whether or not this is so, we may, from equation (4), substitute $r^{\bullet}\delta T^{\bullet}_{ij}$ for δR_{ij} in equation (3) and have

$$\Delta p_i = p_i r^{\bullet} \frac{\delta T_{i.} - \delta T^{\bullet}_{..}}{1 + \delta T^{\bullet}_{..}}.$$

Comparing this with the corresponding equation of the classical model,

$$\Delta p_i = p_i \frac{\delta a_{i.} - \delta a_{..}}{1 + \delta a_{..}} \quad (6)$$

we see that placing genotypic effects on a relative of degree r^{*} instead of reserving them for personal fitness results in a slowing of selection progress according to the fractional factor r^{*}.

If, for example, the advantages conferred by a "classical" gene to its carriers are such that the gene spreads at a certain rate the present result tells us that in exactly similar circumstances another gene which conferred similar advantages to the sibs of the carriers would progress at exactly half this rate.

In trying to imagine a realistic situation to fit this sort of case some concern may be felt about the occasions where through the probabilistic nature of things the gene-carrier happens not to have a sib, or not to have one suitably placed to receive the benefit. Such possibilities and their frequencies of realization must, however, all be taken into account as the effects $(\delta a_{sibs})_A$, etc., are being evaluated for the model, very much as if in a classical case allowance were being made for some degree of failure of penetrance of a gene.

(b) The reduced first moments r_{ij}^{*} differ between genotypes, the sum δT^{*} being common to all. From equation (4), substituting $r_{ij}^{*} \delta T^{*}$ for δR_{ij}^{*} in equation (3) we have

$$\Delta p_i = p_i \frac{\delta T^{*}}{T^{*}} (r_{i.}^{*} = r_{..}^{*}).$$

But it is more interesting to assume δa is also common to all genotypes. If so it follows that we can replace * by $^{\circ}$ in the numerator expression of equation (3). Then, from equation (5), substituting $r_{ij}^{\circ} \delta T^{\circ}$ for δR_{ij}°, we have

$$\Delta p_i = p_i \frac{\delta T^{\circ}}{T^{*}} (r_{i.}^{\circ} - r_{..}^{\circ}).$$

Hence, if a giving-trait is in question (δT° positive), genes which restrict giving to the nearest relative ($r_{i.}^{\circ}$ greatest) tend to be favored;

if a taking-trait ($\delta T°$ negative), genes which cause taking from the most distant relatives tend to be favored.

If all higher reduced moments about $r = r_{ij}^o$ are equal between genotypes it is implied that the genotype merely determines whereabouts in the field of relationship that centers on an individual a stereotyped array of effects is placed.

With many natural populations it must happen that an individual forms the center of an actual local concentration of his relatives which is due to a general inability or disinclination of the organisms to move far from their places of birth. In such a population, which we may provisionally term "viscous," the present form of selection may apply fairly accurately to genes which affect vagrancy. It follows from the statements of the last paragraph but one that over a range of different species we would expect to find giving-traits commonest and most highly developed in the species with the most viscous populations whereas uninhibited competition should characterize species with the most freely mixing populations.

In the viscous population, however, the assumption of random mating is very unlikely to hold perfectly, so that these indications are of a rough qualitative nature only.

(c) $\delta T_{ij}^{\bullet} = 0$ for all genotypes.

$$\therefore \ \delta T_{ij}^o = - \delta a_{ij}$$

for all genotypes, and from equation (5)

$$\delta R_{ij}^o = -\delta a_{ij} r_{ij}^o.$$

Then, from equation (3), we have

$$\Delta p_i = p_i(\delta R_{i.}^{\bullet} - \delta R_{.\ }^{\bullet}) = p_i\{(\delta a_{i.} + \delta R_{i.}^o) - (\delta a_{.\ } + \delta R_{.\ }^o)\}$$

$$= p_i\{ .\ \delta a_{i,} \ (1 - r_{i.}^o) - \delta a_{.\ } . \ (1 - r_{.\ }^o)\}.$$

Such cases may be described as involving transfers of reproductive potential. They are especially relevant to competition, in which the individual can be considered as endeavoring to transfer prerequisites of survival and reproduction from his competitors to himself. In particular, if $r_{ij}^o = r^o$ for all genotypes we have

$$\Delta p_i = p_i(1 - r^o)(\delta a_{i.} - \delta a_{.\ }).$$

Comparing this to the corresponding equation of the classical model [equation (6)] we see that there is a reduction in the rate of progress when transfers are from a relative.

It is relevant to note that Haldane in his first paper on the mathematical theory of selection pointed out the special circumstances of competition in the cases of mammalian embryos in a single uterus and of seeds both while still being nourished by a single parent plant and after their germination if they were not very thoroughly dispersed. He gave a numerical example of competition between sibs showing that the progress of gene-frequency would be slower than normal.

In such situations as this, however, where the population may be considered as subdivided into more or less standard-sized batches each of which is allotted a local standard-sized pool of reproductive potential (which in Haldane's case would consist almost entirely of prerequisites for pre-adult survival), there is, in addition to a small correcting term which we mention in the short general discussion of competition in the next section, an extra over-all slowing in selection progress. This may be thought of as due to the wasting of the powers of the more fit and the protection of the less fit when these types chance to occur positively assorted (beyond any mere effect of relationship) in a locality; its importance may be judged from the fact that it ranges from zero when the batches are indefinitely large to a halving of the rate of progress for competition in pairs.

IV. ARTIFICIALITIES OF THE MODEL

When any of the effects is negative the restrictions laid upon the model hitherto do not preclude certain situations which are clearly impossible from the biological point of view. It is clearly absurd if for any possible set of gene-frequencies any a_{ij} turns out negative; and even if the magnitude of δa_{ij} is sufficient to make a_{ij} positive while $1 + e_{ij}^0$ is negative the situation is still highly artificial, since it implies the possibility of a sort of overdraft on the basic unit of an individual which has to be made good from his own takings. If we call this situation "improbable" we may specify two restrictions: a weaker, $e_{ij}^0 > -1$, which precludes "improbable" situations; and a stronger, $e_{ij} > -1$, which precludes even the impossible situations, both being required over the whole range of possible gene-frequencies as well as the whole range of genotypes.

As has been pointed out, a formula for e_{ij}^* can only be given if we have the arrays of effects according to a double coefficient of relationship. Choosing the double coefficient (c_2, c_1) such a formula is

$$e_{ij}^* = \sum_{c_2,c_1}^* [c_2 \mathrm{Dev}(\delta a_{c_2,c_1})_{ij} + \tfrac{1}{2} c_1 \{ \mathrm{Dev}(\delta a_{c_2.c_1})_i$$

$$+ \mathrm{Dev}(\delta a_{c_2,c_1})_{.j} \}] + \delta T_{..}^{\circ}$$

where

$$\mathrm{Dev}(\delta a_{c_2,c_1})_{ij} = (\delta a_{c_2,c_1})_{ij} - (\delta a_{c_2,c_1})_{..} \text{ etc.}$$

Similarly

$$e_{ij}^{\circ} = \Sigma^{\circ}[''] + \delta T_{..}^{\circ},$$

the self-effect $(\delta a_{1,0})_{ij}$ being in this case omitted from the summations.

The following discussion is in terms of the stronger restriction but the argument holds also for the weaker; we need only replace * by $^\circ$ throughout.

If there are no dominance deviations, i.e., if

$$(\delta a_{\text{rel.}})_{ij} = \tfrac{1}{2} \{ (\delta a_{\text{rel.}})_{ii} + (\delta a_{\text{rel.}})_{jj} \} \text{ for all } ij \text{ and rel.,}$$

it follows that each ij deviation is the sum of the $i.$ and the $j.$ deviations. In this case we have

$$e_{ij}^* = \Sigma \ ^* r \, \mathrm{Dev} \, (\delta a_r)_{ij} + \delta T_{..}^*.$$

Since we must have $e_{..}^* = \delta T_{..}^*$, it is obvious that some of the deviations must be negative.

Therefore $\delta T_{..}^* > -1$ is a necessary condition for $e_{ij}^* > -1$. This is, in fact, obvious when we consider that $\delta T_{..}^* = -1$ would mean that the aggregate of individual taking was just sufficient to eat up all basic units exactly. Considering that the present use of the coefficients of relationships is only valid when selection is slow, there seems little point in attempting to derive mathematically sufficient conditions for the restriction to hold; intuitively however it would seem that if we exclude over- and underdominance it should be sufficient to have no homozygote with a net taking greater than unity.

Even if we could ignore the breakdown of our use of the coefficient of relationship it is clear enough that if δT_{i}^{*}. approaches anywhere near -1 the model is highly artificial and implies a population in a state of catastrophic decline. This does not mean, of course, that mutations causing large selfish effects cannot receive positive selection; it means that their expression must moderate with increasing gene-frequency in a way that is inconsistent with our model. The "killer" trait of *Paramoecium* might be regarded as an example of a selfish trait with potentially large effects, but with its only partially genetic mode of inheritance and inevitable density dependence it obviously requires a selection model tailored to the case, and the same is doubtless true of most "social" traits which are as extreme as this.

Really the class of model situations with negative neighbor effects which are artificial according to a strict interpretation of the assumptions must be much wider than the class which we have chosen to call "improbable." The model assumes that the magnitude of an effect does not depend either on the genotype of the effectee or on his state with respect to the prerequisites of fitness at the time when the effect is caused. Where taking-traits are concerned it is just possible to imagine that this is true of some kinds of surreptitious theft but in general it is more reasonable to suppose that following some sort of an encounter the limited prerequisite is divided in the ratio of the competitive abilities. Provided competitive differentials are small however, the model will not be far from the truth; the correcting term that should be added to the expression for Δp_i can be shown to be small to the third order. With giving-traits it is more reasonable to suppose that if it is the nature of the prerequisite to be transferable the individual can give away whatever fraction of his own property that his instincts incline him to. The model was designed to illuminate altruistic behavior; the classes of selfish and competitive behavior which it can also usefully illuminate are more restricted, especially where selective differentials are potentially large.

For loci under selection the only relatives to which our metric of relationship is strictly applicable are ancestors. Thus the chance that an arbitrary parent carries a gene picked in an offspring is $\frac{1}{2}$, the chance that an arbitrary grandparent carries it is $\frac{1}{4}$, and so on. As regards descendants, it seems intuitively plausible that for a gene which is making steady progress in gene-frequency the true expectation of genes i.b.d. in a n-th generation descendant will exceed $\frac{1}{2}^{n}$, and similarly that for a gene that is steadily declining in frequency the reverse will hold. Since the path of genetic connection with a simple same-generation relative like a half-sib includes an "ascending part" and a "descending part" it is tempting to imagine that the ascending part can be treated with multipliers of exactly ½ and the descending part by multipliers consistently more or less than ½ according to which type of selection is in progress. However, a more rigorous attack on the problem shows that it is more difficult than the corresponding one for simple descendants, where the formulation of the factor which actually replaces ½ is quite easy at least in the case of classical selection, and the author has so far failed to reach any definite general conclusions as to the nature and extent of the error in the foregoing account which his use of the ordinary coefficients of relationship has actually involved.

Finally, it must be pointed out that the model is not applicable to the selection of new mutations. Sibs might or might not carry the mutation depending on the point in the germ-line of the parent at which it had occurred, but for relatives in general a definite number of generations must pass before the coefficients give the true—or, under selection, the approximate—expectations of replicas. This point is favorable to the establishment of taking-traits and slightly against giving-traits. A mutation can, however, be expected to overcome any such slight initial barrier before it has recurred many times.

V. THE MODEL LIMITS TO THE EVOLUTION OF ALTRUISTIC AND SELFISH BEHAVIOR

With classical selection a genotype may be regarded as positively selected if its fitness is above the average and as counter-selected if it is below. The environment usually forces the average fitness a. . toward unity; thus for an arbitrary genotype the sign of δa_{ij} is an indication of the kind of selection. In the present case although it is T.`. and not $R$.`. that is forced toward unity, the analogous indication is given by the inclusive fitness effect δR_{ij}^* for the remaining part, the diluting effect δS_{ij}, of the total genotypic effect δT_{ij}^* has no influence on the kind of selection. In other words the kind of selection may be considered determined by whether the inclusive fitness of a genotype is above or below average.

We proceed, therefore, to consider certain elementary criteria which

determine the sign of the inclusive fitness effect. The argument applies to any genotype and subscripts can be left out.
    Let

$$\delta T^\circ = k\delta a. \qquad (7)$$

    According to the signs of δa and δT° we have four types of behavior as set out in the following diagram:

		Neighbors	
		gain; $\delta T^\circ + $ ve	lose; $\delta T^\circ - $ ve
	gains; $\delta a + $ ve	$k + $ ve *Selected*	$k - $ ve Selfish behavior ?
Individual			
	loses; $\delta a - $ ve	$k - $ ve Altruistic behavior ?	$k + $ ve *Counter selected*

The classes for which k is negative are of the greatest interest, since for these it is less obvious what will happen under selection. Also, if we regard fitness as like a substance and tending to be conserved, which must be the case in so far as it depends on the possession of material prerequisites of survival and reproduction, $k - $ ve is the more likely situation. Perfect conservation occurs if $k = - 1$. Then $\delta T^* = 0$ and $T^* = 1$: the gene-pool maintains constant "volume" from generation to generation. This case has been discussed in Case (c) of section 3. In general the value of k indicates the nature of the departure from conservation. For instance, in the case of an altruistic action k might be called the ratio of gain involved in the action: if its value is two, two units of fitness are received by neighbors for every one lost by an altruist. In the case of a selfish action, $| k |$ might be called the ratio of diminution: if its value is again two, two units of fitness are lost by neighbors for one unit gained by the taker.

The alarm call of a bird probably involves a small extra risk to the individual making it by rendering it more noticeable to the approaching predator but the consequent reduction of risk to a nearby bird previously unaware of danger must be much greater.* We need not discuss here just how risks are to be reckoned in terms of fitness: for the present illustration it is reasonable to guess that for the generality of alarm calls k is negative but $\mid k \mid > 1$. How large must $\mid k \mid$ be for the benefit to others to outweigh the risk to self in terms of inclusive fitness?

$$\begin{aligned} \delta R^{\bullet} &= \delta R^{\circ} + \delta a \\ &= r^{\circ} \delta T^{\circ} + \delta a && \text{from (5)} \\ &= \delta a(kr^{\circ} + 1) && \text{from (7).} \end{aligned}$$

Thus of actions which are detrimental to individual fitness ($\delta a -$ ve) only those for which $- k > 1/r^{\circ}$ will be beneficial to inclusive fitness ($\delta R^{\bullet} +$ ve).

This means that for a hereditary tendency to perform an action of this kind to evolve the benefit to a sib must average at least twice the loss to the individual, the benefit to a half-sib must be at least four times the loss, to a cousin eight times and so on. To express the matter more vividly, in the world of our model organisms, whose behavior is determined strictly by genotype, we expect to find that no one is prepared to sacrifice his life for any single person but that everyone will sacrifice it when he can thereby save more than two brothers, or four half-brothers, or eight first cousins. . . . Although according to the model a tendency to simple altruistic transfers ($k = - 1$) will never be evolved by natural selection, such a tendency would, in fact, receive zero counter-selection when it concerned transfers between clonal individuals. Conversely selfish transfers are always selected except when from clonal individuals.

As regards selfish traits in general ($\delta a +$ ve, $k -$ ve) the condition for a benefit to inclusive fitness is $- k < 1/r^{\circ}$. Behavior that involves

---

* The alarm call often warns more than one nearby bird, of course—hundreds in the case of a flock—but since the predator would hardly succeed in surprising more than one in any case the total number warned must be comparatively unimportant.

taking too much from close relatives will not evolve. In the model world of genetically controlled behavior we expect to find that sibs deprive one another of reproductive prerequisites provided they can themselves make use of at least one half of what they take; individuals deprive half-sibs of four units of reproductive potential if they can get personal use of at least one of them; and so on. Clearly from a gene's point of view it is worthwhile to deprive a large number of distant relatives in order to extract a small reproductive advantage.

Adaptation and Natural Selection

George C. Williams

There remain a number of examples of individuals' acting, at their own expense, in a manner that benefits their conspecific neighbors in general, not specific individuals. Such activity can take place only when the animals occur in unrelated groups larger than two. The important initial problem is why animals should exist in groups of several to many individuals.

It is my belief that two basic misconceptions have seriously hampered progress in the study of animals in groups. The first misconception is the assumption that when one demonstrates that a certain biological process produces a certain benefit, one has demonstrated *the* function, or at least *a* function of the process. This is a serious error. The demonstration of a benefit is neither necessary nor sufficient in the demonstration of function, although it may sometimes provide insight not otherwise obtainable. It is both necessary and sufficient to show that the process is designed to serve the function. A relevant example is provided by Allee.* He observed that a certain marine flatworm, normally found in aggregated groups, can be killed by placement in a hypotonic solution. The harmfulness of such a solution is reduced when large numbers of worms, not just one or a few, are exposed to it. The effect is caused by the liberation of an unknown substance from the worms, especially

---

* W. C. Allee, *Animal Aggregations: A Study in General Sociology,* Chicago: University of Chicago Press, 1931.

dead ones, into the water. The substance is not osmotically important in itself, but somehow protects the worms against hypotonicity. Allee saw great significance in this observation, and assumed that he had demonstrated that a beneficial chemical conditioning of the environment is a function of aggregation in these worms. The fallacy of such a conclusion should be especially clear when it relates to very artificial situations like placing large numbers of worms in a small volume of brackish water. The kind of evidence that would be acceptable would be the demonstration that social cohesion increased as the water became hypotonic or underwent some other chemically harmful change; that specific integumentary secretory machinery was activated by the deleterious change; that the substance secreted not only provided protection against hypotonicity, but was an extraordinarily effective substance for this protection. One or two more links in such a chain of circumstances would provide the necessary evidence of functional design and leave no doubt that protection from hypotonicity was a function of aggregation, and not merely an effect.

The second misconception is the assumption that to explain the functional aspects of groups, one must look for group functions. An analogy with human behavior will illustrate the nature of this fallacy. Suppose a visitor from Mars, unseen, observed the social behavior of a mob of panic-stricken people rushing from a burning theatre. If he was burdened with the misconception in question he would assume that the mob must show some sort of an adaptive organization for the benefit of the group as a whole. If he was sufficiently blinded by this assumption he might even miss the obvious conclusion that the observed behavior could result in total survival below what would have resulted from a wide variety of other conceivable types of behavior. He would be impressed by the fact that the group showed a rapid "response" to the stimulus of fire. It went rapidly from a widely dispersed distribution to the formation of dense aggregations that very effectively sealed off the exits.

Someone more conversant with human nature, however, would find the explanation not in a functioning of the group, but in the functioning of individuals. An individual finds himself in a theatre in which a dangerous fire has suddenly broken out. If he is sitting near an exit he may run for it immediately. If he is a bit farther away he sees others running for the exits and, knowing human nature, realizes that if he is to get out at all he must get out quickly; so he likewise runs for the door, and in so doing, intensifies the stimulus that will cause others to behave in the same way. This behavior is clearly adaptive from the standpoint of individual genetic survival, and the behavior of the mob is easily understood as the statistical summation of individual adaptation.

This is an extreme example of damage caused by the social consequences of adaptive behavior, but undoubtedly such effects do occur, and they may be fairly common in some species. There are numerous reports, at least at the anecdotal level, of the mass destruction of large ungulates when individuals in the van of a herd are pushed off cliffs by the press from the rear. Less spectacular examples of harm deriving from social grouping are probably of greater significance. I would imagine the most important damage from social behavior to be the spread of communicable disease.

The statistical summation of adaptive individual reactions, which I believe to underlie all group action, need not be harmful. On the contrary, it may often be beneficial, perhaps more often than not. An example of such a benefit would be the retention of warmth by close groups of mammals or birds in cold weather, but there is no more reason to assume that a herd is designed for the retention of warmth than to assume that it is designed for transmitting diseases. The huddling behavior of a mouse in cold weather is designed to minimize its own heat loss, not that of the group. In seeking warmth from its neighbors it contributes heat to the group and thereby makes the collective warmth a stronger stimulus in evoking the same response from other individuals. The panic-stricken man in the theatre contributed to the panic stimulus in a similar fashion. Both man and mouse probably aid in the spread of disease. Thus the demonstration of effects, good or bad, proves nothing. To prove adaptation one must demonstrate a functional design.

The Evolution of Reciprocal Altruism

Robert L. Trivers

Altruistic behavior can be defined as behavior that benefits another organism, not closely related, while being apparently detrimental to the organism performing the behavior, benefit and detriment being defined in terms of contribution to inclusive fitness. One human being leaping into water, at some danger to himself, to save another distantly related human from drowning may be said to display altruistic behavior. If he were to leap in to save his own child, the behavior would not necessarily be an instance of "altruism"; he may merely be contributing to the survival of his own genes invested in the child.

Models that attempt to explain altruistic behavior in terms of natural selection are models designed to take the altruism out of altruism. For example, Hamilton (1964) has demonstrated that degree of relationship is an important parameter in predicting how selection will operate, and behavior which appears altruistic may, on knowledge of the genetic relationships of the organisms involved, be explicable in terms of natural selection: those genes being selected for that contribute to their own perpetuation, regardless of which individual the genes appear in. The term "kin selection" will be used in this paper to cover instances of this type—that is, of organisms being selected to help their relatively close kin.

The model presented here is designed to show how certain classes of behavior conveniently denoted as "altruistic" (or "reciprocally altruis-

From *The Quarterly Review of Biology* 46 (March 1971): 35–39, 45–47. Copyright © 1971 Stony Brook Foundation, Inc. Reprinted by permission of the publisher.

tic") can be selected for even when the recipient is so distantly related to the organism performing the altruistic act that kin selection can be ruled out. The model will apply, for example, to altruistic behavior between members of different species. It will be argued that under certain conditions natural selection favors these altruistic behaviors because in the long run they benefit the organism performing them.

THE MODEL

One human being saving another, who is not closely related and is about to drown, is an instance of altruism. Assume that the chance of the drowning man dying is one-half if no one leaps in to save him, but that the chance that his potential rescuer will drown if he leaps in to save him is much smaller, say, one in twenty. Assume that the drowning man always drowns when his rescuer does and that he is always saved when the rescuer survives the rescue attempt. Also assume that the energy costs involved in rescuing are trivial compared to the survival probabilities. Were this an isolated event, it is clear that the rescuer should not bother to save the drowning man. But if the drowning man reciprocates at some future time, and if the survival chances are then exactly reversed, it will have been to the benefit of each participant to have risked his life for the other. Each participant will have traded a one-half chance of dying for about a one-tenth chance. If we assume that the entire population is sooner or later exposed to the same risk of drowning, the two individuals who risk their lives to save each other will be selected over those who face drowning on their own. Note that the benefits of reciprocity depend on the unequal cost/benefit ratio of the altruistic act, that is, the benefit of the altruistic act to the recipient is greater than the cost of the act to the performer, cost and benefit being defined here as the increase or decrease in chances of the relevant alleles propagating themselves in the population. Note also that, as defined, the benefits and costs depend on the age of the altruist and recipient (see *Age-dependent changes* below). (The odds assigned above may not be unrealistic if the drowning man is drowning because of a cramp or if the rescue can be executed by extending a branch from shore.)

Why should the rescued individual bother to reciprocate? Selection would seem to favor being saved from drowning without endangering oneself by reciprocating. Why not cheat? ("Cheating" is used throughout this paper solely for convenience to denote failure to reciprocate; no conscious intent or moral connotation is implied.) Selection will discriminate against the cheater if cheating has later adverse affects on his life which outweigh the benefit of not reciprocating. This may happen if the altruist responds to the cheating by curtailing all future possible altruistic gestures to this individual. Assuming that the benefits of these lost altruistic acts outweigh the costs involved in reciprocating, the cheater will be selected against relative to individuals who, because neither cheats, exchange many altruistic acts.

This argument can be made precise. Assume there are both altruists and non-altruists in a population of size N and that the altruists are characterized by the fact that each performs altruistic acts when the cost to the altruist is well below the benefit to the recipient, where cost is defined as the degree to which the behavior retards the reproduction of the genes of the altruist and benefit is the degree to which the behavior increases the rate of reproduction of the genes of the recipient. Assume that the altruistic behavior of an altruist is controlled by an allele (dominant or recessive), a_2, at a given locus and that (for simplicity) there is only one alternative allele, a_1, at that locus and that it does not lead to altruistic behavior. Consider three possibilities: (1) the altruists dispense their altruism randomly throughout the population; (2) they dispense it nonrandomly by regarding their degree of genetic relationship with possible recipients; or (3) they dispense it nonrandomly by regarding the altruistic tendencies of possible recipients.

Random Dispensation of Altruism

There are three possible genotypes: a_1a_1, a_2a_1, and a_2a_2. Each allele of the heterozygote will be affected equally by whatever costs and benefits are associated with the altruism of such individuals (if a_2 is dominant) and by whatever benefits accrue to such individuals from the altruism of others, so they can be disregarded. If altruistic acts are being dispensed randomly throughout a large population, then the typical a_1a_1 individual benefits by $(1/N)\Sigma b_i$, where b_i is the benefit of the ith altruistic act performed by the altruist. The typical a_2a_2 individual has a net benefit of $(1/N)\Sigma b_i - (1/N)\Sigma c_j$, where c_j is the cost to the a_2a_2 altruist of his jth altruistic act. Since $-(1/N)\Sigma c_j$ is always less than zero, allele a_1 will everywhere replace allele a_2.

Nonrandom Dispensation by Reference to Kin

This case has been treated in detail by Hamilton (1964), who concluded that if the tendency to dispense altruism to close kin is great enough, as a function of the disparity between the average cost and benefit of an altruistic act, then a_2 will replace a_1. Technically, all that is needed for Hamilton's form of selection to operate is that an individual with an "altruistic allele" be able to distinguish between individuals with and without this allele and discriminate accordingly. No formal analysis has been attempted of the possibilities for selection favoring individuals who increase their chances of receiving altruistic acts by appearing as if they were close kin of altruists, although selection has clearly sometimes favored such parasitism (e.g., Drury and Smith, 1968).

Nonrandom Dispensation by Reference to the Altruistic Tendencies of the Recipient

What is required is that the net benefit accruing to a typical a_2a_2 altruist exceed that accruing to an a_1a_1 non-altruist, or that

$$(1/p^2) (\Sigma b_k - \Sigma c_j) > (1/q^2)\Sigma b_m,$$

where b_k is the benefit to the a_2a_2 altruist of the kth altruistic act performed toward him, where c_j is the cost of the jth altruistic act by the a_2a_2 altruist, where b_m is the benefit of the mth altruistic act to the a_1a_1 nonaltruist, and where p is the frequency in the population of the a_2 allele and q that of the a_1 allele. This will tend to occur if Σb_m is kept small (which will simultaneously reduce Σc_j). And this in turn will tend to occur if an altruist responds to a "nonaltruistic act" (that is, a failure to act altruistically toward the altruist in a situation in which so doing would cost the actor less than it would benefit the recipient) by curtailing future altruistic acts to the nonaltruist.

Note that the above form of altruism does not depend on all altruistic acts being controlled by the same allele at the same locus. Each altruist could be motivated by a different allele at a different locus. All altruistic alleles would tend to be favored as long as, for each allele, the net average benefit to the homozygous altruist exceeded the average benefit to the homozygous nonaltruist; this would tend to be true if altruists restrict their altruism to fellow altruists, regardless of what allele motivates the other individual's altruism. The argument will therefore apply, unlike Hamilton's (1964), to altruistic acts exchanged between members of different species. It is the *exchange* that favors such altruism, not the fact that the allele in question sometimes or often directly benefits its duplicate in another organism.

If an "altruistic situation" is defined as any in which one individual can dispense a benefit to a second greater than the cost of the act to himself, then the chances of selecting for altruistic behavior, that is, of keeping $\Sigma c_j + \Sigma b_m$ small, are greatest (1) when there are many such altruistic situations in the lifetime of the altruists, (2) when a given altruist repeatedly interacts with the same small set of individuals, and (3) when pairs of altruists are exposed "symmetrically" to altruistic situations, that is, in such a way that the two are able to render roughly equivalent benefits to each other at roughly equivalent costs. These three conditions can be elaborated into a set of relevant biological parameters affecting the possibility that reciprocally altruistic behavior will be selected for.

1. Length of lifetime. Long lifetime of individuals of a species maximizes the chance that any two individuals will encounter many altruistic situations, and all other things being equal one should search for instances of reciprocal altruism in long-lived species.

2. Dispersal rate. Low dispersal rate during all or a significant portion of the lifetime of individuals of a species increases the chance that an individual will interact repeatedly with the same set of neighbors, and other things being equal one should search for instances of reciprocal altruism in such species. Mayr (1963) has discussed some of the factors that may affect dispersal rates.

3. Degree of mutual dependence. Interdependence of members of a species (to avoid predators, for example) will tend to keep individuals near each other and thus increase the chance they will encounter altruistic situations together. If the benefit of the mutual dependence is greatest when only a small number of individuals are together, this will greatly increase the chance that an individual will repeatedly interact with the same small set of individuals. Individuals in primate troops, for example, are mutually dependent for protection from predation, yet the optimal troop size for foraging is often small (Crook, 1969). Because they also meet the other conditions outlined here, primates are almost ideal species in which to search for reciprocal altruism. Cleaning symbioses provide an instance of mutual dependence between members of different species, and this mutual dependence appears to have set the stage for the evolution of several altruistic behaviors discussed below.

4. Parental care. A special instance of mutual dependence is that found between parents and offspring in species that show parental care. The relationship is usually so asymmetrical that few or no situations arise in which an offspring is capable of performing an altruistic act for the parents or even for another offspring, but this is not entirely true for some species (such as primates) in which the period of parental care is unusually long. Parental care, of course, is to be explained by Hamilton's (1964) model, but there is no reason why selection for reciprocal altruism cannot operate between close kin, and evidence is presented below that such selection has operated in humans.

5. Dominance hierarchy. Linear dominance hierarchies consist by definition of asymmetrical relationships; a given individual is dominant over another but not vice versa. Strong dominance hierarchies reduce the extent to which altruistic situations occur in which the less dominant individual is capable of performing a benefit for the more dominant which the more dominant individual could not simply take at will. Baboons *(Papio cynocephalus)* provide an illustration of this. Hall and DeVore (1965) have described the tendency for meat caught by an individual in the troop to end up by preemption in the hands of the most dominant males. This ability to preempt removes any selective advantage that food-sharing might otherwise have as a reciprocal gesture for the most dominant males, and there is no evidence in this species of any food-sharing tendencies. By contrast, Van Lawick-Goodall (1968) has shown that in the less dominance-oriented chimpanzees more dominant individuals often do not preempt food caught by the less dominant individual with "begging gestures," which result in the handing over of small portions of the catch. No strong evidence is available that this is part of a reciprocally altruistic system, but the absence of a strong linear dominance hierarchy has clearly facilitated such a possibility. It is very likely that early hominid groups had a dominance system more similar to that of the modern chimpanzee than to that of the modern baboon (see, for example, Reynolds, 1966).

6. Aid in combat. No matter how dominance-oriented a species is, a dominant individual can usually be aided in aggressive encounters with other individuals by help from a less dominant individual. Hall and DeVore (1965) have described the tendency for baboon alliances to form which fight as a unit in aggressive encounters (and in encounters with predators). Similarly, vervet monkeys in aggressive encounters solicit the aid of other, often less dominant, individuals (Struhsaker, 1967). Aid in combat is then a special case in which relatively symmetrical relations are possible between individuals who differ in dominance.

The above discussion is meant only to suggest the broad conditions that favor the evolution of reciprocal altruism. The most important parameters to specify for individuals of a species are how many altruistic situations occur and how symmetrical they are, and these are the most difficult to specify in advance. Of the three instances of reciprocal altruism discussed in this paper only one, human altruism, would have been predicted from the above broad conditions.

The relationship between two individuals repeatedly exposed to symmetrical reciprocal situations is exactly analogous to what game theorists call the Prisoner's Dilemma (Luce and Raiffa, 1957; Rapoport and Chammah, 1965), a game that can be characterized by the payoff matrix

	A_2	C_2
A_1	R, R	S, T
C_1	T, S	P, P

where $S < P < R < T$ and where A_1 and A_2 represent the altruistic choices possible for the two individuals, and C_1 and C_2, the cheating choices (the first letter in each box gives the payoff for the first individual, the second letter the payoff for the second individual). The other symbols can be given the following meanings: R stands for the reward each individual gets from an altruistic exchange if neither cheats; T stands for the temptation to cheat; S stands for the sucker's payoff that an altruist gets when cheated; and P is the punishment that both individuals get when neither is altruistic (adapted from Rapoport and Chammah, 1965). Iterated games played between the same two individuals mimic real life in that they permit each player to respond to the behavior of the other. Rapoport and Chammah (1965) and others have conducted such experiments using human players, and some of their results are reviewed below in the discussion of human altruism.

W. D. Hamilton (pers. commun.) has shown that the above treatment of reciprocal altruism can be reformulated concisely in terms of game theory as follows. Assuming two altruists are symmetrically exposed to a series of reciprocal situations with identical costs and identical benefits, then after 2n reciprocal situations, each has been "paid" nR. Were one of the two a nonaltruist and the second changed to a nonaltruistic policy after first being cheated, then the initial altruist would be paid $S + (n - 1)P$ (assuming he had the first opportunity to be altruistic) and the non-altruist would receive $T + (n - 1)P$. The important point here is that unless $T \gg R$, then even with small n, nR should exceed $T + (n - 1)P$. If this holds, the nonaltruistic type, when rare, cannot start to spread. But there is also a barrier to the spread of altruism when altruists are rare, for $P > S$ implies $nP > S + (n - 1)P$. As n increases, these two total payoffs tend to equality, so the barrier to the spread of altruism is weak if n is large. The barrier will be overcome if the advantages gained by exchanges between altruists outweigh the initial losses to nonaltruistic types.

Reciprocal altruism can also be viewed as a symbiosis, each partner helping the other while he helps himself. The symbiosis has a time lag, however; one partner helps the other and must then wait a period of time before he is helped in turn. The return benefit may come directly, as in human food-sharing, the partner directly returning the benefit after a time lag. Or the return may come indirectly, as in warning calls in birds (discussed below), where the initial help to other birds (the warning call) sets up a causal chain through the ecological system (the predator fails to learn useful information) which redounds after a time lag to the benefit of the caller. The time lag is the crucial factor, for it means that only under highly specialized circumstances can the altruist be reasonably guaranteed that the causal chain he initiates with his altruistic act will eventually return to him and confer, directly or indirectly, its benefit. Only under these conditions will the cheater be selected against and this type of altruistic behavior evolve.

Although the preconditions for the evolution of reciprocal altruism are specialized, many species probably meet them and display this type of altruism. . . . Human reciprocal altruism is discussed in detail because it represents the best documented case of reciprocal altruism known, because there has apparently been strong selection for a very complex system regulating altruistic behavior, and because the above model permits the functional interpretation of details of the system that otherwise remain obscure. . . .

HUMAN RECIPROCAL ALTRUISM

Reciprocal altruism in the human species takes place in a number of contexts and in all known cultures (see, for example, Gouldner, 1960). Any complete list of human altruism would contain the following types of altruistic behavior:

1. helping in times of danger (e.g. accidents, predation, intraspecific aggression);

2. sharing food;

3. helping the sick, the wounded, or the very young and old;

4. sharing implements; and

5. sharing knowledge.

All these forms of behavior often meet the criterion of small cost to the giver and great benefit to the taker.

During the Pleistocene, and probably before, a hominid species would have met the preconditions for the evolution of reciprocal altruism: long lifespan; low dispersal rate; life in small, mutually dependent, stable, social groups (Lee and DeVore, 1968; Campbell, 1966); and a long period of parental care. It is very likely that dominance relations were of the relaxed, less linear form characteristic of the living chimpanzee (Van Lawick-Goodall, 1968) and not of the more rigidly linear form characteristic of the baboon (Hall and DeVore, 1965). Aid in intraspecific combat, particularly by kin, almost certainly reduced the stability and linearity of the dominance order in early humans. Lee (1969) has shown that in almost all Bushman fights which are initially between two individuals, others have joined in. Mortality, for example, often strikes the secondaries rather than the principals. Tool use has also probably had an equalizing effect on human dominance relations, and the Bushmen have a saying that illustrates this nicely. As a dispute reaches the stage where deadly weapons may be employed, an individual will often declare: "We are none of us big, and others small; we are all men and we can fight; I'm going to get my arrows," (Lee, 1969). It is interesting that Van Lawick-Goodall (1968) has recorded an instance of strong dominance reversal in chimpanzees as a function of tool use. An individual moved from low in dominance to the top of the dominance hierarchy when he discovered the intimidating effects of throwing a metal tin around. It is likely that a diversity of talents is usually present in a band of hunter-gatherers such that the best maker of a certain type of tool is not often the best maker of a different sort or the best user of the tool. This contributes to the symmetry of relationships, since altruistic acts can be traded with reference to the special talents of the individuals involved.

To analyze the details of the human reciprocal-altruistic system, several distinctions are important and are discussed here.

1. *Kin selection.* The human species also met the preconditions for the operation of kin selection. Early hominid hunter-gatherer bands almost certainly (like today's hunter-gatherers) consisted of many close kin, and kin selection must often have operated to favor the evolution of some types of altruistic behavior (Haldane, 1955; Hamilton, 1964, 1969). In general, in attempting to discriminate between the effects of kin selection and what might be called reciprocal-altruistic selection, one can analyze the form of the altruistic behaviors themselves. For example, the existence of discrimination against non-reciprocal individuals cannot be explained on the basis of kin selection, in which the advantage accruing to close kin is what makes the altruistic behavior selectively advantageous, not its chance of being reciprocated. The strongest argument for the operation of reciprocal-altruistic selection in man is the psychological system controlling some forms of human altruism. Details of this system are reviewed below.

2. *Reciprocal altruism among close kin.* If both forms of selection have operated, one would expect, for example, a lowered demand for reciprocity from kin than from non-kin, and there is evidence to support this (e.g., Marshall, 1961; Balikci, 1964). The demand that kin show some reciprocity (e.g., Marshall, 1961; Balikci, 1964) suggests, however, that reciprocal-altruistic selection has acted even on relations between close kin. Although interactions between the two forms of selection have probably been important in human evolution, this paper will limit itself to a preliminary description of the human reciprocally altruistic

system, a system whose attributes are seen to result only from reciprocal-altruistic selection.

3. *Age-dependent changes.* Cost and benefit were defined above without reference to the ages, and hence reproductive values (Fisher, 1958), of the individuals involved in an altruistic exchange. Since the reproductive value of a sexually mature organism declines with age, the benefit to him of a typical altruistic act also decreases, as does the cost to him of a typical act he performs. If the interval separating the two acts in an altruistic exchange is short relative to the lifespans of the individuals, then the error is slight. For longer intervals, in order to be repaid precisely, the initial altruist must receive more in return than he himself gave. It would be interesting to see whether humans in fact routinely expect "interest" to be added to a long overdue altruistic debt, interest commensurate with the intervening decline in reproductive value. In humans reproductive value declines most steeply shortly after sexual maturity is reached (Hamilton, 1966), and one would predict the interest rate on altruistic debts to be highest then. Selection might also favor keeping the interval between act and reciprocation short, but this should also be favored to protect against complete non-reciprocation. W. D. Hamilton (pers. commun.) has suggested that a detailed analysis of age-dependent changes in kin altruism and reciprocal altruism should show interesting differences, but the analysis is complicated by the possibility of reciprocity to the kin of a deceased altruist (see *Multi-party interactions* below).

4. *Gross and subtle cheating.* Two forms of cheating can be distinguished, here denoted as gross and subtle. In *gross cheating* the cheater fails to reciprocate at all, and the altruist suffers the costs of whatever altruism he has dispensed without any compensating benefits. More broadly, gross cheating may be defined as reciprocating so little, if at all, that the altruist receives less benefit from the gross cheater than the cost of the altruist's acts of altruism to the cheater. That is,

$\sum_i c_{ai} > \sum_j b_{aj}$, where c_{ai} is the cost of the ith altruistic act performed

by the altruist and where b_{aj} is the benefit to the altruist of the jth altruistic act performed by the gross cheater; altruistic situations are assumed to have occurred symmetrically. Clearly, selection will strongly favor prompt discrimination against the gross cheater. *Subtle cheating,* by contrast, involves reciprocating, but always attempting to give less than one was given, or more precisely, to give less than the partner would give if the situation were reversed. In this situation, the altruist still benefits from the relationship but not as much as he would if the relationship were completely equitable. The subtle cheater benefits more than he would if the relationship were equitable. In other words,

$$\sum_{i,j} (b_{qi} - c_{qj}) > \sum_{i} (b_{qi} - c_{ai}) > \sum_{i,j} (b_{aj} - c_{ai})$$

where the ith altruistic act performed by the altruist has a cost to him of c_{ai} and a benefit to the subtle cheater of b_{qi} and where the jth altruistic act performed by the subtle cheater has a cost to him of c_{qi} and a benefit to the altruist of b_{aj}. Because human altruism may span huge periods of time, a lifetime even, and because thousands of exchanges may take place, involving many different "goods" and with many different cost/benefit ratios, the problem of computing the relevant totals, detecting imbalances, and deciding whether they are due to chance or to small-scale cheating is an extremely difficult one. Even then, the altruist is in an awkward position, symbolized by the folk saying, "half a loaf is better than none," for if attempts to make the relationship equitable lead to the rupture of the relationship, the altruist, assuming other things to be equal, will suffer the loss of the substandard altruism of the subtle cheater. It is the subtlety of the discrimination necessary to detect this form of cheating and the awkward situation that ensues that permit some subtle cheating to be adaptive. This sets up a dynamic tension in the system that has important repercussions, as discussed below.

5. *Number of reciprocal relationships.* It has so far been assumed that it is to the advantage of each individual to form the maximum number of reciprocal relationships and that the individual suffers a decrease in fitness upon the rupture of any relationship in which the cost to him of acts dispensed to the partner is less than the benefit of acts dispensed toward him by the partner. But it is possible that relationships are partly exclusive, in the sense that expanding the number of reciprocal exchanges with one of the partners may necessarily decrease the number of exchanges with another. For example, if a group of organisms were to split into subgroups for much of the day (such as breaking up into hunting pairs), then altruistic exchanges will be more likely between members of each subgroup than between members of

different subgroups. In that sense, relationships may be partly exclusive, membership in a given subgroup necessarily decreasing exchanges with others in the group. The importance of this factor is that it adds further complexity to the problem of dealing with the cheater and it increases competition within a group to be members of a favorable subgroup. An individual in a subgroup who feels that another member is subtly cheating on their relationship has the option of attempting to restore the relationship to a completely reciprocal one or of attempting to join another subgroup, thereby decreasing to a minimum the possible exchanges between himself and the subtle cheater and replacing these with exchanges between a new partner or partners. In short, he can switch friends. There is evidence in hunter-gatherers that much movement of individuals from one band to another occurs in response to such social factors as have just been outlined (Lee and DeVore, 1968).

6. *Indirect benefits or reciprocal altruism?* Given mutual dependence in a group it is possible to argue that the benefits (non-altruistic) of this mutual dependence are a positive function of group size and that altruistic behaviors may be selected for because they permit additional individuals to survive and thereby confer additional indirect (non-altruistic) benefits. Such an argument can only be advanced seriously for slowly reproducing species with little dispersal. Saving an individual's life in a hunter-gatherer group, for example, may permit non-altruistic actions such as cooperative hunting to continue with more individuals. But if there is an optimum group size, one would expect adaptations to stay near that size, with individuals joining groups when the groups are below this size, and groups splitting up when they are above this size. One would only be selected to keep an individual alive when the group is below optimum and not when the group is above optimum. Although an abundant literature on hunter-gatherers (and also nonhuman primates) suggests that adaptations exist to regulate group size near an optimum, there is no evidence that altruistic gestures are curtailed when groups are above the optimum in size. Instead, the benefits of human altruism are to be seen as coming directly from reciprocity—not indirectly through non-altruistic group benefits. This distinction is important because social scientists and philosophers have tended to deal with human altruism in terms of the benefits of living in a group, without differentiating between non-altruistic benefits and reciprocal benefits (e.g., Rousseau, 1954; Baier, 1958). . . .

REFERENCES

Baier, K. (1958). *The Moral Point of View* (Ithaca, N.Y.: Cornell University Press).

Balikci, A. (1961). "Development of Basic Socio-Economic Units in Two Eskimo Communities." *National Museum of Canada Bulletin No. 202, Ottawa.*

Drury, W. H., and Smith, W. J. (1968). "Defense of Feeding Areas by Adult Herring Gulls and Intrusion by Young." *Evolution* 22, pp. 193–201.

Fisher, R. A. (1958). *The Genetical Theory of Natural Selection* (New York: Dover).

Gouldner, A. (1960). "The Norm of Reciprocity: A Preliminary Statement." *American Sociological Review* 47, pp. 73–80.

Haldane, J. B. S. (1955). "Population Genetics." *New Biology* 18, pp. 34–51.

Hall, K. R. L., and DeVore, I. (1965). In I. DeVore, ed., *Primate Behavior: Field Studies of Monkeys and Apes* (New York: Holt, Rinehart & Winston), pp. 53–110.

Hamilton, W. D. (1964). "The Genetical Evolution of Social Behavior." *Journal of Theoretical Biology* 7, pp. 1–52.

———. (1966). "The Moulding of Senescence by Natural Selection." *Journal of Theoretical Biology* 12, pp. 12–45.

———. (1969). "Selection of Selfish and Altruistic Behavior in Some Extreme Models." Paper presented at "Man and Beast Symposium" (New York: Smithsonian Institution Press).

Lee, R., and DeVore, I. (1968). *Man the Hunter* (Chicago: Aldine).

Luce, R. D. and Raiffa, H. (1957). *Games and Decisions* (New York: Wiley).

Marshall, L. K. (1961). "Sharing, Talking and Giving: Relief of Social Tension Among !Kung Bushmen." *Africa* 31, pp. 231–49.

Mayr, E. (1963). *Animal Species and Evolution* (Cambridge: Belknap Press).

Rapoport, A., and Chammah, A. (1965). *Prisoner's Dilemma* (Ann Arbor: University of Michigan Press).

Reynolds, L. (1966). "Open Groups in Hominid Evolution." *Man* 1, pp. 111–52.

Rousseau, J. J. (1954). *The Social Contract* (Chicago: Regnery).

Struhsaker, T. (1967). "Social Structure Among Vervet Monkeys *(Cercopithecus aethiops)."* *Behavior* 29, pp. 83–121.

Van Lawick-Goodall, J. (1968). "A Preliminary Report on Expressive Movements and Communication in the Gombe Stream Chimpanzees." In P. Jay, ed., *Primates* (New York: Holt, Rinehart & Winston) pp. 313–74.

Man: From Sociobiology to Sociology

Edward O. Wilson

Let us now consider man in the free spirit of natural history, as though we were zoologists from another planet completing a catalog of social species on Earth. In this macroscopic view the humanities and social sciences shrink to specialized branches of biology; history, biography, and fiction are the research protocols of human ethology; and anthropology and sociology together constitute the sociobiology of a single primate species.

Homo sapiens is ecologically a very peculiar species. It occupies the widest geographical range and maintains the highest local densities of any of the primates. An astute ecologist from another planet would not be surprised to find that only one species of *Homo* exists. Modern man has preempted all the conceivable hominid niches. Two or more species of hominids did coexist in the past, when the *Australopithecus* man-apes and possibly an early *Homo* lived in Africa. But only one evolving line survived into late Pleistocene times to participate in the emergence of the most advanced human social traits.

Modern man is anatomically unique. His erect posture and wholly bipedal locomotion are not even approached in other primates that occasionally walk on their hind legs, including the gorilla and chimpanzee. The skeleton has been profoundly modified to accommodate the change: the spine is curved to distribute the weight of the trunk more

---

evenly down its length; the chest is flattened to move the center of gravity back toward the spine; the pelvis is broadened to serve as an attachment for the powerful striding muscles of the upper legs and reshaped into a basin to hold the viscera; the tail is eliminated, its vertebrae (now called the coccyx) curved inward to form part of the floor of the pelvic basin; the occipital condyles have rotated far beneath the skull so that the weight of the head is balanced on them; the face is shortened to assist this shift in gravity; the thumb is enlarged to give power to the hand; the leg is lengthened; and the foot is drastically narrowed and lengthened to facilitate striding. Other changes have taken place. Hair has been lost from most of the body. It is still not known why modern man is a "naked ape." One plausible explanation is that nakedness served as a device to cool the body during the strenuous pursuit of prey in the heat of the African plains. It is associated with man's exceptional reliance on sweating to reduce body heat; the human body contains from two to five million sweat glands, far more than in any other primate species.

The reproductive physiology and behavior of *Homo sapiens* have also undergone extraordinary evolution. In particular, the estrous cycle of the female has changed in two ways that affect sexual and social behavior. Menstruation has been intensified. The females of some other primate species experience slight bleeding, but only in women is there a heavy sloughing of the wall of the "disappointed womb" with consequent heavy bleeding. The estrus, or period of female "heat," has been replaced by virtually continuous sexual activity. Copulation is initiated not by response to the conventional primate signals of estrus, such as changes in color of the skin around the female sexual organs and the release of pheromones, but by extended foreplay entailing mutual stimulation by the partners. The traits of physical attraction are, moreover, fixed in nature. They include the pubic hair of both sexes and the protuberant breasts and buttocks of women. The flattened sexual cycle and continuous female attractiveness cement the close marriage bonds that are basic to human social life.

At a distance a perceptive Martian zoologist would regard the globular head as a most significant clue to human biology. The cerebrum of *Homo* was expanded enormously during a relatively short span of evolutionary time (see figure). Three million years ago *Australopithecus* had an adult cranial capacity of 400–500 cubic centimeters, comparable to that of the chimpanzee and gorilla. Two million years later its presumptive descendant *Homo erectus* had a capacity of about 1000 cubic centimeters. The next million years saw an increase to 1400–1700 cubic centimeters in Neanderthal man and 900–2000 cubic centimeters in modern *Homo sapiens.* The growth in intelligence that accompanied this enlargement was so great that it cannot yet be measured in any meaningful way. Human beings can be compared among themselves in terms of a few of the basic components of intelligence and creativity. But no scale has been invented that can objectively compare man with chimpanzees and other living primates.

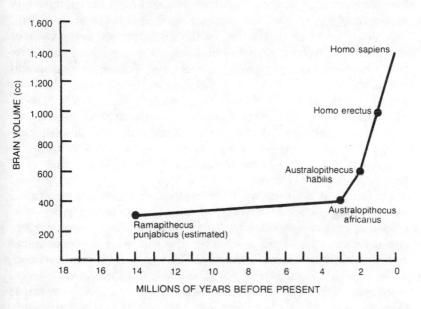

The Increase in Brain Size During Human Evolution. (Redrawn from Pilbeam, 1972.)

We have leaped forward in mental evolution in a way that continues to defy self-analysis. The mental hypertrophy has distorted even the most basic primate social qualities into nearly unrecognizable forms. Individual species of Old World monkeys and apes have notably plastic social organizations; man has extended the trend into a protean ethnicity. Monkeys and apes utilize behavioral scaling to adjust aggressive and sexual interactions; in man the scales have become multidimensional, culturally adjustable, and almost endlessly subtle. Bonding and the practices of reciprocal altruism are rudimentary in other primates; man has expanded them into great networks where individuals consciously alter roles from hour to hour as if changing masks.

It is the task of comparative sociobiology to trace these and other human qualities as closely as possible back through time. Besides adding perspective and perhaps offering some sense of philosophical ease, the exercise will help to identify the behaviors and rules by which individual human beings increase their Darwinian fitness though the manipulation of society. In a phrase, we are searching for the human biogram (Count, 1958; Tiger and Fox, 1971). One of the key questions, never far from the thinking of anthropologists and biologists who pursue real theory, is to what extent the biogram represents an adaptation to modern cultural life and to what extent it is a phylogenetic vestige. Our civilizations were jerrybuilt around the biogram. How have they been influenced by it? Conversely, how much flexibility is there in the biogram, and in which parameters particularly? Experience with other animals indicates that when organs are hypertrophied, phylogeny is hard to reconstruct. This is the crux of the problem of the evolutionary analysis of human behavior. . . .

The first and most easily verifiable diagnostic trait is statistical in nature. The parameters of social organization, including group size, properties of hierarchies, and rates of gene exchange, vary far more among human populations than among those of any other primate species. The variation exceeds even that occurring between the remaining primate species. Some increase in plasticity is to be expected. It represents the extrapolation of a trend toward variability already apparent in the baboons, chimpanzees, and other cercopithecoids. What is truly surprising, however, is the extreme to which it has been carried.

Why are human societies this flexible? Part of the reason is that the members themselves vary so much in behavior and achievement. Even in the simplest societies individuals differ greatly. Within a small tribe of !Kung Bushmen can be found individuals who are acknowledged as the "best people"—the leaders and outstanding specialists among the hunters and healers. Even with an emphasis on sharing goods, some are exceptionally able entrepreneurs and unostentatiously acquire a certain amount of wealth. !Kung men, no less than men in advanced industrial societies, generally establish themselves by their mid-thirties or else accept a lesser status for life. There are some who never try to make it, live in run-down huts, and show little pride in themselves or their work (Pfeiffer, 1969). The ability to slip into such roles, shaping one's personality to fit, may itself be adaptive. Human societies are organized by high intelligence, and each member is faced by a mixture of social challenges that taxes all of his ingenuity. This baseline variation is amplified at the group level by other qualities exceptionally pronounced in human societies: the long, close period of socialization; the loose connectedness of the communication networks; the multiplicity of bonds; the capacity, especially within literate cultures, to communicate over long distances and periods of history; and from all these traits, the capacity to dissemble, to manipulate, and to exploit. Each parameter can be altered easily, and each has a marked effect on the final social structure. The result could be the observed variation among societies.

The hypothesis to consider, then, is that genes promoting flexibility in social behavior are strongly selected at the individual level. But note that variation in social organization is only a possible, not a necessary consequence of this process. In order to generate the amount of variation actually observed to occur, it is necessary for there to be multiple adaptive peaks. In other words, different forms of society within the same species must be nearly enough alike in survival ability for many to enjoy long tenure. The result would be a statistical ensemble of kinds of societies which, if not equilibrial, is at least not shifting rapidly toward one particular mode or another. The alternative, found in some social insects, is flexibility in individual behavior and caste development, which nevertheless results in an approach toward uniformity in the statistical distribution of the kinds of individuals when all individuals within a colony are taken together. In honeybees and in ants of the genera *Formica* and *Pogonomyrmex*, "personality" differences are strongly marked even within single castes. Some individuals, referred to by entomologists as the elites, are unusually active, perform more than their share of lifetime work, and incite others to work through facilitation. Other colony members are consistently sluggish. Although they are seemingly healthy and live long lives, their per-individual output is only a small fraction of that of the elites. Specialization also occurs.

Certain individuals remain with the brood as nurses far longer than the average, while others concentrate on nest building or foraging. Yet somehow the total pattern of behavior in the colony converges on the species average. When one colony with its hundreds or thousands of members is compared with another of the same species, the statistical patterns of activity are about the same. We know that some of this consistency is due to negative feedback. As one requirement such as brood care or nest repair intensifies, workers shift their activities to compensate until the need is met, then change back again. Experiments have shown that disruption of the feedback loops, and thence deviation by the colony from the statistical norms, can be disastrous. It is therefore not surprising to find that the loops are both precise and powerful (Wilson, 1971a).

The controls governing human societies are not nearly so strong, and the effects of deviation are not so dangerous. The anthropological literature abounds with examples of societies that contain obvious inefficiencies and even pathological flaws—yet endure. The slave society of Jamaica, compellingly described by Orlando Patterson (1967), was unquestionably pathological by the moral canons of civilized life. "What marks it out is the astonishing neglect and distortion of almost every one of the basic prerequisites of normal human living. This was a society in which clergymen were the 'most finished debauchees' in the land; in which the institution of marriage was officially condemned among both masters and slaves; in which the family was unthinkable to the vast majority of the population and promiscuity the norm; in which education was seen as an absolute waste of time and teachers shunned like the plague; in which the legal system was quite deliberately a travesty of anything that could be called justice; and in which all forms of refinements, of art, of folkways, were either absent or in a state of total disintegration. Only a small proportion of whites, who monopolized almost all of the fertile land in the island, benefited from the system. And these, no sooner had they secured their fortunes, abandoned the land which the production of their own wealth had made unbearable to live in, for the comforts of the mother country." Yet this Hobbesian world lasted for nearly two centuries. The people multiplied while the economy flourished.

The Ik of Uganda are an equally instructive case (Turnbull, 1972). They are former hunters who have made a disastrous shift to cultivation.

Always on the brink of starvation, they have seen their culture reduced to a vestige. Their only stated value is *ngag,* or food; their basic notion of goodness *(marangik)* is the individual possession of food in the stomach; and their definition of a good man is *yakw ana marang,* "a man who has a full belly." Villages are still built, but the nuclear family has ceased to function as an institution. Children are kept with reluctance and from about three years of age are made to find their own way of life. Marriage ordinarily occurs only when there is a specific need for cooperation. Because of the lack of energy, sexual activity is minimal and its pleasures are considered to be about on the same level as those of defecation. Death is treated with relief or amusement, since it means more *ngag* for survivors. Because the unfortunate Ik are at the lowest sustainable level, there is a temptation to conclude that they are doomed. Yet somehow their society has remained intact and more or less stable for at least 30 years, and it could endure indefinitely.

How can such variation in social structure persist? The explanation may be lack of competition from other species, resulting in what biologists call ecological release. During the past ten thousand years or longer, man as a whole has been so successful in dominating his environment that almost any kind of culture can succeed for a while, so long as it has a modest degree of internal consistency and does not shut off reproduction altogether. No species of ant or termite enjoys this freedom. The slightest inefficiency in constructing nests, in establishing odor trails, or in conducting nuptial flights could result in the quick extinction of the species by predation and competition from other social insects. To a scarcely lesser extent the same is true for social carnivores and primates. In short, animal species tend to be tightly packed in the ecosystem with little room for experimentation or play. Man has temporarily escaped the constraint of interspecific competition. Although cultures replace one another, the process is much less effective than interspecific competition in reducing variance.

It is part of the conventional wisdom that virtually all cultural variation is phenotypic rather than genetic in origin. This view has gained support from the ease with which certain aspects of culture can be altered in the space of a single generation, too quickly to be evolutionary in nature. The drastic alteration in Irish society in the first two years of the potato blight (1846–1848) is a case in point. Another is the shift in the Japanese authority structure during the American occupation following World War II. Such examples can be multiplied endlessly—they are the substance of history. It is also true that human populations are not very different from one another genetically. When Lewontin (1972) analyzed existing data on nine blood-type systems, he found that 85 percent of the variance was composed of diversity within populations and only 15 percent was due to diversity between populations. There is no a priori reason for supposing that this sample of genes possesses a distribution much different from those of other, less accessible systems affecting behavior.

The extreme orthodox view of environmentalism goes further, holding that in effect there is no genetic variance in the transmission of culture. In other words, the capacity for culture is transmitted by a single human genotype. Dobzhansky (1963) stated this hypothesis as follows: "Culture is not inherited through genes, it is acquired by learning from other human beings . . . In a sense, human genes have surrendered their primacy in human evolution to an entirely new, nonbiological or superorganic agent, culture. However, it should not be forgotten that this agent is entirely dependent on the human genotype." Although the genes have given away most of their sovereignty, they maintain a certain amount of influence in at least the behavioral qualities that underlie variations between cultures. Moderately high heritability has been documented in introversion-extroversion measures, personal tempo, psychomotor and sports activities, neuroticism, dominance, depression, and the tendency toward certain forms of mental illness such as schizophrenia (Parsons, 1967; Lerner, 1968). Even a small portion of this variance invested in population differences might predispose societies toward cultural differences. At the very least, we should try to measure this amount. It is not valid to point to the absence of a behavioral trait in one or a few societies as conclusive evidence that the trait is environmentally induced and has no genetic disposition in man. The very opposite could be true.

REFERENCES

Count, E. W. (1958). "The Biological Basis of Human Sociality." *American Anthropologist* 60, no. 6, pp. 1049–85.

Tiger, L., and Fox, R. (1971). *The Imperial Animal* (New York: Holt, Rinehart and Winston).

Wilson, E. O. (1971). *The Insect Societies* (Cambridge: Harvard University Press).

Patterson, O. (1967). *The Sociology of Slavery* (Cranbury, N.J.: Fairleigh Dickinson University Press).

Turnbull, C. M. (1972). *The Mountain People* (New York: Simon and Schuster).

Lewontin, R. C. (1972). "The Apportionment of Human Diversity." *Evolutionary Biology* 6, pp. 381–98.

Dobzhansky, T. (1963). "Anthropology and the Natural Sciences—The Problem of Human Evolution." *Current Anthropology* 4, no. 138, pp. 146–48.

Parsons, P. A. (1967). *The Genetic Analysis of Behavior* (London: Methuen).

Lerner, I. M. (1968). *Heredity, Evolution, and Society* (San Francisco: W. H. Freeman).

PART V

The Contemporary Debate

The Evolution of Sociality

Donald Stone Sade

The reductionistic triumphs of molecular biology having been thoroughly established, many of the great remaining challenges in biology lie in the evolution of the higher levels of organization, especially the social systems that integrate animal populations. The "new synthesis" of ecology, population genetics, and animal behavior brings an integrated theoretical system to confront this remaining biological frontier. At the conclusion of *The Insect Societies*, a synthesis of the population biology, physiology, and social behavior of the world's dominant terrestrial fauna, [E. O.] Wilson asks whether the same quantitative evolutionary theory he successfully used to interpret the social organization of insects could also be applied to societies within other phyla, and especially to those of vertebrates, leading to a unified theory of sociobiology. [*Sociobiology: The New Synthesis*] is his attempt to answer the question by a comprehensive review and synthesis of the literature on social organization, ecology, and evolutionary genetics of all animal groups, from the myxobacteria to humans, whose members show forms of social behavior beyond mating. Occasional examples from the sociology of plant communities are given to illustrate a principle of wide applicability.

No book so ambitious has appeared since Wynne-Edwards's *Animal Dispersion in Relation to Social Behaviour* stirred a tempest of fruitful controversy over the role of group selection in the evolution of animal societies as mechanisms to limit population densities to optimal levels

From *Science* 190 (October 17, 1975): pp. 261–263. Copyright © 1975 by the American Association for the Advancement of Science. Reprinted by permission of the publisher and the author.

through conventional competition. Wilson differs from Wynne-Edwards in crucial matters of logic, selection and interpretation of facts, and style, not to mention access to the abundant new information obtained by the legions of fieldworkers, experimenters, and theoreticians who have swarmed about the subject during the dozen years since *Animal Dispersion* appeared. Both, however, seek the functional similarities or analogs between societies within diverse phyletic groups in order to reveal evolutionary rules of universal application. This approach is in contrast with, but not in contradiction to, a phylogenetical analysis of the features of a group of closely related animals, in which homologous traits and systems are identified and their transformations during evolution studied to reveal the constraints and potentialities inherent in the evolutionary choices made in the ancestry of a given lineage. (The studies of the anthropologist Earl Count on the vertebrate origins of human sociality—see his *Being and Becoming Human: Essays on the Biogram*, 1973—are the most recent major synthesis of the latter sort.) Wilson takes note of the role of phylogenetic constraints in evolution, particularly when contrasting the social insects and vertebrates, but his analysis is primarily functional rather than historical.

A page or two of review cannot begin to summarize even all the major points of this enormous, tightly written, beautifully detailed, abundantly illustrated, and carefully documented book. Not the least of its merits are the enticing tangential leads, such as the discussion of "tradition drift," that adumbrate theories and one hopes books to come. I will try to touch on the points that provide continuity to the book.

The first part of the book is an analysis of modern post-Darwinian evolutionary theory as it relates to social evolution. The attempt to define the boundaries of a group or society, and of the individual, leads immediately to the theory of the genetical structure of animal populations. On the one hand societal boundaries create more or less impermeable genetic barriers, and on the other hand a degree of genetic isolation and inbreeding heightens coefficients of relationship, enhancing the evolution of altruistic behavior through kin selection. The concept of "inclusive fitness," developed especially by W. D. Hamilton, is perhaps the central concept in the book. It states that an individual's genetic fitness is to be measured not only by the survival and reproduction of himself and his offspring but by the enhancement of the fitness of other relatives who share his genes. This allows the evolution of cooperative acts that may be detrimental to the individual's own survival or reproduction and are therefore by definition altruistic. The local population, being, in contrast to casual aggregations, relatively stable in time and relatively closed to immigration, constitutes a "demographic society" in which birth and death rates play an important part in determining group structure. Events of evolutionary importance act to modify these parameters.

In relatively stable environments density-dependent controls, often operating through social mechanisms, result in stabilization of population size at an optimal species-specific equilibrium. Under these conditions rapid reproduction, more characteristic of species adapted to swiftly colonize transitory habitats, is less important than competitive ability in obtaining the more stable resources. These conditions favor the evolution of cooperative behaviors for antipredator defense, increased feeding efficiency, increased survival of offspring, improved population stability, and modifications of the environment.

The demographic profile of the genetically homogenous insect colony is said to be a directly adaptive feature, achieving an energetic (ergonomic) optimal proportion of individuals in each caste through group selection between colonies. Wilson suggests that among vertebrates the demographic profile is a secondary effect of the equilibration of contradictory forces: the inclusive fitness of altruistic acts balanced against the individual advantages of selfish behavior, and the advantage of increased parental investment competing with the advantages of producing more offspring.

The Euler-Lotka formula for the intrinsic rate of natural increase, "little r," is central to the mathematical treatment of these theoretical matters because it summarizes the combined effects of survivorship and natality for the group in competition with other populations, or for some genetical partition of the population compared with other competing genotypes. The use of "little r," calculated from the $l_x m_x$ schedules of a life table, has important implications for the conduct of research, because the action of social mechanisms must be translated into effects on the life-table schedules before their evolutionary results can become manifest. By and large this has not been done, except in modeling hypothetical cases, because most research on social behavior has been too short-term, lacking in sufficient time depth to produce the necessary information.

The first part of the book concludes with an analysis of the controversial concept of group selection. After a careful review of recent genetical and mathematical models, and some zoogeographical and genetical evidence, not confined to the celebrated *t* mutant of wild house mice, Wilson concludes that although interdemic selection cannot be ruled out as never occurring, it is likely to be generally unimportant because of the high rate of extinction of populations required to counteract the forces of individual selection. Kin selection, the favoring of the genes of a group of closely related, cooperating individuals in competition with other groups, through the increased inclusive fitness of the genes favoring altruistic acts, is considered of major importance. Since the favored groups include more than parents and direct descendants, Wilson considers that kin selection is a form of group selection at the opposite extreme from interdemic selection.

The second and longest part of the book reviews the social mechanisms that have evolved as mediators between the ecological pressures to which the population must adapt and the demographic parameters that measure the success of the adjustment. The topics range from the allocation of time and energy to different activities that different species find profitable to a comparison of social symbiosis and parasitism among social insects and birds. Three chapters are devoted to communication, including its mathematical treatment by methods of information theory. These chapters are perhaps the clearest reviews of animal communication in the literature. The theory of causal networks operating in the evolution of social mechanisms is best developed in the chapter on parental care, because that topic has been so completely studied among numerous groups of social animals. Robert Trivers's models of parental investment play a prominent role in the arguments. They represent the effects of extending or shortening the duration of parental care on the differences between cost and benefit in terms of genetic fitness, and indicate that the competing interests of parent and offspring will produce a compromise optimal duration. The most detailed mathematical treatment of social mechanisms is in the discussion of the optimization of the proportion of social insects within each caste. Although the models gain suppport from the confirmation of some of their predictions, such as that the most specialized and numerous castes are found in the stable tropical environments, it is disappointing to learn that the models have not been applied to actual natural populations. Will the study of statuses and roles within vertebrate societies lead to a comparable ergonomics of the division of labor? This is one of the many questions raised in the advanced theory of sociality among insects that await detailed investigation among vertebrates.

In general, social mechanisms are discussed within the framework of the theory outlined in the first part of the book, but without detailed quantitative correspondence between theory and example. The models can be considered to be working hypotheses rather than confirmations of the theory.

The third and last major part of the book is a selective review of social behavior within the major groups of animals that include highly social species. Four groups receive special attention, having achieved degrees of sociality exceeding all others. The colonial invertebrates provide examples of the most perfect societies, in Wilson's view, because the genetic identity of members of the colony allows an extreme degree of altruism. Individual freedom can therefore be completely subordinated to the advantages of the colony, and the physiological plasticity of the individuals allows a degree of specialization one thinks of as more typical of the cells of more familiar animals. In insect colonies social imperfection arises from the independence of the individuals and the occasional competition between workers and queen to produce male offspring, counteracting the high degree of morphological differentiation and specialized division of labor between the castes and the elaborate altruistic behaviors that maintain the colony. The vertebrates have gone in another direction, emphasizing individual recognition, status based upon competition, and individual adaptability. Their societies consist of selfish subgroups of closely related kin, competing with other kin groups at the expense of the integrity of the society as a whole. These trends are carried the furthest among the mammals, which receive the bulk of Wilson's attention. He suggests that man has retained and accentuated these vertebrate characteristics but that greater intelligence has allowed a high degree of cooperative activity with little loss of individual fitness, resulting in man's unique position among the social species. The species accounts are supplemented with very valuable tables summarizing the taxonomy, sociobiology, and bibliography of each group.

Because very few studies on the social life of animals have provided the direct coordination of information on demography, social organization, and genetics necessary for a strict application of the sociobiological theory, the species accounts must stay close to the original reports, which represent theoretical diversity rather than synthesis. However, Wilson is at pains to evaluate and restate their findings as working hypotheses that could lead to a genuine testing of the theory.

More than a hundred pages of glossary, bibliography, and index follow the text, indicating the comprehensive coverage of the book.

The remainder of the review could be devoted to expressions of amazement at the mastery of diverse topics Wilson displays, the clarity of expression, the occasional ironies and twinkles of humor mostly restrained by objectivity, and the perfection of the panoramic drawings by Sarah Landry illustrating the major features of social organization of several species. Conversely, the peevish reviewer might point to the occasional printer's error that by changing a key word alters the author's meaning, or the inevitable although infrequent and unimportant error in fact, such as that the direction of grooming among macaques is a reliable indicator of dominance, that adult male baboons are organized as coalitions rather than in linear dominance hierarchies, or the illustration showing lemurs grooming with the tongue rather than the tooth comb.

More important, however, is to point out that this book is an excellent introduction to the broader field of evolutionary biology. If the problems raised in regard to the evolution of sociality could be solved, then any problem in evolutionary biology could be solved, because the social aspects of populations are the phenotypic characteristics furthest removed from the genotype and therefore the most difficult to account for in terms of current theory. This is a timely book because of the objective analysis it provides of ideas that are gaining popularity, particularly the concepts of inclusive fitness and kin selection. In the conference chambers of scientific meetings I have seen these ideas, like the sweet smoke of a forbidden weed, create a sense of euphoria among their advocates, who seem on the verge of some hidden truth, obscure until the inhalation of these heady notions. Wilson, by contrast, appears to intend his book to be a challenge.

The major value of the book will go beyond the specific models and observations it contains in such abundance and be found in the consistent display of scientific reasoning that insists that theory in all its aspects must be subjected to testing and potential falsification. The advocacy method of reasoning common in the writings of social scientists and popular writers dealing with animal behavior, and especially with notions of human origins, receives deserved flagellation in several barbed passages. But Wilson recognizes that the most insidious weakness of sociobiological theory is the ease with which particular models can gain advocates, for actual testing of these models requires studies of a duration and intensity beyond the current traditions of fieldwork. To conduct sociobiological research on the long-lived, slow-breeding mammals, including the primates, will require revision of the goals of fieldwork and a reallocation of resources for genuine long-term research, even if at the expense of the currently popular 18-month field excursion. As an example, if the Euler-Lotka formula is actually to be applied to data, life tables must be provided, yet in spite of the large investment in research on primate societies there are essentially no life tables available for any primate species other than man.

Wilson acknowledges that sociobiological theory at present is dependent upon the current genetical models of competition between alleles at single loci and that these models may be revised and supplemented as work on polygenes, linkage disequilibria, and epistatic interactions proceeds. Classical selection theory is also currently confronted with evidence and increasingly accepted models emphasizing the role of random processes both in microevolution, as in the maintenance of high levels of genetic polymorphism, and in the broad patterns of emergence and extinction of phyletic groups on a geological time scale. Particularly among the vertebrates, individual adaptability and the flexibility of social systems suggest a degree of indeterminance between the gene and the environmental adaptation that is not fully accounted for in the simplistic single-locus models. Sociobiological studies may lead us into a period of profitable confusion and theoretical indigestion, and finally to a new level of understanding both in sociobiology and in evolutionary theory.

The greatest effort in empirical research should probably be directed to validating the postulated connections between the operation of social mechanisms and the values of the life-table parameters. The arguments about whether individual selection, kin selection, or higher levels of group selection are operating may really turn on how it is most convenient to classify the actual processes after the fact. Can they be distinguished in actual events in real populations? The problem becomes more difficult because random processes such as genetic drift also become important in the small, inbred groups in which kin selection is assumed to operate most effectively.

The quantitative theory of sociobiology has been most successfully applied to the social insects, and the societies of vertebrates remain incompletely explained. The trend in vertebrate evolution toward greater individuality, culminating in the mammals and particularly in man, seems difficult to reconcile with the fact that the most elaborate vertebrate societies are also found within this group. There is no reason to think that all the classes of models have yet been devised, or that all the ways of classifying the processes that result in natural selection have yet been exhausted. It is not proved that the ultimate analogy to the evolution of complex systems is found in the current models based upon capitalistic economic theory, where profits and losses in units of the hypothetical currency of genetic fitness are computed for each compromise in the life history of individuals.

To be complete, sociobiological theory must account for the emergence of man and absorb both anthropology and sociology, providing these disciplines with a truly scientific basis for their practice. The greatest and perhaps final challenge to sociobiology will come when it invades the province of the humanities and attempts to incorporate them, as it must or be proved false, into the strictly materialistic theory of evolutionary biology. In the humanities we see the trend in vertebrate evolution toward individuality carried to its extreme, and artistic expression, being channeled into unique cultural patterns and idiosyncratically enriched, surely is the aspect of the phenotype furthest removed from the determinism of the gene. The highly elaborate, multimodal communication systems among vertebrates may have evolved as devices of social integration in which large amounts of energy are invested to counteract the socially disintegrating trend toward individualization. Here again the humanities may present us with the maximum elaboration of a vertebrate trend. It may be that in order to achieve its final success sociobiology will have to turn somewhat away from the functional models of very general applicability emphasized in the current theory to examine the unique phylogenetic constraints and potentials operating within the specific phyletic line leading to man.

The Biology of Behavior

Robert S. Morison

It is highly probable that the only person qualified to review [Edward O. Wilson's *Sociobiology*] is the author himself. Who else could speak with such familiarity, self-assurance, and apparent authority about a series of topics that range without significant break from the structure of DNA to the current status of behavioral psychology and the sociological traditions of Durkheim, Weber, and Parsons? Certainly this reviewer cannot. I will therefore simply attempt to summarize the book's principal parts and make some surmises about what its immediate reception and possible place in history may be.

In the first place, and most obviously and certainly, the book does us all an enormous service in bringing together (in one oddly shaped volume) most of the important things we think we know about the basic biology of animal behavior. Like other scientific knowledge, sociobiology has been growing at an exponential rate, but it started more recently and the exponent seems even larger than usual. As a result, recent increments, especially in knowledge of primate behavior, leave the breathless observer with the impression that things are happening in quantal jumps. It is indeed somewhat rare for a treatise, which purports to cover the century or so since the *Descent of Man*, to have such a high proportion of references to papers published in the last five years. The bibliography covers sixty-four double column, 10- by 10-inch pages; and it is a rare page that does not include one or more citations of papers published in 1973 or even 1974. Besides the obvious testimony to the industry and determination of the author, this says a lot about the dedication and efficiency of the publisher—to say nothing of his tolerance for last minute changes in proof. And while on the subject, the printing, the proofreading, and the reproduction of the many drawings, photographs, and diagrams are all excellent. Whatever else it may or may not be, this 697-page work is a *tour de force* of collecting, winnowing, interpreting, speculating, and publishing.

The first five chapters outline the basic principles of genetics and population biology. Although these include much of what would be found in any competent treatment of the same topics of comparable length (130 pages), we are immediately aware that something new is going on here. Far from being "sickled o'er with the pale cast of thought" about separating fact from value, Wilson entitles his first chapter "The Morality of the Gene" and takes his first sentence from Camus, "The only serious philosophical question is suicide" (with which, incidentally, he does not agree). The survey ends with a longish chapter on "Group Selection and Altruism," which must contain just about all the available evidence for a biological explanation of virtue. It probably should be pointed out, however, that a nonbiologist could read the entire chapter without being warned that some crusty old theoreticians have never been able to agree that natural selection works on anything but individuals.

Part II gives us twelve chapters on "Social Mechanisms," beginning with "Group Size, Reproduction, and Time-Energy Budgets" and ending with a review of "Social Symbioses." All these strike the nonexpert reviewer as up to date, sophisticated, and wherever possible, admirably quantitative. The three chapters on communication seemed particularly fine for the way they brought the theoretical considerations set forth by Shannon, Chomsky, Hockett, and others into critical interrelation with visual, aural, and odoriferous displays of animals trying to share their hopes, fears, and excitements with their fellows.

Although, as hinted at above, Wilson clearly has his own biases and expectations, his explication of social mechanisms is broadly conceived and executed. As such it amply sets the stage for Part III, which details in some 200 pages the various behavioral adaptations of "The Social Species" from colonial microorganisms to man. The author has devoted most of his career to the Harvard imperative enunciated by William

Morton Wheeler (with biblical assistance) to "go to the ant . . . consider her ways, and be wise." But he does not burden us here with his erudition regarding invertebrates. The selections from his store of field observations and library studies are always apt, crisp and to the point, and no more voluminous than his citations from the rapidly growing literature on dolphins, elephants, wildebeests, and baboons, which he must know largely at second hand.

So there it is; as a carefully selected and synthesized compendium of what we know about the social behavior of animals, it stands alone—almost certainly a landmark, quite possibly a monumental one. But what about the other part that attracted our attention on the very first page—the intention to lay the groundwork for the study of human society in all its richness of fact and value? Perhaps this part of his purpose is stated most clearly where, after describing the "Modern Synthesis" of taxonomy and ecology with neo-Darwinist theory, he continues, "It may not be too much to say that sociology and the other social sciences, as well as the humanities are the last branches of biology waiting to be included in the Modern Synthesis." Maybe so, but one wonders if this is the best way of luring disciples of these historic schools to read the book ushering in the new synthesis. Any pool player appreciates the "unwisdom" of calling one's shots in advance; so what are we to do with the flat statement that ethology and comparative psychology are both destined to be cannibalized by neurophysiology and sensory physiology from one end and sociobiology and behavioral ecology from the other?

As a onetime neurophysiologist, your present reviewer may look forward to meeting his new friends, the sociobiologists, across this not entirely festive dinner table but he wonders a little about the relevant others.

But Wilson is undoubtedly right in observing that, in spite of their "great style and vigor," such attempts to derive man's higher social behavior from phylogenetic analysis as those made by Lorenz, Ardrey, Morris, Tiger, and Fox tended to be "inefficient and misleading" because they selected one plausible hypothesis or another based on a review of a small sample of animal species, then advocated the explanation to the limit. He then goes on to describe the "correct approach" as depending on a careful analysis of behaviors of many closely related primates and extrapolating only the most stabile or conservative to man. Certainly the procedure is more cautious and probably more logical than that followed in the past by Ardrey, Morris, Tiger, and others. But after a long paragraph of discussion, it appears that Wilson himself is not entirely sure of just what we can learn about man by following the route he describes. Indeed, he confesses "that the comparative ethological approach does not in any way predict man's unique traits."

The trouble, of course, is that it is man's unique traits that we are interested in—especially his use of language, his invention of technologies, his passion to understand; above all, his penchant for developing his own social structures with their own rules regarding such peculiarly human notions as right and wrong, justice and mercy.

Fortunately for those of us who share his general commitment to biology as an explanatory, as well as a descriptive, science, Wilson's awareness of the uncertainties does not constrain him to a self-denying ordinance. On the contrary, he devotes the rest of his last chapter to an outline of the evolution of such human traits as "Barter and Reciprocal Altruism; Bonding, Sex, and Division of Labor [women's lib will surely have something to say here, as well as elsewhere in the book]; Role Playing and Polytheism; Communication; Culture, Ritual, and Religion; Ethics"; and so on. In all this, cultural evolution is treated as being closely interwoven with biological evolution, rather than being sharply separated from it in the usual way. Here he gives us some figures to show that gene flow through populations and consequent biological evolution may not necessarily be so slow as to be completely overwhelmed by cultural developments, as we have usually been taught to believe.

In the long run, this emphasis on continuing and current interaction between cultural and constructs and biochemical genes may be Wilson's most enduring theoretical contribution. For the present, it is primarily provocative and one awaits with growing excitement the debates that are sure to follow. When one counts up the possible protagonists of the conventional wisdom in economics, sociology, psychology, and indeed, in biology itself, who must be even now aiming their arrows in his direction, we can only hope that he does not become the Saint Sebastian of sociobiology. One of the arrows incidentally may be fired at rather close range by a young, energetic, and already celebrated population geneticist who has even more interest in social (and political) affairs than Wilson himself. In moments of excitement, he has recently taken the position that man's central nervous system has evolved so far toward infinite plasticity as to transcend completely the remnants of genetic patterning that may have come down to us from former generations.

In general, Wilson seems amply prepared to take care of himself in the inevitable debates. Indeed he is so self-confident as to indulge himself in at least three highly controversial, if not completely unsupported, speculations on quite a different level in the concluding pages of his great work: (1) Mankind will probably achieve an ecologically steady state by the end of the twenty-first century; (2) About the same time (he is less clear about the exact timing here), sociology will become reduced and resynthesized as neurobiology; and (3) Once "we have progressed enough to explain ourselves in these mechanistic terms . . . [we will face] the foreboding insight of Alfred Camus . . . 'in a universe divested of illusions and lights, man feels an alien, a stranger. His exile is without remedy since he is deprived of the memory of a lost home or the hope of a promised land.' " Although Bishop Wilberforce, Feodor Dostoyevsky, Matthew Arnold, and Henry Adams, among others, anticipated Camus, and Theodore Roszak and Jacques Ellul currently share the same insight, each according to his own fashion, it seems an odd way to end a book so full of the excitement of curiosity, the joy of discovery, and the contentment of contemplation.

Indeed, is it really impossible that, following the very mechanisms proposed in this book, man would not evolve the sense of purpose and satisfaction, precisely in his loneliness, the unique ability to do the kind of things Wilson continues to do so well. As one thumbs through the possible scenarios, this seems like a natural selection.

Mindless Societies

C. H. Waddington

Since the discovery of the nature and mode of operation of the basic units of heredity, biologists in search of major new fields to conquer have increasingly turned their attention to what has conventionally been referred to as behavior, mentality, and society. Three of the most important students of animal behavior, Karl von Frisch, Konrad Lorenz, and Niko Tinbergen, who recently shared a Nobel Prize, have all recently published books about their work; but the most sustained attempt to synthesize the whole of our present-day knowledge is undoubtedly that of Professor Edward O. Wilson of Harvard. His book is a formidable work. If I had to find a single word to describe my feelings when I found on my desk this offering from the *NYR*—no fewer than 392 broad-columned galley proofs, with a promise of more to come, containing glossary, bibliography, and index, plus, as a small side dish, a work of a mere 200 pages of sophisticated neurobiology—I think the best I could do would be "dudgeon"—not high dudgeon, but certainly low dudgeon.

A first glance was not very appetizing. The first sentence of *Sociobiology* quotes Camus ("Camus said that the only serious philosophical question is suicide"), only to have it pointed out in the second that there Camus was—not unusually in my opinion—talking Gallic rhetoric through his hat ("That is wrong even in the strict sense in-

From *The New York Review of Books* (August 7, 1975). Copyright © 1975 Nyrev, Inc. Reprinted with permission from *The New York Review of Books,* and the author.

tended"), and in the third sentence we find ourselves involved with the hypothalamus and the limbic system of the brain. H'm. . . . So I turned to the very last sentence, at the bottom of galley 392. Only to find Camus again. This time propounding one of his tautological aphorisms: "In a universe divested of illusions and lights, man feels an alien, a stranger." Well, in such a universe this may be so. This time Wilson remarks, "This, unfortunately, is true. But we still have another 100 years." So I applied what capacity for perseverance I possess to trying to discover what the intermediate 390 galleys told us to do in this 100 years.

It was quickly apparent that there is, as might be expected from Professor Wilson, a great deal of solid and interesting material behind the window dressing. He is well known as one of the most profound professional students of animal societies, particularly those of insects. He very early makes it clear that his book has a well-defined and important aim, and it is rather closely organized around this coherent theme. By "Sociobiology" he means the systematic study of the biological basis of all aspects of social behavior, particularly of animal societies, but also encompassing the social behavior of early man, and the organization of the more primitive contemporary human societies. He foregoes the attempt to deal with more complex forms of human social organization.

He argues that societies have been produced by evolution, that is to say by the natural selection of genetic variants, and that the proper way to understand societies is to discover how natural selection could have brought them into being. He reminds us that biologists who study the evolution of anatomical and physiological characteristics have claimed to have achieved in recent years a New Synthesis, which provides a satisfactory explanation for that entire class of phenomena. Wilson sets himself nothing less than the task of producing an equally satisfying new synthesis about the evolution of the social behavior of animals.

He sees this synthesis as eventually having three major components. At what one might call the most dispersed level would be a theory of the integrated functioning of the cells of the brain ("integrative neurophysiology"), which would itself be related to general cellular biology. This would give rise to a second component, consisting of ethology and physiological psychology. Those fields in turn would form a bridge to the third major component, namely sociobiology and behavior related to the ecological situation of the population of organisms, which in its turn would be linked with general population biology.

This is clearly an extraordinarily ambitious aim. I think one should say immediately that Professor Wilson has been astonishingly successful in achieving it. This book will undoubtedly be for many years to come a major source of information about all aspects of our knowledge of social behavior in animals, from the most primitive types such as corals, through insects, fishes, birds, to the many varieties of mammals and primitive man. It has also some of the clearest discussions yet written of recent advances in general population biology and demography. Many large drawings illustrate the major aspects of social behavior in various groups of animals with exemplary clarity. Unfortunately, I feel in these drawings an exceptional lack of any aesthetic appeal whatever, but perhaps that is not important to their purpose.

There is no point in repeating that this is a very good and very important book. It is more interesting to get down to particular features in which it seems to me something less than perfect.

At the very beginning, when he is still warming up for what he intends to be a long game, Wilson defines "the central theoretical problem of sociobiology: how can altruism, which by definition reduces personal fitness, possibly evolve by natural selection?" This problem was raised, and the essential solution of it actually provided, more than forty years ago in one of the books which founded the theory usually called neo-Darwinism, in which evolution is explained in terms of genes. In *The Causes of Evolution*, published in 1932, J. B. S. Haldane wrote (p. 131): "Insofar as it makes for the survival of one's descendants and near relations, altruistic behavior is a kind of Darwinian fitness, and may be expected to spread as a result of natural selection."

More recently this subject became, for some rather mysterious reason, a fashionable topic for a rather foolish controversy. The argument was represented as turning on whether one cohesive and delimited population, whose members showed some degree of altruistic behavior among themselves, would in competition entirely overcome and eliminate some other population whose members were not so well disposed to their fellows. One has only to look at the results of the arrival of the white man in Tasmania, or in many parts of the United States, to realize that such differential population extinction can occur. However, many people have argued that in theory they would happen only in rather exceptional circumstances.

In a very clear exposition, Wilson shows, first, that these doubts about the superior competitiveness of cohesive and internally altruistic populations are theoretically well founded, but he then has the common sense to demonstrate that the basic theory does not depend on population extinction at all. It only requires that the altruistic behavior should lead to a greater increase in numbers of individuals bearing hereditary factors tending in that direction than of other individuals not similarly genetically endowed. He shows that certain very plausible relations between populations would bring about such situations, and also that a similar differential multiplication might be produced by certain types of competition between individuals, rather than between groups.

This is an argument that has been advanced recently particularly by the English biologist Maynard Smith. I am personally not very convinced that anyone has yet provided a good explanation of how a tendency to altruistic behavior first takes hold in a population, but there certainly are, as Wilson so clearly expounds, several ways in which it might be expected to spread once it got started.

All this is an example of the admirable clarity of Wilson's exposition. The point that remains most obscure is just why he should consider the existence of altruism to be the central theoretical problem of sociobiology. But he does not allow this point about altruism to limit his discussion. He puts under review most of the problems which have recently appealed to students of population biology (except for the peculiar phenomenon of protein polymorphism, which has interested many people, precisely for the paradoxical reason that it seems to have no interesting consequences for the effectiveness of the organisms, either as individuals or as social creatures).

Wilson's discussion of modern selection theory and population dynamics is again a model of clarity. In my opinion he is somewhat too impressed by the distinction that has been made between r-selection and K-selection. These names are derived from coefficients that occur in certain algebraic theories about population growth recently developed by American authors. Many biologists on the other side of the Atlantic feel that the theories are rather schematic, and never fully apply to the complicated situations that arise in the actual ecological situations of nature. Most creatures are probably being subjected both to r-selection and K-selection, though maybe at different stages in their life histories.

In his discussion of modern evolutionary population biology, Wilson is broad-minded enough to bring out the fact, which most orthodox evolutionists try to keep in decent obscurity, that selection operates directly on phenotypes, that is to say on organisms after they have been affected during their development by the environment as well as by the genes they contain. Important effects on the fitness of an organism, and thus on the results of selection, may in some cases be brought about by the influence of stressful environments. It has been found experimentally that if individuals are selected over many generations for their ability to respond successfully to such environments, in the end the modifications may be exhibited even when the environment becomes no longer stressful. This is the process known as genetic assimilation. Wilson admits that "because behavior, and especially social behavior, has the greatest developmental plasticity of any category of phenotypic traits, it is also theoretically the most subject to evolution by genetic assimilation."

However, this is in an early introductory part of his book, and when in the main text he gets down to cases the importance of phenotypic adaptation and genetic assimilation hardly gets a mention. Yet "phenotypic adaptation" is only another way of referring to learning, by a phrase broad enough to encompass modification of physical structure as well as of behavior. If one is going to discuss the evolution of social behavior with the aim of bringing it into connection with human social behavior, which is almost wholly learned, then "learning," and the genetic basis for learning, must have an absolutely central position in the argument. I do not think that Wilson goes far enough to give it the importance it deserves.

This may be partly a defect of one of his great merits. Wilson is perhaps the leading authority in the world on the social life of insects, and insects are notoriously unteachable creatures. Most of them communicate with one another by primarily chemical means, though the bees may have gone slightly further by developing a system of bodily gestures. Neither mode would seem to have the potentiality for anything remotely resembling the semantic richness of the communication systems of apes, or even mammals, let alone the fantastic capacities of human language. It is, I think, a symptom of a certain insensitivity in Wilson to the importance of communication, particularly as a mode of teaching and learning, when he refers to Margaret Mead in this connection only as having employed the world "semiotic" to designate the analysis of communication in the broadest sense. He makes no mention of the fact that she has devoted a large and very illuminating book (*Continuities in Cultural Evolution*, Yale University Press, 1964) precisely to that analysis, covering many forms of transmission of social organization which do not depend on verbal language.

The whole topic of communication among individuals and all the many forms in which it may be carried out seems to me a much more central issue in sociobiology than the problem of altruism, which Wilson singles out as the dominant theme. One can, I think, conceive of a society in which no individual shows any altruism toward any other: anthropologists such as Fortune on the Mundugumor have described human societies that come close to this. But to conceive of a society in which there is no communication among individuals would seem to be a contradiction in terms.

Another field which Wilson explores less deeply than one might hope is the reciprocal interaction between behavior and selection. To a major extent, animals lose out in selection, not so much for doing the wrong thing, but for their inefficiency in performing whatever it is they *are* doing. The nature of the selection is to a very large degree dictated by the nature of their behavior. The accounts of social behavior in animals which Wilson provides very often imply this, but he does not, so far as I can discover, explicitly state it.

That brings one to what is, to my mind, the weakest feature in the whole grand structure which Wilson has built up. Is it not surprising that in a book of 700 large pages about social behavior there is no explicit mention whatever of mentality? In the index, covering more than thirty pages of three columns each, there is no mention of mind, mentality, purpose, goal, aim, or any word of similar connotation. Of course, something very similar to mind or purpose is very often implied. In fact, in searching the index for the latter word, the nearest you get to it is the entry "pursuit, invitation," which refers to the peculiar behavior of certain types of gazelle, apparently "for the purpose" of luring a predator into giving its presence away by starting a pursuit which the gazelle can dispose of by escaping.

Or consider the following account on pages 122 and 123:

A distraction display is any distinctive behavior used to attract the attention of an enemy and to draw it away from an object that the animal is trying to protect. In the great majority of instances the display directs a predator away from the eggs or young. Bird species belonging to many different families have evolved their own particular bag of tricks. . . . New Zealand pied stilts are among the great actors of the animal world: Guthrie-Smith (1925) has described their response to intrusion in the vicinity of the nest as follows:

"Dancing, prancing, galumphing over one spot of ground, the stricken bird seems simultaneously to jerk both legs and wings, as strange toy beasts can be agitated by elastic wires, the extreme length of the bird's legs producing extraordinary effects. It gradually becomes less and less able to maintain an upright attitude. Lassitude, fatigue, weariness, faintings—lackadaisical and fine ladyish—supervene. The end comes slowly, surely, a miserable flurry and scraping, the dying Stilt, however, even *in articulo mortis,* contriving to avoid inconvenient stones and to select a pleasant sandy spot upon which decently to expire. When on some shingle bank well removed from eggs and nests half a dozen Stilts—for they often die in companies—go through their performances, agonizing and fainting, the sight is quaint indeed."

Can there be any point in renouncing the use of words like mind, or goal-seeking, in the face of phenomena of this kind? Is not Wilson guilty of at the very least a certain incoherence, in indulging himself in a delicious mental *frisson* of Camusian alienation, while denying the poor New Zealand stilt, working away so very hard to confuse the sense of reality, even a hint of mentality? I think one is bound to come to the conclusion that the sociobiologists are just "running scared" of ferocious philosophers. A few years ago it may have been tactically wise for quiet behavioral scientists to practice their own distraction procedures against the threat of predatory positivists, but I doubt if there is any longer any need for such super-caution.

Against "Sociobiology"

Elizabeth Allen et al.

Beginning with Darwin's theories of natural selection 125 years ago, new biological and genetic information has played a significant role in the development of social and political policy. From Herbert Spencer, who coined the phrase "survival of the fittest," to Konrad Lorenz, Robert Ardrey, and now E. O. Wilson, we have seen proclaimed the primacy of natural selection in determining most important characteristics of human behavior. These theories have resulted in a deterministic view of human societies and human action. Another form of this "biological determinism" appears in the claim that genetic theory and data can explain the origin of certain social problems, e.g., the suggestion

From *The New York Review of Books* (November 13, 1975), pp. 182, 184–186. Copyright © 1975 Nyrev, Inc. Reprinted with permission from *The New York Review of Books*. [This letter to the Editors was signed by Elizabeth Allen, pre-medical student, Brandeis University; Barbara Beckwith, teacher, Watertown Public High School; Jon Beckwith, professor, Harvard Medical School; Steven Chorover, professor of psychology, MIT; David Culver, visiting professor of biology, Harvard School of Public Health, professor of biology, Northwestern; Margaret Duncan, research assistant, Harvard Medical School; Steven Gould, professor in the Museum of Comparative Zoology at Harvard University; Ruth Hubbard, professor of biology, Harvard University; Hiroshi Inouye, resident fellow, Harvard Medical School; Anthony Leeds, professor of anthropology, Boston University; Richard Lewontin, professor of biology, Harvard University; Chuck Madansky, graduate student in microbiology, Harvard Medical School; Larry Miller, student, Harvard Medical School; Reed Pyeritz, doctor, Peter Bent Brigham Hospital, Boston; Miriam Rosenthal, research associate, Harvard School of Public Health; and Herb Schreier, psychiatrist, Massachusetts General Hospital.]

by eugenicists such as Davenport in the early twentieth century that a host of examples of "deviant" behavior—criminality, alcoholism, etc.—are genetically based; or the more recent claims for a genetic basis of racial differences in intelligence by Arthur Jensen, William Shockley and others. Each time these ideas have resurfaced the claim has been made that they were based on new scientific information. Yet each time, even though strong scientific arguments have been presented to show the absurdity of these theories, they have not died. The reason for the survival of these recurrent determinist theories is that they consistently tend to provide a genetic justification of the *status quo* and of existing privileges for certain groups according to class, race or sex. Historically, powerful countries or ruling groups within them have drawn support for the maintenance or extension of their power from these products of the scientific community. For example, John D. Rockefeller, Sr. said

The growth of a large business is merely a survival of the fittest. . . . It is merely the working out of a law of nature and a law of God.

These theories provided an important basis for the enactment of sterilization laws and restrictive immigration laws by the United States between 1910 and 1930 and also for the eugenics policies which led to the establishment of gas chambers in Nazi Germany.

The latest attempt to reinvigorate these tired theories comes with the alleged creation of a new discipline, sociobiology. This past summer we have been treated to a wave of publicity and laudatory reviews of E. O. Wilson's book, *Sociobiology: The New Synthesis,* including that of C. H. Waddington [*NYR*, August 7]. The praise included a front page *New York Times* article which contained the following statement.

Sociobiology carries with it the revolutionary implication that much of man's behavior toward his fellows . . . may be as much a product of evolution as is the structure of the hand or the size of the brain. [*New York Times,* May 28]

Such publicity lends credence to the assertion that "we are on the verge of breakthroughs in the effort to understand our place in the scheme of things" (*New York Times Book Review,* June 27). Like others before him, Wilson's "breakthrough" is an attempt to introduce rigor and scope into the scientific study of society. However, Wilson dissociates himself from earlier biological determinists by accusing them of employing an "advocacy method" (deliberately selecting facts to support preconceived notions) generating unfalsifiable hypotheses. He purports to take a more solidly scientific approach using a wealth of new information. We think that this information has little relevance to human behavior, and the supposedly objective, scientific approach in reality conceals political assumptions. Thus, we are presented with yet another defense of the status quo as an inevitable consequence of "human nature."

In his attempt to graft speculation about human behavior onto a biological core, Wilson uses a number of strategies and sleights of hand which dispel any claim for logical or factual continuity. Of the twenty-seven chapters of *Sociobiology,* the middle twenty-five deal largely with animals, especially insects, while only the first and last chapters focus on humans. Thus, Wilson places 500 pages of double column biology between his first chapter on "The Morality of the Gene" and the last chapter, "From Sociobiology to Sociology." But Wilson's claim for objectivity rests entirely upon the extent to which his last chapter follows logically and inevitably from the fact and theory that come before. Many readers of *Sociobiology,* we fear, will be persuaded that this is the case. However, Wilson's claim to continuity fails for the following reasons:

1. Wilson sees "behavior and social structure as 'organs,'—extensions of the genes that exist because of their superior adaptive value." In speaking of indoctrinability, for example, he asserts that "humans are absurdly easy to indoctrinate" and therefore "conformer genes" must exist. Likewise, Wilson speaks of the "genes favoring spite" and asserts that spite occurs because humans are intelligent and can fathom its selective advantages. Similar arguments apply to "homosexuality genes" and genes for "creativity, entrepreneurship, drive and mental stamina." But there is no evidence for the existence of such genes. Thus, for Wilson, what exists is adaptive, what is adaptive is good, therefore what exists is good. However, when Wilson is forced to deal with phenomena such as social unrest, his explanatory framework becomes amazingly elastic. Such behavior is capriciously dismissed with the explanation that it is maladaptive, and therefore has simply failed to evolve.

Hence, social unrest may be due to the obsolescence of our moral codes, for as Wilson sees it we still operate with a "formalized code" as simple as that of "members of hunter-gatherer societies." Xenophobia represents a corresponding failure to keep pace with social evolution, our "intergroup responses . . . still crude and primitive."

This approach allows Wilson to confirm selectively certain contemporary behavior as adaptive and "natural" and thereby justify the present social order. The only basis for Wilson's definition of adaptive and maladaptive, however, is his own preferences. While he rejects the "advocacy approach" and claims scientific objectivity, Wilson reinforces his own speculations about a "human nature," i.e., that a great variety of human behavior is genetically determined, a position which does not follow from his evidence.

2. Another of Wilson's strategies involves a leap of faith from what might be to "what is." For example, as Wilson attempts to shift his arguments smoothly from the nonhuman to human behavior, he encounters a factor which differentiates the two: cultural transmission. Of course, Wilson is not unaware of the problem. He presents (p. 550) Dobzhansky's "extreme orthodox view of environmentalism":

Culture is not inherited through genes; it is acquired by learning from other human beings. . . . In a sense human genes have surrendered their primacy in human evolution to an entirely new non-biological or superorganic agent, culture.

But he ends the paragraph saying "the very opposite could be true." And suddenly, in the next sentence, the opposite does become true as Wilson calls for "the necessity of anthropological genetics." In other words, we must study the process by which culture is inherited through genes. Thus, it is Wilson's own preference for genetic explanations which is used to persuade the reader to make this jump.

3. Does Wilson's analysis of studies in nonhuman behavior provide him with a basis for understanding human behavior? An appeal to the "continuity of nature" based on evolutionary theory will not suffice. While evolutionary analysis provides a model for interpreting animal behavior, it does not establish any logical connection between behavior patterns in animal and human societies. But Wilson requires such a connection in order to use the vast amounts of animal evidence he

has collected. One subtle way in which Wilson attempts to link animals and humans is to use metaphors from human societies to describe characteristics of animal societies.

For instance, in insect populations, Wilson applies the traditional metaphors of "slavery" and "caste," "specialists" and "generalists" in order to establish a descriptive framework. Thus, he promotes the analogy between human and animal societies and leads one to believe that behavior patterns in the two have the same basis. Also, institutions such as slavery are made to seem natural in human societies because of their "universal" existence in the biological kingdom. But metaphor and presumed analogy cannot be allowed to mask the absence of evidence.

4. Another way Wilson confronts the difficulties in making the jump from nonhuman to human societies is by the use of *ad hoc* arguments. For example, a major problem exists in Wilson's emphasis on innate biology: how can genetic factors control behavior if social structure within a group can change rapidly over the course of just a few generations? Wilson, of course, does not deny the enormous flexibility and rapid change in human action. But Wilson admits that according to standard population genetics, this period is far too short for the changes observed. He turns instead to the "multiplier effect," which is a concept borrowed from economics. He uses this "effect" in an attempt to show how small genetic changes can be amplified enormously in a limited time span. But nowhere does Wilson present any basis for introducing the multiplier. A crucial point in Wilson's explanation remains purely speculative. Further he relies on the unproven assumption that genes for behavior exist.

5. Many of Wilson's claims about human nature do not arise from objective observation (either of universals in human behavior or of generalities throughout animal societies), but from a speculative reconstruction of human prehistory. This reconstruction includes the familiar themes of territoriality, big-game hunting with females at home minding the kids and gathering vegetables ("many of the peculiar details of human sexual behavior and domestic life flow easily from this basic division of labor"—p. 568), and a particular emphasis on warfare between bands and the salutary advantages of genocide. But these arguments have arisen before and have been strongly rebutted both on the basis of historical and anthropological studies. (See, for instance, A.

Alland, *The Human Imperative* or M. F. A. Montagu, *Man and Aggression*.)

What we are left with then is a particular theory about human nature, which has no scientific support, and which upholds the concept of a world with social arrangements remarkably similar to the world which E. O. Wilson inhabits. We are not denying that there are genetic components to human behavior. But we suspect that human biological universals are to be discovered more in the generalities of eating, excreting and sleeping than in such specific and highly variable habits as warfare, sexual exploitation of women and the use of money as a medium of exchange. What Wilson's book illustrates to us is the enormous difficulty in separating out not only the effects of environment (e.g., cultural transmission) but also the personal and social class prejudices of the researcher. Wilson joins the long parade of biological determinists whose work has served to buttress the institutions of their society by exonerating them from responsibility for social problems.

From what we have seen of the social and political impact of such theories in the past, we feel strongly that we should speak out against them. We must take "Sociobiology" seriously, then, not because we feel that it provides a scientific basis for its discussion of human behavior, but because it appears to signal a new wave of biological determinist theories.

For Sociobiology

Edward O. Wilson

I write to protest the false statements and accusations that comprise the letter signed by Elizabeth Allen and 15 co-signers in the November 13 *New York Review of Books*. This letter, which is directed against my book *Sociobiology: The New Synthesis,* is an openly partisan attack on what the signers mistakenly conclude to be a political message in the book. Every principal assertion made in the letter is either a false statement or a distortion. On the most crucial points raised by the signers I have said the opposite of what is claimed. To date, none of the many other scientists who have reviewed the book in scientific and popular journals have misinterpreted it in this or any other important way.

Allen *et al.* characterize *Sociobiology: The New Synthesis* as the latest attempt to reinvigorate theories which in the past "provided an important basis for the enactment of sterilization laws and restrictive immigration laws by the United States between 1910 and 1930 and also for the eugenics policies which led to the establishment of gas chambers in Nazi Germany." I resent this ugly, irresponsible, and totally false accusation.

To make their case Allen *et al.* have selected bits from *Sociobiology: The New Synthesis* and pieced them together to depict what they claim are my personal and social class prejudices. But not even the interpretations placed on these isolated fragments are accurate. The letter signers, for example, allege that I make institutions such as slavery "seem natural in human societies because of their 'universal' existence in the biological kingdom." I have done no such thing. In the book slavery is stated to occur only in ants and men, and the many distinctions between its practice in the two groups is made clear. In my June 1975 *Scientific American* article on the subject, where I felt freer to editorialize, I went so far as to put the matter as follows: "Does ant slavery hold any lesson for our own species? Probably not. Human slavery is an unstable social institution that runs strongly counter to the moral systems of the great majority of human societies. Ant slavery is a genetic adaptation found in particular species that cannot be judged to be more or less successful than their non-slave-making counterparts. The slave-making ants offer a clear and interesting case of behavioral evolution, but the analogies with human behavior are much too remote to allow us to find in them any moral or political lesson."

Allen *et al.* try to make me appear to be the arch hereditarian by quoting my sentence "The very opposite could be true" after a quotation from Dobzhansky stating that "In a sense human genes have surrendered their primacy in human evolution to an entirely new non-biological or superorganic agent, culture." In fact, my sentence came fourteen lines of mostly technical information after the Dobzhansky quotation, and it really followed the sentence "It is not valid to point to the absence of a behavioral trait in one or a few societies as conclusive evidence that the trait is environmentally induced and has no genetic disposition in man." My meaning, which refers to a lesser technical point, was thus grossly distorted by this elision. A reading of the full paragraph will show that I am far closer to Dobzhansky in my overall view than to the opposite position which seems to be indicated by the mutilated version.

I invite the reader to check all of the other pronouncements in the letter by Allen *et al.* against the actual statements in my book, in the true context in which the statements were made. I suggest that they will encounter very little correspondence, and I am confident that they will be left with no doubt as to my true meaning.

The pivotal indictment which Allen *et al.* try to pin on me is that "Wilson joins the long parade of biological determinists whose work has served to buttress the institutions of their society by exonerating them from responsibility for social problems." I have done no such thing. In fact I have taken care elsewhere to do just the opposite. In an article published in the *New York Times Magazine* on October 12, I felt free to go well beyond the science in the book to discuss some of my personal feelings about the implications of sociobiology. Here is my concluding statement: "The moment has arrived to stress that there is a dangerous trap in sociobiology, one which can be avoided only by constant vigilance. The trap is the naturalistic fallacy of ethics, which uncritically concludes that what is, should be. The 'what is' in human nature is to a large extent the heritage of a Pleistocene hunter-gatherer existence. When any genetic bias is demonstrated, it cannot be used to justify a continuing practice in present and future societies. Since most of us live in a radically new environment of our own making, the pursuit of such a practice would be bad biology; and like all bad biology, it would invite disaster. For example, the tendency under certain conditions to conduct warfare against competing groups might well be in our genes, having been advantageous to our Neolithic ancestors, but it could lead to global suicide now. To rear as many healthy children as possible was long the road to security; yet with the population of the world brimming over, it is now the way to environmental disaster. Our primitive old genes will therefore have to carry the load of much more cultural change in the future. To an extent not yet known, we trust—we insist—that human nature can adapt to more encompassing forms of altruism and social justice. Genetic biases can be trespassed, passions averted or redirected, and ethics altered; and the human genius for making contracts can continue to be applied to achieve healthier and freer societies. Yet the mind is not infinitely malleable. Human sociobiology should be pursued and its findings weighed as the best means we have of tracing the evolutionary history of the mind. In the difficult journey ahead, during which our ultimate guide must be our deepest and, at present, least understood feelings, surely we cannot afford an ignorance of history."

The *New York Times Magazine* article was sent to the editors in August. I would have taken it to Allen *et al.* had I known that their letter was in subsequent preparation, and I would also have asked for the chance to discuss with them their view of the implications of sociobiology. However, in spite of the fact that I have been on friendly terms with some of the signers of the letter for years, and two share the same building with me at Harvard University, I did not know of the letter's existence until three days before it appeared in print.

I make this last point because I feel that the actions of Allen *et al.* represent the kind of self-righteous vigilantism which not only produces falsehood but also unjustly hurts individuals and through that kind of intimidation diminishes the spirit of free inquiry and discussion crucial to the health of the intellectual community.

Fated Genes

Lawrence G. Miller

The search for vast syntheses, incorporating all phenomena under a single rubric, has been a hallmark of twentieth-century science. In sociology, this imperative has taken the form of "grand theory" seeking to explain all social action in similar terms; an example is Talcott Parsons's *The Structure of Social Action*.[1] In evolutionary biology, a parallel quest, more successful in achieving scientific consensus, has resulted in the "modern synthesis" elaborated by Huxley, Haldane, and Dobzhansky in the late 1930s and early 1940s. As a consequence, ecology and taxonomy have been integrated into neo-Darwinist evolutionary theory.

As synthesists seek to extend their purview, these two disciplines tend to converge: from sociology as theorists such as Parsons adopt an evolutionary approach, and more strongly from biology, as ethologists such as Lorenz seek to integrate animal and human behavior. Edward O. Wilson, in *Sociobiology: The New Synthesis*, hopes to stretch convergence into identity; he projects nothing less for his new science than "the systematic study of the biological basis of all social behavior" (p. 4). Relying on the assumption that "sociology and the other social sciences, as well as the humanities are . . . branches of biology," the task of sociobiology is to "reformulate the foundations of the social sciences in a way that draws these subjects into the Modern Synthesis" (p. 4).

Attempts such as Wilson's to provide a biological and specifically

From *Journal of the History of the Behavioral Sciences* (April 1976), pp. 183–190. The author wishes to thank Ms. L. J. Daston for her invaluable assistance. Reprinted by permission of the publisher and the author.

269

evolutionary basis for social behavior are by no means new. Perhaps the most ambitious and most influential effort was that of Herbert Spencer in the last century. In this essay, I will compare the syntheses of Spencer and Wilson, in an attempt to shed light on their respective assumptions and on the perplexing tenacity of evolutionary positivism. I will first provide a brief summary of Spencer's work, and then examine Wilson's arguments in more detail. I will close with some reflections on the roles of ideology and science in social theory.

Talcott Parsons began *The Structure of Social Action* with the rhetorical question, "Who now reads Spencer?" While Parsons's point is well taken, it is far too literal-minded: the evolutionary positivism forged by Spencer has had tremendous influence as a sociological model and as a framework for subsequent argument.[2] Despite the efforts of recent "whiggish" expositors of Spencer, his work must be related to the Victorian social milieu. Only then does the massive *Principles of Synthetic Philosophy* seem anything but a dinosaur.[3] Amidst the Victorian crisis of faith not only in religion but also in the inevitability of human progress, Spencer intended the *Principles* as a beacon: science showed that progress was ordained by Nature, and a code of ethics founded on a scientific basis could assure the inexorable triumph of humanity. The synthetic philosophy was thus an effort to describe a "natural" social order; and the validity of Spencer's conclusions was to be demonstrated by the application of his methodological principles to all phenomena.[4]

Although Spencer would have rejected the appellation "positivist" for its Comtean connotations, his articles of faith are shared by twentieth-century positivists. First, the synthetic philosophy attests to Spencer's belief in the possibility and desirability of a synthesis of all knowledge based on the scientific paradigm of explanation. Second, Spencer's work is characterized by adherence to the universality of natural causation: Newtonian laws of nature exist, apply to all phenomena, and should be sought in their broadest and most general forms. Third, and the *sine qua non* of modern positivists, is Spencer's faith in the primacy of scientific explanation. Parsons has expressed this tenet well: "The phenomena to which a scientific theory is applicable are held to be exclusively understandable in terms of the theory."[5]

Coupled with the positivist precepts in Spencer's work is a principle he embraced with almost religious fervor—the uniformity of nature. All parts of nature are held to be fundamentally similar and therefore will yield to a similar analysis. This assumption has profound effects on the epistemological status of humans: human situations can be seen as biological situations, human institutions as biological instruments for survival. Positivism here assumes a new form; as Spencer himself recognized, positive science could extend beyond Comte's methodological programs to actually delineate the biological regularities of human conduct. And since evolution was for Spencer a natural law, humans and human societies were equally subject to this law, and should be analyzed as such. Spencer was by no means a Darwinist—the outlines of the synthetic philosophy preceded the *Origin of Species*, and throughout most of his life Spencer clung to a Lamarckian mode of natural selection. But evolutionary positivism depended not on a particular theory of evolution but rather on a scientifically modeled evolutionary analysis.

Spencer's brand of positivism had important implications for the human sciences. Sociology became the study of social evolution, so the considerable attention Spencer devoted to the operation of individual societies served primarily to place them in a developmental framework. Ethics was extended beyond the empirical statements of the utilitarians and provided with a theoretical basis. Spencer remained a utilitarian in his individualism, his belief in the principle of utility, and his almost rabid devotion to laissez-faire economics. However, in place of the utilitarians' immutable human nature, Spencer posited a variable human essence, responsive to evolutionary pressure. In particular, human nature was in transition from the selfish individualism of the utilitarians toward an altruistic individualism. Altruism posed a crucial problem for Spencer. On theoretical grounds, the "survival of the fittest" (originally Spencer's phrase) demanded the incessant struggle of individuals: how would altruism evolve? In practical terms, however, altruism existed in Spencer's society and could not be disregarded. Spencer's solution was to suggest that altruism increased individual fitness, thus retaining the individualist premise of natural selection.

Lack of correspondence between theoretical structure and social reality was a continuing problem for Spencer. Several styles of argument were used to avoid both outright dissonance and oversimplification. First, Spencer relied heavily on analogy and metaphor ostensibly as heuristic but actually to carry a heavy explanatory load. His most pervasive analogy was that of the "social organism," human society envisioned with the anatomical structure and physiological function of an animal. Telegraph wires as nerve fibers, roads as blood vessels, and money as red corpuscles illustrate the incredible detail to which Spencer developed this analogy. By careful selection of examples, Spencer used the organic analogy to "document" ideas of societal structure, function, and development based on prior moral and political assumptions: individualism, laissez-faire economics, and evolved human nature.

Similar results were achieved by a second shortcut, the use of common sense explanations coupled with a scientific justification. Religion, for example, was to Spencer born of the fear and ignorance of simple savages, but served in primitive societies as an advantageous cohesive force. Similarly, the nineteenth-century economic division of labor grew out of rational appreciation of its advantages, just as the "physiological division of labor" evolved in organisms under the supremely rational pressure of natural selection. In both cases, Spencer appealed to Victorian conventional wisdom to construct plausible explanations. Judicious mixing of common sense and science enabled Spencer to explain both the successes and failures of his society.

Such flexible explanations point to an important characteristic of the synthetic philosophy: its schizoid explanatory basis. On one hand, Spencer sought to provide a gradualist explanation of past events based on the *natural* laws of evolution. In contrast, his approach to contemporary society was that of a laissez-faire radical, eager to stimulate evolution by artifice. Spencer rationalized this contradiction by asserting that humanity had accumulated sufficient scientific knowledge to determine its own evolutionary course. Ultimately, then, the whole of the synthetic philosophy exists to provide a foundation for Spencer's social recommendations. Since the two are held to be intrinsically connected, and the synthetic philosophy to be based on inviolable scientific principles, then the recommendations must be valid. But evolutionary positivism incorporated individualist and naturalist biases, and Spencer's explanations too often extended analogy to homology. The so-called scientific aspects of the synthetic philosophy cannot be separated from its social and political underpinnings as an effort to justify Spencer's idealized social order.

The remarkable scope of Spencer's enterprise and the eclectic method by which evidence was arrayed rendered the synthetic philosophy obsolete within Spencer's own lifetime. Burrow has aptly described the

Principles as a "suitable mausoleum for an antiquated conception of science."[6] But even if the substantive aspects of Spencer's work were ignored, the evolutionary positivist framework persisted. In America, polemicists such as William Graham Sumner and academic sociologists such as Lester Ward accepted many of Spencer's precepts. The problem of altruism retained particular importance, most clearly in Peter Kropotkin's influential *Mutual Aid.*[7] Kropotkin combined anarchist principles with evolutionary justifications to provide a "scientific" basis for altruism.

Although the positivism in much recent inquiry into human behavior has been tempered or muted, evolutionism remains dominant. Ethologists, among them Lorenz, Tiger, and Fox, and popularizers such as Ardrey and Morris share a common methodology and a common faith that animal observations can be extrapolated to humans. Altruism remains a central concern; to Lorenz, for example, the bond of "love and friendship" is crucial to humanity and will hopefully evolve in the future.[8]

Edward O. Wilson's *Sociobiology: The New Synthesis* represents a recurrence of Spencerian evolutionary positivism. Wilson's goal is threefold: to establish a selection mechanism for social evolution; to illustrate this process from a wide range of animal behavior; and to extend such explanations to human action and human societies. The book is massive, detailed, and heavily documented—ostensibly a work of scientific scholarship corresponding to the status of Spencer's work a century ago. A comparison with Spencer's synthetic philosophy can serve as a useful heuristic in discussing the scientific nature of Wilson's sociobiology.

As noted above, Wilson wishes to draw the social sciences into the evolutionary synthesis and provide them with a biological foundation. In the process, psychology will be "cannibalized" and sociology per se will disappear, as sociobiology and neurophysiology attain primacy. Thus, Wilson shares with Spencer the positivist ideal of the unity of the sciences (or at least of the sciences of life) and the possibility of a total synthesis. In his discussion of reasoning in sociobiology, Wilson further espouses the major tenets of positivism: the unswerving belief in natural causation and the existence of natural laws, and the primacy of scientific argument over other forms of explanation. With Spencer, Wilson also shares the evolutionist's faith in the uniformity of nature, in Wilson's case culminating in the universal application of neo-Darwinist natural selection. Unlike Spencer's simplistic Lamarckianism, Wilson brings to bear sophisticated methods based on "roughly equal parts of invertebrate zoology, vertebrate zoology, and population biology" (p. 4). Sociobiological explanation rests ultimately on a modern genetic foundation.

Citing this scientific basis, Wilson would reject comparison with Spencer, just as he rejects comparison with contemporary theorists such as Lorenz, Tiger, Fox, and Ardrey. They are accused of employing the "advocacy approach": "Their particular handling of the problem tended to be inefficient and misleading. They selected one plausible hypothesis or another based on a review of a small sample of animal species, then advocated the explanation to the limit" (p. 551). Spencer's single-mindedness would have won him similar criticism.

Wilson's evolutionary positivism differs from that of Spencer most obviously in its social context. The crisis of faith Wilson addresses is not religious but scientific. To Wilson, sociology has been content with "empirical description," "unaided intuition," and "first-order correlations" and has therefore achieved only limited success (p. 4). Sociobiology, like the synthetic philosophy in its time, is intended as a beacon: science *can* explain human societies, but only if their true evolutionary nature is recognized. Progress is therefore not inevitable, but rather contingent on comprehending the historical basis of human nature. Then, in the planned society of the near future, sociobiology will "monitor the genetic basis of social behavior" and assure the implementation of those policies deemed consonant with genetics (p. 575). With Spencer, Wilson is concerned with the delineation and maintenance of a "natural" social order.

Although Wilson's arguments are more subtle, better documented, and more convincing to the modern reader than those of Spencer, they are equally flawed. The reliance on evolution and the concern for social order have resulted in similar defects and even similar social and political speculation. Both are, and must be, advocacy theorists.

Evolutionary arguments rely for their major analytical categories on the adaptive/maladaptive dichotomy. Spencer's conception of society as an organism led him to postulate that what existed must have evolved and thus serves an adaptive function. Wilson's argument is similar: "Behavior and social structure, like all other biological phenomena, can be studied as 'organs,' extensions of the genes that exist because of their superior adaptive value" (p. 22). For example, Wilson speaks of spite, indoctrinability, and competition as genetically determined and thus adaptive. There exist "genes favoring spite" (p. 119) so that "true spite is a commonplace in human societies, undoubtedly because human beings are keenly aware of their own blood lines and have the intelligence to plot intrigue" (p. 119). Likewise, "conformer genes" exist to explain why "human beings are absurdly easy to indoctrinate" (p. 562). The result is a reification of contemporary social behavior as adaptive and thus "natural," and a concomitant affirmation of the present social order.

Conversely, Wilson asserts that social institutions which do not appear adaptive have failed to evolve. For example, human societies have become "vastly more complex" but moral codes have not changed: "The average individual still operates under a formalized code no more elaborate than that governing the members of hunter-gatherer societies" (p. 554). A corresponding failure to keep pace with social evolution is manifested by the prevalence of xenophobia: "Part of man's problem is that his intergroup responses are still crude and primitive, and inadequate for the extended extraterritorial relationships that civilization has thrust upon him" (p. 565). The elasticity and a priori character of Wilson's explanations are striking. Further, in arguments from both adaptation and maladaptation, Wilson has inserted norms for human action in the form of "human nature"—human traits are genetically determined, some are deemed natural and adaptive, and others are merely atavistic.

Wilson's conception of human nature recalls that of Spencer. Just as Spencer sought a "true theory of humanity,"[9] Wilson, in modern jargon, is "searching for the human biogram" (p. 548). Both reject the notion of an immutable human essence. Spencer asserted the indefinite flexibility of humans, while Wilson is more circumspect; his human nature includes aggression, allegiance, love, sexual drives, and xenophobia. Both point out that human nature is subject to evolutionary pressure, especially with respect to the development of altruism. And both begin with similar premises: human nature is essentially individualist, so only natural selection can foster altruism.

The central position of altruism in Wilson's synthesis helps to place sociobiology in the context of other efforts to delineate a biological basis for human action, such as those of Spencer and Kropotkin. Wilson presents the "central theoretical problem of sociobiology: how can altruism, which by definition reduces personal fitness, possibly evolve by natural selection?" (p. 3). Wilson's solution involves kin and group selection, which retain the individualist premise of natural selection but present the means by which an individual can gain from altruism. It is important to see altruism as an historical problem of evolutionary positivism rather than a logical problem in Wilson's synthesis. Spencer, Kropotkin, and Wilson all require an explanation of altruism not only to reconcile an inherently individualist theory with social reality, but also to provide an avenue for evolutionary progress. The biological determinism of their theories prevents an appeal to social or institutional change; only a modification in the human nature they have constructed will suffice.

Wilson, then, assumes a conception of human nature and provides a mechanism for its alteration. He uses similar arguments to those of Spencer in attempting to bolster his presuppositions. First, Wilson relies heavily on analogy and metaphor. In some cases, Wilson draws metaphors from population biology to describe human societies. Genetic drift, for example, the random divergence of genetic characteristics, is extended to social drift and tradition drift, both of which are assumed to follow the genetic model. Conversely, metaphors from human societies are frequently applied to animal societies. In describing the social world of insects in terms of slavery and caste, Wilson makes little effort to qualify the two uses of slavery, except to assert that slavery in human societies is less stable.[10] The results of such arguments are twofold: the hazy distinction between analogy and homology of the two types of societies becomes even more blurred; and metaphors tend to subtly corroborate the universality of such social institutions as slavery in the natural world.

A second style of argument common to Wilson and Spencer involves the juxtaposition of common sense and scientific justification. Just as Spencer's explanations of religion and the division of labor were couched in terms most Victorians would immediately recognize, Wilson explains the behavior of children in popular twentieth-century fashion:

It should be of selective advantage for young children to be self-centered and relatively disinclined to perform altruistic acts based on personal principle. Similarly, adolescents should be more tightly bound by age-peer bonds within their own sex and hence unusually sensitive to peer approval. The reason is that at this time greater advantage accrues to the formulation of alliances and rise in status than later. (p. 563).

An obvious rendering of twentieth-century America is presented as natural for *children*. A similar example is the "explanation" of spite cited above. In both cases, the analysis is glib; superficial observation is given an evolutionary basis.

The general plan of Wilson's synthesis in fact rests on equally unsteady foundations. The book is divided into three parts: Social Evolution, Social Mechanisms, and Social Species. The last section culminates in a discussion of humanity as the most developed of the social species. This chapter is presented as following logically and inevitably from what comes before. In fact, the connections are of the metaphorical and speculative sort pointed out above. Wilson's ultimate reliance on the uniformity of nature is merely another premise, not a conclusion. Again the parallel with Spencer is evident: like Spencer, Wilson wants to have it both ways: a gradualist, naturalistic explanation of the past is coupled with a rationalist, active approach to the present. Sociobiology, conceived as a positive science, must not only comprehend but also predict and therefore intervene. Sociobiology, revealed as a theory with political and social bases, is but another advocacy approach to human action.

But merely unmasking sociobiology as a sociopolitical statement will not discredit evolutionary positivism. Spencer's synthesis fell rapidly into disfavor, but its indirect effects in establishing a framework for argument have remained. Sociobiology must be seen as one aspect of the contemporary search for a biological basis for human behavior. Other determinist theories, such as those focusing on I.Q. and the XYY genotype, have been the subject of public controversies for several years and have occasionally shaped social policy.

The appeal of evolutionary positivism clearly transcends the work of any one expositor. It lies first of all in claims to the status of a positive science. Theories then accrue the respect given to the more established sciences and concomitantly promise the certainty that science is assumed to provide. The allure of science cannot be underestimated in an era in which scientism has become the dominant ideology.[11] Second, evolutionary arguments allow social assumptions to be subtly incorported in the form of adaptation or "fitness," particularly assumptions which accord with the individualist bias of natural selection. Finally, evolutionary positivism purports to establish "human nature," a concept which is inherently ideological in the sense that it establishes a certain model of humanity as essential and thus "natural." It may serve to "explain" crime or aggression, justify competition, or pronounce impossible sharing and collective action. Equally important, attention may be deflected from social and political considerations which are tractable, unlike a genetically based human nature. Ultimately, the persistence of evolutionary positivism can be traced to its ideological role in legitimating a conception of social order, be it Spencer's laissez-faire utilitarianism or Wilson's technocratic social engineering.

This is not to deny that humans are organisms or that human action has a biological component. Rather, we must affirm that humans are social beings and that their socialization cannot be removed like a veneer to reveal the naked human nature underneath. Indeed, anthropological and sociological observations indicate that even the most basic and widespread human functions such as sleeping, eating, and excreting are irrevocably socially conditioned.[12] Spencer in his time and Wilson in ours offer the false certainty of evolutionary positivism and "human nature." Those of us concerned with human action can better seek explanations based on a contextual and historical understanding of our society rather than on the illusory pedigree of science.

NOTES

1. Talcott Parsons, *The Structure of Social Action* (New York: McGraw-Hill, 1939).
2. See J. D. Peel, *Herbert Spencer: Evolution of a Sociologist* (New York: Basic Books, 1971), and also Robert A. Jones, "Durkheim's Responses to Spencer," *Sociological Quarterly* 15 (1974), pp. 341–358.
3. The *Synthetic Philosophy* includes *First Principles, Principles of Biology, Principles of Psychology, Principles of Sociology*, and *Principles of Ethics*. A total of nine volumes were published from 1862 to 1893.
4. The best recent source on Spencer is Peel, *op. cit.* The chapter in J. W. Burrow, *Evolution and Society* (Cambridge: Cambridge Univ. Press, 1966) is an excellent brief summary of Spencer's thought.
5. *Ibid.*, p. 205.
6. *Ibid.*, p. 190.
7. Peter Kropotkin, *Mutual Aid* (London: 1902); New York: New York Univ.

Press, 1972). Other turn-of-the-century theories of social evolution include Eduard Bernstein, *Evolutionary Socialism* (London: J. P. Murray, 1899) and L. T. Hobhouse, *Mind in Evolution* (London: Macmillan, 1901) and *Morals in Evolution* (London: MacMillan, 1906).

8. See Konrad Lorenz, *On Aggression* (New York: Harcourt Brace Jovanovich, 1966), especially Chapter 14, "Avowal of Optimism."

9. D. Duncan, *Life and Letters of Herbert Spencer* (London: D. Appleton & Co., 1908), p. 62.

10. For a clear presentation of the slavery metaphor, see also E. O. Wilson, "Slavery in Ants," *Scientific American,* June 1975.

11. See, for example, Trent Schroyer, *Critique of Domination* (Boston: Braziller, 1975).

12. On this point, the work of Mary Douglas is particularly convincing. See her *Purity and Danger* (London: Routledge and Kegan Paul, 1966) and *Natural Symbols* (Baltimore: Penguin, 1973).

Sociobiology—Another Biological Determinism

Sociobiology Study Group
of Science for the People

Biological determinism represents the claim that the present states of human societies are the specific result of biological forces and the biological "nature" of the human species. Determinist theories all describe a particular model of society which corresponds to the socioeconomic prejudices of the writer. It is then asserted that this pattern has arisen out of human biology and that present human social arrangements are either unchangeable or if altered will demand continued conscious social control because these changed conditions will be "unnatural." Moreover, such determinism provides a direct justification for the status quo as "natural," although some determinists dissociate themselves from some of the consequences of their arguments. The issue, however, is not the motivation of individual creators of determinist theories, but the way these theories operate as powerful forms of legitimation of past and present social institutions such as aggression, competition, domination of women by men, defense of national territory, individual-

From *BioScience* 26, no. 3 (March 1976). Published by the American Institute of Biological Sciences. Reprinted by permission of *BioScience* and the authors. [At the time of composition of this article the Sociobiology Study Group of Science for the People consisted of E. Allen, B. Beckwith, J. Beckwith, S. Chorover, D. Culver, N. Daniels, E. Dorfman, M. Duncan, E. Engelman, R. Fitten, K. Fuda, S. Gould, C. Gross, R. Hubbard, J. Hunt, H. Inouye, M. Kotelchuck, B. Lange, A. Leeds, R. Levins, R. Lewontin, E. Loechler, B. Ludwig, C. Madansky, L. Miller, R. Morales, S. Motheral, K. Muzal, N. Ostrom, R. Pyeritz, A. Reingold, M. Rosenthal, M. Mersky, M. Wilson, and H. Schreier.]

ism, and the appearance of a status and wealth hierarchy.

The earlier forms of determinism in the current wave have now been pretty well discredited. The claims that there is a high heritability of IQ, which implies both the unchangeability of IQ and a genetic difference between races or between social classes, have now been thoroughly debunked.

The simplistic forms of the human nature argument given by Lorenz, Ardrey, Tiger and Fox, and others have no scientific credit and have been scorned as works of "advocacy" by E. O. Wilson, whose own book, *Sociobiology: The New Synthesis,* is the manifesto of a new, more complex, version of biological determinism, no less a work of "advocacy" than its rejected predecessors. This book, whose first chapter is on "The Morality of the Gene," is intended to establish sociology as a branch of evolutionary biology, encompassing all human societies, past and present. Wilson believes that "sociology and the other social sciences, as well as the humanities, are the last branches of biology waiting to be included in the Modern Synthesis" (p. 4).

This is no mere academic exercise. For more than a century the idea that human social behavior is determined by evolutionary imperatives operating on inherited dispositions has been seized upon and widely entertained not so much for its alleged correspondence with reality as for its more obvious political value. Among the better known examples are Herbert Spencer's argument in *Social Statics* (1851) that poverty and starvation were natural agents cleansing society of the unfit, and Konrad Lorenz's call in 1940 in Germany for "the extermination of elements of the population loaded with dregs," based upon his ethological theories.

In order to make their case, determinists construct a selective picture of human history, ethnography, and social relations. They misuse the basic concepts and facts of genetics and evolutionary theory, asserting things to be true that are totally unknown, ignoring whole aspects of the evolutionary process, asserting that conclusions follow from premises when they do not. Finally, they invent ad hoc hypotheses to take care of the contradictions and carry on a form of "scientific reasoning" that is untestable and leads to unfalsifiable hypotheses. What follows is a general examination of these elements in sociobiological theory, especially as elaborated in E. O. Wilson's *Sociobiology.*

A VERSION OF HUMAN NATURE

For the sociobiologist the first task is to delineate a model of human nature that is to be explained. Among Wilson's universal aspects of human nature are:

1. territoriality and tribalism (pp. 564–565);

2. indoctrinability—"Human beings are absurdly easy to indoctrinate—they *seek* it" (p. 562);

3. spite and family chauvinism—"True spite is commonplace in human societies, undoubtedly because human beings are keenly aware of their own blood lines and have the intelligence to plot intrigue" (p. 119);

4. reciprocal altruism (as opposed to true unselfishness)—"Human behavior abounds with reciprocal altruism," as for example, "aggressively moralistic behavior," "self-righteousness, gratitude and sympathy" (p. 120);

5. blind faith—"Men would rather believe than know" (p. 561);

6. warfare (p. 572) and genocide (p. 573)—"the most distinctive human qualities" emerged during the "autocatalytic phase of social evolution" which occurred through intertribal warfare, "genocide" and "genosorption."

The list is not exhaustive and is meant only to show how the outlines of human nature are viewed myopically, through the lens of modern Euro-American culture.

To construct such a view of human nature, Wilson must abstract himself totally from any historical or ethnographic perspective. His discussion of the economy of scarcity is an excellent example. An economy of relative scarcity and unequal distribution of rewards is stated to be an aspect of human nature:

> The members of human society sometimes cooperate closely in *insectan* fashion [our emphasis], but more frequently they compete for the limited resources allocated to their role sector. The best and the most entrepreneurial of the role-actors usually gain a disproportionate share of the rewards (p. 554).

There is a great deal of ethnographic and historical description entirely contradicting this conception of social organization. It ignores, for example, the present and historical existence of societies not differentiated in any significant way by "role sectors"; without scarcities differentially induced by social institutions for different subpopulations of the society;

not differentiated by lower and higher ranks and strata (Birket-Smith 1959; Fried 1967; Harris 1968; Krader 1968).

Realizing that history and ethnography do not support the universality of their description of human nature, sociobiologists claim that the exceptions are "temporary aberrations" or deviations. Thus, although genocidal warfare is (assertedly) universal, "it is to be expected that some isolated cultures will escape the process for generations at a time, in effect reverting temporarily to what ethnographers classify as a pacific state" (p. 574).

Another related ploy is the claim that ethnographers and historians have been too narrow in their definitions and have not realized that apparently contradictory evidence is really confirmatory.

Anthropologists often discount territorial behavior as a general human attribute. This happens when the narrowest concept of the phenomenon is borrowed from zoology . . . it is necessary to define territory more broadly. . . . animals respond to their neighbors in a highly variable manner. . . . the scale may run from open hostility . . . to oblique forms of advertisement or *no territorial behavior at all* [our emphasis].

If these qualifications are accepted it is reasonable to conclude that territoriality is a general trait of hunter-gatherer societies. (pp. 564–565)

Wilson's views of aggression and warfare are subject to this ploy of all-embracing definition on the one hand and erroneous historical-ethnographic data on the other. "Primitive" warfare is rarely lethal to more than one or at most a few individuals in an episode of warfare, virtually without significance genetically or demographically (Livingstone 1968). Genocide was virtually unknown until state-organized societies appeared in history (as far as can be made out from the archeological and documentary records).

We have given only examples of the general advocacy method employed by sociobiologists in a procedure involving definitions which exclude nothing and the laying of Western conceptual categories onto "primitive" societies.

HUMANS AS ANIMALS—
THE MEANING OF SIMILARITY

To support a biologistic explanation of human institutions it is useful to claim an evolutionary relationship between the nature of human social institutions and "social" behavior in other animals. Obviously sociobiologists would prefer to claim evolutionary homology, rather than simple analogy, as the basis for the similarity in behavior between humans and other animals; then they would have a prima facie case for genetic determination. In some sections of *Sociobiology*, Wilson attempts to do this by listing "universal" features of behavior in higher primates including humans. But claimed external similarity between humans and our closest relatives (which are by no means very close to us) does not imply genetic continuity. A behavior that may be genetically coded in a higher primate may be purely learned and widely spread among human cultures as a consequence of the enormous flexibility of our brain.

More often Wilson argues from evolutionary analogy. Such arguments operate on shaky grounds. They can never be used to assert genetic similarity, but they can serve as a plausibility argument for natural selection of human behavior by assuming that natural selection has operated on different genes in the two species but has produced convergent responses as independent adaptations to similar environments. The argument is not even worth considering unless the similarity is so precise that identical function cannot be reasonably denied, as in the classic case of evolutionary convergence—the eyes of vertebrates and octopuses. Here Wilson fails badly, for his favorite analogies arise by a twisted process of imposing human institutions on animals by metaphor, and then rederiving the human institutions as special cases of the more general phenomenon "discovered" in nature. In this way human institutions suddenly become "natural" and can be viewed as a product of evolution.

A classic example, long antedating *Sociobiology*, is "slavery" in ants. "Slavemaking" species capture the immature stages of "slave" species and bring them back to their own nests. When the captured workers hatch, they perform housekeeping tasks with no compulsion as if they were members of the captor species. Why is this "slavemaking" instead of "domestication"? Human slavery involves members of one's own species under continued compulsion. It is an economic institution in societies producing an economic surplus, with both slave and product as commodities in exchange. It has nothing to do with ants except by weak and meaningless analogy. Wilson expands the realm of these weak analogies (chapter 27) to find barter, division of labor, role playing, culture, ritual, religion, magic, esthetics, and tribalism among nonhumans. But if we insist upon seeing animals in the mirror of our own social arrangements, we cannot fail to find any human institutions we want among them.

GENETIC BASES OF BEHAVIOR

We can dispense with the direct evidence for a genetic basis of various human social forms in a single word, "None." The genetics of normal human behavior is in a rudimentary state because of the impossibility of reproducing particular human genotypes over and over, or of experimentally manipulating the environments of individuals or groups. There is no evidence that meets the elementary requirements of experimental design, that such traits as xenophobia, religion, ethics, social dominance, hierarchy formation, slavemaking, etc., are in any way coded specifically in the genes of human beings.

And indeed, Wilson offers no such evidence. Instead, he makes confused and contradictory statements about what is an essential element in the argument. If there are no genes for parent-offspring conflict, then there is no sense in talking about natural selection for this phenomenon. Thus, he speaks of "genetically programmed sexual and parent-offspring conflict" (p. 563), yet there is the "considerable technical problem of distinguishing behavioral elements and combinations that emerge . . . independently of learning and those that are shaped at least to some extent by learning" (p. 159). In fact, it cannot be done.

Elsewhere, the *capacity* to learn is stated to be genetic in the species, so that "it does not matter whether aggression is wholly innate or acquired partly or wholly by learning" (p. 255). But it does matter. If all that is genetically programmed into people is that "genes promoting flexibility in social behavior are strongly selected" (p. 549) and if "genes have given away most of their sovereignty" (p. 550), then biology and evolution give no insight into the human condition except the most trivial one, that the *possibility* of social behavior is part of human biology. However, in the next phrase Wilson reasserts the sovereignty of the genes because they "maintain a certain amount of influence in at least the behavioral qualities that underly the variations between cultures." It is stated as *fact* that genetical differences underlie variations between cultures, when no evidence at all exists for this assertion and there is some considerable evidence against it.

Since sociobiologists can adduce no facts to support the genetic basis for human social behavior, they try two tacks. First, the suggestion of evolutionary homology between behavior in the human species and other animals, if correct, would imply a genetic basis in us. But the evidence for homology as opposed to analogy is very weak. Second, they postulate genes right and left and then go on to argue as if the genes were demonstrated facts. There are hypothetical altruist genes, conformer genes, spite genes, learning genes, homosexuality genes, and so on. An instance of the technique is on pages 554–555 of Wilson's book: "Dahlberg showed that *if* a single gene appears that is responsible for success and upward shift in status. . ." and "Furthermore, *there are many* Dahlberg genes. . ." (our emphases throughout). Or on page 562: "*If we assume* for argument that indoctrinability evolves . . ." and "Societies containing higher frequencies of conformer genes replace those that disappear . . ." (our emphasis). Or consult nearly any page of Trivers (1971) for many more examples.

Geneticists long ago abandoned the naive notion that there are genes for toes, genes for ankles, genes for the lower leg, genes for the kneecap, or the like. Yet sociobiologists break the totality of human social phenomena into arbitrary units, which they reify as "organs of behavior," postulating particular genes for each.

EVERYTHING IS ADAPTIVE

The next step in the sociobiological argument is to try to show that the hypothetical, genetically programmed behavior organs have evolved by natural selection. The assertion that all human behavior is or has been adaptive is an outdated expression of Darwinian evolutionary theory, characteristic of Darwin's 19th century defenders who felt it necessary to prove everything adaptive. It is a deeply conservative politics, not an understanding of modern evolutionary theory, that leads one to see the wonderful operation of adaptation in every feature of human social organization.

There is no hint in *Sociobiology* that at this very moment the scientific community of evolutionary geneticists is deeply split on the question of how important adaptive as opposed to random processes are in manifest evolution. More important, there is a strain in modern evolutionary thought, going back to Julian Huxley, that avoids much of the tortured logic required by extreme selectionism, by emphasizing allometry. Organs, not themselves under direct natural selection, may change because of their developmental links to other features that are under selection. Many aspects of human social organization, if not all, may be simply the consequence of increased plasticity of neurological response and cognitive capacity.

The major assertion of sociobiologists that human social structures exist because of their superior adaptive value is only an assumption for which no tests have even been proposed. The entire theory is so constructed that *no tests are possible.* The mode of explanation involves three postulated levels of the operation of natural selection: (1) classical individual selection to account for obviously self-serving behaviors; (2) kin selection to account for altruistic behaviors or submissive acts toward relatives; (3) reciprocal altruism to account for altruistic behaviors toward unrelated persons. All that remains is to make up a "just-so" story of adaptation with the appropriate form of selection acting. For some traits it is easy to invent a story. The "genes" for social dominance, aggression, entrepreneurship, successful deception, and so on will "obviously" be advantageous at the individual level. For example, evidence is presented (p. 288) that dominant males impregnate a disproportionate share of females in mice, baboons, and Yanamamo Indians. In fact, in the ethnographic literature there are numerous examples of groups whose political "leaders" do not have greater access to mates. In general it is hard to demonstrate a correlation of any of the sociobiologists' "adaptive" social behaviors with actual differential reproduction.

Other traits require more ingenuity. Homosexuality would seem to be at a reproductive disadvantage since "of course, homosexual men marry much less frequently and have far fewer children" (Dr. Kinsey disagreed, and what about homosexual women?). But a little ingenuity solves the problem: "The homosexual members of primitive societies may have functioned as helpers . . . [operated] with special efficiency in assisting close relatives" (p. 555). Kin selection saves the day when one's imagination for individual selection fails.

Only one more imaginative mechanism is needed to rationalize such phenomena as friendship, morality, patriotism, and submissiveness, even when the bonds do not involve relatives. The theory of reciprocal altruism (Trivers 1971) proposes that selection has operated such that risk taking and acts of kindness can be recognized and reciprocated so that the net fitness of both participants is increased.

The trouble with the whole system is that nothing is explained because everything is explained. If individuals are selfish, that is explained by simple individual selection. If, on the contrary, they are altruistic, it is kin selection or reciprocal altruism. If sexual identities are unambiguously heterosexual, individual fertility is increased. If, however, homosexuality is common, it is a result of kin selection. Sociobiologists give us no example that might conceivably contradict their scheme of perfect adaptation.

VARIATIONS OF CULTURES IN TIME AND SPACE

There does exist one possibility of tests of sociobiological hypotheses when they make specific *quantitative* predictions about rates of change of characters in time and about the degree of differentiation between populations of a species. Population genetics makes specific predictions about rates of change, and there are hard data on the degree of genetic differentiation between human populations for biochemical traits. Both the theoretical rates of *genetic* change in time and the observed *genetic* differentiation between populations are too small to agree with the very rapid changes that have occurred in human *cultures* historically and the very large *cultural* differences observed among contemporaneous populations. So, for example, the rise of Islam after the 7th century to supreme cultural and political power in the West, to its subsequent rapid decline after the 13th century (a cycle occupying fewer than 30 generations) was too rapid by orders of magnitude for any large change by natural selection. The same problem arises for the immense cultural differences between contemporary groups, since we know from the study of enzyme-specifying genes that there is very little genetic differentiation between nations and races.

Wilson acknowledges and deals with both of these dilemmas by a bold stroke: He invents a new phenomenon. It is the "multiplier effect" (pp. 11–13, 569–572), which postulates that very small differences in the frequency of hypothetical genes for altruism, conformity, indoctrinability, etc., could move a whole society from one cultural pattern to another. The only evidence offered for this "multiplier effect" is a description of differences in behavior between closely related species of insects and of baboons. There is, however, no evidence about the amount of *genetic* difference between these closely related species nor how many tens or hundreds of thousands of generations separate the members of these species pairs since their divergence. The multiplier effect, by which any arbitrary but unknown genetic difference can be converted to any cultural difference you please, is a pure invention of convenience without any evidence to support it. It has been created out of whole cloth to seal off the last aperture through which the theory might have been tested against the real world.

AN ALTERNATIVE VIEW

It is often stated by biological determinists that those who oppose them are "environmental determinists," who believe that the behavior of individuals is precisely determined by some sequence of environmental events in childhood. Such an assertion reveals the essential narrowness of viewpoint in determinist ideologies. First, they see the individual as the basic elements of determination and behavior, whereas society is simply the sum of all the individuals in it. But the truth is that the individual's social activity is to be understood only by first understanding social institutions. We cannot understand what it is to be a slave or a slave owner without first understanding the institution of slavery, which defines and creates both slave and owner.

Second, determinists assert that the evolution of societies is the result of changes in the frequencies of different sorts of individuals within them. But this confuses cause and effect. Societies evolve because social and economic activity alter the physical and social conditions in which these activities occur. Unique historical events, actions of some individuals, and the altering of consciousness of masses of people interact with social and economic forces to influence the timing, form, and even the possibility of particular changes; individuals are not totally autonomous units whose individual qualities determine the direction of social evolution. Feudal society did not pass away because some autonomous force increased the frequency of entrepreneurs. On the contary, the economic activity of Western feudal society itself resulted in a change in economic relations which made serfs into peasants and then into landless industrial workers with all the immense changes in social institutions that were the result.

Finally, determinists assert that the possibility of change in social institutions is limited by the biological constraints on individuals. But we know of no relevant constraints placed on social processes by human biology. There is no evidence from ethnography, archaeology, or history that would enable us to circumscribe the limits of possible human social organization. What history and ethnography do provide us with are the materials for building a theory that will itself be an instrument of social change.

REFERENCES

Birket-Smith, K. (1959). *The Eskimos,* 2nd ed. (London: Methuen).

Fried, M. (1967). *The Evolution of Political Society.* (New York: Random House).

Harris, M. (1968). Law and Order in Egalitarian Societies. Pages 369–391 in *Culture, Man and Nature* (New York: Crowell).

Krader, L. (1968). "Government Without the State." In *Formation of the State.* (Englewood Cliffs, N.J.: Prentice Hall) pp. 53–110.

Lorenz, K. (1940). "Durch Domestikation verursachte Störungen arteigenen Verhaltens." *Zeitschrift für angewandte Psychologie und Characterkunde* 59, pp. 56–75. (As quoted in Cloud, W., 1973, "Winners and Sinners." *The Sciences* 13, pp. 16–21).

Livingstone, F. (1968). "The Effects of Warfare on the Biology of the Human Species." In M. Fried, M. Harris, and R. Murphy, eds. *War: The Anthropology of Armed Conflict and Aggression* (Garden City: Natural History Press) pp. 3–15.

Spencer, H. (1851). *Social Statics.* (London: Chapman).

Trivers, R. (1971). "The Evolution of Reciprocal Altruism." *Q. Rev. Biol.* 46, pp. 35–57.

Wilson, E. O. (1975). *Sociobiology: The New Synthesis* (Cambridge, Mass.: Harvard University Press).

Academic Vigilantism and the Political Significance of Sociobiology

Edward O. Wilson

The best response to a political attack of the kind exemplified by the preceding article, "Sociobiology—Another Biological Determinism," is perhaps no response at all. Some of my colleagues have offered that advice. But the problem is larger than the personal distress that this and earlier activities of the Science for the People group have caused me. The issue at hand, I submit, is vigilantism: the judgment of a work of science according to whether it conforms to the political convictions of the judges, who are self-appointed. The sentence for scientists found guilty is to be given a label and to be associated with past deeds that all decent persons will find repellent.

Thus, in a statement published earlier in *The New York Review of Books* (Allen et al. 1975), the Science for the People group characterized my book *Sociobiology: The New Synthesis* (Wilson 1975a) as the latest attempt to reinvigorate theories that in the past "provided an important basis for the enactment of sterilization laws and restrictive immigration laws by the United States between 1910 and 1930 and also for the eugenics policies which led to the establishment of gas chambers in Nazi Germany." To this malicious charge they added, "Wilson joins the long parade of biological determinists whose work has served to buttress the institutions of their society by exonerating them from responsibility for social problems." The tone of the present *BioScience* article is muted, but the innuendo is clear and remains the same.

This tactic, which has been employed by members of Science for

From *BioScience* 26, no. 3 (March 1976), pp. 183, 187–190. Published by the American Institute of Biological Sciences. Reprinted by permission of *BioScience* and the author.

the People against other scientists, throws the person criticized into the role of defendant and renders his ideas easier to discredit. Free and open discussion becomes difficult, as the critics continue to press their campaign, and the target struggles to clear his name. The problem is increased by difficulties in knowing with whom one is dealing. The statements are often published over long lists of names, shifts in committee membership occur through time, and the authors' names are withheld from some of the documents. (All have occurred during the present controversy.)

Despite the protean physical form taken by the Sociobiology Study Group of Science for the People, the belief system they promote is clear-cut and rigid. They postulate that human beings need only decide on the kind of society they wish, and then find the way to bring it into being. Such a vision can be justified if human social behavior proves to be infinitely malleable. In their earlier *New York Review* statement (Allen et al. 1975) the group therefore maintained that although eating, excreting, and sleeping may be genetically determined, social behavior is entirely learned; this belief has been developed further in the *BioScience* article. In contrast, and regardless of all they have said, I am ideologically indifferent to the degree of determinism in human behavior. If human beings proved infinitely malleable, as they hope, then one could justify any social or economic arrangement according to his personal value system. If on the other hand, human beings proved completely fixed, then the status quo could be justified as unavoidable.

Few reasonable persons take the first extreme position and none the second. On the basis of objective evidence the truth appears to lie somewhere in between, closer to the environmentalist than to the genetic pole. That was my wholly empirical conclusion in *Sociobiology: The New Synthesis* and continues to be in later writings. There is no reasonable way that this generalization can be construed as a support of the status quo and continued injustice, as the Science for the People group have now, on four painful occasions, claimed. I have personally argued the opposite conclusion, most fully and explicitly in my *New York Times Magazine* article of 12 October 1975 (Wilson 1975b). The Science for the People group have not found it convenient to mention this part of my writings.

With the exception of the Science for the People group, all of the many biologists and social scientists whose reviews of *Sociobiology: The New Synthesis* I have seen understood the book correctly. None has read a reactionary political message into it, even though the reviewers represent a variety of personal political persuasions; and none has found my assessment of the degree of determinism in human social behavior out of line with the empirical evidence. The Science for the People group have utterly misrepresented the spirit and content of the portions of *Sociobiology* devoted to human beings. They have done so, it would seem, in order to have a conspicuous straw man against which their views can be favorably pitted, and to obscure the valid points in *Sociobiology* which do indeed threaten their own extreme position. Let me document this interpretation with responses to the specific criticisms made by the 35 cosigners.

RESPONSE TO CRITICISMS

First, it should be noted that *Sociobiology: The New Synthesis* is a large book, within which only chapter 27 and scattered paragraphs in earlier chapters refer to man. The main theses of sociobiology are based on studies of a myriad of animal species conducted by hundreds of investigators in various biological disciplines. It has been possible to derive propositions by the traditional postulational and deductive methods of theoretical science, and to test many of them rigorously by quantitative studies. Once can cite the work on kin selection in social Hymenoptera, the elaboration of caste systems in social insects, the economic functions of vertebrate territories, the ecological causes of ungulate social behavior, the repertory size and transmission characteristics of communication systems, and others. These ideas and data provide the main thrust of general sociobiology.

In my book human sociobiology was approached tentatively and in a taxonomic rather than a political spirit. The final chapter opens with the following passage: "Let us now consider man in the free spirit of natural history, as though we were zoologists from another planet completing a catalog of social species on Earth. In this macroscopic view the humanities and social sciences shrink to specialized branches of biology; history, biography, and fiction are the research protocols of human ethology; and anthropology and sociology together constitute the sociobiology of a single primate species."

It is the intellectually viable contention of the final chapter that the sociobiological methods which have proved effective in the study of animals can be extended to human beings, even though our vastly more complex, flexible behavior will make the application technically more difficult. The degree of success cannot yet be predicted. Chapter 27 was intended to be a beginning rather than a conclusion, and other reviewers have so interpreted it. In it I have characterized the distinctive human traits as best I could from the literature of the social sciences, and I have offered a set of hypotheses about the evolution of the traits stated in a way that seemed to make them most susceptible to analysis by sociobiological methods.

The Science for the People group ignore this main thrust of the book. They cite piece by piece incorrectly, or out of context, and then add their own commentary to furnish me with a political attitude I do not have and the book with a general conclusion that is not there. The following examples cover nearly all of their points.

Roles

The 35 cosigners have me saying that role sectors, and thus certain forms of economic role behavior associated with role sectors, are universal in man. On pages 552 and 554, the reader will find that I did not include role sectors among the widespread or universal traits. What I said was that when role sectors occur, certain economic features are associated with them.

Territory

It is now well known that animal territories commonly vary in size and quality of defense according to habitat, season, and population density. Under some circumstances many species show no territorial behavior, but it is necessary for them to display the behavior under other, specified circumstances in order to be called territorial—an obvious condition. This is the reason I have called the human species territorial. No contradiction in definitions exists; the cosigners have made it appear to exist by simply deleting three key pieces from the quoted statement. Most human societies are territorial most of the time.

Warfare

In *Sociobiology* I presented widespread lethal warfare in early human groups as a working hypothesis, not as a fact, contrary to what the cosigners suggest. And it is a hypothesis wholly consistent with the evidence: military activity and territorial expansion have been concomitants throughout history and at all levels of social organization (Otterbein 1970), and they can hardly fail to have had significant demographic and genetic consequences.

Slavery and Other Terms

The cosigners state that I claim to have found barter, religion, magic, and tribalism among nonhumans. I have made no such claim. The cosigners do not like to see terms such as slavery, division of labor, and ritual used in both zoology and the social sciences. Do they wish also to expunge communication, dominance, monogamy, and parental care from the vocabulary of zoology?

Genetic Bases of Behavior

The cosigners claim that no evidence exists for the genetic basis of particular forms of social behavior. Their statement indicates that they do not use the same criteria as other biologists. To postulate the existence of genes for the diagnostic human traits is not to imply that there exists one gene for spite, another for homosexuality, and so on, as one might envision the inheritance of flower color or seed texture in garden peas. The tendency to develop such behaviors, in a distinctively human form, is part of an immensely complex social repertory which is undoubtedly dependent on large numbers of genes.

My emphasis in *Sociobiology* was on the most widespread, distinctive qualities of human behavior—"human nature" if you wish—and the possible reasons why the underlying genes are different from those affecting social behavior in other species. Certain forms of human social behavior, such as the facial expressions used to convey the basic emotions, are relatively inflexible and transcultural. Human expressions, in fact, are so similar to those of the higher cercopithecoid primates as to suggest the possible existence of true homology (*Sociobiology*, pp. 227–228). Other kinds of response, including those under the categories of aggression, sexuality, and conformity, are of course subject to great variation through differences in experience. But as plastic as these latter behaviors might seem to us, they still form only a small subset of the many versions found in social species as a whole. It seems inconceivable that human beings could be socialized into the distinctive patterns of, say, ring-tailed lemurs, hamadryas baboons, or gibbons, or vice versa. This is the ordinary criterion on which the expression "genetic control of human social behavior" in sociobiology is based. The main idea conveyed by the final chapter of my book is that such a comparison with other social species will place human behavior in a clearer evolutionary perspective.

With reference to genetic variation between human populations, there is no firm evidence. As usual, the cosigners misrepresent what I said. Here is their claim: "It is stated as a *fact* that genetical differences underlie variations between cultures, when no evidence at all exists for this assertion and there is some considerable evidence against it" (emphasis theirs). Here is what I really said, in the very sentences to which they allude (p. 550): "Even a small portion of this [genetic] variance invested in population differences *might* predispose societies toward cultural differences. At the very least, we should try to measure this amount. It is not valid to point to the absence of a behavioral trait in one or a few societies as conclusive evidence that the trait is environmentally induced and has no genetic disposition in man. The very opposite *could* be true" (italics newly added).

Adaptation versus Non-adaptation

The Science for the People group state that I believe all social behavior to be adaptive and hence "normal." This is so patently false that I am surprised the cosigners could bring themselves to say it. I have on the contrary discussed circumstances under which certain forms of animal social behavior become maladaptive, with examples and ways in which the deviations can be analyzed (pp. 33–34). With reference to human social behavior I have said (Wilson 1975b, an article well known to the cosigners): "When any genetic bias is demonstrated, it cannot be used to justify a continuing practice in present and future societies. Since most of us live in a radically new environment of our own making, the pursuit of such a practice would be bad biology; and like all bad biology, it would invite disaster." I then cited examples of maladaptive behavior in human beings. Furthermore, both R. L. Trivers and I have provided varieties of adaptation hypotheses that compete with each other and against the non-adaptation hypothesis, contrary to the assertion of the Science for the People group (see, e.g., *Sociobiology:* pp. 123–124, 309–311, 326–327, 416–418).

Cultural Evolution

The cosigners propose that "sociobiological hypotheses" can be tested by seeing whether certain short-term episodes in history, such as the rise and decline of Islam, occurred too rapidly to be due to genetic change. They conclude that the theory of population genetics excludes that possibility. I agree, and that is why neither I nor any other sociobiologist of my acquaintance has ever proposed such hypotheses. The examples I used in *Sociobiology* to make the same point are the origin of the slave society of Jamaica, the decline of the Ik in Uganda, the alteration of Irish society following the potato famine, and the shift in the Japanese authority structure following World War II (pp. 548–550). I see no reason why the subject was even brought up. (A fuller discussion of the rates of cultural evolution and the complementarity of cultural to genetic evolution can be found in pages 168–175 and 555–562 of *Sociobiology.*)

COMMENTS ON THE DEBATE

I now invite readers to check each of the pronouncements in the article by the 35 cosigners against the actual statements in my book, in the true context in which the statements were made. I suggest that they will encounter very little correspondence, and I am confident that they will be left with no doubt as to my true meaning.

How is it possible for the Science for the People group to misrepresent so consistently the content of a book, in contrast to all of the many other reviewers among their scientific colleagues? There is first the circumstance of the size and composition of the group. It has grown from 16, when it called itself The Genetic Engineering Group of Scientists and Engineers for Social and Political Action (in the magazine *Science for the People*, November 1975), to the present 35 now identified as the Sociobiology Study Group of Science for the People. The membership is heterogeneous: from the best count I can make there are eight professors in several fields of science in the Boston area; other members include at least one psychiatrist, a secondary school teacher, students and research assistants. Furthermore, in conformity with their political convictions the group really does believe in collective decision making and writing, so perhaps the result is not all that surprising. (In the issue of *Science for the People* just mentioned, the two main targets of criticism were myself, for biological determinism, and the Soviet Union, for revisionism.)

But the other, more important cause of the problem, and the reason I have not been able to find the matter as humorous as have some of my colleagues, is the remorseless zeal of the cosigners. By their own testimony they worked for months on the project. They appear to have been alarmed by the impact a critical success of the book might have on the acceptability of their own political views. One of the faculty members, in a *Harvard Crimson* interview on 3 November 1975, stated that the group was formed of persons who became interested "in breaking down the screen of approval" around the book. Clamorous denunciations followed during a closely packed series of lectures, work sessions, and release of printed statements. In October 1975 a second professorial member of the group drafted a 5,000-word position paper for *The New York Times* which characterized me as an ideologue and a privileged member of modern Western industrial society whose book attempts to preserve the status quo (*The New York Times*, 9 November 1975). Later the same person (who shares the identical privileges at Harvard) startled me even more by declaring that "Sociobiology is not a racist doctrine" but "any kind of genetic determinism can and does feed other kinds, including the belief that some races are superior to others" (*Harvard Crimson*, 3 December 1975).

The latter argument is identical to that advanced simultaneously by student members of the Harvard-Radcliffe Committee against Racism, who, citing the Science for the People statement for authority, did not hesitate to label the book "dangerously racist" in leaflets distributed through the Boston area. Both the logic and the accusation were false and hurtful, and at this point the matter was close to getting out of hand.

On various occasions and with only limited success the Harvard faculty has attempted to protect itself from activities of this kind. During an earlier, similar episode 100 of its members published a statement that "In an academic community the substitution of personal harassment for reasoned inquiry is intolerable. The openminded search for truth cannot proceed in an atmosphere of political intimidation." This is the melancholy principle which has been confirmed by the exchange now extended to *BioScience*. In the Boston area at the present time it has become difficult to conduct an open forum on human sociobiology, or even general sociobiology, without falling into the role of either prosecutor or defendant.

THE POLITICAL SIGNIFICANCE OF SOCIOBIOLOGY

Finally and briefly, let me express what I consider to be the real significance of human sociobiology for political and social thought. The question that science is now in a position to approach is the very origin and meaning of human values, from which all ethical pronouncements and much of political practice flow. Philosophers themselves have not explored the problem; traditional ethical philosophy begins with premises that are examined with reference to their consequences but not their origins. Thus, John Rawls open his celebrated *A Theory of Justice* (1971) with a proposition he regards as beyond dispute: "In a just society the liberties of equal citizenship are taken as settled; the rights secured by justice are not subject to political bargaining or to the calculus of social interests." Robert Nozick launches his equally celebrated *Anarchy, State, and Utopia* (1974) with a similarly firm proposition: "Individuals have rights, and there are things no person or group may do to them (without violating their rights). So strong and far-reaching are these rights that they raise the question of what, if anything, the state and its officials may do."

These two premises are somewhat different in content, and they lead to radically different prescriptions. Rawls would allow rigid social control to secure as close an approach as possible to the equal distribution of society's rewards. Nozick sees the ideal society as one governed by a minimal state, empowered only to protect its citizens from force and fraud, and with unequal distribution of rewards wholly permissible. Rawls rejects the meritocracy; Nozick accepts it as desirable except in those cases where local communities voluntarily decide to experiment with egalitarianism.

Whether in conflict or agreement, where do such fundamental premises come from? What lies behind the intuition on which they are based? Contemporary philosophers have progressed no further than Sophocles' Antigone, who said of moral imperatives, "They were not born today or yesterday; they die not, and none knoweth whence they sprung."

At this point the 35 members of the Science for the People group also come to a halt. At the close of their essay they imply the central issue to be a decision about the kind of the society we want to live in; humanity can then find the way to bring this society into being. But which persons are the "we" who will decide, and whose moral precepts must thereby be validated? The group believe that all social behavior is learned and transmitted by culture. But if this is true, the value system by which "we" will decide social policy is created by the culture in which the most powerful decision makers were reared and hence must inevitably validate the status quo, the very condition which the Science for the People group reject. The solution to the conundrum must be that their premise of complete environmentalism is wrong.

The evidence that human nature is to some extent genetically influenced is in my opinion decisive. In the present space I can only suggest that the reader consider the facts presented in *Sociobiology* and in the very extensive primary literature on the subject, some of which is cited in this work. It follows that value systems are probably influenced, again to an unknown extent, by emotional responses programmed in the limbic system of the brain. The qualities that comprise human nature in the Maring of New Guinea as recognizably as they did in the Greeks at Troy are surely due in part to constraints within the unique human genotype. The challenge of human sociobiology, shared with the social sciences, is to measure the degree of these constraints and to infer their significance through the reconstruction of the evolutionary history of the mind. The enterprise is the logical complement to the continued study of cultural evolution.

Even if that formidable challenge is successfully met, however, it will still leave the ethical question: To what extent should the censors and motivators in the emotive centers of the brain be obeyed? Given that these controls deeply and unconsciously affect our moral decisions, how faithfully must they be consulted once they have been defined and assayed as a biological process? The answer must confront what appears to me to be the true human dilemma. We cannot follow the suggestions of the censors and motivators blindly. Although they are the source of our deepest and most compelling feelings, their genetic constraints evolved during the millions of years of prehistory, under conditions that to a large extent no longer exist. At some time in the future it will be necessary to decide how human we wish to remain, in this the ultimate biological sense, and to pick and choose consciously among the emotional guides we have inherited.

This dilemma should engender a sense of reserve about proposals for radical social change based on utopian intuition. To the extent that the biological interpretation noted here proves correct, men have rights that are innate, rooted in the ineradicable drives for survival and self-esteem, and these rights do not require the validation of ad hoc theoretical constructions produced by society. If culture is all that created human rights, as the extreme environmentalist position holds, then culture can equally well validate their removal. Even some philosophers of the radical left see this flaw in the position taken by Science for the People. Noam Chomsky, whose own linguistic research has provided evidence for the existence of genetic influence, considers extreme environmentalism to be a belief susceptible to dictatorships of both the left and the right:

One can easily see why reformers and revolutionaries should become radical environmentalists, and there is no doubt that concepts of immutable human nature can be and have been employed to erect barriers against social change and to defend established privilege. But a deeper look will show that the concept of the "empty organism," plastic and unstructured, apart from being false, also serves naturally as the support for the most reactionary social doctrines. If people are, in fact, malleable and plastic beings with no essential psychological nature, then why should they not be controlled and coerced by those who claim authority, special knowledge, and a unique insight into what is best for those less enlightened? . . . The principle that human nature, in its psychological aspects, is nothing more than a product of history and given social relations removes all barriers to coercion and manipulation by the powerful. This too, I think, may be a reason for its appeal to intellectual ideologists, of whatever political persuasion (Chomsky 1975, p. 132).

Chomsky and I, not to mention Herbert Marcuse (who has a similar belief in the biological conservatism of human nature), can scarcely be accused of having linked arms to preserve the status quo, and yet that would seem to follow from the strange logic employed by the Science for the People group.

In their corybantic attentions to sociobiology, the Science for the People group have committed what can be usefully termed the Fallacy of the Political Consequent. This is the assumption that political belief systems can be mapped one-on-one onto biological or psychological generalizations. Another particularly ironic example is the response to B. F. Skinner's writings. Skinner is a radical environmentalist, whose conclusions about human behavior are essentially indistinguishable from those of the Science for the People group. Yet the particular political conclusions he has drawn are anathema to the radical left, who reject them as elitist, reactionary, and so forth. The cause of the Fallacy of the Political Consequent is the failure to appreciate adequately that scientific theories and political ideas are both complex and tenuously linked, and that political ideas are shaped in good part by personal judgments lying outside the domain of scientific evaluation.

All political proposals, radical and otherwise, should be seriously received and debated. But whatever direction we choose to take in the future, social progress can only be enhanced, not impeded, by the deeper investigation of the genetic constraints of human nature, which will steadily replace rumor and folklore with testable knowledge. Nothing is to be gained by a dogmatic denial of the existence of the constraints or attempts to discourage public discussion of them. Knowledge humanely acquired and widely shared, related to human needs but kept free of political censorship, is the real science for the people.

REFERENCES

Allen, E. et al. (1975). "Against 'Sociobiology'." *The New York Review of Books,* November 13.

Chomsky, N. (1975). *Reflections on Language* (New York: Pantheon Books, Random House).

Nozick, R. (1974). *Anarchy, State and Utopia* (New York: Basic Books).
Otterbein, K. F. (1970). *The Evolution of War* (New Haven, Conn.: Human Relations Area Files Press).
Rawls, J. (1971). *A Theory of Justice* (Cambridge, Mass.: Harvard University Press).
Wilson, E. O. (1975a). *Sociobiology: The New Synthesis* (Cambridge, Mass.: Harvard University Press).
———. (1975b). "Human Decency Is Animal." *The New York Times Magazine,* October 12, pp. 38–50.

Ethics, Evolution, and the Milk
of Human Kindness

Arthur L. Caplan

Sufficient time has elapsed since the publication of Edward O. Wilson's massive new book, *Sociobiology: The New Synthesis* (Cambridge: Harvard University Press, 1975) to permit a large body of critical review articles to accumulate. And accumulate they surely have. Nearly every journal concerned even peripherally with scientific issues has commissioned a review. While many reviewers have acclaimed Wilson's erudition and insight, others have criticized his efforts. This is not, of course, the first time that a new book has received a mixed set of notices. However, *Sociobiology* has been criticized and acclaimed on the basis of so many diverse arguments that it is natural to ask why the book provokes such divergent responses.

Many biologists have praised the book for its biological erudition and analytical insight into complex evolutionary phenomena. Much of the attention given the book has resulted, however, from claims that Wilson commits a series of damning mistakes in extending his evolutionary analysis to human social behavior. These ethical charges will bear the brunt of critical scrutiny in this essay. However, in order to assess the worth of Wilson's evolutionary analysis of human social behavior, it will be necessary first to comment on the book itself and then to explicate the nature of the methodological assumptions underlying Wilson's effort to understand social behavior in all organisms.

Most of Wilson's book is of course devoted to reviewing and critically

From Hastings Center Report (April 1976). Copyright © 1976 by the Institute of Society, Ethics and the Life Sciences, 360 Broadway, Hastings-on-Hudson, N.Y. 10706. Reprinted by permission of the publisher and the author.

analyzing the enormous body of scientific information accumulated over the years concerning the social behaviors that are manifested by both contemporary and fossil organisms. As if this were not in itself a monumental task, Wilson assigns himself the additional chore of attempting to formulate evolutionary explanations for the diversity of social behaviors reported in this literature. Population genetics, population ecology, demography, and biogeography are the tools he employs. Using these disciplines, Wilson hopes to be able to draw together the seemingly disparate patterns of sociality displayed by birds, primates, insects, and man by means of a common evolutionary account of the origin and maintenance of these behaviors. He says: "This book makes an attempt to codify sociobiology into a branch of evolutionary biology and particularly modern population biology. When the same parameters and quantitative theory are used to analyze both termite colonies and troops of rhesus macaques we will have a unified science of sociobiology." This set of variables and quantitative evolutionary principles constitutes the methodological apparatus of what Wilson hopes will become the new integrative science of sociobiology.

A large part of Wilson's book is devoted to laying out the rudiments of evolutionary theory. Readers whose evolutionary education ended with Julian Huxley, Ernst Mayr, Theodosius Dobzhansky, or George Simpson will discover that mathematical modelers and population theorists have been busily extending the idealized assumptions of modern evolutionary theory to encompass more realistic biological situations. No longer need we puzzle about the fate of a single gene in a hypothetical population possessing such unrealistic properties as nonoverlapping generations and a complete absence of migration and genetic drift. Contemporary evolutionary theorists are concerned with studying the evolutionary effects of realistic biological factors such as variable population density, unstable age distributions, and fluctuating migration patterns on natural populations of all shapes and sizes.

Indeed, the richness and abundance of evolutionary theory recounted by Wilson leads one to wonder about the legitimacy of the complaints and fears frequently voiced by an older generation of biologists concerning the neglect of organismic biology in favor of the siren-like reductionist disciplines of molecular genetics, biochemistry, and biophysics. After Wilson's extensive explanatory analysis of such fascinating and intricate behaviors as slave making in ants, parasitism in cowbirds, and mutual symbiosis in fish (all depicted in a set of magnificent illustrations, by the way), it seems doubtful whether molecular biologists will ever be able to convince another graduate student to devote a lifetime of study to *E. coli* or any other microorganism.

So there we have it. Wilson urges that behavioral biology is in need of a good strong dose of evolutionary theory. Social behavior, which he sees as the heart of behavioral inquiry, requires the most powerful evolutionary ministrations. And since what is good enough for the termite and rhesus monkey seems good enough for man, behaviorally speaking, the social behavior of human beings—politics, culture, ethics, and religion—must also be subject to evolutionary analysis. The result will be a new comprehensive science, sociobiology, that will straddle the domains currently occupied by the rather notorious black sheep of the scientific family—ethology, sociology, animal behavior, and comparative psychology.

A number of biologists have found the prospect of such a science tremendously exciting. James Bonner and D. S. Sade, in their reviews of Wilson's book in *Scientific American* (October 1975) and *Science* (October 10, 1975), respectively, see a bright and fruitful future for the nascent science Wilson presents. Sade opts for the incorporation of anthropology into the gaping maw of sociobiology, and apparently not satisfied with this addition, tosses in the bulk of the humanities and the arts for good measure. Sade and Bonner are representatives of a group of "endorser-extenders" that seem to have no objection to Wilson's theoretical approach to social behavior. They see no reason for delay in extending evolutionary investigation to man's complex array of social customs and behaviors. The "murky" findings of such dubious enterprises as sociology will soon, in Bonner's view, be replaced by the precise quantifiable findings of population biology and evolutionary theory.

Allied with these unabashed enthusiasts are a second group of reviewers who teeter briefly on the edge of criticism before plunging headlong into a rousing endorsement of Wilson's work. The reviews of V. C. Wynne-Edwards in *Nature* (January 22, 1976) and Robert Morison in *Natural History* (November 1975) fall into this category of "cautioner-endorsers." Their caution seems to center around two matters of methodological interest. Wynne-Edwards worries whether Wilson is rigorous enough about defining the properties that allow a scientist to confer the label "society" on a biological system. Sponges and polyps and other primitive multicellular creatures that Wilson considers to be the *ne plus ultra* of sociality do not count at all on Wynne-Edwards's typology of social organisms. Since little appears to hang upon the decision concerning how much behavior is enough for sociality, Wynne-Edwards does not hesitate to endorse Wilson's evolutionary explanatory approach. Morison worries that the vagaries of the comparative analysis of behavior may prove troublesome in assessing and explaining human behavior. But he, like Wilson, argues that vagueness and uncertainty are not enough, in and of themselves, to restrain evolutionary inquiry and speculation in this area.

The predominantly critical responses to Wilson's book seem to fall into two general categories. Some biologists have taken exception to Wilson's efforts for purely methodological reasons. Others, however, have objected to the book on moral or ethical grounds. Interestingly, the methodological criticisms leveled at the book are not cited by those reviewers who raise objections on value or ethical grounds. Although these two sorts of critical reviews seem to stand independently of one another, it may be that both the merits and faults inherent in the book demand a simultaneous consideration of both methodological and value issues. Therefore, it is necessary to consider a review which is paradigmatic of the methodological-criticism variety.

C. H. Waddington, in his review in the *New York Review of Books* (August 7, 1975), is unhappy with Wilson's selection of altruistic behavior as the focal point of sociobiological inquiry. Why should biologists devote special attention, Waddington wonders, to altruistic behavior when social communication or the evolution of mentality seem to be equally legitimate problems?

Perhaps Wilson's interest in altruism can be dismissed, as Waddington suggests, as an anomalous idiosyncratic interest motivated by Wilson's fascination with recent population genetic research into kin and group selection. However, Waddington's view can be seen to be invalid once altruistic behavior is viewed in light of the assumptions of contemporary evolutionary theory. This theory, propounded by biologists such as Mayr, Dobzhansky, Simpson, Ford, and Waddington himself, views evolution as the product of organisms striving to maximize their contributions to the gene pool of future generations. The individual is the primary unit of evolutionary change. What Waddington fails to realize is that altruistic behavior, unlike social communication or mentality, cannot be explained on the basis of reproductive advantage accruing to individual organisms displaying social behavior. Caste sterility, warning cries, adoption, food sharing, and dominance hierarchies all represent *prima facie* instances of altruistic behavior, in which an individual sacrifices reproductive ability and personal fitness for the benefit of other organisms. It is difficult to reconcile the willingness of individuals to display sacrificial altruistic behavior with the central tenet of evolutionary theory that all adaptations and behaviors are aimed at maximizing individual success.

Wilson argues that altruistic behavior can be understood only by thinking of the possible advantages accruing to sets of genes or groups of organisms. We can no longer think in terms of individual success but, rather, must see traits and behaviors as increasing the reproductive fitness of sets of genes. Altruism must be considered the prime phenomenon of sociobiological interest because of the shift necessitated in evolutionary theory from explanations based upon individual advantage to those based upon genetic advantage. While Wilson is not always explicit about the reasons for elevating altruistic behavior to the pinnacle of sociobiological interest, Waddington's criticism fails to appreciate the important theoretical shift underlying Wilson's claim.

If Wilson's book had been confined solely to the compilation and explanation of social behaviors in animals by means of a new synthetic evolutionary approach, it is reasonable to assume that the book would have met with the acclaim and approval of most biologists. But the book contains two more interpretive and highly provocative chapters—the first chapter entitled "The Morality of the Gene," and the last, called "Man: From Sociobiology to Sociology." If one had to pinpoint two book chapters written in the last year likely to create controversy in a scientific community already reeling from debates concerning the validity of IQ research, XYY screening programs, genetic transplantation, and the innately aggressive theory of human nature, these undoubtedly would be the chapters.

Sociobiology, as Wilson conceives of the field, draws under its mantle all aspects of social behavior in every species including man. In fact, because his social behavior is so rich and complex, man is perhaps the most interesting of all the species encompassed by sociobiological inquiry. Wilson shows no reluctance to pursue his inquiry into human social behavior. Ethics, aesthetics, politics, culture and religion, in his view, desperately need *biologization*. He cites such altruistic or seemingly altruistic human behaviors as homosexuality, philanthropy, celibacy, slavery, and martyrdom as all needing evolutionary explanations. Like every other structural and behavioral trait, such behaviors must have their origins in selection acting upon genes. A metaphysical commitment to environmentalism must not be permitted to blind scientific inquiry to the fact that much of what we are and how we got that way can be understood in terms of selection pressures on our ancestors' genetic components and organic traits.

Almost inevitably Wilson's willingness to ascribe a hereditary base and evolutionary origin to complex human behaviors, and his attempts to draw explanatory comparisons between animal and human behavior, have drawn a harsh critical response from those reviewers sensitive to the inherent ethical difficulties. In an impassioned letter to the editors in the *New York Review of Books* (November 13, 1975), a Boston-based group of biologists and students warned of the ethical and political dangers lurking behind the "biological determinism" of Wilson's socio-biological approach to human behavior. Wilson's evolutionary explanations of human social behavior, they say, carry the seeds of a genetic justification of regressive sociopolitical policies. Similar speculations in earlier decades blossomed, they claim, into the horrors of eugenics movements, restrictive immigration policies, a rampant competitive ethos in business, and the construction of gas chambers in Nazi Germany. These "value critics" accuse Wilson of treating behavior and social structure simplistically, as the simple end-products of genetic synthesis. He is accused of ignoring the effects of cultural transmissions, of facile comparative generalizations between humans and animals, of *ad hoc* arguments to explain complex human traits, and of a crude and outmoded hereditarianism in his scientific approach to human behavior.

In an equally impassioned response to this letter (December 11, 1975), Wilson decries what he sees as a distortion of the contents and intent of his arguments. Wilson reminds his critics that in *Sociobiology* and in a variety of concurrent articles in various scientific journals and the popular press he explicitly warned against the dangers of simple-minded hereditarianism, *ad hoc* advocacy arguments, facile comparative analogies, and simplistic valuational judgments. Moreover, he argues that sociobiology provides the best means of pursuing an investigation into human nature—a nature that, despite the wishes and desires of various liberal critics, is not infinitely malleable and plastic.

Unfortunately, the personal tone of the debate indicates that the controversy may degenerate into a murky morass of mud-slinging accusations and counter-accusations. This would be most unfortunate, for Wilson's book surely raises fundamental scientific and ethical issues that deserve serious discussion. Can human behavior or any behavioral trait be studied in the same way that structural or physiological organic properties have traditionally been approached by biologists? Is there any methodology for assessing similarities found to exist between animal and human behavior? And, more generally, of what significance are scientific findings and facts to valuational issues in ethics, religion, and politics? And what obligation, if any, should scientists feel about guarding against the possible abuse and misuse of their scientific speculations concerning human nature and human behavior?

It is somewhat puzzling that the "value-critics" of Wilson's book fail to appreciate the theoretical significance of social behavior for evolutionary theorizing despite their admitted ethical distaste for extending evolutionary theorizing to human behavior. It is even more puzzling that, in their haste to formulate ethical criticisms of the book, these same critics seem to commit an important methodological mistake. For much of the hostility to Wilson's evolutionary examination of human social behavior appears to originate in a failure to distinguish clearly between his attempt to give an historical explanation or account of the origin of a trait or behavior, and his attempt to explain the maintenance or persistence of the same trait or behavior in a contemporary population of organisms.

There is a great difference between the explanations that can be invoked to explain the first or rudimentary appearance of a behavior and the explanations that can be used to explain why that same behavior can still be observed in living organisms today. What Wilson tries to do is not so much to explain the *present* manifestation of ethics, culture, and social behavior in contemporary human societies as to explain the *origins* of these behaviors in ancestral societies. It is the conflation of intended historical explanations with explanations of contemporary events that so strongly divides Wilson and his critics.

The error of blurring historical and contemporary accounts should not be a source of controversy once the aims and intentions of sociobiological inquiry are made evident. It is one thing to try and construct evolutionary explanations of rudimentary or primitive altruistic behaviors in ancestral man on the basis of selective environmental forces acting on a variable set of genes. It is quite a different matter to attempt to explain homosexual behavior in twentieth-century American males by means of these same explanatory premises and assumptions. Wilson can make certain assumptions about society, culture, and genetics in the former case that he surely cannot validly make to explain the latter phenomena. While Wilson certainly attempts to explain the origins of human sociality, this attempt can be made entirely independently of an explanation of contemporary human social behavior.

Not only do Wilson's "value-critics" fail to recognize this important distinction, but they also fail to distinguish adequately exactly what it is that they object to in the book on ethical grounds. Just as there are important differences in the assumptions and premises that can be used to explain the origin of a behavior in a population or society and the assumptions and premises used to explain the persistence and presence of the same behavior in a contemporary population or society, there is an important difference between studying the evolution of ethical or social behaviors, and arguing about the ethical validity or worth of behaviors that already exist. One cannot be sure exactly what error these "value-critics" think Wilson has made in engaging in an evolutionary study of human as well as animal sociality.

But perhaps one should not expect a great deal of clarity regarding such value questions. The nature of the relationship between empirical scientific knowledge and moral or value beliefs has long been a bone of contention among philosophers and scientists. It seems painfully obvious to a large number of philosophers and scientists that ethics and science exist in separate worlds, and that it is the most blatant of fallacies to attempt to formulate moral prescriptions on the basis of empirical scientific evidence. It seems equally obvious to an equally large number of philosophers and scientists that scientific findings directly influence the sorts of moral and ethical prescriptions held to be valid at any given moment. The notorious feuds, at the beginning of this century, between those who believed ethics to be reducible to the empirical properties discovered by science and those who denied that any such reduction was possible, have produced a schism between these

two camps that few participants in either group seem willing to acknowledge, much less bridge. But if any answers are to emerge regarding
issues such as the implications of empirical science for ethics, or the
moral responsibilities of scientists, it is necessary at least to be clear
about what the scientists, in this case Wilson, are up to.

There are at least three kinds of questions that can be distinguished
concerning the relationship that obtains between ethics or values and
science:

1. One question concerns the distinction alluded to previously between explaining the origins of a behavior or trait and the presence
of the behavior in a living population. The scientific study of ethics is
concerned with explaining the origins of primitive ethical behavior in
human beings. The evolution of ethics may be a difficult area for scientific
study due to a lack of fossil data concerning primitive behavior; nevertheless it seems to stand as a legitimate subject of scientific investigation
and evolutionary analysis.

2. Entirely distinct from this scientific pursuit is the question of the
ethics of evolution. Although similar-sounding, this question refers to
the problem of determining whether trends or patterns can be seen in
evolution that can be assessed in terms of their ethical worth or merit.

3. The final possible relationship between scientific evolutionary theorizing and ethics can be labeled evolutionary ethics. Scientists interested
in evolutionary ethics are concerned with establishing an ethical or
value system on the basis of a scientific understanding of empirical
evolutionary events.

It is important to distinguish the problem of the evolution of ethics
from the related but distinct question of the ethics of evolution. The
value assessments that can be offered of evolutionary events or the
consequences of the evolutionary process raise issues that are quite
distinct from attempts to understand the origins of ethical behavior.
It may be that scientific speculations concerning human behavioral evolution influence the kinds of value assessments made concerning the
evolutionary process. Nevertheless, disagreements concerning the future
course of evolution should not be allowed to color the legitimacy of
scientific inquiry into the evolution of ethics or any other human activity.

Another question that must be kept distinct is the topic of evolutionary
ethics. This label refers to views which allege that evolution can supply
a foundation or warrant for specific ethical prescriptions and value

systems. Advocates of evolutionary ethics, from Herbert Spencer to Julian Huxley, have claimed that evolution, and in particular human evolution, provides an external standard or foundation upon which it is possible to construct an ethical superstructure. Attempts have been made to justify competition and struggle as well as altruism and cooperation as the moral "goods" to be derived from evolutionary inquiry. It is with regard to this specific topic that the fact/value dichotomy and naturalism/non-naturalism debates loom largest. It is entirely possible for an individual to hold that certain conclusions may be drawn concerning the evolution of human ethics and the ethics of evolution without thereby being committed to a naturalistic belief in the legitimacy of evolutionary ethics.

If I am correct and it is possible to distinguish at least three issues arising concerning the relationship that exists between evolution and ethics, then what, if anything, can be said about Wilson's views on these topics and the views of his critics? Wilson certainly believes that the evolution of ethical and human social behavior constitutes a central problem for the nascent science of sociobiology. He seems to have little interest in discussing the issue of the ethics of evolution, either with regard to value assessment of historical events or prescriptive suggestions as to the future direction evolution should follow. Nor does Wilson appear to be committed to a belief in evolutionary ethics. Instead, contrary to the charges of his critics, Wilson seems merely to urge a new inquiry into the whole issue of ethical naturalism. Wilson seems to say that sociobiological inquiry might produce conclusions that could affect our beliefs about all aspects of human behavior. Surely this claim warrants the sort of serious critical assessment that has been sadly absent in the reviews. Moreover, in their haste to discredit the legitimacy of evolutionary ethics, Wilson's critics make the mistake of attempting to use the very same arguments to deprecate the legitimacy of the independent questions of the evolution of ethics and the ethics of evolution. Little progress can be made toward resolving any of these questions until all parties manage to separate these issues and treat them independently. It is impossible to come to any conclusions concerning the moral responsibilities of scientists and the relationship that exists between their work and particular political beliefs and ideologies unless one understands the aims and intentions underlying the scientific investigation of any problem. Both Wilson and his critics can be faulted for failing to make clear exactly what specific value problems compel their interest in sociobiology.

Many of the objections raised by what I have termed the "value-critics" of Wilson's book are weakened by their inattention to theoretical difficulties that may exist for sociobiology and by the confusion that surrounds ethical issues arising in the context of evolutionary inquiry. There may, however, be a more important reason underlying the diverse nature of the responses that have been made to Wilson's book. For a number of years behavioral biologists have been feuding over the proper methodological approach to studying animal behavior. Europeans, under the influence of ethologists such as Konrad Lorenz and Niko Tinbergen, have tended to lean toward an evolutionary approach to the study of behavior. It is assumed that behavior, particularly innate, species-specific behavior, can be treated as any other organic feature in offering explanations for the presence or uniqueness of a particular behavior. Americans, on the other hand, under the influence of social scientists such as B. F. Skinner, Frank Beach, and T. C. Schneirla have leaned more toward a comparative psychological approach in the study of animal behavior. American researchers have been more concerned with studying the function of behavior than they have been with the origin or maintenance of the trait over long periods of evolutionary history. It may be that Wilson is unpalatable to an American audience because his approach follows in the spirit of the European ethological camp. Perhaps it is not the ethics or the analogies that Wilson's critics find offensive but, rather, the emphasis on heredity and evolution. This claim would ally the "value-critics" of Wilson's book with historical schools of behaviorism and operationalism that I imagine they would find quite distasteful. If I am correct, the sort of response one has to Wilson's book depends upon the sort of methodological approach one brings to bear on behavioral questions. But the subtle historical influences of ethology and comparative psychology in America and Europe on Wilson and his critics remain to be explored.

A Middle Course Between Irrelevance and Scientism

Bernard D. Davis

Arthur Caplan's thoughtful review of E. O. Wilson's *Sociobiology* (Hastings Center Report, April 1976) discusses the problem of evolution and ethics from the point of view of philosophy, which aims at creating a comprehensive system of thought based on clearly defined assumptions and logically consistent inferences. Science, in contrast, aims at understanding the concrete realities of nature, and in its step-by-step approach it is more concerned with the solidity than with the comprehensiveness of its growing body of knowledge. As we grope today for constructive interactions between the two approaches we must recognize that sociobiology can make only limited contributions toward solving social problems. If we expect it to provide "the" basis for an ethical system we will surely be disappointed, and we may miss what it can provide.

I would therefore like to comment on Caplan's statement that Wilson seems "merely" to urge a new inquiry into the issue of ethical naturalism, without being committed to a belief in evolutionary ethics. This is correct, if one accepts Caplan's definition of evolutionary ethics as the search for an evolutionary foundation for specific ethical prescriptions and value systems. But such a deterministic formulation suggests the outmoded view that science can solve all problems, including those involving value judgments. We must reject such scientism. At the same time, we need not accept the opposite extreme—the view that science is irrelevant to such problems. We can take an intermediate position:

Hastings Center Report (October 1976). Copyright © 1976 by the Institute of Society, Ethics and the Life Sciences, 360 Broadway, Hastings-on-Hudson, N.Y. 10706. Reprinted by permission of the publisher and the author.

that even though science cannot solve normative problems, which are in principle incapable of an objectively correct solution, it can nevertheless make valuable contributions. Thus the scientific method can help us to evaluate the means and the consequences of reaching various goals, and these analyses can contribute, along with our value judgments, to our choice of goals. In addition, scientific insights into human nature are surely relevant to the problem of formulating ethical systems: for however wide the range of possible systems, it is clear that any viable system must be consonant with human nature. In other words, our biological evolution has set broad constraints on our behavior, and between these borders our cultural evolution steers our course.

Wilson clearly is committed to this view. More specifically, he reformulates the ancient concept of human nature in terms of behavioral determinants inherited from earlier stages in our evolution, and he anticipates that recognition of these determinants will make our approach to problems of social behavior more realistic and effective. To be sure, he does go farther, and in an extremely long-range speculation he suggests that eventually a complete neuronal understanding of the human brain will provide a firm foundation for ethics. But this remark seems to me tangential, and not relevant to the question of the ethical implications of sociobiology for the present and the foreseeable future.

It would be presumptuous to try here to specify these implications in any detail: that is one of the main jobs ahead. However, certain directions seem evident. The most general one involves the problem of a moral consensus. Ever since evolution undermined the transcendental foundation for ethics, which had guided the bulk of people in the West for millenia, many social critics have concluded that the only logical alternative is unlimited moral relativism. The consequences of this loss of a moral consensus have been disastrous. Humanity desperately needs a replacement that will appeal to enough people to restore an effective consensus. Philosophers have not been notably successful, for while they have continued their ancient search for a basis for ethics that would satisfy their criteria, their logical speculation, by itself, leaves too wide a range to lead to a consensus.

Sociobiology may help to bring us closer to the goal, thereby atoning for the earlier contribution of evolution to moral relativism and to Social Darwinism. Thus the very history and structure of our DNA commits us to the primary evolutionary drive of species survival. With this naturalistic source of constraints we can legitimately narrow the range of acceptable ethical systems to those that are consistent with long-term survival of our species. Sociobiology also provides a naturalistic base for escaping from the shallowness of pure egoistic utilitarianism: our brains are programmed for ethics, just as for language. In either area the specifics that we develop can vary enormously, but common features are built in. Hence philosophers need not apologize if they find intuitionist approaches useful. Finally, one might also suggest, but with less confidence, that the evolutionary drive for improved adaptation to the environment provides support for a perfectionist ethics, emphasizing excellence in those talents that give man his unique position.

When we go beyond these very general implications of sociobiology and seek help in assessing more specific features of ethical systems, our vision becomes more clouded. Wilson seems to anticipate that our increased understanding of the biological roots of human motivation and feeling will begin to be useful in this respect in the near future. I am less sanguine. But even if we cannot specify the relevant biological factors in enough detail to let them serve as a guide to policy, recognition of their existence can influence our viewpoint, if only by leading us to recognize limits to our social goals. For example, if there is a genetic component (as well as a socially conditioned component) to our competitive and our filial drives, to the rational and the irrational aspects of our behavior, and to our individual differences in drives, abilities, and tastes, we cannot hope to eliminate conflicts. We can hope only to moderate and contain them, and to achieve a reasonable balance between altruism and aggression. This aspect of the human condition has always been recognized by traditional moralists, but more recently it has been opposed by utopians imbued with unlimited confidence in the power of environmental manipulation. In a closely related development, the extensive recent discussions of social equality have paid little attention to the need to reconcile such equality with the wide genetic diversity built into our species. The evidence from sociobiology, on both these issues, may help to keep us on a realistic path.

Another interesting feature of Caplan's review is his subdivision of the subject of evolution and ethics into three parts: the evolution of ethics, evolutionary ethics, and the ethics of evolution. He expresses disappointment that Wilson fails to make clear exactly which of these value problems compel his interest in sociobiology. But a biologist might see evolutionary ethics (concerned with present problems) as simply a continuation of the evolution of ethics (concerned with origins): he would analyze both in the same Darwinian terms. As to the third category, the ethics of evolution: if the question concerns the past, any effort to pass judgment on what has been good or bad (in an ethical sense) about evolution, or about the properties of any species, would seem silly. Evolution is simply there, and ethical concepts cannot apply when there are no options under human control. If, on the other hand, Caplan is referring to conscious control over future human evolution (i.e., eugenics), he is reaching into an area that Wilson has wisely considered to be outside the scope of sociobiology.

Finally, I would like to comment on Caplan's own possible moral relativism, in referring to "a harsh critical response from those reviewers sensitive to the inherent ethical difficulties," and in considering both sides of the debate equally impassioned. His safely tolerant position seems to me to miss an important philosophical issue. For while there is no reason to doubt the sincerity of this group of critics ("Science for the People"), we would be naive not to recognize that their criticisms are based primarily on political convictions, rather than on considerations of ethical sensitivity (in the usual, nonpolitical sense) or considerations of scientific validity. This group rejects claims that studies on the genetic and evolutionary aspects of human behavior can help us to find the roots of social problems, and can help us to optimize environments for different individuals. Instead they are convinced that such studies will impede efforts to bring about needed social change and therefore should be discouraged as vigorously as possible. For example, their relentless adverse publicity finally led Dr. Stanley Walzer to discontinue screening of newborns with an extra X or Y chromosome, in a study aimed at determining the possible behavioral effects of these aberrations. The attack on sociobiology similarly went outside the usual range of scholarly criticism (see article by Nicholas Wade in *Science,* March 19, 1976).

Within the political and philosophical framework of our culture espousal of radical political or economic views is a precious right. But intolerance of intellectual freedom is another matter. When its scale is small enough it can be tolerated, but exposure still seems more appropriate than legitimation. From a philosophical perspective such an exposure could well focus on what we might call the ideological fallacy: the belief that one can derive an "is" from an "ought." Surely that doctrine is at least as egregious as the naturalistic fallacy of trying to derive an "ought" from an "is."

Philosophy, Dichotomies, and Sociobiology

Lawrence G. Miller

Like other recent scientific *causes célèbres* such as IQ or XYY, the sociobiology controversy continually teeters on the brink of sloganeering, with accusations of "biological determinism," "environmental determinism," and "academic vigilantism" vying for attention but not careful consideration. Despite our obvious predilection for one side of the controversy, we of the Sociobiology Study Group of Science for the People would welcome a clear exposition of the debate thus far. Unfortunately, the article by Arthur Caplan, "Ethics, Evolution and the Milk of Human Kindness," merely adds to the confusion. In particular, we feel that the article represents a systematic misunderstanding of our critique of sociobiology. We hope to briefly clarify our points here.

Caplan finds three major flaws in our critique, one substantive, two methodological. His substantive point is directed toward the nature of our critique. Caplan divides the critics of sociobiology into two groups: the first group, represented by C. H. Waddington, is characterized as "methodological"; the second, which we occupy, is described as "value-critics." According to Caplan, "The methodological criticisms leveled at the book [E. O. Wilson's *Sociobiology*] are not cited by those reviewers who raise objections on value or ethical grounds." Later, Caplan takes our group to task for "inattention to theoretical difficulties that may exist for sociobiology."

Hastings Center Report (October 25, 1976), pp 20–25. Copyright © 1976 by the Institute of Society, Ethics and the Life Sciences, 360 Broadway, Hastings-on-Hudson, N.Y. 10706. Reprinted by permission of the publisher and the author.

We find these statements puzzling. In our letter to *The New York Review of Books*, which Caplan cites, we explicitly *list* five methodological criticisms of sociobiology: the speculative nature of genetic traits, the confusion of what is with what might be, the reliance on analogy and metaphor, the use of *ad hoc* arguments, and speculations concerning human prehistory.[1] These themes have been further refined and extended in a recent critique which appeared in *BioScience*.[2] We do not ignore methodological issues—in fact, we concentrate on them.

Caplan's criticisms of our methodology are equally puzzling: both are based on dichotomies which have not been present thus far in the sociobiology controversy. First, to Caplan we have made "an important methodological mistake" in our "failure to distinguish clearly between [Wilson's] attempt to give an historical explanation or account of the origin of a trait or behavior, and his attempt to explain the maintenance or persistence of the same trait or behavior in a contemporary population of organisms." To Caplan, Wilson has attempted to explain only the origin of social behavior in our ancestors, rather than the existence of such behavior in ourselves and our contemporaries. Caplan asserts that there is a "great difference" between the two types of explanations, but unfortunately he merely repeats this assertion several times without presenting specific arguments. For example, he contrasts evolutionary explanations of primitive altruistic behavior with those for modern homosexuality, but states only that different assumptions can be made in each case.

Caplan's dichotomy between historical and contemporary explanations is an irrelevant one for two reasons: first, it is not present in the sociobiology controversy; second, it is false. The first point is the more important of the two here, since we are dealing with a review which purports to clarify the sociobiology debate. Contrary to Caplan's assertion, neither Wilson nor any other sociobiologist clings to such a dichotomy; a few quotes should suffice to illustrate this point. In discussing "human nature," for example, Wilson states that "we retain in our heredity, I believe, the capacity to find deep emotional pleasure in natural environments and other living creatures. . . . The capacity to develop this way was ingrained in human nature by millennia of evolution."[3] Thus he explains modern children's affection for pets, wildlife movies, zoos, etc. In a more global vein, sociobiologists Trivers and Devore recently developed a film entitled *Sociobiology: Doing What Comes Naturally;* its descriptive brochure states that it's time we started viewing ourselves as having biological, genetic and natural components to our behavior, and that we should start setting up a physical and social world which matches those tendencies.[4]

In the same brochure they speak of the "male's natural physical freedom and the female's more vulnerable child-bearing nature." Or again, Wilson hopes for a future where sociobiologists will "monitor the genetic basis of social behavior" and "establish a genetically accurate and completely fair code of ethics."[5] We could go on and on, from Wilson's biblical exegesis to his discussion of sex roles and spite, but our purpose here is not to repeat Wilson's arguments but rather to point out that Caplan has misconstrued the focus of the sociobiology debate. Wilson does not, as Caplan would have us believe, confinc himself to explaining the *"origins* of social behaviors in ancestral societies" (our emphasis). Wilson's arguments instead posit a genetic basis for human behavior which has evolved historically and *remains with us,* with specific consequences for our future.

Indeed, Wilson's arguments must take this form—in order to present evolutionary explanations, Wilson constructs a genetic basis for human behavior, one that has evolved from our ancestors and our animal forebears. Since this basis is innate, as it must be for Wilson, then at least some of it remains with us as we continue to evolve. Evolutionary explanations based on genetics do not allow a simple break between past and present; Caplan's historical/contemporary dichotomy is thus not only misleading but false.

Caplan's error here, however, provides a rare chance to clarify an important aspect of the sociobiology controversy: reconstructions of prehistory. Caplan asserts that "Wilson can make certain assumptions about society, culture, and genetics" in the case of primitive behaviors that "he surely cannot validly make" to explain contemporary phenomena. But in fact precisely the opposite of Caplan's statement is true. The assumptions sociobiologists make concerning primitive societies are based on evolutionary speculation, analogies with animal societies, and anthropological evidence from contemporary "primitive" societies. But as we have pointed out in detail elsewhere,[6] the evolutionary speculation is just that, the analogies with animals have no logical or scientific basis, and contemporary primitive societies are highly suspect as indicators of past societies. Indeed, Wilson would be on firmer ground if he chose to advance a contextual explanation of contemporary social phenomena rather than his speculative reconstruction of human prehistory.

The second major dichotomy that Caplan erects is between the "evolution of ethics" and the "ethics of evolution." To Caplan, our group fails to recognize this "important distinction" between "studying the evolution of ethical or social behaviors, and arguing about the ethical validity or worth of behaviors that already exist." Caplan goes on to distinguish three types of relations between ethics and evolution, variations on this theme, and then concludes that "contrary to the charges of his critics, Wilson seems merely to urge a new inquiry into the whole issue of ethical naturalism." To be sure, Caplan presents a valid distinction here; however, it is not one which has been involved in the sociobiology controversy. To use Caplan's terminology, Wilson is primarily concerned with the "evolution of ethics." While Wilson occasionally comments on the implications of his evolutionary analysis, he strenuously attempts to establish his "scientific objectivity" and to distinguish himself from "advocacy theorists" who introduce conclusions based on personal assumptions. Our critique has therefore not sought to respond directly to the *existence* of sexism, hierarchies, aggression, etc. that sociobiologists assert are genetic. What we have attempted to do is to point out the ideological nature of sociobiology, which legitimates such social patterns by "proving" that human behavior is genetically directed. This issue is best illustrated by a passage from an article Wilson wrote for the *New York Times Magazine:*

In hunter-gatherer societies, men hunt and women stay at home. This strong bias persists in most agricultural societies and, on that ground alone, appears to have a genetic origin. No solid evidence exists as to when the division of labor appeared in man's ancestors or how resistant to change it might be during the continuing revolution for women's rights. My own guess is that the genetic bias is intense enough to cause a substantial division of labor even in the most free and egalitarian of future societies. . . . Thus, even with identical education and equal access to all professions, men are likely to play a disproportionate role in political life, business, and science. But this is only a guess, and, even if correct, could not be used to argue for anything less than sex blind admission and free personal choice.[7]

We agree with Wilson's *caveat:* sexism is not justifiable. But the thrust of Wilson's point here and elsewhere is that sexism is inevitable, even if undesirable, since it is genetically determined. We dispute the reasoning and evidence by which Wilson arrived at the genetic basis of sex-role differences.

The components of the human nature constructed by sociobiologists are by no means fortuitous. We have pointed out elsewhere that this human nature bears a striking resemblance to the *status quo,* and have mentioned the difficulties involved in separating the social context of the researcher from his or her work.[8] Yet Caplan again has missed the point; he states that "both Wilson and his critics can be faulted for failing to make clear exactly what specific value problems compel their interest in sociobiology." We will let Wilson and his colleagues speak for themselves here. Our own interest in sociobiology has been made explicit throughout our work: we believe that, intentionally or not, sociobiologists have constructed a theory based on implicit political assumptions and with explicit political implications which they have presented as objective science. Questions concerning the structure of human societies, with which sociobiologists attempt to deal, are fundamentally political questions; scientists have no privileged vantage point from which to provide answers. Yet this is precisely what the sociobiologists claim. Further, they claim that we have "politicized" a scientific discussion by publishing our original critique in a popular journal, *The New York Review of Books.*[9] But surely this is a rather disingenuous stance for the sociobiologists to assume. One merely need look at the statements of the sociobiologists: an article in *The New York Times Magazine,* interviews in *House and Garden* and *People* magazines, a curriculum for high school students entitled "Exploring Human Nature," the film cited above, etc. The issue of sociobiology has been political from the start, due to both the tacit political assumptions incorporated into sociobiology, and also to the popular audience which the sociobiologists have sought.

In the last few sentences of his article, Caplan begins to comprehend our position concerning sociobiology: "Perhaps it is not the ethics or the analogies that Wilson's critics find offensive but, rather, the emphasis on heredity and evolution." But Caplan then goes on once again to polarize the controversy by suggesting that our opposition to human nature "would ally the 'value-critics' . . . with historical schools of behaviorism and operationalism that I imagine they would find quite distasteful." Once again, a dichotomy appears: genetics vs. environment. Once again, the dichotomy is a false one; both extremes present a *passive* view of humans as vehicles either for our genes or our environment. We view humans as *active* agents, striving to shape lives and destinies. Determinist theories, whether genetic or environmental, serve to inculcate an ethos of passivity and thus render us susceptible to active manipulation by others.

NOTES

1. Elizabeth Allen et al., "Against 'Sociobiology'," (*New York Review of Books,* Nov. 13, 1975).
2. Sociobiology Study Group of Science for the People, "Sociobiology—A New Biological Determinism," *BioScience* 26 (March 1976), p. 182.
3. Interview with Edward O. Wilson, *House and Garden.* February 1976, p. 65.
4. The film and brochure are distributed by Document Associates, Inc., 880 Third Avenue, New York, N.Y.
5. E. O. Wilson, *Sociobiology: The New Synthesis* (Cambridge, Mass.: Harvard University Press, 1975), p. 575.
6. Cf. notes 1 and 2.
7. Edward O. Wilson, "Human Decency is Animal." *New York Times Magazine,* October 12, 1975, p. 38.
8. Letter to *Science,* 192 (April 30, 1976), p. 424.
9. E. O. Wilson, "Academic Vigilantism and the Political Significance of Sociobiology," *BioScience* 26 (March 1976), p. 183; also his letter to the members of Science for the People, February 2, 1976.

Sociobiology: Troubled Birth for New Discipline

Nicholas Wade

Sociobiology is the title of an ambitious synthesis that aims to found a new discipline, the systematic study of the biological basis of sociality. Published last June to generally laudatory reviews in the scientific press, the book has since come under heavy criticism for allegedly concealing a reactionary political message. Its theories have been held analogous to those of Nazi eugenics and its author has countercharged his critics with intimidation and inhibiting free inquiry. Beneath the smoke is a scientific issue—which some spectators regard as part of a historic debate—that of the extent to which human social behavior is genetically determined.

Though the controversy about *Sociobiology* is far ranging, the protagonist and his critic-in-chief work in the same building almost within shouting distance of each other. Author Edward O. Wilson is curator in entomology at the Harvard Museum of Comparative Zoology. Richard Lewontin is professor of zoology at the museum.

Slime molds, ants, and apes belong to the three groups of species among which sociality has evolved in nature. Only the last chapter of *Sociobiology,* comprising some 30 of its 600 pages, is devoted to the species at nature's fourth social pinnacle, man. It is this chapter which is the focus of a vehement attack by a phalanx of Cambridge based academics and others. The group, which calls itself the Sociobiology

From *Science* 191 (March 19, 1976), pp. 1151–1155. Copyright © 1976 by the American Association for the Advancement of Science. Reprinted by permission of the American Association for the Advancement of Science, and the author.

325

Study Group, is affiliated with the radically oriented Science for the People. Besides Lewontin and Steven Gould, also a member of Wilson's department, the group includes four other Harvard professors.*

Every other Tuesday for the last 6 months, the group has held meetings to critique Wilson's text. The chief outcome of this assiduous study has been two articles, one published as a letter in the 13 November issue of the *New York Review of Books*, the other a 30-page document of which a condensed version is to appear in *BioScience* together with a reply by Wilson. According to the theme developed in both these articles, Wilson contends that man's social behavior is mostly or wholly determined by his genes. Such a position, which the group labels "biological determinism," conveys a justification of the existing political order of society by implying that it is genetically determined. In any case, the group adds, there is no direct scientific evidence to suppose that any of man's social behavior is determined by the genes.

The Sociobiology Study Group operates as a collective and objects to any suggestion that it has a leader. Attention focuses more equally on Lewontin than on other members, however, because he has actively promoted the campaign against *Sociobiology* by giving lectures and writing letters to the *Harvard Crimson*. Lewontin has long been a prominent and articulate member of Science for the People. He is also a distinguished expert on the subject at hand. He and Richard Levins, another member of the group, are widely regarded as brilliant population geneticists. Both have been elected to the National Academy of Sciences, but Lewontin resigned on a point of principle (issuance by the academy of classified reports) and Levins, a Marxist, declined to accept membership because of the academy's participation in military matters. According to sources close to Wilson, it was he, as an admirer of their work, who was in large measure responsible for bringing Lewontin to Harvard

---

* 35 present members of the collective include the following academics: Jon Beckwith professor, Harvard Medical School; Steven Chorover, professor of psychology, MIT; David Culver, professor of biology, Harvard Medical School; Steven Gould, professor, Harvard University; Ruth Hubbard, professor of biology, Harvard University; Hiroshi Inouye, resident fellow, Harvard Medical School; Anthony Leeds, professor of anthropology, Boston University; Richard Lewontin, professor of biology, Harvard University. Another member, Richard Levins of Harvard University, was not a signatory of the letter to the *New York Review of Books*.

over political opposition in the faculty and for promoting Levins as a candidate for election to the academy. Wilson cites generously from their work and, at least until the present controversy was ignited, is said to have been a reasonably close colleague and friend of Lewontin's.

Whereas Lewontin and his radical colleagues profess to see a political message in *Sociobiology,* its author, who describes himself as a liberal, sees none and says none was intended. Wilson's best known work before *Sociobiology* was *The Insect Societies,* a magisterial survey of the social systems of wasps, ants, bees, and termites. His office, on the floor above Lewontin's, is dominated by a potted orange tree whose leaves have been stitched together by a collective of weaver ants. Nearby containers are homes to colonies of fire ants, leaf-cutting ants, and other exotic myrmecoids. The stray members of these societies that forage through the papers on Wilson's desk do not disturb him; "Inevitable leakage," he says.

The Wilson-Lewontin debate has every outward appearance of an illuminating battle between titans. Unfortunately the main issue is never joined, because Wilson denies that he says what the Sociobiology Study Group claims he says. The group has "utterly misrepresented the spirit and content" of the book, Wilson charges. They "cite piece by piece incorrectly, or out of context, and then add their own commentary to furnish me with a political attitude I do not have and the book with a general conclusion that is not there."

The chief bone of contention thus dissolves into an arid analysis of Wilson's text. This reporter's opinion, for what it is worth, is that Wilson is substantially if not wholly correct in claiming that his critics have seriously distorted what he says. On the issue, for instance, of how much of human social behavior may be genetically determined, the Sociobiology Study Group portrays Wilson's position as thoroughly determinist, even though he says in the book that "the genes have given away most of their sovereignty" and has since stated that maybe 10 percent of social behavior has a genetic basis. The group dismisses these qualifications and says that Wilson's "effective" position is "an extreme hereditarian one." The reader of *Sociobiology* may get the impression that the author believes somewhat more than 10 percent of human social behavior is genetically based, but there is no good reason for assuming he is an extreme hereditarian.

The Sociobiology Study Group consistently misrepresents Wilson's arguments by removing the hedges. A particularly flagrant example concerns "conformer genes." The group attacks him for asserting that such genes must exist, whereas in fact they are merely postulated. "In speaking of indoctrinability, for example," the group says in its letter to the *New York Review of Books,* "he asserts that 'humans are absurdly easy to indoctrinate' and therefore 'conformer genes' must exist." What Wilson actually says is: "Human beings are absurdly easy to indoctrinate—they seek it. If we assume for argument that indoctrinability evolves, at what level does natural selection take place?" The invocation of conformer genes occurs a few sentences later as what is clearly part of the "if we assume for argument." A second example is the charge that, by applying to insect societies such metaphors as "slavery" and "caste," Wilson "promotes the analogy between human and animal societies and leads one to believe that behavior patterns in the two have the same basis." Unwary readers might not guess that Wilson prefaces his comparison with the statement, "Roles in human societies are fundamentally different from the castes of social insects."

Another apparent misrepresentation of Wilson's position occurs on the issue of traits that are adaptive. (An adaptive trait is one that has arisen by evolution and so has a genetic base.) The group accuses Wilson of saying that everything is adaptive. "For Wilson, what exists is adaptive, what is adaptive is good, therefore what exists is good. . . . This approach allows Wilson to confirm selectively certain contemporary behavior as adaptive and 'natural' and thereby justify the present social order." Wilson describes this statement of his position as "patently false" and, far from saying that everything is adaptive, his discussion of man's sociality is prefaced with the statement that "One of the key questions . . . is to what extent the [human] biogram represents an adaptation to modern cultural life and to what extent it is a phylogenetic vestige. Our civilizations were jerrybuilt about the biogram."

In short, the Sociobiology Study Group has systematically distorted Wilson's statements to fit the position it wished to attack, namely that human social behavior is wholly or almost wholly determined by the genes. Such a degree of distortion, though routine enough in political life, is perhaps surprising from a group composed largely of professional scholars. Nevertheless, the group probably deserves some credit for pointing out that the territory Wilson is broaching is fertile ground in which to sow all kinds of social and political dragon's teeth. For example, Wilson indicates in a table (the text is somewhat less definite) that male dominance over females can reliably be concluded to be an inherited human trait. The sociobiology group may have a point in arguing that the ethnographic data on which the assertion is based is itself riddled with sex bias. Since the statement is perhaps not indubitably true, and since its social and political implications are highly controversial, the subject probably deserves more detailed discussion than it receives.

Elsewhere Wilson speculates that homosexuality may have a genetic basis, on the grounds that, although homosexuals tend to have fewer children, they could favor the continuance of their genes by looking after the children of their close kin. The assumptions in this hypothesis could easily become matters of social controversy, as could the possibility which Wilson raises that genetic differences in populations "might predispose societies toward cultural differences."

Wilson had expected his book to be attacked, but not from this quarter. Since he was caught unprepared, it is maybe surprising that those of his positions which are politically vulnerable are so well guarded. But it is probably naive of those who discuss human sociobiology to expect that the political dimensions of their arguments will be ignored. The perils of the subject were instantly spotted by an early reviewer of *Sociobiology*, MIT economist Paul Samuelson. "How do you keep distinct a Shockley from a Wilson? A Hitler from a Huxley?" he asked in his *Newsweek* column last July. "To survive in the jungle of intellectuals," he concluded, "the sociobiologist had best tread softly in the zones of race and sex." Lewontin, who believes that scientists must expect to be held accountable for their nonscientific as well as scientific statements, puts it this way: "Wilson, like most scientists, expects to be able to put out a lot of bullshit about society and not get taken up on it."

Are there in fact dangerous political consequences in even the limited degree of genetic determination that Wilson is postulating for human social behavior? The argument of the Sociobiology Study Group could be valid even if they have distorted the extent of Wilson's postulations. It goes as follows. Biological determinism, the group contends, has repeatedly been invoked in support of evil causes. In the 19th century, social Darwinist Herbert Spencer claimed that it was unnatural to try to eradicate poverty because it interfered with the law of the survival of the fittest. Claims of a genetic basis for intelligence have fueled the assertions of racial differences by William Shockley and others. Determinist theories, the group contended in its letter to the *New York Review of Books*, "provided an important basis for the enactment of sterilization laws and restrictive immigration laws by the United States between 1910 and 1930 and also for the eugenics policies which led to the establishment of gas chambers in Nazi Germany.

"The latest attempt to reinvigorate these tired theories," the letter added in an egregiously raw accusation, was constituted by sociobiology and Wilson's book.

Wilson offers a simple but stout rebuttal argument: "The fallacy of my critics is that to know where we have come from is not to prescribe where we are going." There is a dangerous trap in sociobiology, he wrote in a recent article in the *New York Times:*

> The trap is the naturalistic fallacy of ethics, which uncritically concludes that what is, should be. The "what is" in human nature is to a large extent the heritage of a Pleistocene hunter-gatherer existence. When any genetic bias is demonstrated, it cannot be used to justify a continuing practice in present and future societies. . . . For example, the tendency under certain conditions to conduct warfare against competing groups might well be in our genes, having been advantageous to our Neolithic ancestors, but it could lead to global suicide now. To rear as many healthy children as possible was long the road to security, yet with the population of the world brimming over, it is now the way to environmental disaster.

Even if Wilson's argument is right in theory, could the study of human sociobiology be in practice so fraught with the possibility for misuse as to be not a fit subject for research? Wilson agrees that its current hypotheses and facts are "susceptible to perversion" but argues that the perversion should be discouraged, not the subject. In an interview with the *Harvard Gazette*, the university's official newsletter, Lewontin said in effect that all such research is dangerous: "Any investigations into the genetic control of human behaviors is bound to produce a pseudo-science that will inevitably be misused."

Why does the Sociobiology Study Group fear so much that evidence of a genetic basis for human behavior will be misused when, in their opinion, no such direct evidence exists? According to Lewontin, the very process of doing research, of looking for racial differences in IQ, say, is a political act, whatever the results of the research may be. "Nothing we can know about the genetics of human behavior can have any implications for human society," he says. "But the process has social impact because the announcement that research is being done is a political act."

The process by which the Sociobiology Study Group has pursued its ends is also political and is the subject of a serious countercharge by Wilson. In his letter of rebuttal to the *New York Review of Books* (11 December) he accused the group of "the kind of self-righteous vigilantism which not only produces falsehood but also unjustly hurts individuals and through that kind of intimidation diminishes the spirit of free inquiry and discussion crucial to the health of the intellectual community."

Wilson has a point. In addition to the group's attack, he has had his book labeled as "dangerously racist" by a Harvard-Radcliffe student group calling itself the Committee Against Racism. Citing the Sociobiology Study Group's critique, the committee declared in a recent broadsheet that "Wilson's gene-dependent culture notion amounts to international racism, implying technologically 'backward' cultures have backward genes" and urged readers to raise questions at an impending speech by Wilson. The Sociobiology Study Group has not endorsed the explicit accusation of racism.

"I have wavered about going to several lectures," Wilson told *Science*. "There has been clearly prearranged hostile questioning. Perhaps a braver soul would not have been concerned, but I find it intimidating." Wilson has since withdrawn from a public talk scheduled for 24 March because of the increasing mental strain on his family.

The group's answer to this charge is a mere denial that Wilson is or has any reason to be intimidated. "It is not our intention to frighten him off," says Lewontin. According to Gould, "We may have made some rhetorical mistakes, but we don't intend it as a personal attack. Tactically it would be very bad on our part to conduct this as a personal campaign because it would only make a martyr out of him." Gould adds that "Ed Wilson is a colleague whom we like."

If there is a disingenuous ring about these statements, it is because an attack of the type which the group has mounted on *Sociobiology* is bound to appear as an attack on the author as well, unless accompanied by specific disclaimers. But far from denying that a personal attack was intended, the group's letter to the *New York Review of Books* accuses Wilson of using "a number of strategies and sleights of hand," a phrase which implies deliberate deception, and of failing to separate out his "personal and social class prejudices." The personalization is taken further in the group's impending article in *BioScience*, which states: "It is no accident that the description of this underlying [human] nature bears a remarkable resemblance to the society inhabited by the theorist himself. In Wilson's case it is the modern market-industrial-entre-preneurial society of the United States." The group is thus apparently of the opinion that it is not a personal attack to accuse someone of having written a book which is vitiated by his personal political preju-dices and deliberate efforts to gull the reader.

The group's manner of attack has not only intimidated Wilson but it could well act as a deterrent to others, particularly those less eminent and less able than Wilson to defend themselves. After all, the risk of being publicly compared with Nazi eugenicists by a cohort of Cambridge academics is not the most compelling of invitations to venture into a perplexed and largely uncharted subject.

Yet the group sees the debate as a political issue for which a political rhetoric is appropriate. That should be borne in mind by any who find their style overstated. The group has perhaps usefully drawn atten-tion to the political dimensions of sociobiology and the field's susceptibil-ity to distortion, even though they have had to do much of the distorting themselves to make the point. They would have a better defense against Wilson's countercharges of vigilantism and inhibiting free inquiry if they had argued their case in a less personalized and divisive fashion. But that, nonetheless, is the climate of discussion in which human sociobiology seems likely to develop.

The Implications of Sociobiology

Joseph Alper et al.

In his comments on our critique of E. O. Wilson's *Sociobiology*,[1] Nicholas Wade (News and Comment, 19 Mar., p. 1151) correctly characterizes the basic issue as a political one. Indeed, it is the contention of our Sociobiology Study Group that Wilson's "new synthesis" represents an effort to cloak in modern terminology the age-old political doctrine that the main features of human social existence are biologically determined. As Wade notes, "*Sociobiology* teems with . . . provocative suggestions about human social behavior." It does so, moreover, on many topics of broad ethical, moral, and political import. The main purpose of our critique has been to point out precisely what those suggestions are and to show that Wilson's efforts to "biologicize" human sociality reflect a particular social and political perspective.

According to Wilson, our group has "utterly misrepresented the spirit and content" of his book. He contends that "the issue at hand . . . is vigilantism" and accuses us of condemning his work because its message does not conform to our own political convictions.[2] Wade agrees with Wilson on both points. He says that we have "seriously" and "systematically distorted Wilson's statements to fit the position [we wish] to attack, namely that human social behavior is wholly or almost wholly determined by the genes," and he depicts us as a group of

From the Letters section of *Science* 192 (April 30, 1976), pp. 424–427. Copyright © 1976 by the American Association for the Advancement of Science. Reprinted by permission of the publisher and the author. The letter's cosigners were J. Beckwith, S. L. Chorover, J. Hunt, H. Inouye, T. Judd, R. V. Lange, and P. Sternberg.

ideologues engaged in an unwarranted political attack against a work of objective scholarship. Like Wilson, Wade implies that we are conducting a personal vendetta against the author himself.

Readers of *Science* can only judge the truth of these accusations by reading Wilson's book and our critique[3] for themselves. We strongly urge everyone to do so. We agree with Wade that we previously failed to recognize that Wilson was "hedging" in his statement about the existence of "conformer genes," and we apologize to him for implying that he asserted their existence as a matter of fact. But we can find no other instance in which we misquoted or otherwise misrepresented his position. We have no interest in cutting off debate. We contend that a careful reading of *Sociobiology* will suffice to rebut the charge of distortion and will confirm that the "new synthesis" contains numerous inconsistencies and transparent political messages. Although Wade's superficial and uncritical reading ignores it and Wilson's own statements disclaim it, we contend that there is politics aplenty in *Sociobiology* and that those of us who are its critics did not put it there.

In addition to rejecting Wade's charges we object to his journalistic treatment of the controversy as if it were merely a personal contretemps involving a few newsworthy scientists. By likening it to a "battle between titans" and by singling out one member of our group as Wilson's "critic-in-chief," Wade distorts and, in effect, trivializes the entire matter. The basic issue at hand is *not* one of vigilantism, personalities, or individual motives. We are engaged, rather, in a recurrent dispute over the social and political dimensions of scientific affairs.

Our central point is that sociobiology—like all science—proceeds in a social context; "pure objectivity" is as much a myth for sociobiologists as for science reporters. All attitudes toward sociobiology—ours as much as any—reflect certain political preconceptions which need to be made explicit. The weaker the constraint of fact, and the closer the subject to immediate human concern, the greater the influence of these preconceptions.

There can be no doubt that sociobiology deals with subjects of immediate human concern. We contend, further, that there are *no* constraining facts on several of the subjects with which Wilson's *Sociobiology* deals. One such subject concerns the genetic determination for supposedly universal behavioral differences between men and women. As a matter of fact, the biological basis of sex roles in society is a major issue in the book, and the way Wilson handles it offers an insight into his thought. Given the prevalence of sex discrimination in contemporary American society, we believe that there is an obvious political message in Wilson's assertions that "rampant *machismo*" has evolved in some insects (*Sociobiology,* p. 320) and that "In [human] hunter-gatherer societies, men hunt and women stay home. This strong bias persists in most agricultural and industrial societies and *on that ground alone* [italics ours], appears to have a genetic origin."[4] Although he implicitly acknowledges the lack of compelling proof for his extrapolations from insects to humans and from past to present societies, Wilson goes on to "guess . . . that the genetic bias is intense enough to cause a substantial division of labor even in the most free and egalitarian of future societies."[5] Thus, to the political question of why sex discrimination persists at its obdurate extreme, Wilson answers, in effect, that it is *natural:* "many of the peculiar details of human sexual behavior and domestic life flow easily from [the] basic division of labor" which has evolved through natural selection (*Sociobiology,* p. 568). The political message is clear: the way things *are* is the way they must necessarily be. And to those of us who would change the way things are, Wade quotes Wilson as warning against the effort to "steer" human society "past those stresses and conflicts that once gave the destructive [human] genotypes their Darwinian edge. . . . In this, *the ultimate genetic sense* [italics ours], social control [of human affairs] would rob man of his humanity."

Such assertions about the nature of human nature and society are contestable but they are not scientifically verifiable. For a scientist to promote them is an act that is certainly redolent of political implications. With equal impact, we wish to underscore the responsibility which scientists must bear for the political implications of their academic activities where prescriptions for social policy are consequent.

It deserves emphasis in this connection that natural selection presupposes that genes determine reproductive fitness and hence adaptive success in future generations. Thus, genetic determinism becomes the sociobiologist's ultimate answer to any question about human behavior. All behaviors and social structures which we observe are presumed to exist because they are or were adaptive. The logic is circular, the scenario appears to be predestined, and the result is a kind of parlor game in which prescriptive statements about human nature and human societies are couched in the language of descriptive science.

What we have argued, and continue to assert, is that sociobiological ideas do not arise in a social vacuum but rather reflect the dominant interests and attitudes of the class to which their authors belong. For centuries similar ideas, similarly unproven, have helped to preserve prevailing social conditions by lending an aura of manifest destiny to the particularities of a given time and place. What is natural must be destined, and what is destined cannot, indeed should not, be overcome.

We submit that, despite its bold theoretical poses, Wilson's *Sociobiology* embodies a form of social prophecy which coheres comfortably with the dynamics of modern market societies. It offers, under the guise of scientific objectivity, an invitation to cultivate what Wilson calls a "philosophical ease"[6] toward the unfolding of contemporary human affairs. We find ourselves unable to maintain the ease required to accept discrimination, militarism, and social injustice as natural and inevitable reflections of some vast and insensate sociobiological scheme of things.

NOTES

1. E. O. Wilson, *Sociobiology: The New Synthesis* (Cambridge, Mass.: Harvard University Press, 1975).
2. E. O. Wilson, *BioScience* 26, (1976), p. 183.
3. Sociobiology Study Group of Science for the People, *ibid.*, p. 182.
4. E. O. Wilson, *New York Times Magazine,* October 12, 1975, p. 38.
5. *Ibid.*
6. *Ibid.*

An Alternative Case for Sociobiology

Stephen T. Emlen

Recently, the topic of sociobiology has been the target of much criticism and heated debate. . . . Discussion has centered on the book *Sociobiology: The New Synthesis* by E. O. Wilson,[1] which has been attacked as a dangerously deterministic document with strong political overtones by the Science for the People group[2] and defended by its author.[3]

When the smoke is cleared away, this debate is seen to center largely on the question of the limits of plasticity of human behavior—the degree to which genetic principles of evolutionary adaptation can be applied to the social behavior of man. The attack of the Science for the People group amounts to a resurrection and a rehashing of the old "innate versus learned" controversies that raged during the early phases of the development of the field of ethology. Those debates, although politically enlightening, proved largely unproductive scientifically and, in fact, hampered progress in the fields of both psychology and ethology. It would be a shame if the major contributions and potential importance of the new field of sociobiology were to be lost behind a diatribe of "determinism-environmentalism" rhetoric.

The field of sociobiology did not originate with E. O. Wilson's book. Rather, it has its roots in over a century's accumulation of field natural history studies on a wide range of animals. These studies, when viewed in terms of modern theoretical ecology and population genetics, provide

From the Letters section of *Science* 192 (May 21, 1976): pp. 736–738. Copyright © 1976 by the American Association for the Advancement of Science. Reprinted by permission of the publisher and the author.

the data base from which the general theories of sociobiology are emerging.

One of the strengths of this field is its ability to interpret and partially predict the social structure of a species on the basis of a limited set of environmental or ecological variables—the type of food resource together with its degree of stability and predictability; the dispersion pattern of different resource bases in both time and space; the types and strategies of potential predators or parasites and means for counteracting them; the need (or lack thereof) for rapid information exchange about the environment. These and other ecological parameters impose limits on the range of types of social organization that will be adaptive. With differences in the dispersion of a critical resource, the availability of mates, and other factors, optimal social strategies shift, resulting in a fine tuning of social organization to ecological constraints.

The importance of these predictive hypotheses lies in their broad applicability across phylogenetic lines. Similar ecological determinants seem to apply when we examine such diverse groups as dragonflies or frogs, coral reef fish or marine birds, tropical bats or weaver birds, African ungulates or primates.[4-6] Animals faced with similar ecological "problems" exhibit a predictable convergence in their "solutions," as shown in their social organizations.

The Science for the People group is correct in noting that evolutionary biologists generally assume an observed behavior is the result of natural selection operating at the level of the individual. But the case for the importance of sociobiology need not rest on any premise of rigid genetic determinism of behavior. It is becoming increasingly apparent that social organization, even in so-called "lower" forms, exhibits a surprising amount of plasticity. What adds strength to the hypotheses of sociobiology is that often the form of this plasticity as well as the conditions under which it occurs are, in themselves, predictable. Thus the spatial organization of certain species may shift from being aggressively territorial to being nonaggressively nomadic or gregarious because of changes in predation pressure or in the economic defendability of certain resources.[4,6,7] In fact, the shift from territoriality to nonterritoriality in some species can be predicted with quantitative precision[8] and, in others, can be experimentally induced through manipulation of the distribution of critical resources.[9]

Similar plasticity occurs with respect to mating systems. Shifts between monogamy and serial polygyny and polyandry occur, as do shifts between serial polygyny and the formation of leks (or communal display grounds). Again, these shifts occur where they would be predicted on the basis of changes in predation pressure or in the potential for individual monopolization of critical ecological resources.[10]

The observed plasticity of social behavior should serve as a warning to those who propose overly simplistic genetic explanations for such behavior patterns as monogamous mating systems or territorial imperatives in man. Indeed, it is unfortunate that many early popularizers of animal behavior did precisely this. But most of these writings preceded the synthesis stage of sociobiology, and few, if any, social behaviorists today would adhere to such strict genetic determinism.

Different species are expected to be differentially flexible with respect to making rapid changes in social organization to meet environmental changes. The more stable and predictable the long-term environment for a species, the more we may expect genetic determinism of behavior. Wilson describes this in terms of the "phylogenetic inertia" that an animal carries with it. In species whose environment is highly variable or unpredictable or which show tremendous cultural plasticity (including, but not exclusive to, man), we expect this phylogenetic inertia to be less pronounced and the potential for rapid behavioral change to be greater. But this does not mean human societies are fundamentally different from all other species and are totally free from ecological constraints. Most human societies are still faced with ecological "problems," and we still should expect a limited range of resulting "solutions." Knowing whether the resulting social organization is arrived at through long-term genetic change by natural selection, through individual trial and error learning, or through a cultural transmission of the optimal strategies of resource utilization is not the crux to understanding the potential importance of sociobiology. An organism that has the cultural flexibility to adapt its social organization to changing ecological pressures merely has the capability of arriving at a more optimal social organization more rapidly than one that is locked into the slower process of evolutionary change in gene frequencies dictating changes in its behavior.

Indeed, studies of human societies that still retain a close connection to their environment tend to reinforce the predictions and findings of sociobiology. Understanding human resource bases in ecological terms (type, abundance, dispersion pattern, long-term predictability or reliability of food resources, and so forth) is proving valuable in explaining such features of human social organization as group sizes, types of interactions between neighboring groups, mating systems, and optimal foraging strategies.[11]

The problems and challenges of sociobiology come in attempting to apply it to modern, industrialized societies. Here man no longer lives in harmony with his environment. Western man is buffered from the ecological consequences of his actions, and hence the feedback mechanisms (whether genetic or cultural) that normally promote changes in social organization and "adapt" it to the critical limiting features of the environment are broken. The problem of "adaptation" when such feedback loops are broken was eloquently discussed by Hardin in "The Tragedy of the Commons."[12] The resource bases of modern man are exceedingly complex and highly diversified. Technology and industrialization, exploitation and colonization, and mobile transportation of resources all complicate the picture to the point where sociobiology, at least in its current state, is unable to make strong statements or predictions concerning "optimal and nonoptimal" types of social structure. But this does not decrease either the potential political significance of sociobiology or its possible misuses.

The Science for the People group correctly point out the dangers of misusing biological determinism to justify the status quo. But to whatever degree phylogenetic inertia is of importance in humans (that we are carrying a genetic-behavioral heritage molded by natural selection to be adaptive to a hunting-gathering, pre-urban existence), it would be unwise to cease studies of sociobiology or to ignore the biological consequences of politically imposed social structures—regardless of their ideology.

In contrast to the Science for the People group, I see both the strengths and the dangers of sociobiology as extending far beyond the question of the genetic bases of human behavior. Suppose that studies ultimately reveal that human social behavior is infinitely malleable (which I strongly doubt). If future advances in sociobiology allow us to become increasingly precise in predicting the fine structure of social organizations of animals on the basis of ecological constraints, then why couldn't these principles be applied in reverse? Resource bases or distributions could be manipulated in an attempt to shape a particular, "desired" form of social organization. Who, in this case, should have the power to dictate what the politically or morally "optimal" type of society should be?

These are not hollow questions. In many Third World countries, human cultures exist whose social organization is in tune with their environment. As these nations attempt to rapidly enter the world of 20th-century technology, many industrialization and agricultural reforms are initiated. These frequently result in massive changes in the distribution of the resource bases of the country and lead to significant changes in the potential for monopolization of these resources by certain individuals or groups. This, in turn, can lead to increasingly stratified and nonegalitarian societies. Such changes are occurring constantly, in all corners of the world. Future sociobiological findings could be of importance in helping plan the types of technology that we should export and the detailed manner in which they could be applied in order to minimize the frequently chaotic changes they produce in the cultures of the recipient nations.

Neither the potential benefits nor the political dangers of sociobiology rest solely with the issue of genetic determinism of human social behavior. The best formula for increasing our understanding of sociobiology, while at the same time safeguarding against political misuse of information, lies in promoting basic research in this new field, and in disseminating the findings to as broad an audience as possible.

NOTES

1. E. O. Wilson, *Sociobiology: The New Synthesis* (Cambridge, Mass.: Harvard University Press, 1975).
2. E. Allen et al., *New York Review of Books* 22, 43 (13 November 1975); Sociobiology Study Group: Science for the People, *BioScience* 26, 182 (1976).
3. E. O. Wilson, *BioScience* 26, 183 (1976).
4. P. J. Campanella and L. L. Wolf, *Behaviour* 51, 49 (1974).
5. K. C. Wells, *Anim. Behav.*, in press; S. T. Emlen, *Behav. Ecol. Sociobiol.*, in press; G. W. Barlow, *Am. Zool.* 14, 9 (1974); D. Lack, *Proc. Int. Ornithol. Congr.* 14, 3 (1967); J. Bradbury, in *Biology of Bats*, W. Wimsatt, Ed. (New York: Academic Press, in press); J. H. Crook, *Behaviour* (Suppl. 10) (1964), p. 1; P. J. Jarmen, *ibid.* 48, 215 (1974); R. D. Estes, *IUCN (Int. Union Conserv. Nat. Nat. Resour.) Publ. New Ser.* 1, 116 (1974);

J. H. Crook and J. S. Gartlan, *Nature (London)* 210, 1200 (1966); W. W. Denham, *Am. Anthropol.* 73, 77 (1971); J. F. Eisenberg, N. A. Muckenhirn, R. Rudran, *Science* 176, 863 (1972).

6. J. H. Crook, in *Social Behaviour in Birds and Mammals,* J. H. Crook, Ed. (New York: Academic Press, 1970), p. 103.

7. R. D. Alexander, *Behaviour* 17, 130 (1961); V. C. Wynne-Edwards, *Animal Dispersion in Relation to Social Behaviour* (New York: Hafner, 1962); J. H. Brown, *Wilson Bull.* 76, 160 (1964); J. H. Crook, *Symp. Zool. Soc. London* 14, 181 (1965); V. I. Pagunen, *Ann. Zool. Fenn.* 3, 40 (1966); D. Lack, *Ecological Adaptations for Breeding in Birds* (London: Methuen, 1968); R. D. Estes, *Z. Tierpsychol.* 26, 284 (1969); H. Kruuk, *The Spotted Hyaena: A Study of Predation and Social Behavior* (Chicago: Univ. of Chicago Press, 1972); G. B. Schaller, *The Serengeti Lion* (Chicago: Univ. of Chicago Press, 1972).

8. F. B. Gill and L. L. Wolf, *Ecology* 56, 333 (1975); L. L. Wolf, *ibid.* (in press).

9. J. J. Magnuson, *Can. J. Zool.* 40, 313 (1962); A. Zahavi, *Ibis* 113, 203 (1971).

10. E. A. Armstrong, *The Wren* (London: Collins, 1955), pp. 102–109; N. A. Case and O. H. Hewitt, *Living Bird* 2, 7 (1963); J. Verner, *Evolution* 18, 252 (1964); H. W. Kale II, *Publ. Nuttall Ornithol. Club* 5, 1 (1965); W. Leuthold, *Behaviour* 27, 215 (1966); J. Verner and G. H. Engelsen, *Auk* 87, 557 (1970); H. Hays, *Living Bird* 11, 43 (1972); L. W. Oring and M. L. Knudson, *ibid.*, p. 59; S. T. Emlen and L. W. Oring, in preparation.

11. See, for example, J. H. Stewart, *Smithson. Bur. Am. Ethnol. Bull. 120* (1938); A. P. Vayda and R. A. Rappaport, in *Introduction to Cultural Anthropology: Essays in the Scope and Methods of the Science of Man,* J. A. Clifton, Ed. (Boston: Houghton Mifflin, 1968), p. 477; D. Damas, *Natl. Mus. Can. Bull.* 230 (1969), p. 40; R. Netting, *Addison-Wesley Module* 6–1971, 1 (1971); R. B. Lee, *Hum. Ecol.* 1, 125 (1972); R. D. Alexander, *Ann. Rev. Ecol. Syst.* 5, 325 (1974); R. Dyson-Hudson, E. A. Smith, N. Dyson-Hudson, in preparation.

12. G. Hardin, *Science* 162, 1243 (1968).

Biological Potential vs. Biological Determinism

Stephen Jay Gould

In 1758, Linnaeus faced the difficult decision of how to classify his own species in the definitive edition of his *Systema Naturae.* Would he simply rank man among the other animals or would he create for us a separate status? Linnaeus compromised. He placed us within his classification (close to monkeys and bats), but set us apart by his description. He defined our relatives by the mundane, distinguishing characters of size, shape, and number of fingers and toes. For *Homo sapiens,* he wrote only the Socratic injunction: *nosce te ipsum*—"know thyself."

For Linnaeus, *Homo sapiens* was both special and not special. Unfortunately, this eminently sensible resolution has been polarized and utterly distorted by most later commentators. Special and not special have come to mean nonbiological and biological, or nurture and nature. These later polarizations are nonsensical. Humans are animals and everything we do lies within our biological potential. Nothing arouses this ardent (although currently displaced) New Yorker to greater anger than the claims of some self-styled "eco-activists" that large cities are the "unnatural" harbingers of our impending destruction. But—and here comes the biggest *but* I can muster—the statement that humans are animals does not imply that our specific patterns of behavior and social arrangements are in any way directly determined by our genes. *Potential* and *determination* are different concepts.

The intense discussion aroused by E. O. Wilson's *Sociobiology* has led me to take up this subject. Wilson's book has been greeted by a

From *Natural History Magazine* (May 1976). Copyright © 1976 The American Museum of Natural History. Reprinted with permission of the publisher.

chorus of praise and publicity (for example, the review by R. S. Morison in the November 1975 issue of *Natural History*). I, however, find myself among the smaller group of its detractors. Most of *Sociobiology* wins from me the same high praise almost universally accorded to it. For a lucid account of evolutionary principles and an indefatigably thorough discussion of social behavior among all groups of animals, *Sociobiology* will be the primary document for years to come. But Wilson's last chapter, "From Sociobiology to Sociology," leaves me very unhappy indeed. After twenty-six chapters of careful documentation for the non-human animals, Wilson concludes with an extended speculation on the genetic basis of supposedly universal patterns of human behavior. Unfortunately, since this chapter is his statement on human behavior, it has also attracted more than 80 percent of all the commentary in the popular press.

We who have criticized this last chapter have been accused of denying altogether the relevance of biology to human behavior, of reviving an ancient superstition by placing man outside the rest of "the creation." Are we pure "nurturists?" Do we permit a political vision of human perfectibility to blind us to evident constraints imposed by our biological nature? The answer to both is no. The issue is not universal biology vs. human uniqueness, but biological potentiality vs. biological determinism.

Replying to a critic of his article in the *New York Times Magazine* (October 12, 1975), Wilson wrote

There is no doubt that the patterns of human social behavior, including altruistic behavior, are under genetic control, in the sense that they represent a restricted subset of possible patterns that are very different from the patterns of termites, chimpanzees and other animal species.

If this is all that Wilson means by genetic control, then we can scarcely disagree. Surely we do not do all the things that other animals do, and just as surely, the range of our potential behavior is circumscribed by our biology. We would lead very different social lives if we photosynthesized (no agriculture, gathering, or hunting—the major determinants of our social evolution) or had life cycles like those of certain gall midges. (When feeding on an uncrowded mushroom, these insects reproduce in the larval or pupal stage. The young grow within the mother's body, devour her from inside, and emerge from her depleted external shell ready to feed, grow the next generation, and make the supreme sacrifice.)

But Wilson makes much stronger claims. Chapter 27 is not a statement about the range of potential human behaviors or even an argument for the restriction of that range from a much larger total domain among all animals. It is, primarily, an extended speculation on the existence of genes for specific and variable traits in human behavior—including spite, aggression, xenophobia, conformity, homosexuality, and the characteristic behavioral differences between men and women in Western society. Of course, Wilson does not deny the role of nongenetic learning in human behavior; he even states at one point that "genes have given away most of their sovereignty." But he quickly adds, genes "maintain a certain amount of influence in at least the behavioral qualities that underlie variations between cultures." And the next paragraph calls for "a discipline of anthropological genetics."

Biological determinism is the primary theme in Wilson's discussion of human behavior; chapter 27 makes no sense in any other context. Wilson's primary aim, as I read him, is to suggest that Darwinian theory might reformulate the human sciences just as it has succeeded so spectacularly in other biological disciplines. But Darwinian processes cannot operate without genes to select. Unless the "interesting" properties of human behavior are under specific genetic control, sociology need fear no invasion of its turf. By interesting, I refer to the subjects sociologists and anthropologists fight about most often—aggression, social stratification, and differences in behavior between men and women. If genes only specify that we are large enough to live in a world of gravitational forces, need to rest our bodies by sleeping, and do not photosynthesize, then the realm of genetic determinism will be relatively uninspiring.

What is the direct evidence for genetic control of specific human social behavior? At the moment, the answer is none whatever. (It would not be impossible, in theory, to gain such evidence by standard, controlled experiments in breeding, but we do not raise people in *Drosophila* bottles, establish pure lines, or control environments for invariant nurturing.) Sociobiologists must therefore advance indirect arguments based on plausibility. Wilson uses three major strategies: universality, continuity, and adaptiveness.

1. Universality: If certain behaviors are invariably found in our closest primate relatives and among humans themselves, a circumstantial case for common, inherited genetic control may be advanced. Chapter 27 abounds with statements about supposed human universals. For example, "Human beings are absurdly easy to indoctrinate—they *seek* it." Or, "Men would rather believe than know." I can only say that my own experience does not correspond with Wilson's.

When Wilson must acknowledge diversity, he often dismisses the uncomfortable "exceptions" as temporary and unimportant aberrations. Since Wilson believes that repeated, often genocidal warfare has shaped our genetic destiny, the existence of nonaggressive peoples is embarrassing. But he writes: "It is to be expected that some isolated cultures will escape the process for generations at a time, in effect reverting temporarily to what ethnographers classify as a pacific state."

In any case, even if we can compile a list of behavioral traits shared by humans and our closest primate relatives, this does not make a good case for common genetic control. Similar results need not imply similar causes; in fact, evolutionists are so keenly aware of this problem that they have developed a terminology to express it. Similar features due to common genetic ancestry are "homologous"; similarities due to common function, but with different evolutionary histories, are "analogous" (the wings of birds and insects, for example—the common ancestor of both groups lacked wings). I will argue below that a basic feature of human biology supports the idea that many behavioral similarities between humans and other primates are analogous, and that they have no direct genetic specification in humans.

2. Continuity: Wilson claims, with ample justice in my opinion, that the Darwinian explanation of altruism in W. D. Hamilton's 1964 theory of "kin selection" forms the basis for an evolutionary theory of animal societies. Altruistic acts are the cement of stable societies, yet they seem to defy a Darwinian explanation. On Darwinian principles, all individuals are selected to maximize their own genetic contributions to future generations. How, then, can they willingly sacrifice or endanger themselves by performing altruistic acts to benefit others?

The resolution is charmingly simple in concept, although complex in technical detail. By benefiting relatives, altruistic acts preserve an altruist's genes even if the altruist himself will not be the one to perpetuate them. For example, in most sexually reproducing organisms, an individual shares an average of half the genes of his sibs and one-eighth the genes of his first cousins. Hence, if faced with a choice of saving oneself alone or sacrificing oneself to save more than two sibs or more than eight first cousins, the Darwinian calculus favors altruistic sacrifice, for in so doing, an altruist actually increases his own genetic representation in future generations.

Natural selection will favor the preservation of such self-serving altruist genes. But what of altruistic acts toward nonrelatives? Here sociobiologists must invoke a related concept of "reciprocal altruism" to preserve a genetic explanation. The altruistic act entails some danger and no immediate benefit, but if it inspires a reciprocal act by the current beneficiary at some future time, it may pay off in the long run: a genetic incarnation of the age-old adage, You scratch my back and I'll scratch yours (even if we're not related).

The argument from continuity then proceeds. Altruistic acts in other animal societies can be plausibly explained as example of Darwinian kin selection. Humans perform altruistic acts and these are likely to have a similarly direct genetic basis. But again, similarity of result does not imply identity of cause (see below for an alternate explanation based on biological potentiality rather than biological determinism).

3. Adaptiveness: Adaptation is the hallmark of Darwinian processes. Natural selection operates continuously and relentlessly to fit organisms to their environments. Disadvantageous social structures, like poorly designed morphological structures, will not survive for long.

Human social practices are clearly adaptive. One of my predecessors in these columns, anthropologist Marvin Harris, has delighted in demonstrating the logic and sensibility of those social practices in other cultures that seem most bizarre to smug Westerners (*Cows, Pigs, Wars, and Witches,* Random House, 1974). Human social behavior is riddled with altruism; it is also clearly adaptive. Is this not a prima facie argument for direct genetic control? My answer is definitely "no," and I can best illustrate my claim by reporting an argument I had with a colleague, an eminent anthropologist.

My colleague insisted that the classic story of Eskimo on ice floes provides adequate proof for the existence of specific altruist genes maintained by kin selection. Apparently, among some Eskimo peoples, social units are arranged as family groups. If food resources dwindle and the family must move to survive, aged grandparents willingly remain behind (to die) rather than endanger the survival of the entire family by slowing an arduous and dangerous migration. Family groups with no altruist genes have succumbed to natural selection as migrations hindered by the old and sick lead to the death of entire families. Grandparents with altruist genes increase their own fitness by their sacrifice, for they insure the survival of close relatives sharing their genes.

The explanation by my colleague is plausible, to be sure, but scarcely conclusive since an eminently simple, nongenetic explanation also exists: there are no altruist genes at all, in fact, no important genetic differences among Eskimo families whatsoever. The sacrifice of grandparents is an adaptive, but nongenetic, cultural trait. Families with no tradition for sacrifice do not survive for many generations. In other families, sacrifice is celebrated in song and story; aged grandparents who stay behind become the greatest heroes of the clan. Children are socialized from their earliest memories to the glory and honor of such sacrifice.

I cannot prove my scenario, any more than my colleague can demonstrate his. But in the current context of no evidence, they are at least equally plausible. Likewise, reciprocal altruism undeniably exists in human societies, but this provides no evidence whatever for its genetic basis. As Benjamin Franklin said: "We must all hang together, or assuredly we shall all hang separately." Functioning societies may require reciprocal altruism. But these acts need not be coded into our being by genes; they may be inculcated equally well by learning.

I return, then, to Linnaeus's compromise that we are both ordinary and unique. The central feature of our biological uniqueness also provides the major reason for doubting that our behaviors are directly coded by specific genes. That feature is, of course, our large brain. Size itself is a major determinant of the function and structure of any object. The large and the small cannot work in the same way. We know best the structural changes that compensate for the decrease of surface area in relation to volume of large creatures, for example, thick legs and convoluted internal surfaces such as lungs and villi of the small intestine. But markedly increased brain size in human evolution may have had the most profound consequences of all. The increase added enough neural connections to convert an inflexible and rigidly programmed device into a labile organ. Endowed with sufficient logic and memory, the brain may have substituted nonprogrammed learning for direct specification as the ground of social behavior. Flexibility may well be the most important determinant of human consciousness; the direct programming of behavior has probably become inadaptive.

Why imagine that specific genes for aggression, dominance, or spite have any importance when we know that the brain's enormous flexibility permits us to be aggressive or peaceful, dominant or submissive, spiteful or generous? Violence, sexism, and general nastiness *are* biological since they represent one subset of a possible range of behaviors. But peacefulness, equality, and kindness are just as biological—and we may see their influence increase if we can create social structures that permit them to flourish. Thus, my criticism of Wilson does not invoke a nonbiological "environmentalism"; it merely pits the concept of biological potentiality, with a brain capable of the full range of human behaviors and predisposed toward none, against the idea of biological determinism, with specific genes for specific behavioral traits.

But why is this academic issue so delicate and explosive? There is no hard evidence for either position, and what difference does it make, for example, whether we conform because conformer genes have been selected or because our general genetic makeup permits conformity as one strategy among many?

The protracted and intense debate surrounding biological determinism has arisen as a function of its social and political message. As I have argued in several columns (April 1974, June-July 1975, March 1976), biological determinism has always been used to defend existing social arrangements as biologically inevitable—from "for ye have the poor always with you" to nineteenth-century imperialism to modern sexism. Why else would a set of ideas so devoid of factual support gain such a consistently good press from established media throughout the centuries? This usage is quite out of the control of individual scientists who propose deterministic theories for a host of reasons, often benevolent.

I make no attribution of motive in Wilson's or anyone else's case. Neither do I reject determinism because I dislike its political usage. Scientific truth, as we understand it, must be our primary criterion. We live with several unpleasant biological truths, death being the most undeniable and ineluctable. If genetic determinism is true, we will learn to live with it as well. But I reiterate my statement that no evidence exists to support it, that the crude versions of past centuries have been conclusively disproved, and that its continued popularity is a function of social prejudice among those who benefit most from the status quo.

But let us not saddle *Sociobiology* with the sins of past determinists. What have been its direct results in the first few months of its excellent publicity? At best, we see the beginnings of a line of social research that promises only absurdity by its refusal to consider immediate nongenetic factors. The January 30, 1976, issue of *Science* (America's leading technical journal for scientists) contains an article on panhandling that I would have accepted as satire if it had appeared verbatim in the *National Lampoon*. The authors dispatched "panhandlers" to request dimes from various "targets." Results are discussed only in the context of kin selection, reciprocal altruism, and the food-sharing habits of chimps and baboons—nothing on current urban realities in America. As one major conclusion, they find that male panhandlers are "far more successful approaching a single female or a pair of females than a male and female together; they were particularly unsuccessful when approaching a single male or two males together." But not a word about urban fear or the politics of sex—just some statements about chimps and the genetics of altruism (although they finally admit that reciprocal altruism probably does not apply—after all, they argue, what future benefit can one expect from a panhandler).

In the first negative comment on *Sociobiology,* economist Paul Samuelson (*Newsweek,* July 7, 1975) urged sociobiologists to tread softly in the zones of race and sex. I see no evidence that his advice is being heeded. In his *New York Times Magazine* article of October 12, 1975, Wilson writes:

In hunter-gatherer societies, men hunt and women stay at home. This strong bias persists in *most* [my emphasis] agricultural and industrial societies and, on that ground alone, appears to have a genetic origin. . . . My own guess is that the genetic bias is intense enough to cause a substantial division of labor even in the most free and most egalitarian of future societies. . . . Even with identical education and equal access to all professions, men are likely to continue to play a disproportionate role in political life, business and science.

I can only repeat Kate Millett's complaint that "patriarchy has a tenacious or powerful hold through its successful habit of passing itself off as nature."

We are both similar to and different from other animals. In different cultural contexts, emphasis upon one side or the other of this fundamental truth plays a useful social role. In Darwin's day, an assertion of our similarity broke through centuries of harmful superstition. Now we may need to emphasize our difference as flexible animals with a vast range of potential behavior. Our biological nature does not stand in the way of social reform. We are, as Simone de Beauvoir said, "l'être dont l'être est de n'être pas"—the being whose essence lies in having no essence.

PART VI

Extensions, Implications, and Critiques of Sociobiology

Sociobiology:
A Philosophical Analysis

Michael Ruse

Given the fact that, in the current controversy about the worth of sociobiology, we have very eminent scientists in stark disagreement, it might seem presumptuous for a nonscientist, even a philosopher of science, to dare to comment. However, philosophical comment is not entirely inappropriate, for as so often is the case when scientists fall out, their disagreements are less about brute matters of scientific fact than about rival philosophical commitments and conclusions. In this paper, therefore, I intend to review major claims by both sociobiologists and their opponents, concentrating exclusively on those parts of the controversy which are of philosophical interest. I shall not look at ethical questions raised by the sociobiology controversy, as this has been done elsewhere—by me (Ruse, 1977) and by others in this volume.

I start with the claims of the proponents of sociobiology; I turn then to the critics; and I conclude with a brief look toward the future.

I. SOCIOBIOLOGY AND ITS PLACE IN BIOLOGY

The obvious place to go first, if we want to find out about sociobiology, is E. O. Wilson's massive *Sociobiology: The New Synthesis*. There we learn that "sociobiology is defined as the systematic study of the biological basis of all social behaviour. For the present it focuses on animal societies, their population structure, castes, and communication, together with all of the physiology underlying the social adaptations.

Michael Ruse is in the Department of Philosophy at the University of Guelph, Ontario, Canada.

But the discipline is also concerned with the social behaviour of early man and the adaptive features of organization in the more primitive contemporary human societies." (Wilson, 1975a, p. 4)

Now, let us bypass for the moment the organism which has caused all the trouble, namely man, and concentrate on the first part of Wilson's claim. He (and his fellows) want to look at animal social behaviour from a *biological* viewpoint, considering such behaviour as constituting *adaptations.* Presumably therefore, sociobiology is an attempt to consider animal behaviour from the viewpoint of that biological theory which considers adaptations, namely the modern "synthetic" theory of evolution. And indeed Wilson himself says, "This book makes an attempt to codify sociobiology into a branch of evolutionary biology and particularly of modern population biology." (Wilson, 1975a, p. 4) Hence, already we can start to get glimmerings of what the sociobiologists might hope to achieve. Let me elaborate on this.

Briefly speaking, the modern theory of evolution, a combination of the selectionist ideas of Charles Darwin and the views about particulate inheritance of Gregor Mendel and his successors, starts with the gene— something believed to be on the chromosomes, passed on through the generations, and causally responsible in some kind of ultimate sense, together with the interacting environment, for the gross ("phenotypic") characteristics of organisms, both static and dynamic. The evolutionist's interest in the gene is in the way it functions en masse, that is to say, the way in which the genes in a group of organisms get distributed and relate to each other from generation to generation. What one finds is that in a fairly large interbreeding population, where there are no disruptive forces, gene ratios from generation to generation stay constant—a truth encaptured in the so-called Hardy-Weinberg law. That there are in fact such disruptive forces is of course what leads to evolution, and chief among these forces one might mention immigration and emigration in and out of populations, mutation from one gene form to another, and most importantly, the fact that certain genes express themselves in phenotypic characteristics giving their possessors an edge in the race to reproduce, thus in turn causing the genes to be "selected" favourably in the next generation.

This study of the distributions and transmissions of genes—"population genetics"—is the logical base for all of evolutionary thought, for ultimately almost by definition evolution comes down to changes in gene ratios. Various kinds of evolutionists presuppose this "core," using it to throw light on their own particular area of investigation: for instance, the fossil record (paleontology), the geographical distributions of organisms (biogeography), and so on. Recognizing that some of these latter subdisciplines will borrow from each other also, we might picture evolutionary theory in the fanlike form shown in the figure below. (For more details on the synthetic theory see Ruse, 1973)

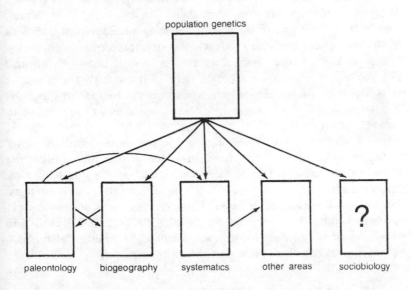

Figure 1
In this figure the rectangles represent various parts of evolutionary theory. The links between population genetics and the subdisciplines are actual. The lower links are just illustrative. No attempt has been made at completeness.

Now, with this picture of evolutionary theory before us, the aim of the sociobiologist is easy to understand. Simply, he or she wants to add another subdiscipline to evolutionary theory: one dealing with animal social behaviour. This means that throughout the sociobiologists' work we should find presupposed the basic truths of population genetics, and I think it is true to say that not only do we find this, but that similarly throughout the sociobiologists' work (and that of their critics) we find no essential feeling that population genetics ought to be violated or ignored. To borrow the well-known language of Thomas Kuhn, in this important sense sociobiologists and their critics, for all their radical-ness, are normal scientists working within an unchallenged paradigm. (See Kuhn, 1970.) Thus, for example, in Wilson's treatment of animal sexuality the discussion begins with an exposition of population genetics theory, and matters take off from there. Sociobiology, I am afraid, does little to solve one of the most interesting philosophical questions about evolutionary theory, namely whether or not it is truly hypothetico-deductive. Indeed, with respect to this matter, it shows its oneness with the rest of evolutionary studies. Parts of it are fairly formal; other parts are fairly loose, particularly when one has to look at questions of how particular genes might help their possessors in the struggle to survive and reproduce.

Given the orthodoxy of sociobiology, in the sense discussed above, we have at once an interesting problem—what Wilson indeed calls "the central theoretical problem of sociobiology." Clearly, natural selection puts a premium on selfishness. Either a gene looks to its own interests, that is a gene causes self-directed characteristics in its possessor, or it gets wiped out. How then do we explain the fact that animals are social, that much of their behaviour towards each other is "altruistic." Let us look at sociobiological thought on this matter.

II. THE GENETICS OF ALTRUISM

The obvious move to explain altruism is to suggest that basically it all reduces to enlightened self-interest, and this essentially is the tack taken by sociobiologists. Until recently, one popular possible mode of explanation was so-called group selection, where an organism's altruism in sacrificing its own genes' interests was thought to be compensated by the benefit to the genes (collectively speaking) of the organism's species. These days, however, that dividend is generally thought to be too tenuous a link, and altruism is thought to be a function only of fairly immediate returns. Three mechanisms are suggested to account for it.

First, we have the possibility of so-called parental manipulation. Consider two organisms A and B, supposing that they each have (on average) four offspring and that unaided about one in four offspring survive. Suppose also however that if an offspring is aided by a sibling its chances of reproducing are improved (say to two in three), even though the altruist itself becomes effectively sterile. Suppose finally that B has genes that will manipulate an offspring into becoming such an altruist. Fairly clearly, these genes for altruism through parental manipulation will be promoted because B is twice as fit, biologically speaking, as A. (More details in Alexander, 1974, and West Eberhard, 1975)

Next, we have kin selection. This involves the idea of one organism, say A, sacrificing some of its own reproductive fitness for the sake of a close relative, say B, because B thereby gains in reproductive fitness and passes on the shared genes of A more efficiently than A could itself. Thus, if I share 50 percent of my genes with my brother, it will pay me (from an evolutionary viewpoint) to give up entirely my own evolutionary hopes if thereby my brother's chances are increased more than twofold. The difference between kin selection and parental manipulation is that in the former the key is shared relationship between altruist and recipient, whereas in the latter theoretically there need be no relationship at all—it is the parent's genes which benefit from the altruism. (See Hamilton, 1964 and 1972.)

Thirdly, we have reciprocal altruism, which according to the model can take place even between members of different species. One organism aids another because it expects help in return, and because cheating and reneging on the return of favours does not pay. This mechanism differs from the two previous, because neither of them supposes any altruistic behavioural returns. Taking an example of R. L. Trivers, a major exponent of this mechanism, suppose that a population faces constant risk of drowning, that unaided one has a 50 percent chance of drowning, but that aided one has a 5 percent chance of drowning. Even if a would-be rescuer has also a 5 percent chance of drowning, genes for altruism will be promoted; for, assuming everyone faces drowning at some time, such altruism reduces drowning chances by about four-fifths. (See Trivers, 1971.)

We have these three models to show how altruism might be promoted. This in itself is not to say that any of the three has actual instantiations. However, restricting ourselves for the moment just to the nonhuman world, and recognizing that it is not always easy to tell actually which mechanism is operating, it seems that even the critics allow that (at least some of the) mechanisms have some actuality. For instance, supporting parental manipulation, we know that some insects constantly use part of their reproductive output ("trophic" eggs) to feed other offspring, or if such eaten eggs are thought not very altruistic, some queens feed their initial offspring in such a way as to make them turn into sterile workers—altruists towards their fertile siblings.

In the case of kin selection, it may have been responsible for much altruism in the insect world, particularly where Hymenoptera are concerned. This is because males in that order are haploid, whereas females are diploid. Because males develop from unfertilized eggs whereas females have both mother and father, a female is more closely related to her sisters than to her daughters (3/4:1/2). Hence, a female can better promote her own genes by rearing sisters than daughters!

Finally, a nice case of reciprocal altruism involves cleaning symbioses in fish. Certain fish groom other fish, to their mutual benefit—cleanliness on the one hand and food on the other. And there are, moreover, strong sanctions against cheating—were the groomed to eat the groomer after grooming, it could never again use that particular groomer.

We have now, I think, a flavour of the problems and explanations of nonhuman sociobiology. Let us turn to the object of controversy: the human.

III. MAN AS A SOCIOBIOLOGICAL SUBJECT

Basically, the sociobiologists would like to take their formal apparatuses and apply them directly to man, thereby explaining man's behaviour both at an individual level and at the wider, social, "cultural" level. However, as Wilson notes; "It is part of the conventional wisdom that virtually all cultural variation is phenotypic rather than genetic in origin." (Wilson, 1975a, p. 550) And certainly, as Wilson admits, vast cultural changes do occur at rates far too rapid to be direct functions of genetic changes. Nevertheless;

although the genes have given away most of their sovereignty, they maintain a certain amount of influence in at least the behavioral qualities that underlie variations between cultures. Moderately high heritability has been documented in introversion-extroversion measures, personal tempo, psychomotor and sports activities, neuroticism, dominance, depression, and the tendency toward certain forms of mental illness such as schizophrenia. . . . Even a small portion of this variance invested in population differences might predispose societies toward cultural differences. (Wilson, 1975a, p. 550)

Wilson envisions something which he calls the "multiplier effect" coming into action here. A small genetic effect might multiply up into a high behavioural change, and thus minor genetic differences might spell major cultural differences.

Although Wilson talks of differences, in the passage quoted above, it is his position that all modes of human behaviour—similarities as well as differences—are causally influenced by the genes. By doing a comparative taxonomic study between various primates (including man), Wilson finds some human characteristics shared fairly widely through the group. This leads him to suspect that such coincidences may be due to genetic factors. Amongst the constants between primates, Wilson finds "aggressive dominance systems, with males generally dominant over females; scaling in the intensity of responses, especially during aggressive interactions; intensive and prolonged maternal care, with a pronounced degree of socialization in the young; and matrilineal social organization." (Wilson, 1975a, p. 551)

Other sociobiologists have been no less ready than Wilson to suggest that their models might also explain the behaviour of *Homo sapiens*. All three genetic models of altruism discussed in the last section have been used to explain aspects of man's behaviour. In the case of parental manipulation, R. D. Alexander, one of its leading exponents, suggests that the theory explains the practice in some human tribes of feeding younger offspring to older offspring in times of food shortages. If again it be felt that there be not much altruism about such "trophic" humans, a clearer case perhaps occurs in certain tribes practicing polyandry. Usually, families in such societies depend on a single resource, the family farm. There is therefore considerable parental pressure on younger brothers to double up with their older brothers, thus ensuring the farm not be split up and that there be plentiful cheap labour without many extra children. Alexander suggests that a case like this so perfectly fits what one would expect from a genetically caused parental manipulation, that such a genetic mechanism may indeed be the cause. (Alexander, 1974)

It is easy to see how kin selection would attract sociobiologists intent on explaining human altruism. Any help to relatives other than mate and offspring seems grist for the kin-selective mill. And, the sociobiologists suggest, such selection may have been even more important in the past, when men formed small, closely knit bands of hunters. Most interestingly, Alexander has suggested that kin selection may be the cause of a phenomenon fairly common throughout the human world, but apparently irreconcilable with any theory of selection. This is the care of children not by the father but by the mother's brother. Alexander argues that this phenomenon is particularly prevalent in societies where biological fatherhood (as opposed to social fatherhood) is often in doubt. He points out that this is a situation favouring kin selection, for (in the case of a male) although one may be in doubt about biological offspring, one is in no doubt about one's relationship to one's sister's children. Hence, genes causing this kind of altruism will be favoured.

In like vein, Trivers thinks that reciprocal altruism can be applied directly to humans.

There is no direct evidence regarding the degree of reciprocal altruism practiced during human evolution nor its genetic basis today, but given the universal and nearly daily practice of reciprocal altruism among humans today, it is reasonable to assume that it has been an important factor in recent human evolution and that the underlying emotional dispositions affecting altruistic behavior have important genetic components. (Trivers, 1971, p. 48)

Finally, let us note that some sociobiologists have tried to put together the various models for altruism. For example, Alexander finds confirmation of and details about the interaction of kin selection and reciprocal altruism in an analysis by the anthropologist M. D. Sahlins (1965). In particular, Sahlins finds two kinds of reciprocity between individuals in primitive human societies: "generalized reciprocity" between relatives, a giving which demands no return; and "balanced reciprocity" between nonrelatives, a giving which does demand return. Alexander identifies these with kin selection and reciprocal altruism respectively, and he feels that such a consilience between anthropology and genetics must be significant.

There is much more that could be written about applications of sociobiology to man, but the general approach should now be apparent. Let us turn to the critics.

IV. AREAS OF CRITICISM

The most vociferous critics of sociobiology, the Sociobiology Study Group of Science for the People, have fired a barrage of charges at sociobiology.* Those that I shall consider here may be grouped under three (not entirely consistent) headings: that sociobiology is incoherent, that it is unfalsifiable, and that it is false. In line with the policy stated earlier, I shall not consider the charges that sociobiology is racist or sexist.

V. IS SOCIOBIOLOGY INCOHERENT?

A major objection levelled by the critics against sociobiology—both human and nonhuman—is that it is predicated on premises which basically do not make any sense. In particular, the critics object that sociobiologists naively assume that the units of heredity, the genes, can be put into direct correspondence with organic physical characteristics, including behavioural characteristics.

Geneticists long ago abandoned the naive notion that there are genes for toes, genes for ankles, genes for the lower leg, genes for the kneecap, etc. Yet the sociobiologists break the totality of human social behavior into arbitrary units, call these elements "organs" of behavior, and postulate particular genes or gene complexes for each. (Allen et al., 1977, p. 21)

Thus, for example, the critics object that when someone like Trivers wants to explain human altruism on his model of reciprocal altruism, the whole enterprise is fundamentally misconceived and muddled because it is just not the case that there are, or even could be, genes corresponding to man's various altruistic traits. The genes just do not work that way.

In reply to this objection two points can be made. First, while it is certainly not the case that organisms can be divided neatly into an

---

* Through the kindness of one of the group's members, I have a detailed, as yet unpublished critical paper by this group, hereafter referred to as Allen et al. (1977). This is essentially a longer version of their published Allen et al. (1976).

"objective" set of characteristics, or that there is a perfect match between characteristics and the genes, there is at least some correlation. To argue otherwise is virtually to reject genetics as presently conceived! Science begins with abstraction; one can certainly abstract characteristics—blue eyes, curly hair, and so on; and one can link up many of these characteristics fairly directly with the genes. Eye colour, for instance, is susceptible to relatively uncomplicated genetic explanation. Of course, matters are not always straightforward; but simply in believing that characteristics can be identified and linked with the genes, sociobiologists are doing no more than any other biologist who turns to genetics.

The second point, in case it be objected immediately that where sociobiologists overstep the bounds is in their trying to extend this abstractive process to behavioural characteristics, is that this extension is neither conceptually misconceived nor necessarily doomed to failure. At least R. C. Lewontin, a leading geneticist and member of the Sociobiology Study Group of Science for the People, in a recent discussion has quite unselfconsciously given a list of "traits" (his language) that can be selected for in *Drosophila* (fruit flies), and has included in this list behavioural traits. "Selection for mating preference can be carried out by allowing free mating in a mixture of two mutant stocks and then destroying all hybrid progeny in each generation." (Lewontin, 1974, p. 90) More generally, the critics destroy their own case, for they admit that there is good evidence that schizophrenia is a genetically controlled disease, and conceptually this is obviously a case of abstracting behavioural traits and linking them to the genes.

In short, although the critics are no doubt right in condemning crude identifications of all gross characteristics with specific genes, generally speaking their strictures fall no more heavily on sociobiologists than they do on other biologists. And such strictures have only limited validity. They do not destroy the sociobiological enterprise.

VI. IS SOCIOBIOLOGY UNFALSIFIABLE?

The critics argue that sociobiology has at its heart the claim that all human behaviour is or was adaptive, and that it shows itself to be a pseudo-theory in that there is no evidence at all that conceivably could be brought to dispute this.

When we examine carefully the manner in which sociobiology pretends to explain all behaviors as adaptive, it becomes obvious that the theory is so constructed that *no tests are possible.* There exists no imaginable situation which cannot be explained; it is *necessarily confirmed by every observation.* The mode of explanation involves three possible levels of the operation of natural selection: 1. classical individual selection to account for obviously self-serving behaviors; 2. kin selection to account for altruistic or submissive acts toward relatives; 3. reciprocal altruism to account for altruistic behaviors directed toward unrelated persons. All that remains is to make up a "just-so" story of adaptation with the appropriate form of selection acting. (Allen et al., 1977, p. 24)

A number of points can be made about this rather persuasive-looking critique. Let us consider some.

First, although the criticism rather implies that there is something ad hoc about the whole sociobiological enterprise—whenever one has a new difficulty, yet another face-saving mechanism is thought up—this is not quite fair. On the one hand, obviously the sociobiologists have got to try to explain all the phenomena—and given the complexity of the phenomena they are considering, it is hardly surprising that they need to invoke a variety of mechanisms. On the other hand, their various mechanisms are not just peculiarly sociobiological fictions, grasped merely to avoid counter examples when one comes to man. Kin selection, for example, is as old as modern evolutionary theory, for it goes back to Darwin and the *Origin,* and indeed is accepted by the critics themselves. "There do exist data supporting the idea that kin selection is effective for some traits in social insects." (Allen et al., 1977, p. 26) Of course, one might question the applicability of kin selection and other mechanisms to man in various instances; but, in itself, actually turning to these mechanisms hardly makes sociobiology a pseudo-theory.

The second point is that it just is not true that sociobiologists claim that all behaviour must be shown adaptive (that is to say, of positive value in the struggle to survive and reproduce). They do argue for nonadaptive behaviour on occasion. For example, Wilson takes human homosexuality to be at least prima facie nonadaptive, because it would seem that homosexual desires make one, biologically speaking, less fit. It is of course true that, generally speaking, sociobiologists try to link behaviour to adaptive advantage. In the homosexuality case Wilson suggests that homosexuality might be a function of superior heterozygote fitness (the heterozygotes $A_1 A_2$ are exceptionally fit, balancing and maintaining less fit homosexual homozygotes $A_1 A_1$). However, inasmuch as they do this linking, sociobiologists do no more than any evolutionary biologist who feels that all characteristics, certainly those of any degree of sophistication and complexity, tend to have adaptive value. In this respect the practices of the sociobiologists seem no different from those of others.

Of course, the critics will hardly be satisfied with this point. "Precisely so," they will argue, "the whole point is that evolutionary theory generally tends towards the unfalsifiable in the claim that everything has adaptive value. Sociobiology in particular is a paradigm of the problems. For all its sweet reasonableness, Alexander's intellectual jesuitry about mother's brother shows full well that in practice, if not in theory, nothing is going to be allowed to stand for sociobiologists as falsifying." In reply, three quick items: First, one can hardly hold their ingenuity against sociobiologists. If they left the mother's brother problem untouched, then their theory would be false, and trying to avoid falsification is hardly a cardinal scientific sin. Karl Popper has made falsifiability the mark of scientific honesty (and in this seems to act as a Pied Piper for all scientists who touch on philosophy), but Kuhn has argued that much scientific success stems from refusing to let a hypothesis be bowled over by every sundry fact—merit can come from not at once admitting falsification. Second, the fact that some sociobiologists refuse to let their theory be falsified does not mean that the theory itself is essentially any less falsifiable than any other. Many nineteenth-century scientists would admit no exceptions to Newtonian mechanics, but history showed that ultimately contrary facts could lead to the theory's eclipse. The same could be so for sociobiology. Third, much of the worrying by critics seems a bit academic, for there surely are conceivable situations which would falsify sociobiology. Take incest avoidance, a common social fact, one certainly justified on genetic grounds, and one the sociobiologists think could be a function of the genes. Widespread existence of societies openly promoting incest, despite the devastating results it brings, would prove a severe (i.e., falsifying) problem for sociobiologists, as would societies where nonrelatives give freely without any hope of return or where such giving significantly reduced the giver's own fitness. That such societies do not exist is hardly the fault of sociobiologists. One should not confuse the need to be falsifiable with the fact of being falsified.

VII. IS SOCIOBIOLOGY FALSE?

The final set of charges we shall consider is that even where sociobiology opens itself up to test, it does so only to show that it is false. "There does exist, however, one possibility of tests of such [sociobiological] hypotheses, where they make specific *quantitative* predictions about rates of change of characters in time and about the degree of differentiation between populations of a species." (Allen et al., 1977, p. 27) But what we find is that rates of cultural change occur far too rapidly to be under the control of the genes—the rise and the fall of Islam took less than thirty generations—and that the genetic differences between populations are just not great enough to bear the kinds of cultural differences we find between populations. "We know from studies of enzyme-specifying genes that at least 85 percent of that kind of human variation lies *within* any local population or nation, with a maximum of about 8 percent between nations and 7 percent between major races." (Allen et al., 1977, p. 28)

There are at least two replies that the sociobiologists make to charges like these, neither of which involves denial of the facts behind the charges. First, they can invoke the multiplier effect, arguing that relatively minor genetic differences can multiply up so that they manifest themselves as rather major cultural differences. As can be imagined, such an argument does not find much favour with the critics, who suggest that the so-called multiplier effect, together with the "threshold effect" according to which organisms have to get to a certain level of complexity for the multiplier effect to take hold, "are pure inventions of convenience without any evidence to support them. They have been created out of whole cloth to seal off the last loophole through which the theory might have been tested against the real world." (Allen et al., 1977, pp. 29–30)

This conclusion seems too harsh. It certainly is the case that small things can multiply up into major effects: remember the case of the king who lost his kingdom "all for want of a horseshoe nail." On the other hand, one must be careful not to overestimate the strength of the sociobiological side. To say that the genetic differences between populations *might* cause cultural differences, and that the multiplier effect *might* operate is a far cry from saying that either claim is true, or indeed very plausible. To be honest, the sociobiologists do not give that much evidence to support their position. Wilson mentions the case of two kinds of baboon with radically different cultures, and he suggests that this difference might be caused by very slight genetic differences, multiplied up. However, as the critics point out, Wilson really has no hard evidence that the genetic differences are slight—and, in any case, one swallow does not a summer make. In short, at this point we might grant the sociobiologists that they have fascinating hypotheses. But these hardly have the status of well-confirmed theory.

This brings me to the second reply the sociobiologists can make to their critics. Even if one grants that much of the difference in cultures over time and space cannot have a great genetic input, one might still argue that much of the similarity—the basic cultural bonds between virtually every human society—has a solid genetic background. Quite aside from the bond of language ability, which is the *sine qua non* of culture and clearly under direct genetic control, we have such things as incest avoidance, various degrees and types of altruism, religious yearnings, and much, much more. All of these could be closely linked to the genes, and none of the critics' objections tells us otherwise.

Of course, once again, even if one grants that the sociobiologists' claims might be true, this is a far cry from saying that they actually are true, or even that they are plausible. Let us therefore, for the moment, reverse the critics' question, and instead of asking if sociobiology is false, let us ask if there is any conceivable reason to think it might be true.

VIII. IS SOCIOBIOLOGY TRUE?

Taking a leaf out of Darwin's *Origin*, a book which reflects its author's sensitivity to philosophical problems, there are at least three ways in which one might approach the confirmation of any biological theory, and sociobiology in particular. First, one might try for direct confirmation; second, one might try for indirect confirmation through predictions; and third, one might argue by analogy. In the *Origin* these three elements are represented by the direct argument for natural selection from the struggle for existence; by the application of selection to all the various subdisciplines; and by the analogy from artificial selection (Ruse, 1975). Let us see where these three routes take us in the sociobiological case.

In the case of direct confirmation, this would seem to centre on men's genes, and their effects on behaviour, individually and collectively. Now, we certainly have all the formal apparatus of both individual and population genetics and the confirmed weight that they carry. The problem of course is the extent to which they can be linked to human behaviour. There is some evidence of a link at the individual level, as discerned from such things as twin studies—for instance, schizophrenia seems partially genetically controlled, and the same may be true of such things as alcoholism. (See McClearn and DeFries, 1973.) After that, though, the evidence starts to run out fast. Wilson's speculations on the causes of homosexuality are not much more than that—speculations. And Trivers is almost brazen in his ignorance. "There is no direct evidence regarding the degree of reciprocal altruism practiced during human evolution nor its genetic basis today." (Trivers, 1971, p. 48) In short, we are not that much beyond the starting point with respect to direct evidence for genetic control of individual behaviour, and coming to the group (as we saw for the multiplier effect) the case is even thinner.

The same is more or less true of indirect evidence too, understanding here predictions about behaviour produced by the theory. We have seen that Alexander is making noble efforts to fit his theories to well-established anthropological data, but these are early days. Two important factors still seem absent. First, from a psychological viewpoint one would like evidence of Alexander's theories' implications actually being involved in predictions of new and surprising phenomena (rather than being always *post facto*). One of the strongest marks of theory confirmation is when it reveals new, unexpected facts not "built in" to the theory. A major reason why kin selection at the nonhuman level seems so convincing is that it does lead to such predictions (Wilson, 1975a, p. 416). Second, one would like more evidence that alternative, nongenetic theories are inadequate. For instance, although genes might cause incest avoidance, given the dreadful effects of incest, it is easy to imagine the elders of a tribe banning it and thereby setting up a tradition. I hasten to reemphasize that these are still early days, and that I am not denying Alexander's case. There is, for instance, some evidence from kibbutzim that children brought up together—even when openly not related—still feel emotional bars to interbreeding. So the genes might be crucial in this and like instances. But we hardly have solid theory yet.

Third and finally we have analogy: something which has again raised the critics' ire. Now, in one sense the whole sociobiological enterprise seems predicated on analogy—and probably fairly so. We know that gross morphological characteristics in man and animals are under control of the genes. We know also that much animal behaviour is under control of the genes. Therefore, whatever the importance of nongenetic culture, whatever our present paucity of direct evidence, it seems incredible that little in man's behaviour is related to the genes. Moreover, given that some of man's behaviour is without doubt genetic, we can push the analogy further. Not withstanding John Locke's horror stories about parental mistreatment of children (Locke, 1894, pp. 72–73), altruism towards one's own offspring and mate is pretty general. And given its crucial role in the evolutionary scheme and its phenomenologically emotive nature (most strikingly, we tend not to show much reason about falling in love), the genes surely provide major backing. But this does seem to be the thin end of an analogical wedge for genetic backing for other kinds of altruism. Not firm proof, perhaps, but good guidelines nevertheless.

How much further can we take analogy? The sociobiologists certainly want to make more of analogy. As we saw, Wilson wants to argue from the behavioural similarities between man and the apes to the genetic backing of such things as human male dominance. With some reason, the critics have complained about the sociobiologists on this score. Behavioural similarities are taken as evidence of genetic causes; behavioural dissimilarities are taken as evidence of genetic causes! At worst, this is inconsistent; at best, this assumes what one sets out to prove. But, this said, analogy at this point is not necessarily bad. Consider an example. If I want to buy a good pair of new shoes, two things will probably guide me. First, is the store I am buying the shoes from the same kind of store as led to good shoes in the past? Second, are the kind of shoes I am buying of a kind which have proven good in the past? In the case of sociobiology, we have two similar questions. Are the organisms from which I am arguing to man close to man? Is the behaviour from which I am arguing to man close to man's behaviour? Depending on the extents to which one can answer these questions, one's analogies to man will be strong or weak.

I would suggest that, in the light of these guidelines, one probably can argue analogically to some genetically caused human behavioural traits—particularly those which seem not to involve much reason. However, one does seem to face a paradox. One wants not just behavioural analogies to man, but analogies which point to genetic foundations. Now in the case of organisms remote from man, like insects, one can be fairly certain that virtually all of their "culture" is genetic. Unfortunately, as one gets closer to man, the possibilities of nongenetic culture rises. Instances of it certainly occur in the great apes. In short, as one strengthens the analogy between nonhumans and humans one decreases the certainty that the behaviour being considered is primarily genetic! Perhaps even with remote organisms some analogies about behaviour are so strong that one can feel sure of some similar genetic backings, but when we come to such things as analogy proving innate male dominance over females, given the possibility of nongenetic factors intervening, I start to get dubious. And this is a feeling in no way abated by the fact that Wilson's only direct evidence for the genetic foundations of male dominance is that men have (genetically) more mathematical ability and women have more verbal ability (Wilson, 1975b). His conclusion does not at all follow.

My general conclusion about sociobiology, therefore, is that although its advocates have made a start, much of their work remains in the realm of fascinating, unsupported hypothesis. It is, as the Scots say, "not proven." But, ever optimistically, let us ask about the future. In particular, what is sociobiology threatening to do to the social sciences? In the past quarter century we have seen the encroachment of the physical sciences on the biological sciences. Is the next quarter century to see the encroachment of the biological sciences on the social sciences? Let us close this essay with a brief look at this question.

IX. SOCIOBIOLOGY AND THE SOCIAL SCIENCES: REDUCTION OR REPLACEMENT?

When one science or theory muscles in on another, as it were, there seem basically to be two things that can happen. On the one hand, the interloper can wipe out the old science. The explanations of the old science are dropped entirely and the new science takes over. This process of "replacement" is exemplified by the nineteenth-century Darwinian revolution. There, the anatomist Richard Owen's explanation of homologies (isomorphisms between organisms of different species) as manifestations of Platonic archetypes was dropped entirely in favour of Darwin's explanation of homologies as indicative of common ancestry. On the other hand, the interloper might absorb the old science into itself—perhaps this process of "reduction" expresses the way in which the old biological genetics has been taken up into the new molecular genetics. Although there is much controversy about the precise nature of reduction, popularly it is thought to imply the showing of the old theory as a deductive consequence of the new. Rarely, in fact, would a straightforward deduction be possible between old and new— at the very least one would need translation principles between the language of old and new (e.g., from talk of Mendelian genes to talk of DNA), and often the new would not imply the old but show areas where explanations were needed which could then be filled by the old. (See Ruse, 1973, for more on reduction and replacement.)

I suspect that if one looks long enough and hard enough at any instance of scientific change, what one finds is that it is neither clearly replacement nor reduction, but some kind of amalgam of the two. Certainly in the sociobiological case, the approach seems to be one where, if successful, social sciences like anthropology would be partially replaced by sociobiology and partially reduced to it. On the one side, if one accepts the basic truth of sociobiology, then no longer can one take a position (like that of the extreme behaviourists) which holds that all men and women are inherently identical, and that individual and group differences are all functions solely of environment. One cannot, say, put down religious yearnings just to childhood training, nor can one explain homosexuality purely in terms of sexual influences during development. However, on the other side, there is no question of just throwing out all of present psychology, sociology, and so on. Much of it would be connected fairly directly to sociobiological explanations.

Take homosexuality. Suppose one had some psychological, Freudian or neo-Freudian explanation of its causes—suggesting, for instance, that for male homosexuals dominant mothers are a crucial causal factor. One could easily, without inconsistency, link this to a genetic theory of parental manipulation. Suppose, for example, that it is biologically advantageous for just the oldest male siblings to reproduce (for otherwise, limited, essential resources will be diluted). One can readily suppose that mothers are genetically programmed to be overprotective about their youngest children, thus unwittingly radically altering their sexual preferences. Certainly in many societies there are strong pressures on youngest children to adopt sexually neutral roles, and apparently it is more common proportionately for younger rather than older children (sons at least) to be homosexual and for the children of older mothers (proportionately) to be homosexual.

In a case such as this, one hardly has formal deductive links explicitly spelled out between biology and social science, but in outline the situation does seem closer to reduction than replacement—although I must confess that spelling out a case like this inclines me to think that much of the reduction of the social sciences would be of the weakest kind, where the old becomes an integral part of the new and thus is trivially deductible from the combination. Schematically, we have something like this:

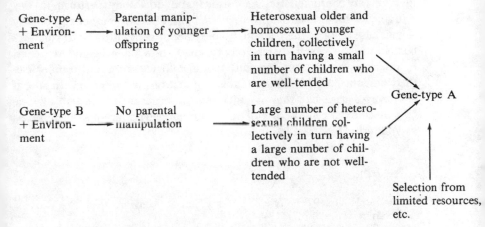

Obviously lots of simplifying assumptions occur here, but it can be seen how the older nonbiological theory is filling gaps in the newer biological theory rather than being deduced directly from it.

Perhaps a rather stronger kind of reduction is true of other cases: in economics, for example, Wilson points out that, given the correlation between much of sociobiological theory and much of economic theory, by postulating links or identities the latter can be shown to be a special case of the former. Here possibly, we are pointing towards a direct deduction. (See Wilson, 1977.) The critics would argue that this is hardly surprising, since so much of biological theory was inspired in the first place by politico-economic theory. While not denying that this may be so—one thinks particularly here of Darwin's debt to Malthus—I fail to see why this should be taken, as it is taken by Sahlins (1976), as a criticism.

One final point. There is no case being argued here that the coming of sociobiology means the end of social science. First, there is still need for the collection of basic empirical data about human behaviour, individually or in groups. This is wanted whether one explains through genes or not. Second, there is still the obviously great domain of human behaviour not directly under the genes—the rise and fall of Islam, for example. And third, there is the fact that explanations involving genes are never of the genes alone, but always of the genes as they interact with their environment. In the full scale of things, the explanations involve the characteristics so formed and how they perform in the struggle for survival and reproduction. Thus, in the (hypothetical) homosexual case one has the genetical theory about genes leading to parental behaviour, the psychological theory about how such behaviour leads to offspring homosexuality, and the sociological-cum-anthropological theory about how such homosexuality functions in the group. In short, assuming a case like this to be typical in structure, there will always be a place for the study of individual human behaviour and the cultures to which it gives rise.

REFERENCES

Alexander, R. D. (1974). "The Evolution of Social Behavior." *Ann. Rev. Ecology and Systematics* 5, pp. 325–84.
Allen, E. et al. (1976). "Sociobiology—Another Biological Determinism." *BioScience* 26, no. 3, pp. 182–186.
———. (1977). "Sociobiology." Forthcoming.
Hamilton, W. D. (1964). "The Genetical Theory of Social Behavior." *J. Theo. Bio.* 7, pp. 1–52.
———. (1972). "Altruism and Related Phenomena, Mainly in Social Insects." *Ann. Rev. Ecol. Syst.* 3, pp. 193–232.
Kuhn, T. S. (1970). *The Structure of Scientific Revolutions,* 2nd ed. (Chicago: Chicago University Press).
Lewontin, R. C. (1974). *The Genetic Basis of Evolutionary Change* (New York: Columbia University Press), p. 90.
Locke, J. (1894). *An Essay Concerning Human Understanding,* ed. A. C. Fraser (Oxford: Oxford University Press).

McClearn, G. E. and J. C. DeFries (1973). *Introduction to Behavioral Genetics* (San Francisco: Freeman).

Ruse, M. (1973). *The Philosophy of Biology* (London: Hutchinson).

———. (1975). "Charles Darwin's Theory of Evolution: An Analysis." *Journal of Historical Biology* 8, pp. 219–41.

———. (1977). "Sociobiology: Sound Science or Muddled Metaphysics?" *PSA 1976* 2, pp. 48–73.

Sahlins, M. D. (1965). "On the Sociobiology of Primitive Exchange." In M. Banton, ed., *The Relevance of Models for Social Anthropology* (London: Tavistock), pp. 139–236.

———. (1976). *The Use and Abuse of Biology: An Anthropological Critique of Sociobiology* (Ann Arbor: University of Michigan Press).

Trivers, R. L. (1971). "The Evolution of Reciprocal Altruism." *Quarterly Review of Biology* 46, pp. 35–47.

West Eberhard, M. J. (1975). "Evolution of Social Behavior by Kin Selection." *Quarterly Review of Biology* 50, pp. 1–34.

Wilson, E. O. (1975a). *Sociobiology: The New Synthesis* (Cambridge, Mass.: Harvard University Press).

———. (1975b). "Human Decency is Animal." *The New York Times Magazine,* October 12, pp. 38–50.

———. (1977). "Biology and the Social Sciences." *Daedalus,* forthcoming.

A Methodological Critique of Sociobiology

Richard M. Burian

E. O. Wilson's *Sociobiology: The New Synthesis*[1] is a controversial book. The heart of the controversy extends far beyond the difficulties of explaining particular behaviors, animal and human. At its deepest levels it concerns Wilson's attempt to develop a new conceptual framework within which to describe and explain fundamental animal social behaviors, including human social behaviors. Wilson hopes, by establishing a new descriptive apparatus, a set of explanatory schemata, and a stock of fundamental principles on which explanations are to be based, to found a new scientific discipline—one which will lay bare "the biological basis of all social behavior" (p. 4). The controversy over these claims is of great interest not only to biologists, but also to social scientists, philosophers, and ordinary people.

It is entirely reasonable for Wilson to attempt to reconceive and redescribe social behavior; if we are to have any hope of explaining social behavior we must allow various forms of reconceptualization, even radical ones. Nonetheless, as one of Wilson's chief critics, writing in another context, has pointed out, not all reconceptualizations are scientifically useful:

I am grateful to the American Council of Learned Societies for a Study Fellowship which supported the present work. Portions of this paper were read at the Brandeis University Philosophy Colloquium. I am grateful to Linda Burian, Catherine Elgin, Stephen Gould, and Richard Lewontin for extremely helpful discussions, and to Robert Holt for saving me from an important technical error.

Richard Burian is in the Department of Philosophy at Drexel University, Philadelphia, Pennsylvania.

The problem of theory building is a constant interaction between constructing laws and finding an appropriate set of state variables such that laws can be constructed. We cannot go out and describe the world in any old way we please and then sit back and demand that an explanatory and predictive theory be built on that description.[2]

In this paper I argue that the particular ways of categorizing and explaining social behavior to which sociobiology is committed offer no hope of bringing its program to successful fruition.

I

The framework of sociobiology implies a form of biological determinism. By this I mean that the explanation of social behavior is supposed to proceed exclusively from genetic parameters, ecological parameters, natural-historical descriptions of organisms, and the evolutionary history of the relevant organisms. Indeed, the debate over sociobiology constitutes yet another round in the nature/nurture controversy, for sociobiology is yet another articulation of the view that we are what we are and do what we do by our very nature.

The criticisms of current sociobiological theory which I will now consider[3] can be couched so as to challenge the particular form of biological determinism implicit in the current theory. (Many of them have been extended into criticisms of all forms of biological determinism. I will only consider their application to sociobiology in this paper.) These criticisms may be grouped under two headings:

1. Sociobiology does not offer a proper framework for the description of social behaviors.

2. Sociobiological theory and practice are so deeply flawed methodologically as to vitiate the major claims of the theory and the derivation of further consequences from it.

I shall first consider the descriptive difficulties and show their substantive importance and then turn to more narrowly methodological difficulties.

II

A great deal of criticism has been directed at the descriptive apparatus used by Wilson and other sociobiologists. Much of this criticism is, I think, just—though the reader should check this for herself. I will summarize and illustrate such criticisms under three headings:

1. By a process of *back metaphor*, very distinct animal and human behaviors are lumped under common anthropomorphic descriptions. For example, "xenophobia" is applied to aggression against newcomer animals, whatever form that aggression may take; "altruistic behavior" is applied to such distinct "behaviors" as forgoing reproduction in sterile castes of insects and the feeding of the adults of certain wasps by their larvae;[4] "aggression" is applied to an incredible variety of "competitive" behaviors including fighting, ritualized posturings, marking items with chemicals, and so on.

2. In the effort to make behaviors thus classified susceptible to genetic explanation, Wilson often places intolerable strain on the descriptive apparatus of his otherwise glorious natural history. (Cf. his objection on page 4 to sociology for attempting to explain human behavior "without reference to evolutionary explanations in the true genetic sense"). The most extreme example I have noticed illustrates the way in which the *importation of genetic considerations* into natural historical descriptions undermines one's confidence:

> The origin of new gibbon groups has never been observed in nature, but its course can be safely inferred from circumstantial evidence. As Berkson et al. (1971) have noted, young gibbons become aggressive at puberty, and adults placed close together are very hostile. Young adults tend to be excluded, especially at feeding sessions. It is probable that as relations between the parents and young adults become more abrasive, the offspring scatter to form families of their own. Carpenter observed one such pair that might have been in the process of forming an incestuous union, *although their sexes and origin could not be ascertained* (p. 529, my emphasis).

Although no conclusions are drawn in the present instance from the presumption that Carpenter's gibbons were in the process of forming an incestuous pair bond, it is hard to avoid the sense that Wilson's natural history is distorted by his constant search for genetic relationships suggesting kin selection processes and by the constant employment of genetic terminology in his descriptions. (Why is human cultural evolution described as built "upon the *genetic* potential in the brain" (p. 565, my emphasis) rather than upon, say, the capacity for intelligent representation of, and choice among, alternative actions? Are we really supposed to believe that the first Good Samaritan appeared "as a rare mutant" (p. 120) and that kin and group selection preserved the fortunate mutation?)

3. In his descriptions of humans, Wilson not only aggregates diverse behaviors, but he often accepts naively ethnocentric descriptions and makes unwarranted generalizations concerning the characteristic behavior of humans and the effects of that behavior. To take three reasonably typical examples of what Wilson calls "general traits of the species" (p. 548), consider the following: (1) "The best and most entrepreneurial of the role-actors usually gain a disproportionate share of the rewards" (p. 554); (2) "Homosexual men marry much less frequently and have far fewer children than their unambiguously heterosexual counterparts" (p. 555); and (3) "Men would rather believe than know" (p. 561) and are therefore "absurdly easy to indoctrinate" (p. 562). Richard Lewontin has called such claims "barroom wisdom." The worry is not that they are false (though I suspect that they are), but that they are naively accepted as good examples of inductively established laws of human nature which, as such, provide the material which sociobiology must explain. By thus trivializing the explanatory task of his discipline, Wilson secures the illusion of explanation—and discourages efforts to identify and describe phenomena which genuinely deserve explanation.

To appreciate fully the difficulties raised by these problems with the descriptive apparatus of sociobiology, one needs to know a bit about the immense difficulty of achieving adequate explanations in genetics. This situation is extremely interesting, and will occupy us for the next few pages.

Any genetic theory must distinguish between genotypes and phenotypes. If it is to explain such matters as the limits of phenotypic variation, the history of phenotypic variation, the capacity for phenotypic variation, etc., it must set forth the relevance of a given genotype to the phenotype of the organism in a fairly precise manner. The fundamental outlines of this task have been secured for two sorts of cases—where breeding experiments have revealed discrete phenotypic traits to be under direct genetic control and where the phenotypes in question are the sequence of amino acids in proteins and enzymes. The latter case is the famous story of DNA. But in higher organisms a very small percentage of DNA makes the body's proteins—in man it has been estimated that it makes as little as 0.5 percent; certainly no more than

5 percent of the total DNA does this job. No one knows how protein synthesis is turned on and off in higher organisms, nor precisely what the rest of the DNA does, nor how all of this is connected with the development of the organism. Except in a few of the cases where the absence (or the presence of a variant form) of a particular protein has discrete observable phenotypic effects (as in albinism or Tay-Sachs disease), we really do not know how the sequence of protein production brings about the gross morphology (or other gross phenotypic traits) at stake or how it affects the behaviors (or ranges of behavior) of the organism.

Given our immense ignorance, we *suppose* that the genes somehow affect a trait of interest, and attempt to find out how it varies and whether its mean or its variance in the populations of concern can be altered by artificial or natural selection. By the formally sophisticated bookkeeping of Mendelian population genetics it is then sometimes possible to determine that a trait is under fairly straightforward genetic control. Typically, even where the trait itself is under such control, that control is so linked with the control of other traits that its presence or absence in a natural population is not a sign of the adaptive value of the trait itself. For example, the gene (or complex of genes) which determines the characteristic coat color of Siamese cats also causes a developmental disorder which prevents the optic nerves of the animals from crossing as they normally would in the brain. (This is why Siamese cats are cross-eyed.) Thus the scarcity of Siamese cats in natural populations of cats is not due to selection against their coat color, but (if it is due to selection at all) to selection against the whole phenotype which, in the genetic context, results from the Siamese coat color gene or genes. Worse yet, it is a formal result of population genetics that in finite populations random process alone tends to eliminate alternative alleles—i.e., to give the *appearance* of selection. (This effect is most marked in small populations.) Only where one can test whether selection is operating by correlating phenotypic change with change in environmental variables over many generations can one be sure that selection is operating—and even then it takes great ingenuity to determine which trait or combination of traits is affected by the selective process.

But the situation is still worse, for my use of the term "trait" has been naive. To count as a trait, a property of an organism must be under genetic control. And it is far from obvious when one describes a property how accessible to genetic control it is. My favorite example is due to Stephen Gould. For a variety of reasons which need not concern us here morphologists have been particularly interested in the changing shape of the chin as one passes through the primate lineage from apes to humans. The issue has been why the chin behaved contrary to expectation. And the answer appears to be that it is because *the chin is not a trait at all.* That is, the shape of the chin is determined by the ratio of growth in two growth fields (alveolar and mandibular), and although each of these growth fields is under direct genetic control, *their ratio is not.*

The point of all of this is that in general we have very little idea whether a specifically described behavior is under genetic control or not. If we start from arbitrarily chosen behaviors, *even if they are of selective and ecological significance,* we have no real basis for supposing that those behaviors are traits. And the principles (if any) by means of which we classify behaviors may well, by focusing on anthropocentric or noticeable phenotypic features of those behaviors, bias our classifications in such a way as to favor the description of behaviors which are not subject to genetic control. Thus even if we grant (as we should not) that Wilson's generalizations about animal and human behavior capture the regularities which require explanation, there is little or no reason to suppose that the behaviors picked out by his (or any available) descriptive apparatus are under direct genetic control. There is no immediate prospect of overcoming these difficulties. To repeat, "we cannot go out and describe the world in any old way we please and then sit back and demand that an explanatory and predictive theory be built on that description."

III

I turn now to the methodological flaws which are alleged against current sociobiological theory and practice. I shall concentrate on two criticisms which are of interest in the present context. The first is that sociobiological theory is too powerful—that it explains *all* behaviors, that no conceivable behavior would fail to confirm the theory.[5] The second criticism is that sociobiology systematically excludes alternative explanations and contains no adequate apparatus for comparing alternative explanations of a given behavior or social structure whether the explanation is sociobiological or not.

1. The power of the theory resides in the richness of the explanatory stories it allows, the system of retreats to alternative stories, and some special ad hoc devices. To provide a logically satisfactory evolutionary explanation of the occurrence of a given trait, only three claims are needed: first, that there was a dimension of phenotypic variation in the population which *could* result in the trait; second, that such variation was heritable (i.e., that it had a genetic basis); and third, that some appropriate selective regime (or random fixation process) favored the trait. For these claims to be true it need not be the case that there is *currently* variation of the kind required, for if the selective regime is strong enough, it eliminates variation away from the optimum. Thus, even in the absence of current variation (or, for that matter, of heritability in the current variation), a trait could well have been fixed in a population by natural selection. Again, the selective regime may involve individual selection, kin selection, or group selection—which is to say that selective forces may go in opposing directions. To set up the germ of an evolutionary explanation, all that is needed is to find some one level of selection which favored the trait in question strongly enough.

To put the point cynically: it becomes a highly amusing parlor game to see who can devise the best evolutionary account showing how an arbitrarily chosen behavior could have become fixed in a given population. But in the unlikely event that one should fail altogether to find an appropriate story, explanatory resources are still available. Wilson, for example, invokes the "multiplier effect" to explain the immense speed with which social behavior changes when compared with the rate of change in the genetic composition of a population. He argues that a small change in behavior can be amplified in its effects by the social context in which it occurs. Consider his example of the differences between two very closely related species of baboon: olive baboon males seek to "appropriate" females only around the time of their estrus, whereas hamadryas baboon males maintain a permanent "proprietary attitude" toward females. "This trait alone is enough to account for profound differences in social structure, affecting the size of the troops, the relationship of the troops to one another, and the relationship of the males within each troop" (p. 11). Wilson also invokes what he calls the "threshold effect" (p. 573) to explain why the incremental increase in intelligence in primate phylogeny did not trigger cultural evolution via multiplier effects in any species other than *Homo sapiens*. This is a classic example of an ad hoc hypothesis with no independent support and no independent *raison d'être*. With all this apparatus, Wilson can tell a logically satisfactory story to account for any behavior one chooses. But the untestability and arbitrariness of the components prevents it from being of genuine explanatory interest.

2. This brings me to the second set of methodological criticisms. How do we weigh such stories? Wilson officially espouses the methodology of strong inference[6] (pp. 27 ff.), a form of eliminative induction. The methodology, devised in another context for application to all sciences, requires one, in this context, to do one's best to enumerate all alternative stories which *might* account for a given phenomenon, to find testable details regarding which the stories disagree, to carry out the tests, and to eliminate those stories which are falsified. Complete success in this procedure would yield exactly one uneliminated story. One is then entitled to accept this story provisionally, always realizing that a better story may yet be invented which can eliminate the current survivor.

In the present context, this procedure is clearly utopian. Even dismissing the multiplier and threshold effects, the stories which the sociobiological framework allows will typically differ over such matters as the plasticity of a given trait to genetic change, the selective regime or sequence of environments to which a given population or species was exposed over the last few hundred generations, the minimum population size and the population structure during that period, the degree of linkage between a trait of interest and other traits, the relative importance of individual and kin selection to the case, and so on. Such issues can virtually never be resolved. The most one can do is to eliminate one or two stories which conflict dramatically with one's pet hypothesis and then maintain that the evidence is consistent with the proposed hypothesis. This—the reader should check my claim—is what Wilson does time and time again. Foreseeably, it is the best anyone can do.

The problem is slightly worse than I have yet suggested. Various nonsociobiological explanations have been proposed for many of the behaviors of interest to sociobiologists. As long as one employs the descriptive and explanatory apparatus of sociobiology, these explanations will be excluded from consideration—for all described behaviors will be treated as having underlying descriptions based on genetic, ecological, and narrowly behavioral parameters.[7] Thus the possibility that there are adequate, strictly cultural explanations of such phenomena as rapid changes in social structure or in the forms of interaction among humans is systematically ignored. The result is that the spirit of Wilson's official methodology is consistently violated. The impossibility of weighing genetic vs. nongenetic explanations within the apparatus of sociobiology elevates the violation of the canons of strong inference into a methodological principle.

IV

In spite of all I have said so far, a defender of sociobiology could argue that these methodological difficulties are of strictly local importance. That is, it is still possible to argue that ad hoc uses of the multiplier and threshold effects are eliminable artifacts of Wilson's presentation and that the difficulty of testing alternative sociobiological explanations is not due to methodological weaknesses, but rather to the incredible difficulty of obtaining the facts which are needed to carry out the tests. As for the comparison of sociobiological and (for example) cultural explanations, this can be handled in part on a case-by-case basis and in part by arguments to show that the sociobiological framework is applicable to all cases of interest.

This sort of defense of the large-scale program to which sociobiology is committed is initially plausible; failed theories are the stepping-stones to successful ones, to the successful culmination of a program of research. It is important not to cut off a promising line of research prematurely because it encounters technical and methodological difficulties at an early stage of work.

The methodological difficulties of sociobiology, however, penetrate to the very heart of the research program. The defense against methodological criticism just suggested cannot be sustained. I shall establish these claims in the next two sections of the paper by showing first, that the difficulties with the descriptive apparatus yield a deep incoherence at the very foundation of the program and, second, that the current results in genetics and ecology conflict with the central claims of the program. In the final section of the paper I will draw some philosophical morals from this case study.

V

"The central theoretical problem of sociobiology," writes Wilson (p. 3), is this "How can altruism, which by definition reduces personal fitness, possibly evolve by natural selection?" His official account of altruism runs as follows:

When a person (or animal) increases the fitness of another at the expense of his own fitness, he can be said to have performed an act of *altruism.* Self-sacrifice for the benefit of offspring is altruism in the conventional but not in the strict genetic sense, because individual fitness is measured by the number of surviving offspring. But self-sacrifice on behalf of second cousins is true altruism at both levels; and when directed at total strangers such abnegating behavior is so surprising (that is, "noble") as to demand some kind of theoretical explanation (p. 117).

For the sake of the argument, I will pretend that we can make proper sense of the claim that a gene is altruistic. (I do not, however, believe that this is so. Cf. the next section.) I will show that even so no connection has been established, nor foreseeably can be, between genetic and conventional altruism. More specifically I will show (1) that *the genetic definition of altruism has no content when applied to vertebrate behavior;* (2) that Wilson's back-metaphorical apparatus, by illegitimately confusing altruism "in the conventional sense" with altruism "in the strict genetic sense," produces the illusion of explaining specific behaviors genetically; and (3) that the difficulty of identifying altruistic behaviors in the manner required by the explanatory apparatus infects the explanatory program of sociobiology at its deepest levels.

Genetic altruism is, properly speaking, a relation of a genotype to other genotypes given the background of environments in which the organisms of concern live. (A genotype with altruistic effects in one environment may have no such effects in other environments. What matters is the net statistical effect of the genotype on the fitness of the organisms possessing it.) Thus, given a genotypic, phenotypic, and ecological context, an altruistic allele is one which, when compared with alternative alleles at the same locus, reduces the average number of viable offspring produced by the organisms which carry it and which, by direct action of those organisms, increases the number of offspring of the conspecific organisms with which they interact.

Genetically controlled sterility of worker and soldier castes of social Hymenoptera clearly requires the existence of altruistic genes.[8] It is of central importance, however, that organisms which sacrifice themselves for others, even for nonkin, need not have altruistic genes or genotypes. The very same gene which (let us say) disposes an organism to sacrifice itself in extremely rare circumstances, resulting in the death of, say, one out of ten bearers of the gene, may result in a remarkable increase in the progeny of the other nine. In such a case the net effect of an allele disposing its bearers to perform the "self-sacrificing behavior" will be to *increase* their average individual fitness. The proper definition of genetic altruism, unlike Wilson's, does not allow one to treat a gene as altruistic because it causes an act of self-sacrifice in some of its bearers or because it causes surrender of some resource such as food to conspecific organisms; rather, the sole ground on which a gene will be classified as altruistic is that its average effect on the phenotype reduces the average fitness of its bearers and increases that of the conspecific organisms with which its bearers have social interactions.

To make the point clearer, consider two examples, one extreme and one controversial: (1) In his section on altruistic behaviors, Wilson discusses certain long-lived, highly visible ("aposematic," i.e., self-advertising), highly unpalatable butterflies which by their postreproductive longevity "train" predators not to eat like-marked butterflies (pp. 124–125). Although Wilson holds that kin selection increases longevity in such cases, it is in any event clear that the postreproductive self-sacrifice of such a butterfly, far from being genetically altruistic, increases its individual fitness by reducing the likelihood of predation on its offspring. (2) Similarly, the cases of larval trophallaxis (see above, n. 4) are questionable as cases of genetic altruism since the larvae would probably starve (hence suffering a drastic loss of individual fitness) if they did not return processed food to the adults. The fact that larvae regurgitate otherwise unavailable essential foodstuffs does show that they "contribute, by virtue of their behavior patterns, to the homeostatic machinery of the colony" and that there is "biochemical division of labor between adults and young," but these findings do not suffice to "demonstrate . . . that larvae can behave altruistically [in the genetic sense] toward adults" (p. 345).

Once again, the descriptive apparatus has deceived us into accepting mistaken explanations—but this time because of the conceptual confusion of genetic with conventional altruism. There is no reason to suppose that animals which sacrifice themselves are, in general, altruistic in the genetic sense of having genes which, by causing self-sacrifice, lower the average individual fitness of their bearers. No stories about dramatic cases of self-sacrifice, no postulation of genes which significantly affect only a single trait or a single behavior, can show the genetic definition of altruism to have been met in a particular phenotypically circumscribed case.

To characterize an act as conventionally altruistic, insofar as the characterization rests on the intention with which the act was performed, is not to characterize its effects with any degree of precision. And to characterize an act as conventionally altruistic in its effects is not to characterize the effects of similar acts. John Doe's attempt to rescue Richard Roe from drowning may eventuate in Doe's death or in Doe's acquiring a fortune in reward from Roe. Either way, his act was conventionally altruistic. Yet whether or not a putative gene which increases the likelihood that its bearer, say John Doe, will jump in and attempt to rescue a drowning person is an altruistic gene remains utterly obscure. To ascribe the property of the act (conventional altruism) to the gene which, let us say, disposes one to perform it is rather like ascribing the properties of a musical composition ("harmonious") to the person who composed it.

These comments in no way depend on the human example. Do the genes which putatively dispose juveniles of certain animals to expose themselves to predation by remaining on the edge of the troop decrease their individual fitness (by increasing their exposure to predation) or increase it (by increasing their opportunity to become, in time, the dominant member of an established troop with a good territory)? Indeed, of the nine or so major examples of putatively altruistic behaviors discussed by Wilson on pp. 121–129, there is only one (self-sacrifice in combating predators by the sterile soldier castes in a great variety of insects) which seems to escape this criticism. In general, there is no way of isolating and identifying the genes disposing for or against the behaviors of interest, and hence no way of determining whether their net effect is genetically altruistic or not. The soldier caste case is an exception to the extent that these behaviors are linked to what is presumably genetically determined sterility. (However, cf. n. 8)

By now the role of back metaphor should be clear. It is virtually impossible to know which behaviors are the expression of altruistic genes, especially in vertebrates where there are no sterile castes and where the extreme plasticity of social behavior and social structure make assessment of the average effects of a behavior on the individual fitness of the individuals emitting it extremely difficult. We have supposed (though there is no good reason for doing so) that the definite descriptions of genes in terms of the conventionally altruistic behaviors they dispose organisms to emit do, in fact pick out definite genes. We still have no reason whatsoever except for the back metaphor to suppose that these genes are genetically altruistic. Without the unfounded misidentification of altruistic genes as those which cause or dispose organisms to emit such conventionally altruistic behaviors as food sharing, self-sacrifice, raising strangers' offspring, protecting conspecifics against predation, and so on, no connection has been forged between the genes described by the concept of an altruistic gene and the actual behaviors of actual organisms. The misidentification allows sociobiologists to offer the illusion of explanation, no more.

VI

This brings us to the relation of sociobiology to population genetics and (less centrally) ecology. I am not concerned here with the immensely interesting technical issues which lie at the interfaces of these sciences, but with large-scale worries about the divergences between each of them and sociobiology.

1. For heuristic purposes, Wilson speaks a genetically atomistic language. He writes, by and large, as if the traits he is concerned with are controlled by single genes which vary independently of one another, do not significantly alter the effects of other genes, and do not have major effects on other phenotypic traits. He does not seriously believe, of course, that there is a one-to-one relation between genes and traits. He knows full well that most traits of interest are subject to polygenic control and that most genes of interest are pleiotropic, i.e., affect many traits. He is also aware of the recent emphasis in genetics on the unity of the genotype, i.e., on the subtle linkages among genes and on the influence of other genes on a given gene's phenotypic expression.

I grant that it is heuristically sound to soft-pedal these complications, but I fear that it will be devastatingly difficult for the sociobiological program to take them into account. At the heart of that program is the assumption that individual genes make a stable contribution to the individual and inclusive fitnesses of their bearers and that these fitnesses determine whether or not natural selection will eliminate those genes. As I understand it, current genetic theory leaves such claims in doubt. Consider Ernst Mayr's reflections on the unity of the genotype:

1. Since the fitness of a gene depends in part on the success of its interaction with its genetic background, it is no longer possible to assign an absolute selective value to a gene. A gene has potentially as many selective values as it has possible genetic backgrounds.
2. The target of selection does not consist of single genes but rather of such components of the phenotype as the eye, the legs, the flower, the thermo-regulatory or photosynthetic apparatus, etc. . . . As a result any given selection pressure affects simultaneously whole packages of genes which may or may not be tied together by special devices, such as linkage, epistatic balances, etc. . . .
3. At no stage in the life of an individual is the interaction of genes more obvious than during ontogeny. The adult individual is the end-product of the entire epigenetic process. The endeavor to dissect this into the effects of individual genes can only rarely be successful. . . .
The genes are not the units of evolution nor are they, as such, the targets of natural selection. Rather, genes are tied together into balanced adaptive complexes, the integrity of which is favored by natural selection.[9]

To the extent that Mayr's claims are well supported, they undermine all of the sociobiological calculations I have seen to date, for these calculations have assigned fixed fitnesses to genes which were treated wholly atomistically. Thus there is considerable technical difficulty ahead in connecting the current sociobiological calculational apparatus to a realistic genetics—and little likelihood of successfully assessing the contribution to fitness of a genotype (*not* a gene) disposing an organism to emit a conventionally altruistic behavior.

The extremely troublesome technical issues here are not the main point, however. If the unity of the genotype, the complexity of the target of selection, and the effects of epigenesis on fitness are taken seriously, then *genetic altruism—and indeed an exact fitness—cannot be a property of genes or alleles.* Clearly, the average effect of an allelic kind (or of a complex of genes) in the population is not a property of an individual allele (or gene complex). Nor is it, strictly speaking, a property of that allelic *kind* (or gene complex) either, any more than the average mortality in humans from cholera infection is a property of *Vibrio comma*, the microorganism causing cholera. In philosophical language, fitnesses are not properties of *tokens* (individual instances of an allelic kind) nor of *types* (allelic kinds); fitnesses are a statistic reflecting extremely complex relations involving genes, their genetic environments, epigenetic factors, phenotypes, and the environments to which the bearers of the genes are exposed.

It is often possible, to be sure, to carry out successful calculations while one employs the misleading shorthand of treating fitnesses as properties of allelic kinds. This works when enough of the other parameters are held constant in their effects or are varied uniformly enough so that genic variation at the target locus is the principal cause of variation in fitness. But this shorthand goes wrong where nongenetic variation seriously alters the expression or the effects on fitness of the genes in question—as in the case of social behavior played out against the background of highly variable social structures.

I should add that this problem raises very serious foundational difficulties, which I cannot explore on this occasion, for the discipline of population genetics. Although these difficulties are especially acute and especially obvious when one deals with genes whose effects are highly sensitive to environmental and cultural variables (as any genes affecting social behaviors must be), it is by no means only in sociobiology that such difficulties are encountered.

2. Related to the difficulty of assessing the relevant fitnesses is the difficulty of assessing the relative importance of individual, kin, and group selection. As J. Maynard Smith points out,

the argument [over relative importance] is quantitative, not qualitative. Group [and kin] selection will have evolutionary consequences; the only question is how important these consequences have been. If there are genes which, although decreasing individual fitness, make it less likely that a group (or deme or species) will go extinct, then group selection will influence evolution. It does not follow that the influence is important enough to play the role suggested for it by some biologists.[10]

In complex cases, such quantitative issues cannot be resolved while employing the atomistic genetics of which I have just been complaining. And even when the genetic simplicity and epigenetic and environmental stability of a particular case allow one to employ an atomistic genetics, the quantitative questions are extremely hard to resolve properly. To do this, one must identify the genotype which causes or disposes members of the population of concern to emit a certain behavior by some form of genetic analysis, and compute the individual, kin, and group selection coefficients for this genotype by following its effects over a number of generations on the survivorship and fecundity of the individuals who possess it, on their kin, and on the groups to which they belong. Anyone familiar with the difficulty of genetic analysis of behavioral traits, of determining kinship relations and population structure in natural populations, and of following a natural population over several generations in this kind of detail, will appreciate the fact that the likelihood of attaining quantitatively rigorous estimates of the relevant selection coefficients is virtually nil. Yet without such quantitatively rigorous results, there remain innumerable stories, consistent with observation, about the selective regime which produced the characteristics of the members of the population. We can insist on logical consistency and on consistency with observation, but this is not enough to resolve the issues at hand.

3. Some recent models in ecology suggests that under the most extreme competitive pressures, selection can alter the behavioral traits (such as the size of preferred food particles or preferred habitat) of an isolated population in as few as ten generations. For widespread species (which experience different selective pressures in different places) with considerable gene flow between populations—and *Homo sapiens* is a perfect example of such a species—selection typically requires at least a few hundred generations to alter major traits. As Wilson points out, the time from the beginning of the Roman Empire to the present is approximately one hundred human generations (p. 569). Thus there is considerable question whether natural selection has had enough time to "track" the effects of changes in behavior and in social structure in humans during historical times. Indeed, such questions are also serious for many other vertebrate species.

The degree of rigor with which a behavior in a widespread species is controlled by natural selection depends on at least the following: (1) the degree to which the behavior is under direct genetic control, (2) the degree to which the behavior alters fitness, (3) the stability over space and time (say one hundred generations?) of its contribution to fitness, and (4) the structure of the population in each generation—i.e., whether there is (perhaps intermittent) gene flow between subpopulations, whether there is significant inbreeding, whether neighbors are kin, and so on. Where phylogenetic inertia is high, genetic inertia is probably high too, but where it is low we know very little about the importance of selective processes in fixing different traits in different species. What we do know is that (except in small peripheral isolate populations) *the rate of change in the frequency of extremely rare (or extremely common) genetically determined traits is quite low even under stringent selection*[11] and that *kin and group selection require even longer to establish a trait than individual selection does.*

The range of behaviors which animals (including humans) can emit is, of course, genetically constrained. Humans will never fly without the aid of mechanical devices. But no one knows how to locate the limits which the genetic makeup of an organism imposes on the behaviors it can emit—except that they include all the behaviors which the organism exhibits. When a behavior is invented, elaborated, or accepted within a generation or a few generations, the time scale is so short that one must assume that genetic change did not play a significant role in establishing it. Behaviors acquired in this way are typical of human beings and common enough among vertebrates. (Two especially clear vertebrate examples are [1] the invention of sweet potato washing, peanut digging, and placer mining of rice grains scattered in sand by Japanese macaques, discussed by Wilson, pp. 170 ff., and [2] the invention of the practice, now widespread, of cream theft by English tits. The birds pierce the foil caps of milk bottles delivered and left on the stoop, and drink the cream from the top.) Such opportunistically acquired behaviors must be classed as genetically permitted, and their maintenance in the population must be determined by ecological and cultural, not genetic factors. Over the short run, selection may play an eliminative role for drastically detrimental behaviors—but no more.

VII

It is of no little sociological interest that sociobiology has met with considerable success in the academic world; publishers, universities, professional associations, and many working scientists believe that it has already established itself as a legitimate scientific discipline. Many of them are wrongly persuaded by Kuhn's unsatisfactory account of the formation of a new "paradigm"[12] that Wilson's book brought about a scientific revolution and that sociobiology is entering what ought to be a long period of development as a "normal science." Nonetheless, in spite of the fact that sociobiology has passed the sociological tests of discipline formation, and in spite of the fact that it has generated a number of successful predictions,[13] there are good methodological reasons why this Kuhnian scenario ought not be played out. I have shown that there is no legitimate new discipline here, that the price of making the sociobiological paradigm autonomous (i.e., of allowing it to set its own problems and the standards of acceptability for their solution) will be to allow pseudo-solutions to pseudo-problems.

My criticisms show that the exemplary solutions of the exemplary problems of this field—like the problems themselves—are conceptually confused and that the major aspirations of the program cannot be realized. The criticisms based on considerations taken from the neighboring sciences show that the autonomy cannot legitimately be preserved—indeed, they show that there are strong objections based on contemporary genetic knowledge to the genetics on which the sociobiological program is erected. If we are to bind the biological sciences together into a relatively more unified body of knowledge, sociobiology will have to accede to genetics on these issues.

Because my criticisms are primarily methodological in character, I have refrained from criticizing a great deal of the bad philosophy which underlies much of the Wilsonian program.[14] Even so, we have seen that the disciplinary imperialism which sociobiology seeks to practice ("Today sex ratio in the ants and bees, tomorrow all of the social sciences!") is utterly ungrounded. Methodological criticism can show the futility of major research programs in science. This is an important lesson for both scientists and philosophers to learn.

NOTES

1. Cambridge, Mass.: Harvard University Press, 1975. All otherwise unidentified page references in the text of this paper are to this book.
2. Richard Lewontin, *The Genetic Basis of Evolutionary Change* (New York: Columbia University Press, 1974), p. 8.
3. The best presentation of most of the criticisms I discuss in the next two sections is Richard Lewontin, "Sociobiology—A Caricature of Darwinism," in P. Asquith and F. Suppe, eds., *PSA 1976*, Vol. 2 (East Lansing, Michigan: The Philosophy of Science Association, 1977), pp. 22–31.

4. This is an example of the phenomenon of trophallaxis, discussed in a number of places by Wilson. On pp. 344–345 he summarizes the evidence that in certain species of wasps the larvae manufacture essential carbohydrates which the adults require but can no longer produce for themselves.

5. Lewontin, *op. cit.*

6. John Platt, "Strong Inference," *Science* 146 (1964), pp. 347–353.

7. This is another indication of the importance of the descriptive apparatus. Recall the example of "Good Samaritan" behavior in humans. The field of competing explanations ought not be restricted to those which require the initial occurrence of such behavior to be based on a rare mutation (p. 120). Again, if one wishes to explain the putative ease of indoctrinating human beings, must one assume that the variability in indoctrinability is ultimately genetic, i.e., that, speaking loosely, some "societies [contain] higher frequencies of conformer genes" (p. 562) than others?

8. Even here I have reservations. Where caste (and with it sterility) is controlled by pheromones, foods, etc., the sterility of workers and soldiers may result from *exploitation by reproductives* rather than *genetic* sacrifice of fitness by workers and soldiers whose genotype may be indistinguishable from that of reproductives.

9. Ernst Mayr, "The Unity of the Genotype," *Biologisches Zentralblatt* 94 (1975), pp. 382, 386.

10. John Maynard Smith, "Group Selection," *Quarterly Review of Biology* 51 (1976), p. 277.

11. Consider albinism, a genetically determined trait. Suppose one wished to eliminate all of the (recessive) genes causing albinism in humans by preventing albinos from reproducing. Assuming that this policy is followed rigorously and that these genes have little effect on the fitness of heterozygotes, the frequency of the genes in the nth generation, q_n, is given by

$$q_n = \frac{1}{(1 + nq_0)}$$

where q_0 is the initial frequency of the undesired genes. Since albinism occurs in less than one birth in ten thousand among humans, $q_0^2 < 10^{-4}$ and $q_0 < 10^{-2}$. Therefore it would take at least one hundred generations (roughly 2,500 years) to cut the number of these genes in half and roughly three hundred generations (7,500 years) to reduce their frequency to one-fourth of their present value! (I owe this argument to Richard Lewontin.)

12. Thomas Kuhn, *The Structure of Scientific Revolutions,* 2nd ed. (Chicago: University of Chicago Press, 1970) and "Second Thoughts on Paradigms," pp. 459–482 in F. Suppe, ed., *The Structure of Scientific Theories* (Urbana, Ill.: University of Illinois Press, 1974).

13. One of the most highly touted of these was R. L. Trivers and H. Hare's startling prediction that parental investment (as measured by the mass of male and female offspring) in certain ants and bees would vary from 1:1 to 1:3 male to female according to the degree to which workers or queens

control the survivorship of offspring. Cf. "Haplodiploidy and the Evolution of Social Insects," *Science* 191 (1976), 249–263. However, cf. also the criticisms of the data, arguments, and conclusions of this article in R. D. Alexander and P. W. Sherman, "Local Mate Competition and Parental Investment in Social Insects," *Science* 196 (1977), pp. 494–500.

14. There is much more bad philosophy than I have discussed, some of it of considerable importance. It is perhaps worth listing three examples. (1) There is a confusion between *ontological* claims (e.g., that all organisms are made of matter and nothing else) with methodological and epistemological claims about the relations among sciences or among theories (e.g., that anthropology, linguistics, psychology and sociology may be made into branches of (socio)biology—cf. Chaps. 1 and 27 and elsewhere). (2) There is the displacement of *agency* and *teleology* from organisms onto genes. "The organism is only the DNA's way of making more DNA" (p. 3), from which Wilson concludes that the various subsystems of organisms, including the emotive systems of higher organisms, "are *engineered* [my emphasis] to perpetuate DNA" *(ibid)*. Thus the "external" agency of genes aiming at their own ends is supposed to govern the structure and determine the behavior of organisms. Human love, hate, aggression, fear, expansiveness, withdrawal (p. 4), spirituality, and altruism (p. 120) are joined "in blends designed not to promote the happiness and survival of the individual, but to favor the maximum transmission of the controlling genes" (p. 4). This metaphysics of genetic agency is, of course, at the center of all talk of "selfish genes". Without it, the temptation to conflate genetic with conventional altruism would surely be considerably reduced. Yet it is fundamentally at odds with our depersonified physico-chemical understanding of the composition and nature of genes. (3) There is Wilson's claim that the humanities, including ethics and aesthetics, can be made into branches or subdisciplines of sociobiology. He supposes (pp. 562 ff.) that a positive morality (rather than the information required to apply positive morality to real-life circumstances) can be derived from sociobiological considerations and that an aesthetic (rather than a description of the aesthetics of others) can be similarly derived (p. 564). The misunderstandings which are required to make these claims seem plausible are so grotesque that it is simply better for me to note them without further comment.

Principles and Methods of Comparative Analyses in Sociobiology

Walter J. Bock

Comparative analysis has always played a central role in ethological studies, as illustrated by the lecture "Analogy as a Source of Knowledge" presented by Konrad Lorenz (1974) when he received the Nobel Prize in Physiology and Medicine in 1973. Indeed, twenty years earlier, while a student at Cornell University, I heard a series of lectures by Lorenz in which he described ethology as the latest daughter of that grand old lady of biology—comparative anatomy. A number of papers and symposium volumes have been devoted to the subject of comparative study in animal behavior; the recent volume *Evolution, Brain and Behavior: Persistent Problems* (Masterton, Hodos and Jerison, 1976) provides a good sample of diverse approaches to comparative analysis as well as references to the earlier literature. Recent analyses of sociobiology by Wilson (1975) and of animal awareness by Griffin (1976) are strongly dependent on methods of comparison because the authors seek to develop general biological principles and to extrapolate conclusions from one group to another. Yet neither author gives the theoretical principles of biological comparison underlying his synthesis or the practical

I would like to thank Professor F. E. Warburton for providing me with examples of the genetical control of behavior and for discussing critical points of this analysis. The research upon which my ideas of biological comparison and classification are based was done under a series of grants from the National Science Foundation; this paper was written during the tenure of grant DEB-76-14746 from the National Science Foundation. The foundation's support is gratefully acknowledged.

Walter J. Bock is in the Department of Biology at Columbia University, New York.

methods of comparison used. This problem is not unique to these analyses, but is widespread in the field of animal behavior as well as in all other fields of biology.

How are comparisons made in biology and what type of interpretations may be reached at the conclusion of a comparative study? It is not valid to claim that everyone knows how to compare or to speak of a single comparative method. Comparison is more than simply placing the biological objects in juxtaposition on the table and noting their points of similarity and dissimilarity. More worrisome are statements by workers in nonbiological fields about the usefulness of the method of comparative analysis in biology (e.g., in comparative anatomy and systematics) and the value to be gained in their science by the application of this powerful conceptual tool.

I know of only a few discussions of the theory and methods of comparative biology. Textbooks in comparative anatomy are sadly deficient in such discussions and I know of no book-length analysis to which a student could be referred. My analysis will be based largely upon several of my earlier papers; the reader is referred to Bock (1977a,b) for additional details and references to earlier studies.

No single comparative method exists in biology and it is invalid to speak of "the" comparative method as is often done. Although it may be possible to formulate a set of general principles, the details of the particular methods used in any analysis will depend largely on the intended goals of that study. All comparative methods must be based on theory and that theory must be an appropriate one for the particular science. As I will consider only comparisons in biology (including psychobiology, sociobiology, and anthropology—all sciences dealing with biological organisms), the basic theory underlying the principles and methods of comparison will be that of organic evolution.

Therefore it will be necessary in this essay to outline (1) the essential parts of evolutionary theory and of the mechanism of evolutionary change, (2) the basic principles and methods of comparative biology, and (3) the application of these ideas to sociobiology.

EVOLUTIONARY THEORY

A clear distinction must be made between evolutionary theory—the concept that living organisms change over time—and the mechanisms by which evolution takes place. Darwin in his *On the Origin of Species* had two tasks before him. The first was to argue that animals and plants change with respect to time; the second was to provide a mechanism by which this change occurs.

Organic Evolution

The theory of organic evolution states that the features of biological organisms may modify with respect to time. The minimum period of time is one generation, so that any observed differences between parents and offspring may be considered as an evolutionary change. Modifications in the features of an individual during its life span would be excluded from evolutionary changes. Modifications can be of any type; they do not have to be genetically based changes, and hence the definition of organic evolution should not include reference exclusively to genetically based or inheritable modifications. If this restriction were included in the definition of evolution, then it would be impossible to ascertain whether most observed differences between organisms were actually evolutionary modifications. This definition of evolution makes it necessary to distinguish between heritable evolutionary changes and nonheritable evolutionary changes, and to discuss the mechanisms by which each type of modification can occur.

Evolutionary theory is not equivalent to the theory of natural selection, nor is Darwinian theory equivalent to the theory of natural selection. At the minimum, evolutionary change must be divided into phyletic evolution and speciation (for those organisms arranged in species). Phyletic evolution can occur without speciation, but speciation must include phyletic evolution. The mechanisms of phyletic evolution are the formation of phenotypical variation as the population reproduces generation by generation and the action of natural selection. If the phenotypical variation is genetically based, then the evolutionary changes will be heritable ones. In addition to phyletic evolution, the mechanism of speciation is the appearance of intrinsic isolating mechanisms in two or more phyletic lineages which have split from a single ancestral lineage.

Levels of Organization

Evolution, like most other biological concepts, occurs at many different levels of organization, including individual features, whole organisms, populations, species, communities of species, and the whole biosphere. Most, if not all, evolutionary principles hold for a particular level of organization and cannot be extrapolated simply to other levels. Fitness, for example, is a concept on the level of individuals and has no meaning if applied to features or to populations. The ideas of comparison to be discussed below apply to individual features of organisms be they members of the same or different species and/or of different phyletic lineages.

Definitions

Because several critical definitions will be formulated herein, and because of considerable difference of opinion on the nature of definitions in evolutionary biology, I would like to specify the type of definition to be used. All definitions will be stipulative: they will stipulate properties of the word being defined. The stipulative definition does not necessarily provide the methods by which objects in nature can be recognized as corresponding to the definition. Thus a set of recognizing methods must be provided in addition to the definition; these permit recognition of objects that correspond to the definition. I have referred to the stipulations as the defining criteria and to the methods of recognition as the recognizing criteria (Bock, 1974, pp. 383–385; 1977b, pp. 873–875). These criteria may refer to quite different properties of the object under consideration, and each set of criteria must not necessarily be circular. Thus species are defined as groups of interbreeding populations that do not interbreed with other such groups of populations—even though most species are actually recognized by morphological criteria.

Operational definitions which are advocated by some evolutionists will not be used because I believe that they are difficult if not impossible to formulate within evolutionary biology. It must be emphasized that operational definitions are not the only valid approach, although this has been argued by some workers.

Nature–Nurture

One of the most persistent arguments in biology is whether the phenotypic appearance or the variation in a feature is determined either completely genetically or completely environmentally. This extreme formulation is not supported by observations and should be discarded. A more reasonable statement is that the phenotype of any feature has a genetical basis as well as an environmental influence. The environment acts on developmental mechanisms by which the information in the genotype is used to form the phenotype. For any particular genotype, a range of phenotypic expressions exist which depend on the environment. Even after development is completed, modification of the environment can cause alteration in the phenotypic expression in many features—such as the mechanism of physiological or somatic adaptation (Bock and von Wahlert, 1965).

Ample evidence exists that demonstrates the genetical basis of many behavioral features. These can be found in almost any textbook of human genetics, such as Stern (1973) or Levitan and Montagu (1971) or in texts of behavior genetics such as Fuller and Thompson (1960) or Ehrman and Parsons (1976). Two examples are the nest material-carrying behavior in lovebirds *(Agapornis)* studied by Dilger (Ehrman and Parsons, 1976, p. 89) and the disease American foulbrood of honeybees studied by Rothenbuhler (Ehrman and Parsons, 1976, p. 38). The hybrid between two species of lovebirds (*A. roseicollis* and *A. fischeri*) has a carrying behavior that combines those of the two parental species. Breeding experiments suggest that this behavior is controlled polygenetically. In honeybees, the larvae are killed by a pathogen *(Bacillus larvae)* necessitating nest cleansing behavior by the adults. Genes at two loci control this behavior, one *(u)* for uncapping of the diseased larvae and one *(r)* for removal of the cadavers. Both genes are recessive so that the genetic makeup of the bees in a hygenic colony is *uurr*. Many other examples can be found in studies of monozygotic and dizygotic twins. (See Mittler, 1971.)

The general conclusion may be offered that all behavioral features have a genetical as well as an environmental basis. The onus of proof for any claim that a particular behavioral feature, including social behavior, does not have any genetical basis must lie with the worker making this claim, not with those opposing it.

Species and Phyletic Lineages

Not all living organisms are arranged into species, nor is there any intrinsic necessity for species to appear in the course of organic evolution. Species appear, however, to be a consequence of sexual reproduction. The species is defined as a collection of interbreeding populations which are reproductively isolated from other groups of populations (Mayr, 1963). Species are isolated from other species by intrinsic isolating mechanisms. The species concept is nondimensional in that it loses meaning with increasing distance and time from a particular reference population. Thus it has greatest application to sympatric species existing at one point in time.

A phyletic lineage is the continuity of a species through time as the result of successive generations of reproduction. The cross-section of a phyletic lineage at any point in time represents a species. Cross-sections of the same phyletic lineage at different points in time represent neither the same species nor different species, but ancestral-descendant sections of the same phyletic lineage.

Thus, different species are sections of different phyletic lineages and their relationship to one another (and hence their comparisons) is different from that between different time segments of the same phyletic lineage.

Phyletic evolution is change in a single phyletic lineage with respect to time; it does not result in new species. Speciation is the splitting of a phyletic lineage into two or more separate lineages. Phyletic evolution can occur without speciation, but speciation requires phyletic evolution. Extinction is the disappearance of a phyletic lineage with no descendants.

Phyletic Evolution

Heritable phyletic evolution occurs by the interaction of two separate mechanisms. The first is the formation of genetically based phenotypic variation as the population reproduces generation by generation. This variation is produced mainly by the reshuffling of existing genetical material by recombination, crossing over, and other genetical mechanisms. Mutation serves to introduce new genetical material slowly into the gene pool. The formation of genetically based variation is strictly chance-based with respect to present and future selection forces—it is the accidental component of evolution.

The second mechanism is natural selection, which is the interaction between the environment and the phenotype of individual organisms resulting in differential survival and reproduction of individual organisms. Natural selection requires a "struggle for existence" between individuals. Selection is the design aspect of evolution. It does not predetermine the nature of the genetically based variation that appears and is exposed to selection.

The constant interaction between the formation of genetically based variation and of natural selection is the basis for the concept of accident vs. design in evolution (Mayr, 1962), and adaptation vs. paradaptation (Bock, 1977a).

Speciation

Speciation occurs when a phyletic lineage is split into two separate lineages and these evolve intrinsic isolating mechanisms with respect to each other (Mayr, 1963). This requires phyletic evolution in at least one of the lineages. The intrinsic isolating mechanisms evolve as the result of pleiotropic effects. The two phyletic lineages must be kept separate by some external isolating mechanism—which for most organisms is a geographic-ecological barrier—during the period prior to the evolution of the intrinsic isolating mechanism. Thus, during the allopatric phase of speciation, the populations diverge somewhat and the intrinsic isolating mechanisms evolve. These mechanisms must be 100 percent effective when the external barrier breaks down and the two species become sympatric.

Speciation is not complete when the two new forms become sympatric. During the neosympatric period, the two species interact with one another to reduce ecological competition and to reduce the cost of reproduction (Bock, 1972). These species interactions result in strong mutual selection on the two species and consequent divergence between them. The greatest amount of divergence between species generally occurs during this neosympatric phase of speciation. Speciation is completed only after this period of divergence, when the two species are no longer exerting mutual exclusionary selection on each other.

Adaptive Radiation and Major Change

No separate mechanisms exist for adaptive radiation and for macroevolutionary change. An adaptive radiation of new species results from continued speciation and phyletic evolution. Macroevolution results from a continual series of microevolutionary changes. Explanation of any major change is dependent upon the arrangement of the microevolutionary steps into the proper sequence (Bock, 1970).

COMPARISON

Biological comparison must be based upon the theory of organic evolution and the mechanisms of evolutionary change. I would like to inquire into what is compared in and what are the desired conclusions of a comparative analysis. I want to examine what are the principles and methods of comparison and what conclusions are permitted from different types of comparative studies.

Comparisons and Goals

Comparisons may be made between phenotypic features of any two different individual organisms, be they members of the same species, different species, or different time segments of the same phyletic lineage. Thus any behavioral feature may be compared in the same way as any morphological structure.

The goal of comparative studies is to formulate generalizations which are valid for more than one individual and usually more than one species. One may be interested in mechanisms of muscle contraction that are valid for all striated muscles regardless of the groups in which they are found. A synthesis of sociobiology would, one hopes, permit the formulation of generalizations that are valid for groups exhibiting social behavior regardless of their systematic position.

Types of Comparison

Not all comparisons are the same. Nor, excluding the obvious comparison of conspecific individuals, are all comparisons between members of different species. Two types of comparison must be distinguished (see Bock, 1977a). I have called these horizontal and vertical. Horizontal comparisons are between members of different phyletic lineages, that is, between different species. Comparison between conspecific individuals may be considered to be a special case of horizontal comparison. Vertical comparisons are between members of different time segments of the same phyletic lineage; these are not between different species nor within the same species.

The results and interpretations of each type of comparison are different and one cannot simply extrapolate the results from one type of comparison to another. Horizontal similarities are not necessarily the same as vertical similarities, nor are vertical differences the same as horizontal differences. If evolutionary change of a particular feature in a phyletic lineage has been under the control of selection, then the observed difference would be adaptive with respect to that selection force. But differences between features in several lineages that evolved under the control of the same selection force would not be adaptive or nonadaptive, but paradaptive with respect to that selection—that is, the differences are indifferent with respect to that selection force. These paradaptive differences are the result of different genetical modifications that occurred in each lineage, not of difference in selection forces.

Other categories of comparison may be distinguished, such as historical vs. nonhistorical, but these may fall under the heading of horizontal vs. vertical.

Comparisons are made between features of different individuals, but it is not known prior to the completion of the study whether the comparison is a horizontal or a vertical one—with the exception, of course, of comparisons between recent species, which must be horizontal. One must complete the analysis and, on the basis of the possible interpretations, conclude whether the comparison was a horizontal or vertical one. This will permit the conclusion as to whether the individuals under comparison are members of different or of the same phyletic lineage.

Homology

The concept of homology is one of the core ideas in comparative studies. Homology can be applied to any phenotypical feature or to any property or aspect thereof. Exactly the same principles and methods hold whether structural or behavioral features are being homologized. I will base my discussion on that in Bock (1977b) and in earlier papers cited therein. Homology may be defined as follows. Features (or conditions of a feature) in two or more organisms are homologous if they stem phylogenetically from the same feature (or the same condition of the feature) in the immediate common ancestor of these organisms. Thus homology is defined in terms of phylogeny and phylogeny can be defined in terms of evolution. Homology is not defined in terms of similarity; that word appears nowhere in the definition. Homology is a relative concept; hence the nature of the relationship must always be stated when discussing particular homologous features, and the presumed nature of the feature in the common ancestor must be described in a conditional phrase. Statements about homologues lacking this conditional phrase are incomplete and meaningless. Thus wings of bats and wings of birds are nonhomologous as aerodynamic surfaces but are homologous as tetrapod forelimbs.

The opposite of homology is nonhomology, not analogy. The term analogy has been defined and used in several different ways; it is of very limited value in comparative studies and is best dropped from usage. The term homoplasy is likewise not needed because it means the same as similar. No meaning exists in phrases such as "the concept of resemblance." Resemblance is an observation made within certain limits of accuracy.

Homologous features may be ascertained when the organisms are members of different phyletic lineages (a horizontal comparison in which the homologous features correspond to a feature in the common ancestor—where the phyletic lineages branched) or when the organisms are members of the same phyletic lineage (a vertical comparison in which an ancestor-descendant sequence is proposed and the ancestral feature is one of the two features being homologized). The methods of study in these two types of homologization will differ.

Homologies are defined in terms of phylogeny, but all homologous features are recognized with a different criterion. Indeed the *only* criterion available for testing statements about homologues (horizontal ones) is similarities between the features being compared. These similarities may be structural, developmental, or functional, or may refer to any other attribute of the feature. Similarity of the phenotypes of features can be used to test homologues because these similarities may be interpreted as ancestral similarity. Homologous features are self-identical at the point just prior to the divergence of each lineage from the common ancestor. After the divergence of the two phyletic lineages, the features can become different because of different patterns of evolution in each lineage. But those attributes of the features which have not changed during these periods of phyletic evolution will remain the same as in the ancestral feature and hence will be similar in the homologous features. Correlation with other homologous features and presence in closely related species are not valid criteria because they lead to circular arguments. Vertical sequences of homologues would be tested by similarities in addition to the formulation of transformation series.

The methods (i.e., similarities) used to test homologous features have low resolving power to distinguish between homologues and nonhomologues. Consequently many errors are made in ascertaining and judging homologous features. These are of two types, namely (1) concluding features are homologous when they are nonhomologous, and (2) concluding features are nonhomologous when they are homologous. Errors of the first type are the more serious, but it must be emphasized that many errors of both types are made whenever homologues are determined.

Once homologues are ascertained, together with their conditional phrases, and these phrases are arranged into hierarchies, the homologous features can be used to establish classifications of organisms. The order of study is always to determine the homologies prior to and independently of the classifications that they support (see Bock, 1977b, for procedures).

Comparisons can be made of homologous features in which one may be interested in the amount of morphological and functional divergence between different homologues as a measure of the degree of evolutionary change. Or one may wish to contrast homologues possessing similar functions with those possessing dissimilar functions. Moreover, it is possible and often very useful to compare nonhomologous features. Nonhomologous convergent features may provide clues to the important functional and adaptational correlations with particular selection forces. Or one may wish to examine nonhomologous, nonconvergent features which represent different adaptive answers to the same selection force to determine the possible range of such adaptive interactions.

Determining the homology of behavioral features is in principle exactly the same as determining it for morphological features. Behavioral features in two or more organisms that stem phylogenetically from the same behavior in the common ancestor are homologous. Conditional phrases must be included. And the test of homologous behavioral features is by similarities. The nature and greater flexibility of many behavioral traits may make their homologization more difficult. Fewer points of similarity may be available with which to test behavioral homologues, and it may be more difficult to separate homologous from nonhomologous behavioral traits. But these aspects of behavioral features do not make them different in any essential way from morphological or any other phenotypical features in the analysis of homology. After all, all of these features are part of the organism's phenotype and the concept of homology applies equally to all parts of the phenotype.

Phylogenetic Analysis

A final part of comparative study is the establishment of phylogenetical sequences of features and of organisms. This has been done, in part, with the arrangement of conditional phrases describing homologues into hierarchies. Phylogenetic analysis starts with establishing homologous features and then moves to arranging these homologues into transformation series that correspond with the most likely sequence of evolutionary changes. The polarity of these transformation series are then established with the primitive feature being a pleisomorph and the advanced feature an apomorph; apomorphous features evolve from pleisomorphs. The apomorphs are then studied to distinguish between homologous apomorphs and nonhomologous apomorphs; the former are synapomorphs (Hennig, 1966). (The details of phylogenetic analysis are summarized in Bock, 1977b, but see also Hennig, 1966, and other phylogenetic systematists who advocate somewhat different methods.)

COMPARISON AND SOCIOBIOLOGY

Sociobiology deals with the behavioral interactions of conspecific organisms that live in certain types of assemblages (societies). I am not here concerned with the nature of these assemblages or that they grade into other types of groups of conspecific individuals and into solitary individuals. Of importance is that the features pertinent to sociobiology are behavioral traits which serve as communication between members of the conspecific society. How can these behavioral traits be compared and what types of conclusions may be reached at the end of a comparative analysis?

The answer is, of course, that behavioral features are compared with the same principles and methods as are any other phenotypical features, and one hopes to ascertain generalizations (scientific statements) which are valid for as many social organisms as possible. Immediate problems arise because the social insects are protostomes and the social vertebrates are deuterostomes; their common ancestor is a primitive wormlike coelomate animal. It is hardly likely that the aspects of social behavior in insects and in vertebrates are homologous as social behavior. This does not mean that comparisons cannot be made and that generalizations cannot be reached, but their formulation must be made with care because nonhomologous features are being compared. Comparison of social behavior among vertebrates can be done with more assurance, but even in this phylum the major groups of social organisms—the teleost fishes, the birds, and the mammals—have been separated for long periods of time. The lineages leading to birds and mammals both go back to early reptiles living at the beginnings of the Permian, if not the Carboniferous—at least 270 million years ago. Comparisons and generalizations would be safest if made within the primates, most members of which exhibit social behavior.

What are the units to be compared in sociobiology? Certainly any behavioral trait, be it a display, or part of a display, or the display plus the associated morphology, may be compared. Calls, songs, and odors are all part of the organism's phenotype and available for comparison. The song of a bird is absolutely equivalent to the movements of the wings during flight. If agreement exists that wing movement during flight or food handling in the bill can be homologized, so too can song. Spider webs and bird nests are also properly included in the phenotype of these animals.

Behavioral features are compared and homologized like any other phenotypical trait. Some problems exist in anthropomorphic statements applied to nonhuman animal behavior in comparisons between humans and other animals, for it is difficult to know when such statements can be applied validly. We may not know enough about human behavior and hence about the details of anthropomorphic traits to know how to apply these to nonhuman animals.

While it is possible to use behavioral features, including those used in social behavior, for phylogenetic and systematical studies, such studies would be difficult in comparison with the use of morphological studies.

Moreover, far more interesting comparative analyses in sociobiology can be made by exploring questions as to the evolution and adaptive significance of behavior.

CONCLUSION

Syntheses such as Wilson's treatment of sociobiology and Griffin's treatise on animal awareness gain biological interest in direct proportion to the comparativeness of the study. Certainly these two analyses fulfill this critical requirement. The bulk of Wilson's volume, for example, is a detailed description of social behavior observed in a broadly diverse assemblage of organisms which he uses as the data base to formulate general principles of social behavior. The validity and applicability of these generalizations will increase with proper understanding and use of the principles and methods of comparative biology.

REFERENCES

Bock, W. J. (1970). "Microevolutionary Sequences as a Fundamental Concept in Macroevolutionary Models." *Evolution* 24, pp. 704–722.
————. (1972). "Species Interaction and Macroevolution." In *Evolutionary Biology*, ed. Dobzhansky, Hecht, and Steere (New York: Appleton-Century-Crofts). Vol. 5, pp. 1–24.
————. (1974). "Philosophical Foundations of Classical Evolutionary Classification." *Syst. Zool.* 11, pp. 375–392.
————. (1977a). "Adaptation and the Comparative Method." In *Major Patterns in Vertebrate Evolution,* edited by Max Hecht. (New York: Plenum). NATO Advanced Study Institute, Series A, Vol. 14, pp. 57–82.
————. (1977b). "Foundations and Methods of Evolutionary Classification." In *ibid.,* pp. 851–895.
———— and G. von Wahlert. (1965). "Adaptation and the Form-Function Complex." *Evolution* 19, pp. 269–299.
Ehrman, L. and P. A. Parsons. (1976). *The Genetics of Behavior* (Sunderland, Mass.: Sinauer).
Fuller, J. L. and W. R. Thompson. (1960). *Behavior Genetics* (New York: J. Wiley & Sons).
Griffin, D. R. (1976). "The Question of Animal Awareness." *Evolutionary Continuity of Mental Experience.* (New York: Rockefeller University Press).
Hennig, W. (1966). *Phylogenetic Systematics* (Urbana: University of Illinois Press).
Levitan, M. and A. Montagu. (1971). *Textbook of Human Genetics* (New York: Oxford University Press).

Lorenz, K. (1974). "Analogy as a Source of Knowledge." *Science* 185, pp. 229–234.

Masterton, R. B., Hodos, W., and Jerison H., eds. (1976). *Evolution, Brain and Behavior: Persistent Problems.* (Hillsdale, N.J.: Erlbaum).

Mayr, E. (1962). "Accident or Design: The Paradox of Evolution." In *The Evolution of Living Organisms* (Melbourne: Melbourne University Press), pp. 1–14. Reprinted in Mayr, *Evolution and the Diversity of Life* (Cambridge, Mass.: Harvard University Press, 1976).

———. (1973). *Animal Species and Evolution* (Cambridge, Mass.: Harvard University Press).

Mittler, P. (1971). *The Study of Twins.* (Harmondsworth, England: Penguin Books).

Stern, C. (1973). *Principles of Human Genetics,* 3rd ed. (San Francisco: W. H. Freeman and Co.).

Wilson, E. O. (1975). *Sociobiology: The New Synthesis* (Cambridge, Mass.: Harvard University Press).

The Methodology of Sociobiology from the Viewpoint of a Comparative Psychologist

Ethel Tobach

Wilson purports to present a new synthesis of behavioral biological principles which will set sociobiology on a par with molecular biology and developmental biology as a branch of evolutionary biology, rather than a new theory (Wilson in *Animal Behaviour* 24, p. 716). Nonetheless, his exhaustive presentation of those principles has resulted in a statement of a theory of the evolution of behavior. This is brought about in two ways. First, he sets up a series of postulates that constitute such a theory. These postulates are as follows. The process of natural selection is the "process whereby certain genes gain representation in the following generations superior to that of other genes located at the same chromosome positions." (Wilson, 1975, p. 3) The individual, as a gene-transmitting agent, is the product of the evolutionary process. Social behavior is the fundamental process whereby the individual, through interaction with others of the same species, participates in that gene-transmission process. "Sociobiology is the systematic study of the biological basis of all social behavior." There is no behavior other than that related to gene transmission.

Wilson's theory can be described as hereditarian (cf. Lorenz, Skinner, and Jensen). He proposes that the gene is the ultimate unit whereby structure (morphology), function (physiology) and behavior are preprogrammed in the individual. He does state that there are constraints imposed on the gene by the environment or experience of the individual. However, he does not formulate his corollary concepts, such as social

Ethel Tobach is in the Department of Animal Behavior at the American Museum of Natural History, New York.

organization and parental behavior, within these constraints. The function of the gene is definable by the statistical analysis of the conditions under which the gene is expressed during development (Ebert and Sussex, 1965; Srb, Owen, and Edgar, 1952). Although Wilson presents a great deal of information about many aspects of genetic processes, and although he cautions against concluding the characteristics of a species on the basis of nonexhaustive observations, these caveats are frequently forgotten. The concept of heritability is a strict statistical definition derived from population genetics of a well-defined character (Topoff, 1974). Wilson applies it to all aspects of behavior, from that of the zooid in colonial organisms to the culture of people. In the latter, he admits, there is little possibility of separating the heritable and environmental components, either in the population or in the individual. Nonetheless, he views all structure, physiology and behavior as definable in terms of the heritable and the experiential or environmental.

To consider heritability the fundamental characteristic of behavior presupposes that behavioral, morphological and physiological characters are equally definable in precise terms which permit experimental manipulation in controlled population-genetic types of experimentation. Wilson points out that there are many steps between the genetic coding for an enzyme, a protein, or some molecular entity and the complicated developmental expression of this biochemical level of function in tissues, organs, and behavior, particularly social behavior. Nonetheless, he forgets this important point frequently; for example, "dominance" in primates, a term which is not precise, is viewed as being genetically based and modified by the behavior of the nursing female and her relationship to conspecifics.

According to Wilson's own definition of a theory (Wilson, 1975, p. 27), the above is an example of "postulational-deductive" thinking.

Second, in sketching the future development of behavioral biology, he sees sociobiology and behavioral ecology rising from the ashes of other disciplines. Ethology and comparative psychology will be cannibalized by "neurophysiology and sensory physiology from one end and sociobiology and behavioral ecology from the other." In "a subjective conception [graphic, ET] of the relative number of ideas in various disciplines in and adjacent to behavioral biology," by the year 2000, ethology and physiological psychology are united and comparative psychology no longer exists (Wilson, 1975, pp. 6–7). As neurophysiology and sensory physiology will remain in the future, a brief examination of the history, theoretical basis and methodology of the two "expendable" sciences, ethology and comparative psychology, may be in order.

Comparative psychology as a term was first used by Flourens (Jaynes, 1969) but it is generally agreed that Romanes (Boring, 1950) seriously formulated the discipline as a development of Darwin's theories and writings. The history of comparative psychology reflects stresses and strains of the growth of other fields, as well as the changes in the philosophy of science (Jaynes, 1969; Tobach, Adler and Adler, 1973). Today, comparative psychology is frequently confused with ethology and animal behavior. Indeed, most academic faculties do not know of the discipline as such, and do not feature it in their catalogs. One of the major theories in the field is represented by T. C. Schneirla and his followers. Schneirla's theory, based on the concept of levels of organization and integration, stressed the complementarity of field and laboratory research, an evolutionary approach to physiological and behavioral studies of different species, and an application of the comparative method based on process rather than analogy, homology, or a mechanical application of concepts from one science to another, as in logical positivism. His comparative method stressed the dissimilarities as much as the similarities among species or behavioral phenomena. Above all, he was concerned with a careful application of Ockham's Razor (Schneirla, 1971).

He was particularly critical of vitalistic thinking. These theoretical and philosophical considerations led him to a position significantly opposed to the concepts of instinct and inheritance as an explanation for the development and evolution of behavior. In this respect, then, he represented the antithesis, methodologically and theoretically, to ethology.

Ethology was first formulated as the study of customs, traditions and habits in regard to human behavior (Jaynes, 1969). It was transformed into a science of the evolution of behavior based on innate behavioral patterns which were considered taxonomic units, primarily through the writings of Lorenz (1950) and Tinbergen (1951). Coming from a primarily zoological tradition in Europe, the pioneer workers in ethology based their methodology on observations of animals in their natural habitat and in captivity. Observing nondomesticated animals in captivity was a continuance of the tradition started by the earliest zoologists and carried on by the followers of Darwin, such as comparative psychologists and biologists interested in evoluton. Nonetheless, the stress on field work and on animals that were "wild" led to the reputation of ethology as being more "naturalistic" while comparative psychology was considered more experimental and laboratory-oriented. Contemporary comparative psychology and ethology are not monolithic disciplines. Ethological thinking today is undergoing many modifications and the neo-ethologists such as Hinde, Crook and Bateson do not use the orthodox definition of ethology—that is, the study of innate patterns of behavior. Rather they have attempted a rapprochement among Schneirla, Skinner and ethological formulations as they have modified them (Hinde, 1970; Crook, 1970; Bateson, 1966). Comparative psychology similarly represents a spectrum of conceptualizations that relies on hereditarian viewpoints as well as views related to those of Schneirla (Tobach, Adler and Adler, 1973).

This brief presentation may indicate that the fields of comparative psychology and ethology are not mutually independent of each other. In both disciplines there are scientists who are hereditarian in view. In both disciplines there are scientists who are mostly engaged in field work or laboratory research, with exotic species or with domestic (laboratory-bred) species. In both disciplines there are those who work on the physiological level or on the behavioral level only. In both disciplines there are those who are comparative and evolutionary in their approach and those who are strictly phenomenon-oriented, or species-oriented (e.g., concentrating on feeding behavior in different species, or on all levels of integration in a particular species).

What then is the distinction among the three disciplines—ethology, comparative psychology and sociobiology? The distinction is not in the names themselves, but in the philosophical assumptions of a particular scientist or group of scientists, no matter what they call themselves. But there is a significant issue that leads to a categorization principle for those who are studying the evolution of behavior. The major issue in behavioral science today is that of the way in which genetic theory is related to evolutionary theory. The two dominant views are based on the hereditarian concept or on the concept of levels of organization and integration. Hereditarian concepts are based on the reductionist view that genes are the ultimate unit of living matter and as such offer the ultimate explanation of all phenomena of living matter. Structural, physiological, behavioral or ecological phenomena are viewed as equivalent in their requirements for explanation and study. This frequently takes the form of relying on mathematical models and physical analogies. As a consequence of these modes of thought, hereditarian theories and formulations are characterized by the use of anthropomorphic and zoomorphic explanations and descriptions (Tobach, 1976).

The hereditarian view is also reductionistic in that all processes are seen as variations of the primary process of gene transmission. This leads to analogous thinking, which blurs the differences among phenomena and emphasizes the similarities. An example of this in Wilson is his discussion of social drift, tradition drift and genetic drift. Let us start by defining "genetic drift," which Wilson states is a precise and mathematically clear concept. In the glossary of *Sociobiology* he defines it as "evolution (change in gene frequencies) by chance processes alone" (p. 585). In the text (p. 64) it is defined as "the alteration of gene frequencies through sampling error." He offers the formulae which precisely determine the size of the sample which can lead to different levels of genetic loss and thus defines genetic drift further as an appropriate term for the process of random change in gene frequencies. These formulations are based primarily on experimentation with two-allele Mendelian systems, and assumes that no other factors, such as temperature, food resources, predators, etc. are operating.

Behavior is seen by him as the pacemaker of evolution in regard to its effect on the probability of the natural selection of particular morphological and physiological characteristics resulting from the behavior of the individual. Because the individual is the fundamental unit in gene transmission, this leads to social drift by virtue of the variability of the individual's behavior. Social drift is seen as composed of a genetic basis and an experiential basis, and is accordingly an interaction between genetic drift and tradition drift; tradition drift is equated with experiential variation. This reasoning leads to analogous thinking, as for example, where variations among human cultures are seen equivalent to a mixture of two populations of Barbary apes. Wilson adopts the analogous thinking of Cavalli-Sforza and Feldman, who, he says, "suggested that in human societal evolution the equivalent of an important mutation is a new idea" (p. 14). One possible consequence of these postulates is the following.

Genetic drift is an explication of chance factors in gene frequencies.

Tradition drift, because it is related to experience, is viewed either as an example of selection, or of contingency in the Skinnerian sense, or as a candidate for conversion to chance, as in the case of genetic drift. Social drift is composed of genetic and tradition drift. The aim is to convert tradition drift, which is possibly definable and determinable by the immediate adjustive value of the behavior in a given situation in a given population, into a random process definable as a sampling error. The concept of the process of idea selection is derived from the proposition that one individual in a transmission of a new idea is active and the receiver of the new idea is passive. Further, good ideas are presumed to survive, while bad ideas are selected against (not adopted by different human cultures).

The concept of "good" and "bad" ideas is also genetically determined (Wilson, 1975, p. 3).

These centers [hypothalamus and limbic system of the brain] flood our consciousness with all the emotions—hate, love, guilt, fear and others—that are consulted by ethical philosophers who wish to intuit the standards of good and evil. . . . They evolved by natural selection. That simple biological statement must be pursued to explain ethics and ethical philosophers, if not epistemology and epistemologists, at all depths.

Thus, the good and bad ideas to which an individual might react passively or actively would be selected for on the basis of the gut feeling about ethics, morals or values, as Wilson describes it, which arises from neural structures which have been preprogrammed to respond. Should one suppose that those who fought against slavery, or who are fighting against racism and sexism, have one set of inherited characteristics programming what shall be considered a "good" idea, while those who defend slavery have another?

The concept of ethics as an inherited behavior pattern is a reflection of the reductionism of hereditarianism. This type of analogous thinking expresses itself in anthropomorphism and zoomorphism. Anthropomorphism is the attribution of human characteristics to animals other than humans, and zoomorphism equates the behavior of humans with that of other animals. Although Wilson recognizes the unsuitability of this type of thinking, the misunderstanding of Morgan's Canon which he indicates in *Sociobiology* (p. 30) may be related to his consistency in being reductionistic, anthropomorphic and zoomorphic.

One of the early, major contributions of comparative psychology was the formulation of a principle by Lloyd Morgan, which came to be known as Morgan's Canon. Wilson interprets that canon as calling for explanation of behavior "exclusively by the simplest mechanisms." Morgan did not propose simplicity as the guideline. Instead, he said in 1894, "In no case may we interpret an action as the outcome of the exercise of a higher psychical faculty, if it can be interpreted as the outcome of one which stands lower in the psychological scale." Later, in 1908, he used the phrase "lower in the scale of psychological development"; in 1930, he talked of "lower in the order of mental development"; and finally, in 1933, he advised psychologists "not to interpret what is observed at an earlier and lower stage of evolutionary advance in such relational terms as are appropriate to the interpretation of a higher and lower stage."

Morgan was talking about an evolutionary, developmental ordering of behavioral phenomena. (Darwin and the writers of his era were more likely to talk about psychological, mental or psychical phenomena; today we usually use the term "behavior".) Morgan's thinking was in close agreement with Darwinian theory, and with that of others such as Woodger (1920), who elaborated the concept of levels of organization. He was postulating that it was invalid to confound different levels of behavioral plasticity. Simplicity was not at issue. The response of an amoeba to light, to the metabolic by-products of another amoeba, or to temperature is very complex; to talk of the amoeba's motivation to be with other amoebas would be attributing a behavioral ability to the animal which is not warranted.

Wilson, like others, may have confused the principle of parsimony, Ockham's Razor, and Morgan's Canon. William of Ockham, apparently influenced by John Duns Scotus, wrote the following in the fourteenth century: "What can be explained by the assumption of fewer things is vainly explained by the assumption of more things" (Boehner, 1962). This has become known as "Ockham's Razor." The law of parsimony, or Hamilton's Law (nineteenth century), as Pearson (1908) pointed out, expresses Ockham's Razor in a more complete and adequate form, but is sufficiently different not to be confused with it. Hamilton's law states, "Neither more, nor more onerous, causes are to be assumed, than are necessary to account for the phenomena." Morgan's Canon is an expression of the need to beware of excess on the level of explanation and interpretation, not on the level of the characteristics of the phenomenon itself, which may be complex.

The concept of levels of organization and integration requires neither reductionism nor an excess of assumptions and causal phenomena. Both are hallmarks of the hereditarian concept. The concept of levels proposes that matter is hierarchically organized in terms of complexity; that each level subsumes the preceding level; that each level has its own characteristics and requirements for study and interpretation; and that there is continuity between levels of particular processes, such as transduction of energy or genetic replication, but that on each level the forms and processes are different and have their own laws. Within the organism one can schematize levels of organization beginning with the biophysical, biochemical level of function at membranes and within cells; to the physiological level of tissues, organs and systems; to the intersystemic physiological level; and finally to the level of the total organ behavioral function. A second aspect of the levels of organization and integration can be seen in regard to social organization, where the formation of bonds through reciprocal stimulation (Schneirla, 1971) varies as to temporal character, the types of individuals participating in bond formation, the kind and quality of energy which is involved in the reciprocal stimulation, and the ability of the individual organism to modify behavior with or without the actual experience of reciprocal stimulation (ability to store past experience of a related but not necessarily identical type; ability to abstract and generalize; ability to project future consequences of behavior and social interaction, etc.). In this way, the social organization of insects is seen as qualitatively and significantly different from that of human beings not only because of the differences in the genetic processes or of the reproductive processes but because of the differences in the levels of organization and integration of the individual members of the social group and the differences in the temporal and other characteristics of reciprocal stimulation and bond formation. The concept of levels as developed above by Schneirla eliminates anthropomorphism and zoomorphism. It makes it possible to understand the continuities in the evolution of behavior, such as reciprocal stimulation, within the context of the discontinuities that bring about speciation.

Wilson also uses a concept of levels of organization. In discussing social organization, the "cut-off point or, to be more precise, the level of organization at which we cease to refer to a group as a society and start labeling it as an aggregation or nonsocial population" always involves some "ambiguity" (p. 8). The ambiguity stems from the nonhistoric nature of the units he assembles in a building-block fashion, based on a holism in which the triumphant reductionism of molecular biology expresses itself in his hereditarian view of behavior. He defines a society as "a set of particular organisms," and confesses that "it is difficult to extrapolate the joint activity of this ensemble from the instant of specification, that is, to predict social behavior."

What is it that cannot be predicted and why? One cannot predict from one level to another if one does not know the history of the levels and their interrelationship. One also needs to know the contemporary situation in which the level is being studied, and the history of that contemporary situation (how and when the individuals arrived in spatial contiguity, for example). One can predict from one level to another by using the principles and tools that are appropriate to the next level. Prediction is possible within one level, based on the analysis of the chronology of events and processes on that level; prediction is possible if one approaches the problem historically. But without the historical dimension, in terms of phylogeny, ontogeny and population history, as in human history the "emergent," "holistic" qualitative changes from one level to another remain mysterious and nonmaterial.

For example, knowing that circulating titers of hormones change the firing frequency of a set of motor neurones (physiological level) does not enable us to predict whether a fish will swim towards or away from another fish (behavioral level). Knowing the ontogenetic history of the two fish, the history of the circumstances in which they are being observed together, enables us to predict the probability of events on the behavioral level of integration without referring to the subsumed physiological level. Prediction is eminently feasible within one level, as the operant conditioning techniques demonstrate repeatedly. However, only a limited type of explanation can be gained within one level. Causal explanations on any one level require the integration of many levels.

Although Wilson's concept of levels is nonhistoric, static and structural (the social "emerges" from individual, dyad or tryad interactions), he does propose a process that differentiates an aggregation from a social group: "cooperation". How does one define cooperation? Intuitively (p. 7). The concept of intuition is frequently used throughout the book, but there is no definition either in the glossary or the text. The third edition of *Webster's Unabridged Dictionary* gives the following definitions: 2a. The act or process of coming to direct knowledge or certainty without reasoning or inferring: immediate cognizance or conviction without rational thought: revelation by insight or innate knowledge: immediate apprehension or cognition. 2d. In Bergsonism: a form of knowing that is akin to instinct or a divining empathy and that gives direct insight into reality as it is in itself and absolutely. 2e. quick and ready insight.

Cooperation is also not defined in the glossary or text. Rather the discriminating processes distinguishing population and society are gene flow and communication. Communication again starts from an intuitive understanding to become mathematically analyzable, and is defined in the panchrestic way, which by analogy reduces the interaction between a neurohormonal cell in the brain and a cell in the thyroid gland to a telephone call.

Coordination indirectly also involves a concept of levels of organization. It is defined as "interaction among units of a group such that the overall effort of the group is divided among the units without leadership being assumed by any one of them. Coordination may be influenced by a unit in a higher level of the social hierarchy, but such outside control is not essential" (Wilson, 1975, p. 10). By this definition, "the formation of a fish school, the exchange of liquid food back and forth by worker ants, and the encirclement of prey by a pride of lions are all examples of coordination among organisms at the same organizational level" (pp. 10–11). The criterion that removes the consideration of the differences among these examples is that of leadership. What is leadership? In the glossary (p. 588) it is defined. "Narrowly used in sociobiology, leadership means only the role of leading other members of the society when the group progresses from one place to another." "Leading" is described on p. 213: "A few vertebrate and insect species use signals that seem explicitly designed to initiate and to direct the movement of groups." It also means dominance to terminate fighting among subordinates (p. 287) and the power of the tyrant among many insects (p. 287). The anthropomorphic conceptualization of the interactions of members of the social organizations inherently derives from a lack of consideration of the differences among levels of phyletic as well as phenomenal organization.

The confounding of levels operates not only among nonhuman animal species, but particularly in regard to human beings in comparison with other species.

Division of labor is based on these memorized distinctions, in a fashion analogous to the physiological determination of castes in social insects. But whereas social organization in the insect colonies depends on programmed, altruistic behavior by an ergonomically optimal mix of castes, the welfare of human societies is based on trade-offs among individuals playing roles. When too many human beings enter one occupation, their personal cost-to-benefit ratios rise, and some individuals transfer to less crowded fields for selfish reasons. When too many members of an insect colony belong to one caste, various forms of physiological inhibition arise, for example the underproduction or overproduction of phero-mones, which shunt developing individuals into other castes. (Wilson, 1975).

This would appear to make some fine distinction between the two types of organisms. Two points should be remembered, however. The value systems that lead to selfish behavior and role playing are also programmed in people, as the physiological processes are programmed in the insect. Also, the societal problems of employment and human welfare are reduced to a simplistic process of individual ergonomics. The processes whereby overproduction of one particular caste in insects, or of too many Ph.D.'s in physics, are seen as comparable "biological" phenomena.

The most telling application of his concept of levels of organization is in Chapter 27, which Wilson himself calls the most vulnerable chapter (Wilson, 1976). One example is his analysis of the factors that cement "the close marriage bonds that are basic to human social life." "The traits of physical attraction are, moreover, fixed in nature. They include the pubic hair of both sexes and the protuberant breasts and buttocks of women. The flattened sexual cycle and the continuous female attrac-tiveness" are the cement. This reductionist analysis ignores not only the variations in standards of "attractiveness" in different societies, the variety in types of "marriages" and the changes in the relationship of women and men to child-rearing practices, but it emphasizes physiologi-cal and morphological processes that are limited in societal meaning to the issue of production of offspring. The societal practices in regard to reproduction are many levels removed from physiology; property and other economic constraints play the significant roles in this respect (Sahlins, 1977).

In discussing human behavior, Wilson frequently acknowledges that "there is no way of knowing whether the divergence is ultimately genetic in origin or triggered entirely by experiential events at an early age" (p. 555). Here he is discussing class and caste in human society, but for "divergence" one might substitute any of the other processes he discusses in this chapter. It is important to note, however, that in his grand scheme for experimental analysis in sociobiology, his basic assumption is not to be tested. That is the assumption that all explanations start with genetic function. This is accepted in his program for determining the components of heritability and experience in behavior. Although Wilson's own research is not directed at this question, to demonstrate the various mechanisms of altruism, such research is inherently required. It is this research question which is most vulnerable to criticism as a valid procedure in the study of the evolution of behavior (Topoff, 1974).

The reduction of explanation to genetic function is basically the key to the weakness of Wilson's extrapolation of the postulates of sociobiology to all levels of social organization. The alternative concept to hereditarianism, the concept of levels of organization and integration, incorporates all levels of function, including genetic processes. It does so, however, by integrating them in the historic development of species and individuals, without seeing genes as the ultimate explanation. In this way, it avoids the weaknesses of Wilson's sociobiologic theory.

REFERENCES

Animal Behaviour 24 (1976): Multiple review of Wilson's *Sociobiology,* pp. 698–718.

Bateson, P. P. G. (1966). "The Characteristics and Context of Imprinting." *Biology Review* 41, pp. 177–220.

Boehner, P. (1962). *Ockham* (Edinburgh: T. Nelson & Sons, Ltd.).

Boring, E. G. (1950). *A History of Experimental Psychology* (New York: Appleton-Century-Crofts).

Crook, J. H. (1970). *Social Behaviour in Birds and Mammals* (New York: Academic Press).

Ebert, J. D. and I. M. Sussex. (1965). *Interacting Systems in Development* (New York: Holt, Rinehart and Winston).

Hinde, R. A. (1970). *Animal Behaviour: A Synthesis of Ethology and Comparative Psychology.* (New York: McGraw-Hill Book Co.).

Jaynes, Julian. (1969). "The Historical Origins of 'Ethology' and 'Comparative Psychology'." *Animal Behaviour* 17, pp. 601–606.

Lorenz, K. (1950). "The Comparative Method in Studying Innate Behaviour Patterns." *Sym. Soc. Exp. Biol.* 4, pp. 221–268.

Morgan, C. Lloyd. (1894). *An Introduction to Comparative Psychology* (London: Walter Scott, Ltd.).

———. (1908). *Animal Behaviour* (London: Edward Arnold).

———. (1930). *The Animal Mind* (London: Edward Arnold).

———. (1933). *The Emergence of Novelty* (London: Williams & Norgate).

Pearson, Karl. (1900). *The Grammar of Science* (London: A. & C. Black).

Sahlins, Marshall. (1977). *The Use and Abuse of Biology* (Ann Arbor: The University of Michigan Press).

Schneirla, T. C. (1970). *Selected Writings.* (San Francisco: W. H. Freeman).

Srb, A., Owen, R. D., and Edgar, R. S. (1965). *General Genetics* (San Francisco: W. H. Freeman).

Tinbergen, N. (1951). *The Study of Instinct* (Oxford: Oxford University Press).

Tobach, E., Adler, H. E., and Adler, L. L. (1973). *Comparative Psychology at Issue.* Annals of the New York Academy of Sciences 223.

Tobach, E. (1976). "Evolution of Behavior and the Comparative Method." *International Journal of Psychology* 11, pp. 185–201.

Topoff, Howard. (1974). "Genes, Intelligence and Race." In *The Four Horsemen,* E. Tobach (New York: Behavioral Publications).

Wilson, E. O. (1976). "Author's Reply." *Animal Behaviour* 24, pp. 716–718.

———. (1975). *Sociobiology: The New Synthesis* (Cambridge, Mass.: Harvard University Press.).

Woodger, J. H. (1967). *Biological Principles: A Critical Study* (New York: Humanities Press).

The Use and Abuse of Biology

Marshall D. Sahlins

Our discussion of the kinship-based societies, which constitute the historic converse of appropriative and possessive individualism, and, so far as representative status in history is concerned, the normal human condition, supports the following judgments on the theory of kin selection.

First, no system of human kinship relations is organized in accord with the genetic coefficients of relationship as known to sociobiologists. Each consists from this point of view of arbitrary rules of marriage, residence, and descent, from which are generated distinctive arrangements of kinship groups and statuses, and determinations of kinship distance that violate the natural specifications of genealogy. Each kinship order has accordingly its own theory of heredity or shared substance, which is never the genetic theory of modern biology, and a corresponding pattern of sociability. Such human *conceptions* of kinship may be so far from biology as to exclude all but a small fraction of a person's genealogical connections from the category of "close kin"; while, at the same time, including in that category, as sharing common blood, very distantly related people or even complete strangers. Among those strangers (genetically) may be one's own children (culturally).

Second, as the culturally constituted kinship relations govern the real processes of cooperation in production, property, mutual aid, and marital exchange, the human systems ordering reproductive success

From Marshall D. Sahlins, *The Use and Abuse of Biology* (Ann Arbor: The University of Michigan Press, 1976), pp. 56–61. Copyright © 1976 The University of Michigan Press. Reprinted by permission of the publisher, and the author.

have an entirely different calculus than that predicted by kin selection and, *sequitur est,* by an egotistically conceived natural selection. Indeed, the relation between pragmatic cooperation and kinship definition is often reciprocal. If close kinsmen live together, then those who live together are close kin. If kinsmen make gifts of food, then gifts of food make kinsmen—the two are symbolically interconvertible forms of the transfer of substance. For as kinship is a code of conduct and not merely of reference, let alone genealogical reference, conduct becomes a code of kinship. We can be sure, then, that the categories of kinship are eminently practical, precisely in the measure that they are freely conceptual—and so become the very language of social experience.

Yet as Durkheim taught, there is no social experience for men apart from its conceptualization, and in the matter at hand it follows that giving birth is just as much a pretext of kinship as giving gifts. The first is equally subject to a social interpretation of relationships, and no more beholden than the second to genetic axioms. A third conclusion, then, is that kinship is a unique characteristic of human societies, distinguishable precisely by its freedom from natural relationships. When sociobiologists use the term "kinship," and mean by that "blood" connections, they imagine they are invoking the common tongue, and the common experience, of men and animals, or at least of men as animals. For them, this pre-Babelian concept refers to nothing else than facts of life: a connected series of procreative acts, upon which natural selection must operate. Yet in cultural practice it is birth that serves as the metaphor of kinship, not kinship as the expression of birth. Birth itself is nothing apart from the kinship system which defines it. But as an event within this cultural order, birth becomes the functional index of certain values of childhood and parentage, values which are never the only ones conceivable yet which integrate the persons concerned, within and beyond the family, in ways independent of their degrees of genetic connection. The relationships that may be traced on genealogical lines, such as matrilineal or patrilineal descent, respond to considerations of social identity and opposition external to the biological nexus as such; they are relationships imposed upon it, that organize it in the interest of a relative social scheme—and thereby distort it. This does not mean people will not trace their genealogies more or less widely and bilaterally. On the contrary, they will do so precisely because different kinds of consanguineal links are used to operate such distinctions as in-group and out-group and to stipulate the relations between them. So bilateral reckoning, for example, can be expected to become important just in the measure that patrilineal or matrilineal descent introduces a bias of kinship solidarity since it is the difference of kinship through males or females—itself irrelevant to genetic distance—that makes all the difference in social behavior. Genealogy thus serves to situate individuals in relation to one another, but according to qualitative values of solidarity that could never be discovered in the genetic connections as such.

Hence we say that the determination of kinship through acts of birth is just as arbitrary and creative as its establishment through acts of exchange or residence. Furthermore, as in the case of "aggression" and other human dispositions, the various emotions that may be mobilized around birth, though they be potentialities of biological evolution itself, are given a social effect only by the meanings (i.e., the kinship) culturally assigned to the event. Unique in this capacity of creative interpretation, humans alone formulate systems of kinship properly so-called; even as genealogy, being the product of this same capacity, operates in human society as the ideology of kinship, not its source. Because kinship categories give arbitrary values to genealogical relationships, sociobiologists have been forced to suppose that the categories are cultural mystifications of truer biological practices. It would be more accurate to say that insofar as kinship employs a code of births, it is a genealogical mystification of truly cultural practices. Paradoxically, then, whenever we see people ordering their social life on the premises of genealogy, it is good evidence that they are violating the dictates of genetics.

Fourth, it follows that human beings do not merely reproduce as physical or biological beings but as social beings: not in their capacities as self-mediating expressions of an entrepreneurial DNA but in their capacities as members of families and lineages, and in their statuses as cross cousins and chiefs. It follows too that what is reproduced in human cultural orders is not human beings *qua* human beings *but the system of social groups, categories, and relations in which they live.* The entities of social reproduction are precisely these culturally formulated groups and relations. Individuals of the same group may then figure as particulate expressions of the same inherent substance: they have a coefficient of relationship of 1, whatever their genealogical distance.

Conversely, their own persistence is not figured individually or as the mortality chances of their own genetic stock. They have an eternal existence as names as well as a spiritual destiny as ancestors or great men, for which the only guarantee may be a moral existence during life far removed from the selfish demands of an inclusive fitness. In these senses it can be understood that human reproduction is engaged as the means for the persistence of cooperative social orders, not the social order the means by which individuals facilitate their own reproduction.

The final, most fundamental conclusion must be that culture is the indispensable condition of this system of human organization and reproduction, with all its surprises for the biogenetic theory of social behavior. Human society is cultural, unique in virtue of its construction by symbolic means. E. O. Wilson says, "the highest form of tradition, by whatever criterion we choose to judge it, is of course human culture. But culture, aside from its involvement with language, which is truly unique, differs from animal tradition only in degree" (1975, p. 168). Literally, the statement is correct. If we were to disregard language, culture would differ from animal tradition only in degree. But precisely because of this "involvement with language"—a phrase hardly befitting serious scientific discourse—cultural social life differs from the animal in kind. It is not just the expression of an animal of another kind. The reason why human social behavior is not organized by the individual maximization of genetic interest is that human beings are not socially defined by their organic qualities but in terms of symbolic attributes; and a symbol is precisely a meaningful value—such as "close kinship" or "shared blood"—which cannot be determined by the physical properties of that to which it refers.

Toward a Coevolutionary Theory of Human Biology and Culture

William H. Durham

BIOLOGICAL AND CULTURAL EVOLUTION

According to neo-Darwinian evolutionary theory, the genetic traits of a given population of plants or animals track, over generations of time, one or more optimal character states that are specific to the organism and its environment. Changes in phenotype are thought to result most commonly from individual-level natural selection (together with some forms of kin and group selection), which acts to preserve those genotypes that direct the formation of phenotypes best suited to the prevailing conditions. This theory has now proven to be very successful in explaining the genetically coded traits of most organisms.

Particularly in human beings, however, there is an important nongenetic or cultural component of phenotypes. What was apparently selected for during the organic evolution of human beings was *an unusual capability for modifying and extending phenotypes on the basis of learning and experience.* Within limits, culture enables us to alter and build onto aspects of morphology, physiology, and behavior without any corresponding change in genotype. This means, of course, that natural selection by itself is neither adequate nor appropriate for explaining

I thank Robert Boyd, Kathleen Durham, David Gordon, Brian Hazlett, Sarah Blaffer Hrdy, Frank Livingstone, Marlene Palmer, Elizabeth Perry, Roy Rappaport, Peter Richerson, Eric Smith, Victoria Sork, Joel Samoff, Alfred Sussman, John Vandermeer, and Jim Wood for thoughtful discussion and criticism of this work.

William H. Durham is in the Department of Anthropology at Stanford University, Stanford, California.

the culturally acquired phenotypic traits of human beings.

Anthropologists realized long ago that nonbiological process or processes were behind the cultural component of human phenotypes, and they have led the search for alternative models or theories for the evolution of this important cultural aspect. A wide variety of theories are explicit and implicit in the anthropological literature (see, e.g., Kaplan and Manners, 1972) and a number of them have been successful at explaining some within-group and between-group variations in human culture. Curiously, a large number of these models represent a process of selective retention analogous in some sense to natural selection (Campbell, 1965 and 1975; Durham 1976a), although the phenotypes retained in time would be those which best suited a given *cultural* criterion. Unfortunately, there has been little agreement to date regarding the effective criterion or criteria behind any such cultural selection. The list of candidate criteria now includes free energy, satisfaction, profit, population regulation, homeostasis, and even ease of replication of a cultural instruction. Again, each has proven useful for the analysis of cultural characteristics in certain societies, but none has proven adequate for a general theory.

Part of the problem has been that, in the search for theories to explain cultural phenomena, one key factor has been continually overlooked, and that factor has much to do with the relationship between human biology and culture. Many scholars have failed to appreciate that the organic evolution of the *capacity* for culture had, at least at one time, important implications for the actual *process* of cultural evolution. What was presumably genetically selected for in our ancestors was an increasing ability to modify phenotypes through learning and experience, but it was selected for only because those ancestors persistently used that abilty to enhance their survival and reproduction.The capacity for culture, one could say, continued to evolve not merely because it *enabled* superior adaptations, but also because it was used to *produce* superior adaptations. Our hominid ancestors must therefore have had ways of keeping culture "on track" of the adaptive optima as those optima varied from place to place and time to time. The conclusion is important: as the capacity for culture evolved, *the developing culture characterizing a group of people, whatever else it was, must have been adaptive for them in terms of survival and reproduction.*

It is important to note that this conclusion does not require that the cultural meaning of things was consciously or unconsciously related to their survival and reproduction consequences. It means only that, however culture changed and evolved, and whatever meaning was given by people to their cultural attributes, the net effect of those attributes was to enhance human survival and reproduction. There is an important deduction from this argument. Although a coevolutionary theory can potentially contribute to an understanding of the adaptive significance of cultural attributes, it is not necessarily the key to understanding the meaning and symbolic significance people may give to those attributes (see also Sahlins, 1976).

Obviously things have changed since the days when the capacity for culture was evolving because it was used by protohominids to produce superior adaptations. It is appropriate to ask whether culture is still used by human beings as a way to enhance their survival and reproduction. Have we lost the ability to keep culture "on track"? Has cultural evolution by some other principle of optimization, for example, more recently run counter to individual survival and reproduction, and has culture therefore lost its original adaptive significance for human existence?

It is, of course, impossible to give a definitive answer at this time, but for a number of reasons I am inclined to think that there is still an important adaptive dimension to human cultural attributes. These reasons can be divided into two parts: those related to the action of cultural selection within groups, and those related to cultural selection between groups.

CULTURAL SELECTION WITHIN GROUPS

For convenience in the description of levels of cultural selection, I will define *social group* to be any subset of a deme or breeding population containing individuals whose survival and reproduction are directly and substantially interdependent because of interactions among them. It can be thought of as a collection of individuals whose behavior creates at least a given arbitrary amount of interdependence so that the collection is bounded by frontiers of far less interdependence. Of course there are a whole variety of forms of interdependence, including ties arising from goods and services exchanged between members, but for most of the arguments that follow, the specific nature of interdependence is not important. It may be helpful here to think of a deme as some entire ethnolinguistic population or "culture" and to think of social groups as smaller, more interdependent camps, bands, or villages within that population.

Basic to any theory of cultural change and adaptation, of course, is the way in which distinct human social groups acquire their cultural attributes. In this section, I propose the hypotheses (1) that the cultural characteristics of human social groups result to a large extent from internal, individual-level selective retention, and more importantly, (2) that this process generally selects for cultural attributes that enhance the ability of their carriers to survive and reproduce.

My reasons are these. First, I believe that there is ample evidence that some process of selective retention continues to operate on the accumulation and modification of cultural attributes within human societies. People remain somehow selective in their receptivity to cultural innovation, for we know that many more innovations are introduced by invention and diffusion that are retained at length within any given society. Second, I believe that this ongoing selective retention is, and always has been, influenced by a number of human biases which tend to keep people from selectively retaining cultural attributes that run counter to their individual survival and reproduction, provided they have a choice. Of these, perhaps the most important are learned biases. Robert LeVine (1973) has argued that the process of socialization teaches children from an early age not only adherence to social norms and traditional patterns of behavior, but also selectivity in the adoption of new forms—a selectivity based on what is held to be adaptive and "for their own good".

Two properties of this bias make it particularly important. First, the development of this selectivity is at least partly in the *combined interest* of the parents, the child, and even the social group as a whole. To some extent, all participants in the process have their own survival and reproduction at stake (this is not to deny some amount of conflict between these interests). Second, it is urgent. Because of the unusual vulnerability of children, the ability or inability to discriminate between positively and negatively adaptive practices in childhood can have direct and immediate consequences in addition to long-term effects.

A second sort of bias might be called the bias of "satisfaction" (see Ruyle, 1973 and 1977). Presumably throughout the organic evolution of hominids there was a persistent, genetic selective advantage for a neurophysiology which rewarded with sensory reinforcements and a feeling of "satisfaction" those acts likely to enhance survival and reproduction, and which produced unpleasant, distressing, or painful feedback in response to potentially dangerous behaviors. When the capacity for culture began evolving, there was already some built-in bias of this kind, biologically programmed in the design of the prehuman nervous system. Eugene Ruyle, among others, has argued that the selective retention of cultural traits has continued to be influenced by the general sense of "satisfaction" that they do or do not bring to their bearer. While we disagree over the definition and relative utility of the concept of satisfaction, I concur with Ruyle that cultural evolution has probably not ignored nor completely overridden the feedback from the neurophysiology that we are born with (cf. Durham, 1977). I agree that "square wheels, crooked spears, and sickly children are unlikely to provide much satisfaction" (Ruyle, 1977, p. 54), but I feel that this is because they are unlikely to do much for survival and reproduction.

There is potentially a third source of bias to be found in the learning structures and functions of the human brain, although I hasten to add that this possibility remains not well documented at present. A knowledge of the structures and functions of the human brain is certainly crucial to understanding the relationship between biology and culture, but I have not been persuaded by hard-core genetic structuralists (e.g., Laughlin and d'Aquili, 1974) that there is a determinism rather than a bias to be found therein. To my knowledge, the best evidence of any learning "canalization" that might affect culture comes from studies by Seligman (1971) showing that some common human phobias are learned with an exposure and rapidity that suggests that these may represent a form of "prepared learning." Other examples of prepared learning have been documented for nonhuman animal species, where they are thought to result from built-in neurophysiological mechanisms of the brain. To the extent that there is a bias on culture imposed by the biochemistry and physiology of the human brain, the organic evolution of that organ would mean a bias in favor of the selective retention of more rather than less adaptive cultural traits.

A fourth kind of bias, which might be called "circumstantial bias", has been suggested recently by Cloak (1977) and Alexander (1978). This kind of bias may occur when the customary organization of child-rearing practices and enculturation in a social group ensure some regularity of learning and reinforcement for culture carriers. Consider the simple example where parents customarily rear and enculturate their own children. "Wherever that is true, a cultural instruction whose behavior helps its human carrier-enactor (or his/her relatives) to acquire more children thereby has more little heads to get copied into." As a result, cultural instructions that enhance survival and reproduction will differentially propagate through social groups as generations go by, "until most extant cultural instructions have that effect" (Cloak, 1977, p. 50).

These four biases (and possibly others unrecognized and undiscovered) taken together represent a reasonably strong probabilistic "force" tending to keep culture on track of the adaptive optima. This force would operate at the level of individual human beings and bias them as culture carriers. As a result, individuals would tend to select and retain from competing variants those cultural practices whose net phenotypic effect best enhances their individual ability to survive and reproduce (Durham, 1976a and b). Hypothetically, this process of cultural selection would result in the spread and maintenance of cultural attributes that are adaptive in the general biological sense of contributing to their bearer's reproductive success. To be more explicit, I hypothesize that cultural features of human phenotypes are commonly *designed to promote the success of an individual human being in his or her natural and sociocultural environment* and, to be consistent with the biological meaning of adaptation, I suggest that *success is best measured by the extent to which the attribute permits individuals to survive and reproduce and thereby contribute genes to later generations of the population of which they are members* (adapted from Williams, 1966, p. 97).

Several implications of this hypothesis deserve elaboration. First, it suggests that successful adaptation be measured by the long-term representation of an individual's genes in a population, a quantity which ecologists and evolutionary biologists often call "individual inclusive fitness" (see, for example, Williams, 1966; Alexander, 1974; West Eberhard, 1975), even though the phenotypic traits in question here need have no special genetic basis whatsoever. This suggestion often leaves both biologists and anthropologists a bit uncomfortable—anthropologists because even cultural ecologists are not accustomed to think in explicit terms of "reproductive success" and "genetic representation" and biologists because they are used to thinking that transmissible repro-ductive differentials measured between phenotypes are always the result of differences in genotype. Indeed, for rigorous population genetics, fitness is conventionally defined *between genotypes* in a given environ-ment. With culture, however, inter-individual differences in the long-term representation of genes can result from acquired phenotypes that have no special underlying genotype. Put differently, the representation of a wide variety of genotypes may actually benefit (they may or may not benefit equally) from a given cultural phenotypic change. To mini-mize confusion on this matter I therefore suggest that *individual inclusive fitness* be used to refer to the long-term representation of an individual's genes in a population, and *genotypic inclusive fitness* be used to refer to the differential representation of explicit genotypes. Where differences in phenotypes result from genetic differences between organisms, indi-vidual inclusive fitness contributes to the genotypic fitnesses of particular genotypes and there is no problem. However, for humans where pheno-types may be culturally altered, extended, and transmitted, individual inclusive fitness differentials can result from phenotypes with no special genotypic basis. The analysis of the adaptive significance of cultural attributes thus requires a focus on individuals, their phenotypes, and associated differences in reproductive success. With these qualifications in mind, I suggest that relative, individual inclusive fitness (as approxi-mated by the long-term differential reproductive success of an individual and appropriately weighted kin) remains the best measure by which to assess the adaptiveness of a given biological and/or cultural trait.

Second, an important distinction must be made between "the extent and effectiveness of design for survival" and the actual reproduction record of a given individual or sample (cf. Williams, 1966). There may always be chance effects that render a trait in a given case maladaptive or suboptimal. Furthermore, the extent and effectiveness must be judged relative to the particular environment in which the adaptation arose. Third, the analysis of the adaptiveness of a characteristic must always be made in consideration of the alternative phenotypes historically or presently available in a given social context. At any given time, the nature of culture change and the rate of this change will be affected by the availability of alternative forms and the degree of relative advan-tage and disadvantage among them. Adaptiveness must then be seen as a statement of relative, not absolute, advantage among phenotypes.

To summarize, I hypothesize (1) that human beings are not just passively receptive to cultural innovation but (2) that we have and develop a number of selective biases which result in (3) a tendency to acquire those aspects of phenotype which past experience and some degree of prediction suggest to be most advantageous for personal inclusive fitness. Although the resulting process of cultural selection would normally result in adaptive phenotypic attributes, I should point out that it is actually easier to conceive of cultural influences getting "off track" in the evolution of a phenotype than it is for biological influences. Maladaptive cultural practices *can* be maintained at substantial frequency in a population, particularly when the biases previously mentioned are overridden or prevented from functioning by force, threat, misinformation, or restrictions on alternatives. Maladaptive behaviors can also recur through the conscious or deliberate choice of individuals to behave counter to their reproductive interests, but I am suggesting that this behavior is not likely to become a long-lasting cultural tradition. I am reminded of the "rather extreme example" mentioned in Ruyle (1973, p. 206) of "a religious sect in nineteenth-century Russia whose cultural pool contained a total ban on sexual intercourse. Lacking an adequate alternative method of recruitment, the sect disappeared."

Where circumstances do permit the preceding biases to operate, however, culture would hypothetically evolve to an important extent by the selective retention of nongenetic traits that enhance the ability of human beings to survive and reproduce in their particular habitats (Durham, 1976a and b). In principle, this cultural selection may proceed consciously or unconsciously and it may ironically proceed according to any number of other "proximate" or "cognized" criteria (like free energy yield, homeostasis, etc.) that are closely correlated with the reproductive success of human beings in the environment concerned. In fact, the process may proceed through selective retention not related in any obvious way to reproduction or survival as long as the net effect enhances (or at least does not reduce) the relative fitness of the culture carrier. In this way, cultural characteristics may take on a meaning and value which themselves are not explained by individual inclusive fitness, although their adaptive consequences may be.

Michael Harner (1973, p. 152) implied a way to summarize this hypothesis for cultural selection within groups when he wrote that "culture is learned and transmitted through human effort; therefore it seems unlikely that cultural institutions and traits can be successfully passed on through centuries and millenia without having some regular reinforcement for their maintenance." For the sake of simplicity, let us say that the individual effort involved in culture increases monotonically over the range of a metric phenotypic trait that is culturally variable. Further, let us assume that these "phenotypic costs" to an individual from the effort and/or risk associated with the cultural trait are proportional over the range to any "fitness costs," however slight, of maintaining and perpetuating the practice (see the cost curve figure). What I

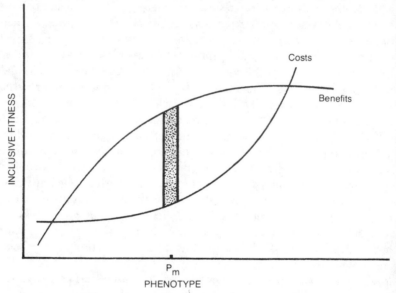

am suggesting here is that individual-level cultural selection would act in time to increase the frequency of any available phenotype whose resulting net fitness benefits (total benefits minus costs) conferred a differential reproductive advantage relative to other phenotypes. In other words, the reinforcement proposed by Harner is largely to be found in the inclusive fitness benefits of culture. Cultural selection as used here could then be "directional," "stabilizing," or "disruptive" analogous to the modes of natural selection, depending on the shape of the cost and benefit curves. The cost curve figure shows a hypothetical case for stabilizing cultural selection. In an environment where the costs and benefits shown as a function of phenotype persist for some time, the hypothesized process of cultural selection would result in convergence on the intermediate phenotype P_m which effectively maximizes human survival and reproduction in that environment. It should be emphasized that such a trait would spread by individual-level selective retention to all individuals in the given social group for whom these costs and benefits apply. The trait could also spread by diffusion to other groups in the same deme or even other demes. If it continued there to confer individual fitness benefits, this phenotype could spread still further by individual-level selective retention.

One final qualification must be included in this argument. A large number, perhaps even a majority, of the identifiable cultural aspects of human phenotypes involve extremely low fitness costs and/or benefits for their carriers. Cultural traits in some cases may be virtually inconsequential to inclusive fitness and there may be essentially no relative fitness advantage among existing alternative forms. With little basis for fitness discrimination, the hypothesized process of cultural selection would not be effective for these traits. The spread and perpetuation of recognizably low-cost attributes are then likely to be better explained in other ways (like momentary phenotypic reward or arbitrary symbolic value). As I have argued elsewhere (Durham, 1976a), the importance of inclusive fitness to our understanding of human cultural attributes is therefore expected to be conditionally dependent upon the degree to which an attribute taxes the highly variable time, energy, and resource budgets of individuals. My belief is that there are few, if any, cultural practices that are maintained in the absence of force or threat and persist even though individual parents would achieve substantially higher fitness without them or by available alternative practices.

This argument suggests that where cultural evolution proceeds through a process of selective retention within groups, resulting attributes are not likely to require what may be called "fitness altruism" by any individual. Cultural selection, like natural selection, would incessantly oppose any phenotype whose net effect was to assist reproductive competitors in the same population. (Alexander, 1974, makes this point for genetic selection.) This does not mean that cultural selection somehow precludes mutual assistance. On the contrary, cooperative phenotypes would have a cultural selective advantage in any circumstance where joint effort results in mutually enhanced fitness. Nor does this imply that cultural selection within groups necessarily opposes all forms of self-sacrifice. There are now a number of theories showing ways in which genetically based social altruism may actually increase fitness and thereby evolve by natural selection: for example, through reciprocity (Trivers, 1971), mate selection (Blaney, 1976), social rewards (Ghiselin, 1974), and kin selection (Hamilton, 1964). To the extent that cultural evolution is complementary to organic evolution, as I propose, analogous processes may favor cultural forms of social altruism that actually require no net fitness altruism (see also Durham, n.d.).

CULTURAL SELECTION BETWEEN GROUPS

Where the spread of some cultural trait within a group or population can be traced to an individual-level process, the preceding arguments may appear plausible. Problems arise, however, when a trait spreads through a deme or between demes because of some group-level process. Where the selective retention of cultural evolution results from group selection, it is not altogether obvious that individual-level fitness costs and benefits are particularly relevant to understanding changes in the distribution of phenotypes.

As with organic evolution, where an individual- versus group-selection debate has been argued for over a decade, the important question concerns not the possibility of cultural selection at group and higher levels, but rather the relative effectiveness and direction of selection at those levels. When the two processes work in the same direction, either for or against a given cultural variant, there is no problem. They are likely to have complementary and reinforcing effects. Two questions arise, however, when individual- and group-level processes run in opposition. (1) Can group-level cultural selection retain cultural traits advantageous to group reproduction (making it less likely that the group will go extinct or more likely that the group will propagate and colonize), even though they decrease individual inclusive fitness and are therefore altruistic? (2) Can individual-level cultural selection maintain traits advantageous to individuals while simultaneously being detrimental to the group?

Again, a definitive answer is difficult at present because of our general ignorance of the processes behind cultural change and because of the paramount importance of situation-specific variables (like rates of innovation, diffusion, group extinction, etc.) to the outcome. However, if we assume that individual-level selection operates continuously and rapidly when choice is available, it is reasonable to hypothesize that the answer to (1) is negative, in general, judging from parallel arguments in organic evolutionary theory (reviewed in Maynard Smith, 1976). The *origin* of an altruistic phenotype by cultural processes would require that groups be small for there to be, through "cultural drift" or some "founder effect," no alternative phenotype more individually beneficial within the groups to be selected. In addition, the *maintenance* of the altruistic trait would then depend on there being low rates of introduction of alternative "selfish" variants to groups of altruists (as through diffusion, migration, and invention) at the same time as rapid extinction of groups where any selfish variant is found. These conditions may well obtain in special circumstances, and there groups of altruists could prevail. In general, though, group selection is not likely to be the mechanism maintaining the frequency of altruistic cultural traits. Where fitness altruism exists, it is more likely a result of incomplete or impeded individual-level selection, and therefore only a characteristic of certain individuals within a group.

When individual selection is not permitted to function as described above, it is hypothetically possible for group selection to aid in the perpetuation of altruistic cultural attributes. Consider a social system in which force or misinformation may be used by some members of a social group to create a degree of altruism in others that is not likely to result from the operation of individual selection under noncoercive conditions. If that altruism is then put to use to lower the probability of group extinction or raise the probability of group reproduction, group selection could favor that social system, which in turn would perpetrate the coercive practices creating real altruism. A few altruists could be especially effective in group selection by intergroup aggression.

My hypothesis would be that the answer to question (2) is also likely to be negative. In most cases, the long-term reproductive success of an individual human being is dependent upon a stable, functioning social group for any number of group benefits (e.g., increased security or efficiency of resource harvest, defense of resources and progeny). Where these benefits are real and apparent, individual-level cultural selection would act to constrain selfishness to a group-preserving form. This argument implies that cultural selection cannot be seen as leading to some sort of universal adaptive optimization, but rather to relatively beneficial compromises required by group living. In order to obtain the benefits of sociality for self and descendants, an individual must behave in ways that at least do not eliminate some net benefit of sociality for others. Where social benefits are real and apparent, the result of cultural selection would likely be norms, rules and cultural controls on excessively selfish individual behaviors in the interest of preserving group integrity.

That individual- and group-level cultural selection are unlikely to be successful in opposing one another in the long run does not mean that group selection is without important consequences for understanding cultural evolution. As a number of authors have now argued, the *acceleration* of changes made possible by group-level extinction and replacement may be the key to understanding the rapid pace of the evolution of *Homo sapiens* (see discussion in Durham, 1976a). Once a trait like P_m gets established by individual-level cultural selection within a social group, that trait may then give its bearers an advantage as a group in competition with other groups. Group selection may then result, reinforcing the spread of the cultural trait within the population. This form of group selection has the interesting property of conserving or even enhancing the original relative fitness value of the trait for the individual culture carriers.

A COEVOLUTIONARY SYNTHESIS

In the preceding sections, I have proposed that processes of cultural selection operating within and between human social groups generally result in the selective retention of cultural traits, including behaviors, that past experience and some degree of prediction suggest to be most advantageous to the inclusive fitnesses of individual members. To the extent that this proposition is valid, cultural selection would remain functionally complementary to natural selection, although there need be no genetic basis to the selected aspects of phenotype. Operationally, the process would also be independent of organic evolution—rendering it thus more rapid, better able to track environmental change or stability, and at times even responsive to perceived human need. At the same time, cultural attributes which evolved in this way could have the interesting property of reducing or eliminating organic selection pressures. Similar phenotypic traits acquired by different genotypes may make the genotypes equally or more equally "fit" (Durham, 1976a). As Dobzhansky (1951) once put it, "The transmission of culture short-circuits biological heredity." On the other hand, cultural change has the opposite potential of creating new and different organic selection pressures (cf. Washburn, 1959 and 1960; Geertz, 1973).

The combination of these features gives reason to believe that cultural selection may account for the origin and maintenance of more forms of human social behavior than do mutation and transgenerational changes in the frequency of presumed behavior genes. It will be seen that this theory of cultural evolution shifts the burden of proof for any explicitly biological basis for adaptive human behaviors over to the sociobiologists. Until we have direct and compelling evidence that a given human behavior has a discrete genetic basis, the demonstration that such behavior has adaptive functions does not by any means prove it to be the product of natural selection. Chances are good that it is partly, largely, or even entirely a product of cultural selection. Biologists interested in human adaptations would therefore do well to make explicit allowance for the cultural mechanism for the transmission of traits in a population.

While distinguishable on the basis of their means of transmission, biological and cultural inheritance by the arguments above would be functionally complementary. Indeed, the biological influences molded by natural selection and the cultural influences molded by cultural selection could easily be confounded in human phenotypes. Consequently, I suggest that models for the evolution of human social behaviors should explicitly integrate both the genetic and the cultural inheritance mechanisms.

Simply stated, my hypothesis is that the selective retention in biological *and* cultural evolution generally favors those attributes which increase, or at least do not decrease, the ability of individual human beings to survive and reproduce in their natural and social environments. This perspective has the advantage of explaining both how human biology and culture can often be adaptive in the same sense (cf. Durham, 1976a), and how they may interact in the evolution of human attributes. In addition, a coevolutionary view can explain the adaptive significance of human social behaviors without forcing them into natural selection models—indeed without forcing *any* separation of the confounded influences of genes and culture.

For the analysis of adaptive patterns in human social behavior I therefore suggest that "Selection" (capital S) be used to refer to the selective retention of differentially advantageous phenotypic traits by the fitness criterion regardless of whether the predominant process is a variety of cultural selection or of natural selection.

A coevolutionary perspective implies that for both biological and cultural reasons the interdependence of individual fitnesses among members of a social group can be viewed as the social glue that holds human (and nonhuman) groups together. It further suggests that the *kinds* of fitness interdependence among individuals (e.g., interdependence based on kinship, control of resources, or exchange of goods and services) and the *relative degree* of interdependencies can be used to define "social structure" in a population. Social structure from this point of view reflects the fact that not all individuals in a social group are interdependent in the same way or to the same degree. Indeed, structural asymmetries in dependence relations can give rise to a degree of manipulative control by some over the behavior of others (Durham, n.d.). In extreme cases, these structural constraints on the adaptations of individuals within society can result in behaviors which appear to require altruistic reproductive sacrifice. I should point out, however, that to those in control, manipulated behaviors may accrue handsome survival and reproduction benefits. For those being manipulated, on the other hand, such behavior can actually be seen as another adaptive compromise required by powerful structural constraints. For this reason, social structure defined by fitness relations deserves to be considered an integral part of an individual's environment. Structural influences on the adaptations of individuals may have major effects upon the joint biocultural evolution of social behaviors within a group.

Human intergroup aggression constitutes a particularly suitable form of social behavior for testing the coevolutionary approach and many of the preceding arguments about biology, culture, and levels of selection. Not only is intergroup warfare commonly held to be dysfunctional for the individual participants, but it is also one of the more obvious mechanisms for high frequency group selection in human organic and cultural evolution. Coevolutionary theory suggests the following hypothesis. Human social behaviors, including intergroup aggression, are generally adaptive (i.e., individual fitness-enhancing) for all participants. Where there are exceptions, so that net reproductive sacrifice is demanded of some or all participants, this is either because of some unusual degree of group selection or because of coercive manipulation within a social system. From this, the need arises to analyze how human intergroup aggression is organized and conducted, paying special attention to the distribution of costs and benefits among the participants.

Elsewhere, I have begun an attempt at such an analysis by comparing aspects of intergroup warfare as waged by members of some "primitive" human societies with models for the coevolution of adaptive intergroup aggression in social groups faced with resource competition (Durham, 1976b and n.d.). The models suggest that "individually sacrificial participation in organized group aggression" may have non-obvious fitness benefits in two ways. First, where human groups compete for limited resources, participants in successful group aggression may themselves directly benefit from the fitness value of resources defended or acquired. The requirements for this to be adaptive are only that the spoils must be shared not throughout the deme but within the group or subgroup of aggressors, so that the fitness value of resources gained by each participant exceeds his or her accumulated costs. Second, intergroup aggression may have circuitous benefits such that when the participants do not each derive direct resource benefits from the conflict, their fitness costs are more than compensated by other benefits from within the group. For this to be adaptive, at least one important figure in the group must secure resource benefits from the war, and the benefactors must provide other goods and/or services upon which the other participants' fitnesses depend. What appears to be the self-sacrificing participation of warriors in this case may actually be an imperative for them to continue receiving other benefits from within the group.

These two models for group aggression suggest that knowledge of group structure (i.e., fitness interdependencies among individuals within the group), of the factors or resources constraining the reproductive success of some or all individuals, and of fitness costs likely to be incurred when rival groups clash, allows the prediction or explanation of group-level human behavior. In both cases, this information gives direct means for predicting the characteristics of groups from the behavior of individuals.

The reinterpretation of ethnographic descriptions of primitive warfare in terms of these models reveals that at least some cases of human intergroup aggression can be seen as biocultural adaptation to conditions of competition for limiting resources. The evidence suggests that to an important extent processes of organic and cultural evolution both result in the selective retention of phenotypic traits that enhance the ability of individual human beings to survive and reproduce in a given environment. This finding calls into question the continued practice of analyzing human social behaviors in terms of natural selection models alone, for such analyses consider only one aspect of what may be truly coevolutionary influences on human social behavior.

SUMMARY AND CONCLUSION

Because the capacity for culture allows human beings to modify aspects of phenotype without any concomitant genotypic change, I have argued that it makes no sense to view the evolution of human attributes, including social behavior, solely in terms of the natural selection models of sociobiology. Instead, I have suggested that a process of "cultural selection" functionally complements natural selection by retaining in time those cultural variants whose net effect best enhances the inclusive fitnesses of individuals. Where cultural selection operates in this way, human phenotypes would then evolve *subject to both biological and cultural influences* in the direction of character states that maximize inclusive fitness under prevailing environmental conditions (for additional discussion, see Durham, 1976 a and b).

As I have argued, this coevolutionary perspective has the advantage of explaining both how human biology and culture are often adaptive in the same sense, and how they may interact in the evolution of human attributes. This theory, moreover, contains an important irony. If cultural differences between human societies are largely the result of individual-level cultural selection for more rather than less adaptive traits (possibly reinforced by a process of group selection), then our capacity for culture is a capacity to reduce or even eliminate many of the organic selection pressures that would have favored the refinements of genetic control required by theories which rely solely on the mechanism of natural selection. Put differently, the operation of cultural selection—what some would call only a "proximate" mechanism—may at times replace and preclude the operation of natural selection—which then cannot be considered the "ultimate" mechanism. In short, this theory can explain the biocultural evolution of human attributes without presuming a genetic basis or predisposition for all adaptive forms. To the extent that humans do behave in ways that maximize their individual inclusive fitnesses, this would suggest that it is generally for both cultural and biological reasons.

This coevolutionary view of human biology and culture may be of help to human ecologists and cultural ecologists who have studied human adaptation but have often failed to identify exactly who benefits from a given practice and how in fact they do benefit. It suggests, for example, a renewed emphasis on individuals and their problems of survival and reproduction in society. This may lead to new interpretations of ethnographic studies which have commonly focused on group-level behaviors. It also suggests new directions for future research. Measures of reproductive success may prove useful both as analytic tools for understanding specific social behaviors and as modeling devices for formulating new research questions. This kind of approach should be most helpful where the "costs" of a given practice can be factored out in terms of time, energy, and resources and where it is possible to detect associated differentials in reproductive benefit. Thus I suggest that coevolutionary analysis is most appropriate in studies of medical anthropology, nutrition and food taboos, human intergroup aggression, population regulation and demography, migration, trade and exchange, and other "high-cost" practices. I believe that the theory is also adequate for predicting its own limitations. Considering the abundance of day-to-day cultural practices which involve little time, energy, or resource cost, I reemphasize that this argument does not say that everything we do is best explained in terms of reproductive success.

The approach suggested here bears some resemblance to recent works by Ruyle (1973), Cloak (1975), Campbell (1975), Richerson and Boyd (in press), and Dawkins (1976, Chapter 11). These authors hypothesize, as I do, that the mechanism of cultural evolution can operate independently of the mechanism of natural selection. But they go further than I go to suggest that the differential replication of cultural attributes is independent of the individual fitness criterion as well. Dawkins, for example, proposes the term "meme" to refer to the basic conceptual unit of cultural transmission; he argues in a fashion similar to the other authors that competition among memes results in a selection process (analogous to natural selection) favoring "memes which exploit their cultural environment to *their own advantage*" (p. 213, emphasis added). Like Dawkins, I believe that it is important to ask what gives memes stability and penetrance in their cultural environment, but unlike Dawkins and the others, I argue that the fate of a meme in its pool usually depends upon the meme's fitness costs and benefits to *carriers.* A coevolutionary perspective does not postulate the gradual and cumulative organic evolution of an organ (the brain) that often functions antagonistically to natural selection. It seems to me that other interpretations do.

In conclusion, instead of prolonging once again the debate of biology versus culture, nature versus nurture, and instinct versus learning, I believe real gains in understanding human social behavior can now be made in several ways. First, we must concentrate our efforts on theories which integrate human biology and culture in the study of human adaptation (see also Durham, 1976b). Again, I suggest that "Selection" (capital S) be used to refer to the selective retention of differentially advantageous phenotypic traits by the fitness criterion regardless of whether the predominant process is a variety of cultural selection or of natural selection. Second, we need to examine the specific processes of selective retention in operation so that more may be learned about the mechanisms of cultural selection within and between groups. This endeavor has the interesting prospect of adding a historical dimension to theories of adaptation, allowing practices observed in the "ethnographic present" to be studied in light of their specific paths of coevolution.

Third, we need to develop theories of transition between organizational levels, so that knowledge of behavior on one level can be used to predict behavior on another level. Paradoxically, in all of this, there is a new danger of overemphasizing individuals as independent entities. Gains will be made when individual-level theorists remember that the adaptations of individuals are not independent, nor dependent solely because of shared genes. The effort to understand the characteristics of groups and social systems beginning with a focus on individuals will need a better theory of "interest group" activities, where interest groups are defined by any form of fitness interdependence, including control of access to strategic resources. Related to this is a need for incorporating social structure into coevolutionary models for human social behavior.

Finally, in addition to any understanding of the present gained by a coevolutionary view of the past, the insights from these endeavors should prove useful as tools for contemporary social change.

REFERENCES

Alexander, R. D. (1974). "The Evolution of Social Behavior." *Ann. Rev. Ecol. Syst.* 5, pp. 325–383.

———. In press. "Evolution, Human Behavior, and Determinism." *Proc. Phil. Sci.*

Blaney, P. H. (1976). Comment on "Genetic Basis of Behavior—Especially of Altruism." *Amer. Psych.* 31, p. 358.

Blurton Jones, N. G. (1976). "Growing Points in Human Ethology: Another Link Between Ethology and the Social Sciences?" In P. P. G. Bateson and R. A. Hinde, eds., *Growing Points in Ethology* (Cambridge, England: Cambridge University Press), pp. 427–450.

Campbell, D. T. (1965). "Variation and Selective Retention in Sociocultural Evolution." In H. R. Barringer, G. I. Blankstein, and R. W. Mack, eds., *Social Change in Developing Areas: A Re-interpretation of Evolutionary Theory* (Cambridge, Mass.: Schenckman), pp. 19–49.

———. (1975). "On the Conflicts between Biological and Social Evolution and between Psychology and Moral Tradition." *Amer. Psych.* 30, pp. 1103–1126.

Cloak, F. T. Jr. (1975). "Is a Cultural Ethology Possible?" *Human Ecology* 3, no. 3, pp. 161–182.

———. (1977). Comment on "The Adaptive Significance of Cultural Behavior." *Human Ecology* 5, no. 1, pp. 49–52.

Dawkins, R. (1976). *The Selfish Gene* (Oxford: Oxford University Press).

Dobzhansky, T. (1951). "Human Diversity and Adaptation." Cold Spring Harbor Symposium on Quantitative Biology 15 (1950), pp. 385–400.

Durham, W. H. (1976a). "The Adaptive Significance of Cultural Behavior." *Human Ecology* 4, no. 2, pp. 89–121.

———. (1976b). "Resource Competition and Human Aggression, Part I: A Review of Primitive War." *Quart. Rev. Biol.* 51, no. 3, pp. 385–415.

———. (1977). Reply to comments on "The Adaptive Significance of Cultural Behavior." *Human Ecology* 5, no. 1, pp. 59–68.

———. n.d. "Resource Competition and Human Aggression, Part II: Dependence and Manipulation." Unpublished manuscript.

Geertz, C. (1973). *The Interpretation of Cultures* (New York: Basic Books).

Ghiselin, M. T. (1974). *The Economy of Nature and the Evolution of Sex* (Berkeley, Calif.: University of California Press).

Hamilton, W. D. (1964). "The Genetical Evolution of Social Behavior." *J. Theor. Biol.* 7, pp. 1–52.

Harner, M. J., ed. (1973). *Hallucinogens and Shamanism* (New York: Oxford Press).

Kaplan, D. and R. A. Manners. (1972). *Culture Theory* (Englewood Cliffs, N.J.: Prentice-Hall).

Laughlin, C. D. and E. G. d'Aquili. (1974). *Biogenetic Structuralism* (New York: Columbia University Press).

LeVine, R. A. (1973). *Culture, Behavior, and Personality* (Chicago: Aldine).

Maynard Smith, J. (1976). "Commentary: Group Selection." *Quart. Rev. Biol.* 51, no. 2, pp. 277–283.

Richerson, P. J. and R. Boyd. In press. "A Dual Inheritance Model of the Human Evolutionary Process." *Journal of Human and Social Biology.*

Ruyle, E. E. (1973). "Genetic and Cultural Pools: Some Suggestions for a Unified Theory of Biocultural Evolution." *Human Ecology* 1, no. 3, pp. 201–215.

———. (1977). Comment on "The Adaptive Significance of Cultural Behavior." *Human Ecology* 5, no. 1, pp. 53–55.

Sahlins, M. (1976). *The Use and Abuse of Biology* (Ann Arbor: University of Michigan Press).

Seligman, M. (1971). "Phobias and Preparedness." *Behavior Therapy* 2, pp. 307–320.

Simpson, G. G. (1972). "The Evolutionary Concept of Man." In B. Campbell, ed., *Sexual Selection and the Descent of Man* (Chicago: Aldine), pp. 17–39.

Washburn, S. L. (1959). "Speculations on the Interrelations of Tools and Biological Evolution." In J. M. Spuhler, ed., *The Evolution of Man's Capacity for Culture* (Detroit: Wayne State University Press), pp. 21–31.

———. (1960). "Tools and Human Evolution." *Sci. Am.* 203, pp. 63–75.

West Eberhard, M. J. (1975). "The Evolution of Social Behavior by Kin Selection." *Quart. Rev. Biol.* 50, no. 1, pp. 1–33.

Williams, G. C. (1966). *Adaptation and Natural Selection* (Princeton, N.J.: Princeton University Press).

Sociobiology and Politics

Steven A. Peterson and Albert Somit

Humans have long speculated about the nature of political man and the wellsprings of political behavior. Given the recent advances in biology, it was almost inevitable that some students of politics would look to the life sciences for guidance. In political science, this movement has been termed "biopolitics," the study of the linkage between biology and politics.

With the recent emergence of sociobiology, political scientists have become even more sensitive to the relevance of work being done in biology for understanding political man. In this essay, we discuss the implications of sociobiology for political science. First, since it both preceded and established a receptivity to sociobiology, we note briefly the development and major concerns of biopolitics. Second, we discuss some of the possible implications of sociobiology for political science, with special attention to long-standing issues in political philosophy. Finally, we point out some limitations in the sociobiological approach to politics.

I. THE RISE OF CONTEMPORARY BIOPOLITICS

Over the centuries there have been repeated attempts to use biological theory—or biological metaphor—to explain political behavior.[1] For example, John of Salisbury argued in *Policraticus* that society was analo-

Steven A. Peterson is in the Department of Political Science at Alfred University, Alfred, New York. Albert Somit is in the Political Science Department at SUNY-Buffalo, New York.

gous to a biological organism. He portrayed the commonwealth as similar to the body, with the king as its head, the church as its soul, and all other members of the polity performing lesser functions.[2] Thomas Hobbes probably developed one of the more detailed metaphors. In his introduction to *Leviathan,* he referred to the state as an artificial being, likening sovereignty to the soul, magistrates to joints, reward and punishment to nerves, the wealth and riches of members of the state to strength, concord to health, and sedition to illness. At a later point, Hobbes remarked that money was the nourishment of the state, acting as blood in the real person; that public payments and tax collection were analogous to arteries and veins respectively; and that colonies were the offspring of the state.[3]

We find others, such as Arthur de Gobineau, utilizing a racial analysis. De Gobineau's studies led him to conclude that there was a clear hierarchy of races and that this correlated with political accomplishments.[4] Perhaps the best known manifestation of a "biological analysis" of political life was Social Darwinism which, in some quarters, was used to justify laissez-faire economics and class stratification, and to espouse one or another theory of social superiority. Public policy on certain occasions reflected this tendency, as can be seen in the United States Supreme Court's decision in *Lochner* v. *New York*[5] and the exclusive immigration law of 1924.

From our contemporary vantage point, these earlier racial or evolutionary efforts seem inadequate and doomed to intellectual failure. All too often, those who attempted to use evolutionary theory simply did not understand the basic concepts involved. Indeed, the scientific knowledge of the era was not yet able adequately to explain biological, let alone social, phenomena. Further, Darwinian theory was distorted to bear the burden of an argument for which it was not intended.

There followed an inevitable reaction. By the 1920s and the 1930s, many social scientists drew a sharp line between humans and other forms of animal life. The behavior of other species was seen as largely determined by instinct, while human behavior was treated as almost totally learned, with little if any relationship to genetic legacy. Among the behaviorists after Watson, even this distinction became blurred as they argued that behavior in both humans and animals was the result of learning and/or "conditioning." The Lockean tabula rasa became the reigning orthodoxy, and was viewed as accounting for political and social, as well as individual, behavior.

By the 1950s and 1960s, this outlook came under increasing attack. Freudian psychology, with its emphasis on the inherent nonrational nature of much of human behavior, prepared the way for change. From here, it was but a short step to assuming a direct link between biology and human action, since any innate behavioral tendencies must be rooted in man's genetic makeup. More important, though, were significant advances in biology itself. Research in neurology, psychopharmacology, and psychoneurology made it evident that human behavior was heavily influenced by biological substrates; the modern synthetic theory of evolution provided an explanation for much of what had previously been puzzling; the genetic code was broken, the process by which genetic information was transmitted from generation to generation was clarified, and the possibilities of genetic engineering emerged from what previously had been "mere" science fiction. Perhaps most important of all, ethology was transformed, almost within a decade, from an obscure to a surprisingly popular field as Konrad Lorenz, Nikolaas Tinbergen, and Karl von Frisch received Nobel Prizes for their works and popularized ethological doctrine made the best-seller lists.[6]

As the life sciences moved rapidly forward, some social scientists began, by the mid-1960s, to speculate about the implications of biology and ethology for human behavior in general and political behavior in particular. The latter writings marked the emergence of what is now called biopolitics.[7] Over the ensuing ten years, those working in this area have produced a considerable literature.[8] We can divide this corpus into four broad categories:

1. The case for a more biologically oriented political science;
2. Ethological and evolutionary aspects of behavior;
3. Physiological and pharmacological aspects of political behavior; and
4. Issues of public policy raised by recent advances in the life sciences.

The first area is made up of attempts to argue, or demonstrate, in a rather general way, that a more biologically oriented political science is desirable and would prove profitable to the discipline.[9] The second seeks to utilize ethological or evolutionary concepts (aggression, attention structure, territoriality, male bonding, personal space, etc.) to account for human political behavior and even for political structures.[10]

The third category represents the effort to relate physiological factors to political behavior. There appears to be an increasing interest in conducting empirical studies within this area, an encouraging trend since such studies are more likely to persuade the data-oriented practitioner of the soundness of such an approach.[11] Fourth, there are those who suggest that recent advances in biology and the life sciences have important public policy implications. Harold Lasswell coined the term "somatarchy" to describe the situation in which drugs might be used to control mass behavior and thus assure stability for a regime. Plainly, the study of policy issues raised by advances in biomedical technology will receive more and more attention. Obvious topics will include psychosurgery, environmental issues, genetic engineering, and mind control.

The preceding has outlined the major approaches to biopolitics. In a relatively short time, a substantial literature has been produced; panels on biopolitics have become regular features at professional meetings; an increasing number of the discipline's "elite" have accepted, at least in principle, the validity of biopolitics;[12] and (a further encouraging sign) a second generation of scholars committed to this approach is emerging.

Given, then, the existence of a biologically oriented area within political science, it is not surprising that sociobiology has attracted considerable interest among political scientists. This interest has been fanned by the publication of E. O. Wilson's *Sociobiology*,[13] by several succeeding volumes—a basic text by Barash,[14] a popularized work by Dawkins,[15] and an important critique by Sahlins[16]—and by the furious controversy which erupted over the scientific and ideological aspects of sociobiology.[17] These are significant issues, but are dealt with in detail elsewhere in this volume. We turn our attention, therefore, to the implications which sociobiology might have for political science in general and political philosophy in particular.

II. IMPLICATIONS FOR POLITICAL PHILOSOPHY

One of the perennial—and probably central—questions in political philosophy is that of the nature of political man, an issue which ultimately arises whether we deal with individual thinkers or with competing ideological schools. In this section, we briefly indicate the salience of this question for political philosophy, and suggest the manner in which sociobiology might assist in the resolution of a debate which has persisted for some twenty-five centuries.

There are at least two dimensions of the nature of humans which are relevant for us: first, whether they are inherently good or evil, and second, whether they are political "by nature" or become so via a process of "socialization". Peter Kropotkin, in common with many other anarchists, argued man's inherent goodness, insisting that humans were naturally cooperative and that the state was both unnecessary and evil.[18] Hobbes, on the contrary, asserting that man was selfish (or, at the very least, completely self-centered), moved to the logical conclusion that a strong state was urgently needed to cope with man's acquisitive tendencies and that, without the state, life would be "solitary, poor, nasty, brutish, and short."[19] There are, of course, other philosophers, such as Karl Marx and Robert Owen, who held that human nature is neither good nor evil but, rather, a reflection of the objective conditions under which humans are raised and live.

We also find philosophers differing as to the "naturalness" of the state and of political society. Aristotle declared that man was by his very nature a political animal.[20] Near the opposite end of the spectrum is Locke, who believed that humans learn to be political, i.e., they discover, via reason, the necessity for political life.[21] Plato took yet another stance, insisting that some men were by nature born to be producers, others to be warriors, and a very small minority with the potential to be philosopher kings. From this, he derived a "republic" in which each person would perform the duties and responsibilities for which he or she had been equipped by nature.[22]

Just as the nature of man forms a foundation on which individual theorists have erected their political philosophies, the same issue underlies, and is a point of dispute among, competing political ideologies. Four examples should suffice. First, classical conservatism assumes that much of political behavior is nonrational and that people differ profoundly in ability and intelligence. The shortcomings of human nature require a strong state and/or powerful traditions if social order is to be preserved. Calculated attempts to radically change either of these through social engineering efforts are pointless as well as unwise, since man's rational abilities are not capable of comprehending the consequences of attempts at directed social change.

Liberalism, alternatively, proceeds from a conception of human beings as desiring freedom, as essentially rational, and as capable of effecting deliberate political change (reform) via the use of rational faculties.

(The economic parallel, of course, is capitalism, in which the key assumption is that the individual, conceptualized as economic man, applies a cost-benefit calculus to maximize economic gain.) Third, socialism insists that man is, or is capable of becoming, essentially cooperative and nonacquisitive, and thereby concludes that people can happily— and efficiently—share the means of production and the output of that process. While there are many types of socialism, the unifying element found in most of them is the belief that collective, social ownership of the means of production provides a viable—and the only morally justified—foundation on which society can be built. Fourth, as noted above, the anarchist tends to believe that humans are, by nature, so peaceful and cooperative that political society is, at best, unnecessary and, much more often, inherently evil.

The preceding examples illustrate the manner in which convictions about the nature of political man divide ideological schools as well as individual thinkers. At this juncture, sociobiology can be drawn on to support specific tenets by almost all of the disputants. Sociobiology seems to bolster aspects of both polar positions in the controversy over whether man is naturally good or naturally evil. The sociobiological notion of a genetic basis for altruism in humans suggests an inherent goodness. Wilson, for example, says that "human nature abounds with reciprocal altruism consistent with genetic theory."[23] Contrariwise, interindividual competitiveness may also legitimately be seen as a part of the human species-typical repertoire since, as Campbell argues, aggressiveness could enhance reproductive success and, therefore, be selected for.[24] Thus, specific components of quite diverse views may be lent credence by sociobiology.

On the other hand, it does seem that sociobiology supports more nearly the Aristotelian, conservative notion of "natural" political behavior than the rival Lockean, liberal formulation. The conservative postulate that human behavior is rooted in the nonrational seems in tune with the sociobiological insistence that much of our behavior is a product of evolutionary adaptation and conceivably "designed" to maintain stability in society. There is also indirect support for the conservative emphasis on natural differences—and the consequent need for subordination and superordination in political societies. Social differentiation occurs, for instance, in social insects, with their various castes, and while the primates are rather distinct from the many insect species, this has not prevented some from hypothesizing a natural, genetic basis for class divisions.[25] While such a position is at best highly tendentious, it is consistent with the conservative framework.

At the same time, the sociobiologists' concept of reciprocal altruism supports that part of liberal theory emphasizing free market exchange. Reciprocal altruism entails assisting others on the presumption that others will help one in the future even if there be no immediate, forthcoming benefits. If, by helping others, one increases the chances that one will be aided later in return, there could be selective advantage to "altruism." Wilson suggests that money and free exchange of goods are forms of reciprocal altruism,[26] an idea that leads Sahlins to charge that sociobiologists such as Hamilton, Trivers, and Wilson sanctify "possessive individualism".[27]

Evenhandedly, sociobiology also lends some support to the socialists' collectivist tradition. *Homo sapiens* has spent most of its evolutionary history in small hunting bands, a period probably involving the collective use of a group "territory." This "fact" is at least not inconsistent with the socialists' advocacy of collective control of the means of production. Of course, since most humans no longer live in hunting bands, an argument based upon a mode of living long past may be open to some skepticism.

Kropotkin and many anarchists, we observed above, maintain that man is inherently cooperative. Here again, work on the genetics of altruism indicates that this particular proposition of the anarchists may stand up. Wilson mentions that man has achieved a very high level of cooperation with little sacrifice of personal survival and reproductive success and that cooperation may well confer selective advantage.

The preceding analysis must remain speculative at this time. Nonetheless, it does point out that separate, diverse elements of different philosophical viewpoints, based upon almost contrary views of human nature, hold up under sociobiological analysis. A logical future step would be to attempt the construction of a philosophical edifice resting on a coherent sociobiological foundation, rather than by using building blocks drawn from widely varying theories. While such an effort would be premature now, there is the potential for such an undertaking if sociobiology's promise can be realized.

III. IMPLICATIONS FOR POLITICAL SCIENCE IN GENERAL

Since sociobiology is concerned, perhaps above all, with the mechanisms and consequences of adaptive evolution, it may sensitize students of politics to the fact that political institutions, no less than living organisms, must be capable of adjusting to changing environmental conditions (using the term in its broadest sense) and to the consequences for individuals and institutions alike of the ability to adapt as circumstances require. Thus, for example, Peter Corning has undertaken an ambitious project in which he sets out functionally to analyze political institutions in terms of their survival consequences.[28] While Corning's attempt to construct evolutionary indicators is not altogether successful, his failure is less important than his imaginative effort to assess the value of social structures and institutions in terms of concepts derived from evolutionary theory.

In a somewhat different application of sociobiology, Donald Campbell examines the significance of social norms and institutions for individuals, with special emphasis on altruistic behavior. He assumes that humans have selfish tendencies because biological evolution would select these as a result of interindividual genetic competition. To achieve social order, however, societal norms for altruism would be developed via social, as contrasted to biological, evolution. These social and political norms, then, could function to override or limit genetic selfishness.[29]

Second, as indicated above, it is conceivable that sociopolitical institutions evolve through a process analogous to natural selection, but change more rapidly than human morphological or behavioral characteristics. This would—or does—suggest at least a partial explanation for "deviant" or "antisocial" behavior in humans. The state and the city have emerged as major features of human social and political life only in the past few thousand years. Although man's genetic nature may have been modified over that same span, it is highly improbable that this evolution has been able to keep pace with the massive changes in our social, political, and economic institutions. If this is the situation, there is the obvious possibility that we do not have an adequate genetic "fit" with the social environment we have created for ourselves. There would be, in such a circumstance, an increasing likelihood of conflict between genetically influenced individual predispositions and the social norms and political structures within which the individual must function. The task for both biology and political science would be that of finding some way in which to restore a viable balance between the two.

Third, other ethological concepts may help cast light on phenomena of interest to those in other areas of the discipline. As many political scientists have already begun to realize, the persistent appearance of political factions and cliques, the almost predictable nature of bureaucratic rivalries, and even the process technically known as political socialization may be at least analogous to what the ethologists call, respectively, territorial behavior, group bonding and imprinting. And, as one political scientist has already attempted to show, the study of primate social life may better help us understand the nature of human hierarchical ordering—a near universal manifestation—and, interestingly enough, may serve to identify a serious limitation in the applicability of Rawl's recent attempt to construct a "practicable" theory of justice.[30]

Lastly, sociobiology has manifest implications for political scientists concerned with public policy. To take the most frequently cited example, there is the question of the relationship between international and domestic violence and possible innate human tendencies toward aggression and violence. As a leading student of international affairs has observed, there are at least three basic levels of analysis from which to begin the search for the causes of war—human nature, the nature of states, and the structure of the international system.[31] Sociobiology offers the possibility of casting light upon the interaction between individual behavior and the functioning of such macro-structures as the state by the utilization of concepts—and even research techniques—derived from ethology and population genetics. It holds out to the political scientist the prospect of better understanding socialized forms of aggression and, conceivably, of ultimately devising means of dealing with a phenomenon as old as recorded history.

IV. THE PRESENT LIMITATIONS OF SOCIOBIOLOGY FOR POLITICAL SCIENCE

Manifestly, there are limitations on the contributions which sociobiology can presently make to the study of politics. There are formidable conceptual problems yet to be resolved. Sociobiological explanations, it has often been argued, tend to underestimate the role of culture. Sahlins points out that since a culture, through a repository of shared symbols, shapes the individual's view of the world, "reality construction" via the medium of language may have largely emancipated human culture from direct genetic influence.[32] Even if this is not the case, and one concedes the importance of our genetic legacy, how are we to measure the relative influence upon human behavior of biological and nonbiological factors? To ask this question is to reopen a controversy which has raged for decades—"nature vs. nurture," "learned vs. innate." The contemporary form of the debate indicates that this dispute is far from resolved.[33]

Methodological problems must also be acknowledged. Because of ethical and technical difficulties encountered in directly studying the possible biological bases of *human* behavior, conclusions based on studies of other species are frequently cited as relevant to *Homo sapiens.*[34] This practice is open to serious objection on two counts. There is grave danger in applying to one species conclusions based upon observations of another species, especially when one analogizes from animal behavior, even that of primates, to humans. Furthermore, some of the conclusions advanced may have been drawn from inadequate evidence. Put somewhat differently, ethological data sometimes are extraordinarily "soft". On careful scrutiny, they are frequently suspect in terms of the criteria usually applied to sampling, measurement, observer effect, recording, and reliability. Too often only a few individuals or groups are studied. In other instances, observations are conducted for limited spans of time and may miss essential features which recur at intervals or which would become apparent only after thousands of hours of dedicated voyeurism. Doubts can also be raised about the validity of many measurement schemes. There are a wide variety of these and findings may be problematic if different studies utilizing different metrics are compared. The animal's awareness of being observed may affect behavior and lead to faulty conclusions. Audio and movie equipment often break down in the field and handwriting may be too slow and inefficient to record all relevant occurrences. And, to note one more recurrent shortcoming, reliability checks are not always used, making evaluation of studies sometimes difficult.[35]

Furthermore, in the present state of sociobiology, hypotheses cannot readily be tested in a convincing manner. Given the conceptual and methodological problems noted above, arguments are often advanced in "as if " form. That is, those adopting the sociobiological approach assert that behavior under scrutiny manifests itself as if it were genetically controlled, i.e., that it is therefore consistent with sociobiological formulations. This is hardly conclusive, since other "as ifs" can be adduced in many cases. To argue that a particular social structure or behavior appears as if it were genetically determined and *is* therefore genetically controlled, is to assume what one is attempting to prove.

It should be apparent, given the preceding comment, that our earlier observation that sociobiology may eventually help resolve some major philosophical issues does not mean that we can expect final answers in the immediate future. It would be premature to place too great a faith in sociobiology as a solution to the problems of political science, since both are far from advanced as disciplines. To find that liberalism, socialism, anarchism, and classical conservatism are all, *to some extent,* consistent with sociobiological expectations is to demonstrate that we are not yet able to make final judgments on the validity of the assumptions underlying these doctrines through the medium of sociobiology alone.

In summary, sociobiology can be useful for political inquiry if we remain modest about its present value and understand both its capabilities and what it cannot yet, if ever, do. The difficulties of testing political hypotheses by utilizing concepts and techniques drawn from sociobiology are formidable. Nonetheless, this new field will eventually compel political scientists to take into consideration the biological factors which may influence our political behavior; and, there is good reason to believe, it may in the future contribute significantly to the ability of the political scientist to understand and explain, if not predict and control, the phenomena and problems which are his professional province.

NOTES

1. Cf. Steven A. Peterson, "Biopolitics: Lessons from History," *Journal of the History of the Behavioral Sciences* 12 (1976), pp. 354–366.
2. John of Salisbury, *The Statesman's Book of John of Salisbury* (New York: Knopf, 1927). Translated by John Dickinson.
3. Thomas Hobbes, *Leviathan* (Baltimore: Penguin, 1968). Reprint of 1651 edition.
4. Arthur de Gobineau, "Essay on the Inequality of the Human Races," in *Gobineau: Selected Political Writings* (New York: Harper & Row, 1970), edited by Michael D. Biddiss.

5. 198 U.S. 45 (1905).
6. E.g., Robert Ardrey, *The Territorial Imperative* (New York: Atheneum, 1966); Konrad Lorenz, *On Aggression* (New York: Bantam, 1966); Desmond Morris, *The Naked Ape* (New York: Dell, 1967).
7. Albert Somit, "Toward a More Biologically Oriented Political Science," *Midwest Journal of Political Science* 12 (1968), pp. 550–567.
8. For an early survey of the literature, see Albert Somit, "Biopolitics," *British Journal of Political Science* 2 (1972), pp. 209–238. A recent volume representative of this subfield is Albert Somit, ed., *Biology and Politics* (Paris: Mouton, 1976).
9. Glendon Schubert, "Politics as a Life Science: How and Why the Impact of Modern Biology Will Revolutionize the Study of Political Behavior," in Somit, *Biology and Politics*.
10. Cf. Roger Masters, "The Impact of Ethology on Political Science," *ibid.;* Henry Beck, "Attentional Struggles and the Silencing Strategies in a Human Political Conflict: The Case of the Vietnam Moratoria," in *The Social Structure of Attention,* eds. M. R. A. Chance and R. R. Larson (New York: Wiley, 1976); Fred Willhoite, "Ethology and the Tradition of Political Thought," *Journal of Politics* 33 (1971), pp. 615–641.
11. Dean Jaros, "Biochemical Desocialization: Depressants and Political Behavior," *Midwest Journal of Political Science* 16 (1972), pp. 1–28; David C. Schwartz, "Health Processes and Body Images as Predictors of Political Attitudes and Behavior," a paper presented at the International Political Science Association meeting, Montreal, 1973; David C. Schwartz, "The Influence of Health Status on Basic Attitudes in an American Political Elite," a paper presented at the International Political Science Association meeting, Edinburgh, 1976; David C. Schwartz, "Somatic States and Political Behavior: An Interpretation and Empirical Extension of Biopolitics," in Somit, *op. cit.;* Bernard Tursky et al., "A Bio-Behavioral Framework for the Analysis of Political Behavior," in Somit, *op. cit.*
12. Cf. David Easton, "The Relevance of Biopolitics to Political Theory," in Somit, *op. cit.*
13. Cambridge, Mass.: Harvard University Press, 1975.
14. David P. Barash, *Sociobiology and Behavior* (New York: Elsevier, 1976).
15. Richard Dawkins, *The Selfish Gene* (New York: Oxford, 1976).
16. Marshall Sahlins, *The Use and Abuse of Biology* (Ann Arbor: University of Michigan Press, 1976).
17. Stephen T. Emlen, "An Alternative Case for Sociobiology,"*Science* 192 (1976), pp. 736–738; Cheryl M. Fields, "Sociobiology Furor Subsides But Debate Over Field Continues," *Chronicle of Higher Education* 13 (December 1976), p. 5; Nicholas Wade, "Sociobiology: Troubled Birth for New Discipline," *Science* 191 (1976), pp. 1151–1155.
18. Peter Kropotkin, *Mutual Aid* (Boston: Extending Horizons Books, n.d.).
19. Hobbes, *op. cit.*
20. Aristotle, "Politics," in *On Man in the Universe* (New York: Black, 1943), edited by Louise R. Loomis.

21. John Locke, *Two Treatises of Government* (New York: Hafner, 1947 reprint edition).
22. Plato, *The Republic* (New York: Oxford, 1945), edited by Francis Cornford.
23. Wilson, *op. cit.,* p. 120.
24. Donald T. Campbell, "On the Conflicts Between Biological and Social Evolution and Between Psychology and Moral Tradition," *American Psychologist* 30 (1975), pp. 1103–1126.
25. Cf. B. Eckland, "Genetics and Sociology: A Reconsideration," *American Sociological Review* 32 (1967), pp. 173–194.
26. Wilson, *op. cit.,* pp. 551–553.
27. Sahlins, *op. cit.*
28. Peter A. Corning, "Evolutionary Indicators: Applying the Theory of Evolution to Political Science," 1971. Revision of a paper presented at the International Political Science Association meeting, Munich, 1970.
29. Campbell, *op. cit.*
30. Fred Willhoite, Jr., "Equal Opportunity and Primate Particularism," *Journal of Politics* 37 (1975), pp. 270–276.
31. Kenneth Waltz, *Man, the State and War* (New York: Columbia University Press, 1959).
32. Sahlins, *op. cit.* See also Dawkins, *op. cit.*
33. For the basic perspective on this dispute, see Daniel S. Lehrman, "Semantic and Conceptual Issues in the Nature–Nurture Problem," *Development and Evolution of Behavior,* eds. Lester Aronson *et al.* (San Francisco: Freeman, 1970); Konrad Lorenz, *Evolution and Modification of Behavior* (Chicago: University of Chicago Press, 1965); T. C. Schneirla, "Behavioral Development and Comparative Psychology," *Quarterly Review of Biology* 41 (1966), pp. 283–302.
34. On comparison, for example, see: Konrad Z. Lorenz, "Analogy as a Source of Knowledge," *Science* 185 (1974), pp. 229–234; Roger D. Masters, "Functional Approaches to Analogical Comparison Between Species," *Social Science Information* 12 (1973), pp. 7–28.
35. See, for example, Robert Plutchik, "The Study of Social Behavior in Primates," *Folia Primatologica* 2 (1964), pp. 67–92.

Altruism, Ethics, and Sociobiology
Ruth Mattern

With the development of a powerful theory of evolution by natural selection, biologists have become increasingly optimistic about explaining human characteristics in the same way that features of animals are explained. Altruistic behavior presents an interesting case in point. In 1932, Haldane suggested that the increase of altruistic behavior could be explained within the theory formed by the synthesis of Darwinian theory and population genetics (Haldane, 1932, p. 131). A series of biologists since then have worked out this suggestion in more detail (Wilson, 1975a, 108–110). This development culminates in recent writings by E. O. Wilson, who explicitly declares human ethical behavior—like altruism in animals—to be explicable by appeal to natural selection on inherited traits. And Wilson goes even further than this. One of the most interesting features of his discussion is his contention that sociobiology promises a new perspective on ethics; Wilson claims not only that sociobiology sheds considerable light on the problem of explaining ethical behavior in humans, but also that this insight warrants a "biologicized" ethics which should replace previous philosophical approaches to ethics. This claim merits careful attention, especially in light of the fact that much of the controversy surrounding sociobiology concerns its ethical implications.

Wilson's optimism about a new approach to ethics stems from his

For helpful discussions related to previous drafts of this paper, I am grateful to Professors Elizabeth Flower and Abraham Edel.

Ruth Mattern is in the Philosophy Department at the University of Pennsylvania, Philadelphia.

confidence in the power of his theory to explain ethical behavior. For this reason, it is important to ask whether the theory accomplishes here what Wilson claims it does. Some of the relevant issues about this matter are the topic of the first section of this paper, where I suggest some limitations in the sociobiologist's attempt to explain ethical behavior.

Granting that sociobiology could have some success in explaining ethical behavior, problems remain about the possible ethics derivable from such an explanation. In the second section, I try to locate these problems and to distinguish various versions of the thesis that sociobiology is relevant to ethics.

Others have made evaluations of the explanatory ambitions of sociobiology, and I do not discuss here the general issues raised by this topic.[1] Nor will I try to settle complex philosophical issues about ethics within the scope of this paper. My aim is to clarify issues, to distinguish between some claims that are easily conflated, and to show where the sociobiologist moonlighting as ethicist needs to proceed with caution.

I

Wilson brings a wealth of evidence about altruistic behavior to bear on his interpretation of the biological basis of altruistic behavior in humans. This evidence concerns animal behavior; as Wilson writes, "The main theses of sociobiology are based on studies of a myriad of animal species conducted by hundreds of investigators in various biological disciplines" (Wilson, 1976). His main strategy is to show, first, the plausibility of explaining altruistic behavior in animals in terms of natural selection. This involves several assertions. (1) Altruistic behavior in animals serves a biological function; i.e., it is adaptive. (2) Altruistic behavior in animals has a genetic basis; i.e., predispositions to altruistic behavior are inherited. These are steps in support of the contention that (3) altruistic behavior in animals evolved by natural selection. I take it that establishing these claims is part of the task of the first twenty-six chapters of Wilson's *Sociobiology: The New Synthesis.* Whether his argumentation for these contentions succeeds is not my present concern; I wish to focus attention on the second stage of the argument, which extends this explanation of altruistic behavior in animals to altruistic behavior in humans. This argument, put forward in the last chapter, proceeds via the assumption that (4) altruistic behavior is found in both animals and humans, to the conclusion that (5) altruistic behavior in humans is adaptive, has a genetic basis, and evolved by natural selection.

What I have labeled claim (4) is the crucial claim for my present purposes. I do not wish to question it on the grounds that it appeals to an analogy between phenomena in two different contexts; analogy is a common, useful strategy for extending the scope of scientific claims. My question about claim (4) is whether it can serve as a bridge to the concluding claim (5) interpreted as a claim about ethical behavior in humans.

To bring human ethical behavior within the scope of his explanatory scheme, Wilson need not merely say that *some* human behavior is similar to animal "altruism". He needs to claim that the human altruistic behavior which we call ethical is essentially similar to what he calls "altruism" in animals, similar enough to warrant applying the same concept of altruism to both sorts of behavior. In fact, though, there appear to be two different concepts of altruism involved. The distinction may be clarified by reflecting on the implausibility of saying that ethical behavior occurs in animals at all; as Simpson writes, man is the only ethical animal (Simpson, p. 310). We do not say that birds which give warning calls to protect others in their group are acting in an ethical manner, even if such behavior does fall within the scope of Wilson's concept of altruism. Surely Wilson would agree that the notion of ethical behavior does not extend as far as he extends his concept of altruism; presumably he would not say that parasites can act ethically, even though he does say that even a parasite "can be altruistic" in the sense that "feeding ability or reproduction is curtailed in spite of competition from other genotypes" (Wilson, 1975a, p. 116).

This point suggests that the concept of altruism with ethical implications is not the same as the concept of altruism presented at the beginning of the argument; claim (4) is supposed to link animal and human ethical altruism, but the term "altruism" in this claim may be ambiguous. Further reflection indicates that there are indeed two different concepts involved. Ordinarily we are inclined to say that human altruistic behavior counts as ethical only because it is done with the *intention* and primary *motive* of benefiting other individuals. We call an act altruistic if this is the case, regardless of whether the agent succeeds or not in bringing about the effects he intends. Wilson's reason for calling some animal behavior "altruistic", though, has nothing to do with these mental features of ethical behavior; his concept of altruism only has to do with the actual *consequences* of the behavior, namely the increase of the fitness of others at the expense of the agent's own fitness (Wilson, 1975a, p. 106). Of course, *some* human behavior might be labeled "altruistic" because of its consequences, but it is far from clear that all human altruism merits this classification for that reason.

Wilson entitles one of his articles "Human Decency is Animal" (Wilson, 1975b) because he wants to contend that human ethical altruism can be subsumed under the biological laws explaining animal altruism. If there are two different concepts of altruism involved, however, then the biological explanation of animal altruism will not automatically guarantee the explicability of ethical altruism on the same terms. But there is still a possibility that the biological explanation will apply to that sort of altruism too; the difference between the two concepts of altruism only shows the need for further argumentation, without in itself ruling out the possibility of its success.[2]

Can Wilson extend his biological explanation to ethical behavior? There is some reason for doubting whether *all* instances of ethical altruism in humans will fall within the scope of the sociobiological explanation that he sketches. Wilson appeals to kinship selection, as he explains in his response (Wilson, 1975a, pp. 3–4) to "the central theoretical problem of sociobiology":

How can altruism, which by definition reduces personal fitness, possibly evolve by natural selection? The answer is kinship: if the genes causing the altruism are shared by two organisms because of common descent, and if the altruistic act by one organism increases the joint contribution of these genes to the next generation, the propensity to altruism will spread through the gene pool. This occurs even though the altruist makes less of a solitary contribution to the gene pool as the price of its altruistic act.

The "kinship selection" theory requires that the altruistic behavior enhance the competitive capacities of those having the genetic predisposition to altruism. But much ethical altruism is aimed at the good of all humans, not merely of close relatives or those with similar genes. Furthermore, some altruistic behavior is intended to benefit not merely the members of our own species, but the members of other species.

Concern about the humane treatment of animals, or an ethics like Albert Schweitzer's "respect for life" doctrine, are phenomena which present apparent exceptions to Wilson's explanation. Even if one interprets the "unit of selection" in the broadest possible way in order to accommodate various sorts of altruism, it is quite dubious that one can include all ethical altruistic behavior within that version of the explanation by natural selection.

Faced with this problem, the sociobiologist might attempt to establish only a weaker thesis about the problematic cases. He might admit that there are some instances of ethical altruism which do not fit directly within the scope of his explanation, but assert that these instances were *derived* in some way or other from gene-based altruism. That is, sociobiology might try to show the plausibility of positing a rudimentary form of altruism in early humans, and try to establish that all altruistic behavior in present humans can be traced back to this primitive behavior in early humans. Wilson's discussion of altruism in animals may be viewed as relevant to the first part of this contention, for the altruistic behavior of animals may well be an illuminating model for understanding primitive human altruism. But there would still be a significant problem in carrying out the second part of this program. To explain all altruistic behavior as derived from altruism in primitive humans, the sociobiologist would need to rule out the competing hypothesis that some human altruistic behavior stems simply from the realization that cooperation is better than competition. Even the weaker sociobiological explanation would not apply to all instances of ethical altruism, unless it could be shown that all altruism derived by cultural or genetic transmission from the altruism of early humans.

This, I believe, goes beyond what Wilson has actually established. It would be surprising if, contrary to appearances, *no* ethical altruism has its origin in beliefs that an altruistic way of life is preferable. Perhaps Wilson gives less attention to this alternative hypothesis than he should because of his tendency to interpret moral beliefs as mere emotive expressions of underlying biological states; he interprets moral claims as arising from "the emotive centers" of the "hypothalamic-limbic system," which "evolved by natural selection" (Wilson, 1975a, pp. 3, 563). But it is one thing to say that this system evolved by natural selection, and quite another thing to say that each specific moral belief is explainable in terms of natural selection. Sometimes (Wilson, 1975a, p. 129) it appears that Wilson does believe the second, stronger claim.

A science of sociobiology, if coupled with neurophysiology, might transform the insights of ancient religions into a precise account of the evolutionary origin of ethics and hence explain the reasons why we make certain moral choices instead of others at particular times.

The evidence which Wilson cites, though, does not suffice to show that natural selection provides an account of the origin of each moral belief. In short, the explanation of altruistic behavior by natural selection is subject to increasingly severe strain the more we concentrate on those examples of altruism which are labeled ethical.

II

On the basis of his belief in a sociobiological explanation of human behavior, Wilson suggests that ethics should be "biologicized"; "Scientists and humanists should consider together the possibility that the time has come for ethics to be removed temporarily from the hands of the philosophers and biologicized" (Wilson, 1975a, p. 562). Wilson develops this suggestion in two different directions. One direction emerges at the beginning of his first chapter on "The Morality of the Gene"; there (p. 3) he writes that the "emotional control centers in the hypothalamus and limbic system of the brain"

flood our consciousness with all the emotions—hate, love, guilt, fear, and others—that are consulted by ethical philosophers who wish to intuit the standards of good and evil. What, we are then compelled to ask, made the hypothalamus and limbic system? They evolved by natural selection. That simple biological statement must be pursued to explain ethics and ethical philosophers, if not epistemology and epistemologists, at all depths.

He returns to the same theme in the last chapter of his book (p. 563):

In the first chapter of this book I argued that ethical philosophers intuit the deontological canons of morality by consulting the emotive centers of their own hypothalamic-limbic system. This is also true of the developmentalists, even when they are being their most severely objective. Only by interpreting the activity of the emotive centers as a biological adaptation can the meaning of the canons be deciphered.

Part of what Wilson is claiming here is that ethical beliefs are explained in terms of natural selection. But obviously he is asserting more than this. He is claiming not merely that a philosopher's having a particular ethical belief is explicable by appeal to that philosopher's hypothalamic-limbic system and the evolution of that type of system; he is also claiming that the very *content* of ethical beliefs is a matter to be understood only by reference to the emotional control centers. One cannot be sure exactly what position Wilson is endorsing here, but it sounds as though he is denying the cognitive significance of ethical claims, interpreting moral contentions as mere expressions of emotions rather than as true or false assertions.[3] If he is in fact advancing a noncognitivist reading of ethical claims, then one must question whether he has given adequate support to that view. He never really does *argue* that the pronouncements of ethical philosophers are merely outpourings of "the emotive centers of their own hypothalamic-limbic system."

Sometimes Wilson suggests a second, quite different approach to ethics. For he sometimes writes as though ethical claims are not mere emotive responses, but that they follow directly from biological claims. He suggests, that is, that ethics should be naturalized, since its cognitive content rests on biological empirical claims. An example of his approach to ethics as a "specialized branch of biology" is his derivation (1976) of human rights from sociobiological facts:

To the extent that the biological interpretation noted here proves correct, men have rights that are innate, rooted in the ineradicable drives for survival and self-esteem, and these rights do not require the validation of ad hoc theoretical constructions produced by society.

Here Wilson appears to commit himself to the view that some biological claims serve to *justify* some ethical conclusions.

The sociobiologist endorsing an ethical naturalism could hold either a stronger or a weaker version of this thesis. The stronger version would be that biological claims are *sufficient* for ethical conclusions, while the weaker version would merely contend that biological facts are *necessary* for ethical conclusions. Wilson does not distinguish these two versions of naturalism or make it clear which he asserts, but some of his comments suggest that he actually believes the stronger thesis. The comment about rights quoted above, for instance, seems to imply that biological facts will suffice to generate some ethical conclusions without further ethical premises. His remark about the possibility of removing ethics from the hands of philosophers also suggests that biological claims will be enough to give ethical conclusions.

Wilson's attempts to make this strong naturalism plausible leave much unexplained. The specific example cited in his *BioScience* article, the derivation of rights from genetically based drives, is not developed to the point of plausibility. He infers natural rights from "ineradicable drives for survival and self-esteem"; but he does not explain how a normative claim about rights is to be inferred from a factual claim about drives. Nor does he succeed in circumventing the traditional philosophical questions about what sorts of beings have rights and how conflicting rights are to be weighed.

To see the need for proceeding carefully here, let us look more closely at the hints which Wilson does give about the relevance of sociobiology to ethical contentions. What is distinctive about his biological theory is that it ascribes a very important role to genetic influence; it is his belief that some drives are ineradicable and innately determined which leads Wilson to say that men have innate rights. But there are many examples of genetically influenced drives for which there are not corresponding rights. Presumably virtually every animal has an "ineradicable drive for survival"; but few would agree that every animal, including the lowliest of insects, has a *right* to life. Similarly, showing that a psychotic rapist acted out of an ineradicable and genetically influenced drive would presumably not suffice to show that he had a right to act as he did. If claims about genetic influence are to be used as premises in moral reasoning in the strong way that Wilson suggests, a much more sophisticated elucidation of that relevance would need to be made.

An analogous problem arises in the attempt to draw moral conclusions from sociobiological claims about altruism. In the last section, I criticized the assumption that the concept of altruism appearing in Wilson's sociobiological claims is the same concept of altruism which appears in ethical claims. This still left open the possibility that some instances of ethically altruistic behavior are examples of behavior explainable by sociobiological laws. I do not argue that *no* instances of ethical altruism are explicable in this way, though I do question whether *all* instances of ethical altruism would fall within the scope of Wilson's theory. We must ask now whether the claim that some instances of ethically altruistic behavior can be explained by natural selection would suffice to establish any normative claim about altruism. It is far from obvious that this sociobiological claim would be enough to justify any normative conclusion. Explaining a fact in biological terms and making a moral assertion do not appear to be identical activities, nor is it obvious how one could arrive at moral conclusions about altruism without using more than sociobiological premises. To show that ethics was merely a specialized branch of biology, one would need to establish a conceptual connection between the concepts in the two sorts of claims. A form of sociobiology attenuated enough to be plausible seems to be too weak to take ethics out of the hands of philosophers.

The biologist wishing to say that ethics is nothing but biology would also need to come to terms with the traditional philosophical problem of the "naturalistic fallacy", and confront the issue whether it is ever possible to derive ethical claims from factual ones.[4] Many philosophers have contended that such a derivation is impossible, and proving a strong assimilation of ethics to biology would require showing its possibility. Wilson does mention the naturalistic fallacy at one point, but he does not explain why he thinks that his own reduction of ethics to a branch of biology would not be an example of this fallacy (Wilson, 1975b).[5]

Both parties in the controversy about the political implications of sociobiology have tended to assume without question that normative conclusions follow directly from scientific premises. Critics of sociobiology say that if all behavior is genetically determined, this would constitute a defense of the status quo. The Sociobiology Study Group of Science for the People, a group which is particularly critical of sociobiology because of its social implications, wrote (1976, p. 182) that theories like sociobiology

operate as powerful forms of legitimation of past and present social institutions such as aggression, competition, domination of women by men, defense of national territory, individualism, and the appearance of a status and wealth hierarchy.

Neither side of the dispute has approached with sophistication the problematic status of derivations of value claims from scientific ones. Both parties would do well to confront straightforwardly the claim made by T. H. Huxley in the nineteenth century that a study of the evolution of ethics does not in itself imply an ethics of evolution (Huxley, 1893, p. 402). The denial of the possibility of deriving normative conclusions from scientific premises should either be accepted or refuted, but not ignored.

If the sociobiologist does not wish to take on the burden of these problems, he could avoid them by retreating to a weaker form of ethical naturalism.[6] He could hold that biological facts are *relevant* to the justification of moral claims, without endorsing the view that they are *sufficient* for such justification. Various facts about humans might serve to make some moral claims more appealing than others, and rule out some possible approaches to ethical problems; but the facts alone would not show what should be done.

This weaker form of ethical naturalism would not commit one to saying that ethics ought to be taken out of the hands of philosophers, even temporarily. In fact, the point that biological facts are relevant to ethical theorizing is a familiar one in some traditions of philosophical ethics. Wilson's narrow focus on intuitionistic approaches to ethics makes his picture of philosophy a caricature. He has overlooked the long and rich history of attempts to relate theories of human nature to ethical claims, a history including figures as eminent as Aristotle and Dewey. If Wilson's recommendation that we "biologicize" ethics is merely the suggestion that we should utilize empirical facts in constructing an ethics for humans, then this recommendation should not be viewed as inaugurating a radical new approach to moral theory.

In at least one respect, Wilson's sociobiology might make a helpful contribution to this tradition. Some previous attempts to establish the rationality of ethical behavior are based on a narrow reading of natural human drives as egoistic. Wilson's theory, if successful, could show that the set of natural drives includes natural inclinations to benefit others. Such an extension of the set of "natural" drives was anticipated by some other writers; Darwin himself, for example, suggested a similar approach in his treatment of ethical behavior in *The Descent of Man* (Darwin, 1871, Ch. 4). In this respect, too, Wilson's contribution is more a development and refinement of previous traditions than a radical departure from all previous thought. This is not to deny, of course, that the advances made by Wilson's version of this approach may be important ones.

To assess the significance of sociobiology's contribution to ethics, one would need to elucidate the special relevance of the sorts of natural features to which Wilson calls attention, the genetically influenced attributes. Ethical theorists appealing to assumptions about human nature have often concentrated on features thought to be universal among humans.[7] An ethical theory whose assumptions were general in this way would have a broader scope than an ethical theory drawing on empirical claims peculiar only to some members of the species. However, there is no essential connection between the claim that a feature has a genetic basis and the claim that it is universal within a species. A gene-based feature need not be found in all members of a kind.

Biological facts are relevant to ethics because they inform the theorist of some constraints on his ethical claims; we cannot be obliged to do what we are not capable of doing. But limitations on abilities will restrict obligations in this way regardless of whether these limitations were imposed by the environment or by the genes. Biological considerations are also relevant to ethics because they inform us of what is already accepted as valuable to humans, what they do not need to be persuaded to treat as important. But what we are naturally inclined to do need not be restricted to what our *genes* predispose us to do. If culture molds and adds to natural attributes in profound ways, as it certainly seems to do, the whole set of features thus produced is the factual basis which may be relevant to moral claims.

More generally, there is some reason for questioning whether biology in general, or sociobiology in particular, would play as large a role in an ethical naturalism as Wilson suggests. We may distinguish two possible versions of an ethical naturalism contending that biological facts are necessary but not sufficient for ethical theories; one version would claim that biological assertions are the only empirical claims needed, while another version would allow that other sorts of empirical claims are also relevant. Judging from his comments about the relation of ethics to biology, Wilson would opt for the former version even if he surrendered the view that biological claims are sufficient for ethical ones. But it is not clear why other sorts of facts would not also constitute part of the factual basis relevant to moral claims. Perhaps Wilson already assumes that many other sorts of facts (such as psychological ones) are reducible to biological ones; if so, that is a large step which needs discussion.

III

Wilson's sociobiology is a striking attempt to provide a biological framework for understanding humans, but one must proceed with caution in trying to pull ethical conclusions out of this theory. If the sociobiologist asserts that biological facts alone suffice to establish ethical conclusions, he must explain how one can possibly derive normative conclusions without normative premises. Perhaps that can be done, but its possibility would need to be argued with care, not simply assumed. If the sociobiologist admits that the concept of altruism appearing in ethical claims does not appear in the claims justified by sociobiology, he also incurs the obligation of explaining how a relatively weak assimilation of claims about altruism to sociobiological laws could warrant a strong naturalism.

If the sociobiologist merely wishes to assert that his claims constitute the necessary basis for ethical theory rather than a sufficient condition for such a theory, he would avoid the whole problem of deriving ethical conclusions from purely factual claims. But even this moderate ethical naturalism may be too daring, if it asserts that biology alone provides an account of the facts relevant to ethics.

From the analysis so far, we must have some reservations about the contention that ethics ought to be "biologicized" in the strong sense that Wilson intends. Some important examples of ethical behavior may elude the grasp of his theory, and some facts about the behavior within the scope of his theory may need to be investigated by other approaches. Also, it seems implausible that a sociobiological approach to ethics would be incompatible with all philosophical approaches to the field. Wilson's focus on a few philosophers to the exclusion of all the naturalistic schools of ethical theories may be responsible for some of the excesses of the view he asserts. If sociobiology does give some insights about the nature of ethical beings, it will be performing a task which supplements rather than replaces ethical theorizing.

NOTES

1. For a discussion of some of the general problems about sociobiology as a scientific theory, see Michael Ruse's paper "Sociobiology: A Philosophical Analysis" in this volume.

2. I appeal here to the common philosophical distinction between a concept and the extension of a concept; the point is that the *instances* of altruism which we call ethical might fall within the scope of Wilson's explanation even if there is not a *conceptual* connection between the two concepts of altruism.
3. For a classic statement of the noncognitivist view of ethical claims, see A. J. Ayer, *Language, Truth and Logic* (London: Gollancz, 1936).
4. For a survey discussion of positions about naturalism and the naturalistic fallacy, see Paul W. Taylor, *Principles of Ethics: An Introduction* (Encino, Calif.: Dickenson, 1975), pp. 175–207. For an anthology on this issue, see W. D. Hudson, ed., *The Is/Ought Question: A Collection of Papers on the Central Problem in Moral Philosophy* (New York: St. Martin's Press, 1969).
5. What Wilson refers to as the "naturalistic fallacy" here is the assumption that whatever is, ought to be. But one may reject this version of the naturalistic fallacy while still believing that some factual claims imply normative ones, and this is apparently what Wilson does believe.
6. For a discussion of various versions of ethical naturalism with special attention to the relevance of biological theories, see Abraham Edel, *Ethical Judgment* (New York: The Free Press, 1955). pp. 115–50.
7. Consider, for example, the appeal to universal features of humans in Spinoza's *Ethics* as the basis for the ethical theory advanced in the latter part of that book.

REFERENCES

Appleman, Philip, ed. (1970). *Darwin: A Norton Critical Edition* (New York: Norton).

Aristotle. *Ethica Nicomachea.* In Richard McKeon, ed., *The Basic Works of Aristotle* (New York: Random House, 1941), pp. 935–1112.

Ayer, A. J. (1936). *Language, Truth and Logic* 2nd ed. (New York: Dover).

Darwin, Charles. (1871). *The Descent of Man.* (New York: Appleton and Co., 1896). Abridged version in Appleman, ed., pp. 199–276.

Dewey, John. (1898). "Evolution and Ethics," *The Monist* 8, pp. 321–341.

Edel, Abraham. (1955). *Ethical Judgment: The Use of Science in Ethics* (Glencoe, Ill.: Free Press).

Haldane, J. B. S. (1932). *The Causes of Evolution* (London: Longmans, Green).

Hudson, W. D., ed. (1969). *The Is/Ought Question: A Collection of Papers on the Central Problem in Moral Philosophy* (New York: St. Martin's Press).

Huxley, Thomas Henry. (1893). "Evolution and Ethics." In Appleman, ed., pp. 402–404.

Ruse, Michael. "Sociobiology: A Philosophical Analysis." In this volume.

Simpson, G. Gaylord. (1951). *The Meaning of Evolution* (New York: Mentor).

Sociobiology Study Group of Science for the People. (1976). "Sociobiology—Another Biological Determinism," *BioScience* 26, no. 3, March 1976.

Taylor, Paul W. (1975). *Principles of Ethics: An Introduction* (Belmont, California: Dickenson Publishing Co.).

Wilson, Edward O. (1975a). *Sociobiology: The New Synthesis* (Cambridge, Mass.: Harvard University Press).
————. (1975b). "Human Decency is Animal," *The New York Times Magazine,* October 12, 1975.
————. (1976). "Academic Vigilantism and the Political Significance of Sociobiology," *BioScience* 26, no. 3, March 1976.

Sociobiology Is a Political Issue

Joseph Alper, Jon Beckwith, and Lawrence G. Miller

In this article we wish to expand our discussion of certain issues brought up briefly in previous critiques. The question of the political implications of sociobiology has become increasingly controversial. We believe it is important to point out the political content of the theory. We also seek to show how in concrete terms, sociobiological ideas in their most politicized form are being disseminated. The political content of sociobiology is especially evident in its treatment of sex roles. We will, therefore, discuss the central role of sexism in the formulation of sociobiological theories and in its social impact.

SOCIOBIOLOGY GOES PUBLIC

Sociobiology has been proclaimed as a scientific theory of the dynamics of human and animal societies. The publicity which surrounded the appearance of E. O. Wilson's *Sociobiology: The New Synthesis* emphasized the supposed importance of this new field for social planning. "In charting the future course of society, Wilson believes man will need all the help he can get from the new field of sociobiology."[1] Robert Trivers, one of the leading theorists of sociobiology, has stated:

The authors are particularly grateful to Freda Salzman and Marian Lowe for pointing out the importance of the sexist assumptions and structure of sociobiology and for helping us develop the analysis presented here. In addition, we thank Barbara Beckwith, Tedd Judd, Bob Lange, Judy Livingstone and Pat Walicke for their detailed critique of the curriculum, *Exploring Human Nature*.

Joseph Alper, Jon Beckwith, and Lawrence G. Miller are members of the Sociobiology Study Group of Science for the People.

It's time we started viewing ourselves as having biological, genetic, and natural components to our behavior, and that we start setting up a physical and social world to match those tendencies.[2]

What kind of world do sociobiologists see as matching "those tendencies?" Since, according to sociobiology, the tendencies to sex-role division of labor, competition and hierarchies are, to some extent, genetically controlled, there are limitations on how much these aspects of our behavior can be changed. While Wilson has pointed out the dangers of the "naturalistic fallacy of ethics which uncritically concludes that what is, should be,"[3] he has still consistently offered us advice on *what can be* derived from sociobiological wisdom.

How we structure our societies, how we deal with inequalities and other fundamental social questions, ideally depends on ethical principles. But what is the origin of these ethical principles? Sociobiology, according to Wilson, suggests an "evolutionary approach to ethics."[4] Perhaps ethics should be "temporarily removed from the hands of the philosophers and biologicized." In developing these principles, we must be aware that "while few would disagree that justice is an ideal state for disembodied spirits," "the human genotype and the ecosystem in which it evolved were fashioned out of extreme unfairness."[5] In other words, no matter how much we might wish for a fair and egalitarian society, we must recognize the limitations on how far we can move in reaching these goals. The limitations derive from an understanding of our evolutionary history. For instance, as we discuss in detail below, Wilson suggests that sociobiological theory leads to the prediction that women are unlikely to occupy certain of the high-status positions in society.

In summing up his work on the last page of his book, Wilson foresees constraints on possible social changes:

If the planned society were to deliberately steer its members past those stresses and conflicts that once gave the destructive phenotypes (aggression, dominance, violence) their Darwinian edge, the other phenotypes (cooperativeness, creativity) might dwindle with them.[6]

This is rather a new twist in biological determinist theorizing. It does not say that we cannot change unwanted aspects of our behavior, but rather that if we change them too much, we may lose other more desirable qualities.

Perhaps if such statements were limited to academic journals and academic discussions, they would not be of much concern to us. However, no matter how academic the intent of the proponents, theories which deal with human behavior and human social arrangements have often had significant social impact. This has been particularly true of genetic theories of human behavior from Social Darwinism and eugenics to the recent studies on genetics and intelligence and on criminality.[7] In the case of sociobiology it is not merely that these ideas will eventually leave the university and become widely known because of their own intrinsic appeal; but rather that sociobiologists themselves have been extremely active in ensuring that their theories and the implications of the theories receive the widest public attention.

E. O. Wilson and Harvard University Press launched a massive public relations campaign rare for a technical book in the natural sciences. Even before its publication, a front page article appeared in the *New York Times,* announcing the book and its "revolutionary" implications for human societies.[8] Subsequently, three full-page ads were taken in the *New York Times Book Review* section. Wilson was extensively interviewed, on TV and in the press, and stories appeared in *People* magazine,[9] *House and Garden* magazine,[10] *The National Observer*[11] and the Boston *Globe,*[12] with such titles as "Sociobiology is a New Science with New Ideas on Why We Sometimes Behave Like Cavemen" and "Sociobiology: New Theory on Man's Motivation." This attempt to reach the public with sociobiological theories has continued since the publication of Wilson's book with recent articles in the magazines *Mother Jones*[13] and *Psychology Today* (an interview with Irven DeVore).[14]

In addition, sociobiologists have been proclaiming the importance of their field at a wide range of professional meetings. At the 1976 annual convention of the American Group Psychotherapists' Association, they stated that "clinicians and students of human groups will be able increasingly to base their work on foundations rooted in zoology and primatology." Sociobiologists organized several major sessions at the 1976 meetings of the American Anthropological Association, and Wilson gave major addresses at the eastern meetings of the American Psychological Association and the American Sociological Association in 1977.

One of the areas where, in the past, biological determinist theories have had their most immediate impact is education. This has been no less true for sociobiology. College and university sociobiology courses have proliferated. In an article in *The American Biology Teacher* (a magazine for high school biology teachers), Paul Gastonguay called for the teaching of sociobiology in high schools, arguing that "several crucial dilemmas faced by our present day society can be quantifiably related to analogous phenomena in other animal species."[15] There already exists a high school curriculum, *Exploring Human Nature,*[16] prepared by Harvard sociobiologists Irven DeVore and Robert Trivers. This curriculum, which is used in over one hundred school systems in twenty-six states,[17] essentially presents sociobiological theory as fact, assuming without question that human behaviors can be explained according to evolutionary principles. Then the students are asked to look at the world around them and explain various social behaviors in terms of their adaptive significance. For instance, the following questions are posed in that way. "What in our evolutionary past led to the human family?" "Why don't females compete? Why aren't males choosy?" "How did the pair bond become part of human nature?" The curriculum is constructed so as to play down the role of cultural factors and cultural evolution in such behaviors. A section entitled "How are Behaviors Inherited?" includes the following statement:

But some men, because of their genetic construction, will make better soldiers and will probably be happier in their profession than many others. Fortunately modern society offers many different occupations, and differently endowed persons are likely to find one that suits their dispositions.

The obvious popular appeal of sociobiology, created in part by the extensive proselytizing efforts of Wilson and his colleagues, has led to a second wave of sociobiology books and films. In the last year, at least two new, more popular books have appeared: R. Dawkins's *The Selfish Gene* (with a foreword by R. Trivers),[18] and D. P. Barash's *Sociobiology and Behavior* (with a foreword by E. O. Wilson).[19] An illustration of how sociobiological thinking is extended in these books appears in the following quotation from Dawkins's book:

[Our genes] swarm in huge colonies, safe inside gigantic lumbering robots, sealed off from the outside world, communicating with it by tortuous indirect routes . . . they created us body and mind; and their preservation is the ultimate rationale for our existence.[20]

In the foreword to Barash's book, Wilson warns us that sociobiology will "help us learn what we really are and not just what we hope we are." According to Barash, sociobiology helps us to understand "why women have almost universally found themselves relegated to the nursery, while men derive the greatest satisfaction from their jobs."[21]

In these books, sociobiology is taken to its ridiculous extremes. For instance, Barash uses the principles of this new science to explain a variety of aspects of our social behavior.

Sociobiological theory would predict that adults with the most to gain and the least to lose would be the most eager adopters, and certainly this is true in the United States where childless couples are the predominant adopters.[22]

Do we really need sociobiology to explain this societal phenomenon?

Possibly the most blatant example of the social implications of sociobiology and a possible harbinger of things to come is a new film entitled *Sociobiology: Doing What Comes Naturally.*[23] The film, which is based mainly on interviews with Wilson, DeVore and Trivers, is designed for high school and college students. It lays heavy emphasis on sex role differences, arguing against the "assertions of the women's liberation movement."[24] While war is not condoned, Trivers, in this film, says that a major motivation for war is the innate need for men to proliferate their genes by impregnating the women of the defeated enemy. Social class differences are implied to be genetically programmed. Ant societies are used as a model: "Once a worker, always a worker. There is no upward mobility here."[25] While the film is clearly a vulgarization of sociobiological ideas (a woman in hot pants is used to symbolize women's natural role as sex objects), its claims and its symbols are a logical extension of the statements by sociobiologists in the film. The film openly presents a justification for a sexist and class society.

THE ASSUMPTIONS OF SOCIOBIOLOGY

The kind of society for which sociobiology provides a rationale is determined by the very assumptions upon which this new "science" is based. Sociobiologists, like other scientists, make critical assumptions when formulating their theories. Some of these assumptions are well-grounded, supported by data from other fields: for example, the existence of genes and the predictable effects of some kinds of evolutionary pressure upon animal populations. Others, especially those concerning humans, are simply speculative. For instance, the view that contemporary "primitive" societies are similar to societies which preceded our own has been extensively criticized.[26] In our earlier critiques we have analyzed in detail other fundamental assumptions of the theory.[27] We have shown that the hypotheses that *human* social behavior is subject to evolutionary pressures, and that a genetically based human nature exists, are both open to serious questions. Thus, evolutionary arguments founded on animal data cannot be directly applied to the complex interactions both within and between human societies; and while humans are animals and have certain obvious genetic traits, the extent to which genes influence complex social behavior is essentially unknowable at present.

These assumptions form the basis of sociobiological theory. Thus, human behavior can be explained in biological terms, and biological solutions can be suggested for human problems. But since a biological basis for human behavior cannot be determined "scientifically," the political and social biases of the sociobiologists must play a large role in the formulation of their theory of human nature. Thus, despite the sociobiologists' supposed disregard for social, historical and political factors which shape human action, these factors are incorporated into the theory in the form of the behavioral traits suggested as fundamental to human society. The view of a society characterized by such traits as "indoctrinability," "spite," "male dominance over women," "deception and hypocrisy," and "xenophobia," ultimately reflects a particular social, political and historical analysis. From this analysis flow specific political consequences.

THE SEXISM IN SOCIOBIOLOGY

The inherent political and social implications of sociobiology can perhaps be best illustrated by an investigation of the treatment of sex roles. D. P. Barash, in his book on sociobiology, emphasizes the importance of sex differences in the theory: "Sociobiology relies heavily upon the biology of male-female differences and upon the adaptive behavioral differences that have evolved accordingly. Ironically, mother nature appears to be a sexist."[28] These statements are of course accompanied by the usual hedges; e.g., "sexism is recognition of male-female *differences;* however it does not imply either sex is *better;* "[29] and the biological underpinnings of the theory may or may not apply to humans. Wilson himself, in discussing male-female division of labor, maintains that "even with identical education and equal access to all professions, men are more likely to play a disproportionate role in political life, business, and science," and "my own guess is that the genetic bias is intense enough to cause a substantial division of labor even in the most free and most egalitarian of future societies."[30] It is our contention that this sexism (using the word as ordinary people do) in sociobiology is so embedded in the theory that it can not be simply excised. Furthermore, such disclaimers as Barash's that "evaluation of male-female differences in human behavior should not be construed as supporting its propriety"[31] or Wilson's pious hopes that his guesses even if correct "could not be used to argue for anything less than sex-blind admission and free personal choice"[32] ignore the realities of our society which has discriminated against women and minority peoples for so many years.

The sexism in sociobiology is an outgrowth of the theory itself. The sociobiological theory of human behavior begins by attempting to identify those traits that are common to people in all cultures, assuming of course, that such universal traits exist.[33] The universality of a trait is then deemed to be an argument for the biological basis of that trait.[34] In addition to searching for universals, Wilson maintains (again with the appropriate hedges) that conservative traits, those that remain constant throughout the order Primates, are "the ones most likely to have persisted in relatively unaltered form into the evolution of *Homo.* "[35] The social traits that are both universal and conservative serve as the basis for sociobiological hypothesis formation. These traits, listed in Table 27.1 of *Sociobiology,* are "aggressive dominance systems with males dominant over female; scaling of responses, especially in aggressive interaction; prolonged maternal care; pronounced socialization of young; and matrilinear organization."[36] Since it is argued that males are naturally more aggressive than females, we see that all of the important traits listed by Wilson are based on sex differences. Furthermore, many of the other social traits that are taken to be universal can be derived from those more fundamental traits. Territoriality, xenophobia, and waging war, cited as universals by sociobiologists, are all related to aggression. Or in the words of Fox, as quoted by Wilson, the dominant male in hominid societies was likely to be "controlled, cunning, cooperative, attractive to the ladies, good with the children, relaxed, tough, eloquent, skillful, knowledgeable and proficient in self-defense and hunting."[37] The implicit and explicit sexism in this list needs no comment.

The arguments given above for the biological nature of sex-related behaviorial traits focus on the universality of these traits in all human cultures and on the appearance of these traits in other primates. Attention is also drawn to the relation between these traits and differences in sex hormone levels in males and females and to the fact that these traits manifest themselves at an early age before differential socialization could occur. Probably the most important work discussing the biological basis of sex differences is *The Psychology of Sex Differences,* by E. Maccoby and C. Jacklin,[38] which is cited by Wilson in his *New York Times* article. A detailed critique of the evidence in support of the thesis that men are naturally more aggressive than women is given by Chasin.[39] Chasin points out that the evidence on nonhuman primates is selected to confirm the biological determinists' hypotheses. Different species of primates differ dramatically in their aggressiveness, and even groups within the same species differ depending on the habitat. Thus, baboons living on the plains (one of the sociobiologists' favorite species) show the classic patterns of male dominance, while forest baboons of the same species show little aggression and no male dominance hierarchies. The cross-cultural evidence cited by Maccoby and Jacklin is similarly circumscribed. Chasin discusses the Tasaday people of the Philippines, Pygmies, the Chinese, and the !Kung bushmen before they were resettled as examples of people living in societies in which boys are not more aggressive than girls and in which the sexual division of labor is much less pronounced then is the case in our own society.

The hormone research indicating that higher levels of male hormones result in more aggressive behavior is inconclusive at best. For example, it is conceivable that increases in male hormone levels are the result of rather than the cause of the aggressive behavior. Finally, the arguments that aggressive behavior appears before socialization can occur are difficult to accept in view of the evidence showing that babies of different sexes are treated differently from birth.[40] The possibility that parents' reactions to their child's behavior is influenced by their preconceptions of proper and expected male or female behavior is discounted by Maccoby and Jacklin.

The tendency to discuss only the evidence supporting the thesis that sex-related behavior is biologically controlled might be seen as resulting simply from the sexist biases that pervade our society and which may even operate below the level of consciousness. (Indeed, Maccoby and Jacklin maintain that they are feminists!)[41]

But deeper than the sexist biases in the sociobiologists' selection of the universal traits is the sexism that is inherent to the structure of the theory of sociobiology as it exists today. Sociobiology relies almost totally on Darwinian sexual selection as the mechanism for the evolutionary development of characteristics. This theory of sexual selection operates in the following manner. A single male animal can impregnate many females. Thus, in order for a species to produce as many offspring as possible it is necessary for all the females to be reproductively active, but only a small fraction of the males need contribute their sperm. In order for the fittest offspring to be produced, only the fittest males should engage in reproduction. In evolutionary biology an individual's fitness is measured by its success in propagating its genes in the next generation. Fitness is equated with reproductive success and so competition among the males for the available females is inevitable. It is this competition that gives rise to the biological basis for aggression, aggressive dominance systems with male dominant over female, territoriality, and entrepreneurship. Males possessing the most aggressive traits therefore succeed in propagating their genes through successive generations by means of their and their offspring's superior mating ability. Males are more aggressive and cunning than females because the evolutionary pressures of sexual selection force them to be so. This theory of sexual selection, however, is only one of a number of possible forms of natural selection and its importance in the evolution of the human species is an untested hypothesis.

The implications of this theory are striking. The important traits that have been selected for in evolutionary history are male traits. Only males need compete; therefore selection operates on the genetic variability in males. Genetic variability in females is relevant to the evolutionary process only when females choose from among competing males. Females are thus the passive carriers of the selected male genes. Is it a coincidence that the conventional stereotypes of the passive woman acted upon by aggressive men carries over into the sociobiologists' view of the female role in the evolution of the species?

Sociobiology cannot be divorced from its sexism. Not only are the postulated human universals sexist, but the asserted mode of their propagation in evolution is sexist as well. This pervasiveness of the sexism in sociobiology is camouflaged by the careless and sexist language used by the sociobiologists. An insistence on the use of the word "person" instead of "man" when referring to a member of the human species is often viewed as frivolous nitpicking, but in sociobiology the distinction is crucial. The title of Chapter 27 of Wilson's book is "Man: From Sociobiology to Sociology," but the human universal traits of "man" that are cited by Wilson are really traits of stereotypical males. Aggression and territoriality are universals in males and are not species universals. Once the sexism of the language is exposed and the ambiguous use of the word "man" made clear, it becomes manifest that sociobiology carries with it the implication that human social behavioral traits evolved primarily through selection on male traits. Much of "Man's" evolutionary history is really the history of "men." Female social behavior, which is not readily explainable on the basis of sexual selection, is—like the creation of Eve in Genesis—just an afterthought.

CONCLUSION

Sociobiological theories, then, contain both implicit and explicit political implications and have been promoted in a fashion emphasizing these implications. As we have pointed out elsewhere, theories similar to sociobiology are not new: what have been termed evolutionary positivist theories extend back at least a century, and have included Social Darwinism and some contemporary ethology. The explosion of interest in sociobiology manifested by many publications indicates a revival of interest in these theories. This revival is one example of the increasing reliance upon science to explain a host of social problems and the proposal of scientific solutions to such problems. This reliance has been clearly demonstrated in recent controversies concerning the importance of scientific notions of intelligence (I.Q.) and of biological bases of criminality (XYY chromosome). In those controversies the assumption of the genetic basis of human behavior has been used to rationalize social inequalities and deviant behavior. Problems such as the failure of compensatory education and the increasing crime rate, both of which are rooted in the structure of society, are studied as scientific problems susceptible to scientific analysis. Given the social context in which these theories were developed, it is not surprising that they were very rapidly presented to the public as scientific truth and have had significant social consequences.

As sociobiologists have been quick to point out, sociobiology promises an extension of this trend. For example, the role of women in society is now a highly debated issue. The struggle over the passage of the Equal Rights Amendment and the recent Supreme Court decision denying pregnancy benefits to workers (General Electric Co. *v.* Gilbert, 1976) are only two of its manifestations. Sociobiological arguments concerning innate sex-role differences clearly have relevance to the debates on these issues. Since these arguments are presented as objective science, they can be used to provide "rational" solutions to essentially political problems. Considering the history of the use of biological determinist ideas, there is good reason to fear that the development of sociobiological theories in the present social context will have pernicious social consequences.[42]

NOTES

1. N. McCain, "Sociobiology: New Theory on Man's Motivation," Boston *Sunday Globe,* November 16, 1975.
2. From sound track of *Sociobiology: Doing What Comes Naturally.* A film distributed by Document Associates, Inc., 880 Third Avenue, New York, N.Y.
3. E. O. Wilson, "Human Decency is Animal," *The New York Times Magazine,* October 12, 1975.
4. E. O. Wilson, *Sociobiology: The New Synthesis* (Cambridge, Mass.: Harvard University Press, 1975), p. 564.
5. *Ibid.,* p. 562.
6. *Ibid.,* p. 575.
7. Ann Arbor Science for the People, *Biology as a Social Weapon* (Minneapolis: Burgess, 1977).
8. B. Rensberger, "Sociobiology: Updating Darwin on Behavior," *New York Times,* May 28, 1975, p. 1.
9. "Sociobiology is a New Science with New Ideas on Why We Sometimes Behave Like Cavemen." Interview in *People* magazine, November, 1975.

10. "Getting Back to Nature—Our Hope for the Future," Interview in *House and Garden*, February, 1976, p. 65.
11. P. Young, "Is Behavior Inherited?" *The National Observer*, August 16, 1975, p. 1.
12. N. McCain, *op. cit.*
13. R. Brown, "The Monkeys Who Kill their Young," *Mother Jones*, January, 1977, p. 32.
14. S. Morris, "The New Science of Genetic Self-Interest," *Psychology Today* 10, no. 9 (1977), p. 42.
15. P. R. Gastonguay, "A Sociobiology of Man," *The American Biology Teacher*, November 1975, p. 481.
16. Education Development Center, *Exploring Human Nature* (Cambridge, Mass.: EDC, 1973).
17. Information obtained from Educational Development Center.
18. R. Dawkins, *The Selfish Gene* (New York: Oxford University Press, 1976).
19. D. P. Barash, *Sociobiology and Behavior* (New York: Elsevier, 1977).
20. Dawkins, *op. cit.*, p. 21.
21. Barash, *op. cit.*, p. xv.
22. *Ibid.*, p. 313.
23. *Sociobiology: Doing What Comes Naturally.* A film distributed by Document Associates, Inc., 880 Third Avenue, New York, N.Y.
24. *Ibid.*, from the brochure advertising the film.
25. *Ibid.*, from the sound track.
26. See, for instance, M. H. Fried, *The Evolution of Political Society* (New York: Random House, 1967), especially pp. 170–174.
27. See other articles in this volume and "Sociobiology: A New Biological Determinism" (an expanded version of the *BioSciences* article) in Ann Arbor Science for the People, *op. cit.*
28. Barash, *op. cit.*, p. 283.
29. *Ibid.*
30. Wilson, *The New York Times Magazine*, *op. cit.*
31. Barash, *op. cit.*, p. 283.
32. Wilson, *The New York Times Magazine*, *op. cit.*
33. See M. Sahlins, *The Use and Abuse of Biology* (Ann Arbor: University of Michigan Press, 1976) for evidence that important human social behavioral traits are not universal.
34. For a discussion of the fallacy in this argument, see R. C. Lewontin, "The Analysis of Variation and the Analysis of Causes," in N. Block and G. Dworkin, *The IQ Controversy* (New York: Pantheon, 1976), p. 179.
35. Wilson, *Sociobiology: The New Synthesis*, p. 551.
36. *Ibid.*, p. 552.
37. *Ibid.*, p. 569.
38. E. Maccoby and C. Jacklin, *The Psychology of Sex Differences* (Stanford: Stanford University Press, 1974).

39. B. Chasin, "Sociobiology: A Sexist Synthesis," *Science for the People Magazine* 9, no. 3 (1977), p. 27.
40. S. Goldberg and M. Lewis, "Play Behavior in the Year Old Infant: Early Sex Differences," *Child Development* 40, no. 21 (1969).
41. Maccoby and Jacklin, *op. cit.,* p. 12.
42. Recent examples of the overt political use of sociobiology include the August 1, 1977, cover story in *Time* magazine and an article in April 10, 1978, issue of *Business Week* entitled "A Genetic Defense of the Free Market."

SELECTED BIBLIOGRAPHY

The bibliography included here is intended solely as a preliminary guide to the vast body of literature on sociobiology. The number of books and articles on the subject and cognate fields is enormous and continuously increasing—thus making any attempt at a comprehensive bibliography impossible. Instead, it is hoped that the interested reader will be able to pursue source materials in the diverse disciplines related to sociobiology using the references cited here. Additional bibliographical material may be found in E. O. Wilson's *Sociobiology: The New Synthesis*, David P. Barash's *Sociobiology and Behavior*, and Albert Somit's *Biology and Politics*. A number of journals in biology and the social sciences regularly publish articles pertaining to sociobiology. Among these are *The American Naturalist*, *Current Anthropology*, *The Journal of Theoretical Biology*, *The Journal of Social and Biological Structures*, *Social Science Information*, *Science*, *Animal Behaviour*, *The Quarterly Review of Biology*, and *Nature*.

Alcock, J. *Animal Behavior: An Evolutionary Approach.* Sunderland, Mass.: Sinauer Associates, 1975.

Alexander, R. D. "The Search for an Evolutionary Philosophy of Man." *Proceedings of the Royal Society of Victoria*, 84, 1971, pp. 99–120.

_____. "The Evolution of Social Behavior." *Annual Review of Ecology and Systematics* 5, 1974, pp. 325–83.

_____. "The Search for a General Theory of Behavior." *Behavioral Science* 20, 1975, pp. 77–100.

_____, and Sherman, P. W. "Local Mate Competition and Parental Investment in Social Insects." *Science* 196, 1977, pp. 494–500.

_____. "Natural Selection and Social Exchange." *Social Exchange and Developing Relationships.* Edited by Burgess, R. L., and Huston, T. L. New York: Academic Press, 1976.

Alland, A. *The Human Imperative.* New York: Columbia University Press, 1972.

Allee, W. C. *Animal Aggregations.* Chicago: University of Chicago Press, 1931.

_____. *The Social Life of Animals.* New York: W. W. Norton, 1938.

_____, Emerson, A. E., Park, O., Park, T., and Schmidt, K. P. *Principles of Animal Ecology.* Philadelphia: W. B. Saunders Co., 1949.

Allen, G. "Genetics, Eugenics, and Class Struggle." *Genetics* 79, 1975, pp. 29–45.

Altmann, S., ed. *Social Communication Among Primates.* Chicago: University of Chicago Press, 1967.

Alverdes, F. *Social Life in the Animal World.* London: Harcourt, Brace, 1927.

Ann Arbor Science for the People Editorial Collective. *Biology As a Social Weapon.* Ann Arbor: Burgess, 1977.

Ardrey, R. *The Territorial Imperative.* New York: Atheneum, 1966.

_____. *The Social Contract.* New York: Atheneum, 1970.

_____. *The Hunting Hypothesis.* New York: Atheneum, 176.

Aronson, L. et al., eds. *Development and Evolution of Behavior.* San Francisco: W. H. Freeman, 1970.

Baerends, A. et al., eds. *Function and Evolution in Behavior*. Oxford: Clarendon Press, 1975.

Baier, K. *The Moral Point of View*. New York: Random House, 1965.

Baldwin, J. M. *Development and Evolution*. New York: Macmillan Company, 1902.

Barash, D. P. "Some Evolutionary Aspects of Parental Behavior in Animals and Man." *American Journal of Psychology, 89, 1976, pp. 195–217.*

———. *Sociobiology and Behavior*. New York: Elsevier, 1977.

Bardwick, J. M. *Psychology of Women*. New York: Harper & Row, 1971.

Barkow, J. H. "Prestige and Culture: A Biosocial Interpretation." *Current Anthropology* 16, 1975, pp. 553–72.

Barnett, S. A. *A Study in Behaviour: Principles of Ethology and Behavioural Physiology Displayed Mainly in the Rat*. London: Methuen, 1963.

Bateson, P., and Hinde, R., eds. *Growing Points in Ethology*. Cambridge: Cambridge University Press, 176.

Beach, F. "The Snark Was a Boojum." *American Psychologist* 5, 1950, pp. 115–24.

———. ed. *Sex and Behavior*. New York: Wiley, 1965.

Benthall, J., ed. *The Limits of Human Nature*. New York: E. P. Dutton & Co., 1974.

Benzer, S. "Genetic Dissection of Behavior." *Scientific American* 229, 1973, pp. 24–37.

Bigelow, R. *The Dawn Warriors: Man's Evolution Towards Peace*. Boston: Little, Brown, 1969.

Birney, R. C., and Teevan, R. C., eds. *Instinct*. Princeton: D. Van Nostrand Co., 1961.

Block, N. J., and Dworkin, G., eds. *The I.Q. Controversy*. New York: Pantheon, 1976.

Bock, W. J. "Adaptation and the Comparative Method." In *Major Patterns in Vertebrate Evolution*. Edited by M. Hecht. New York: Plenum, 1977.

Boorman, S. A., and Levitt, P. R. "Group Selection on the Boundary of a Stable Population," *Theoretical Population Biology* 4, 1973, pp. 85–128.

Bowler, P. J. *Fossils and Progress*. New York: Science History Publications, 1976.

Brock, D. W. "The Justification of Morality." *American Philosophical Quarterly* 14, 1977, pp. 71–78.

Brown, J. L. "Alternate Routes to Sociality in Jays—With a Theory for the Evolution of Altruism and Communal Breeding." *American Zoologist* 14, 1974, pp. 63–80.

———. *The Evolution of Behavior*. New York: W. W. Norton, 1975.

Burrow, J. W. *Evolution and Society*. Cambridge: Cambridge University Press, 1966.

Campbell, B. G., ed. *Sexual Selection and the Descent of Man 1871–1971*. Chicago: Aldine, 1972.

Campbell, D. T. "Evolutionary Epistemology." In *The Philosophy of Karl R. Popper*, edited by P. A. Schilpp. La Salle: Open Court, 1966.

_____. "On the Conflicts Between Biological and Social Evolution and Between Psychology and Moral Tradition." *American Psychologist* 30, 1975, pp. 1103–26.

Caplan, A. L. "Genetic Aspects of Human Behavior: Philosophical and Ethical Issues." In *The Encyclopedia of Bioethics,* edited by W. T. Reich, pp. 1070–72. New York: The Free Press, 1978.

_____. "In What Ways Are Recent Developments in Biology and Sociobiology Relevant to Ethics?" *Perspectives in Biology and Medicine* 1, Vol. 21, 1978.

Carneiro, R. L. "A Theory of the Origin of the State." *Science* 196, 1970, pp. 733–38.

Cavalli-Sforza, L. L. "Similarities and Dissimilarities of Sociocultural and Biological Evolution." In *Mathematics in the Archeological and Historical Sciences,* edited by F. R. Hodson. Edinburgh: University Press, 1971.

_____, and Feldman, M. W. "Models for Cultural Inheritance." *Journal of Theoretical Population Biology* 4, 1973, pp. 42–55.

Chagnon, N., and Irons, W., eds. *Sociobiology and Human Social Organization.* Scituate, Mass.: Duxbury Press, 1978.

Chance, M. R. A., and Jolly, C. J. *Social Groups of Monkeys, Apes and Men.* New York: E. P. Dutton, 1970.

Charnov, E. L., and Krebs, J. R. "The Evolution of Alarm Calls: Altruism or Manipulation?" *American Naturalist* 109 (1974): 107–112.

Chase, A. *The Legacy of Malthus.* New York: Alfred A. Knopf, 1977.

Christian, J. J., "Social Subordination, Population Density, and Mammalian Evolution," *Science* 168, 1970, pp. 84–90.

Cloak, F. T., Jr. "Is a Cultural Ethology Possible?" *Human Ecology* 3, 1975, pp. 161–82.

Cody, M. L. *Competition and the Structure of Bird Communities.* Princeton: Princeton University Press, 1974.

Cohen, J. E. *Casual Groups of Monkeys and Men: Stochastic Models of Elemental Social Systems.* Cambridge: Harvard University Press, 1971.

Count, E. W. "The Biological Basis of Human Sociality." *American Anthropologist* 60, 1958, pp. 1049–85.

_____. *Being and Becoming Human: Essays on the Biogram.* New York: Van Nostrand Reinhold, 1973.

Cowan, R. S. "Nature and Nurture: The Interplay of Biology and Politics." *Studies in the History of Biology* 1, 1977, pp. 133–208.

Crook, J. H., ed. *Social Behavior in Birds and Mammals.* New York: Academic Press, 1970.

Darling, F. F. *Bird Flocks and the Breeding Cycle: A Contribution to the Study of Avian Sociality.* Cambridge: Cambridge University Press, 1938.

Darlington, C. D. *The Evolution of Man and Society.* New York: Simon and Schuster, 1969.

_____. *Genetics and Man.* New York: Schocken Books, 1969.

Darwin, C. *On the Origin of Species by Means of Natural Selection.* London: J. Murray, 1859.

———. *The Descent of Man and Selection in Relation to Sex.* London: J. Murray, 1871.

———. *The Expression of Emotions in Man and Animals.* 2nd ed. London: J. Murray, 1904.

Davis, B. D. "Evolution, Human Diversity and Society." *Zygon* 11, 1976, pp. 80–95.

Dawkins, R. *The Selfish Gene.* New York: Oxford University Press, 1976.

DeVore, I., ed. *Primate Behavior.* New York: Holt, Rinehart & Winston, 1965.

Dewsbury, D. A. *Comparative Animal Behavior.* New York: McGraw Hill, 1978.

Dobzhansky, T. *The Biology of Ultimate Concern.* Edited by Ruth N. Anshen. New York: New American Library, 1967.

———. *Genetics of the Evolutionary Process.* New York: Columbia University Press, 1970.

———. "The Myths of Genetic Predestination and of Tabula Rasa." *Perspectives in Biology and Medicine* 2, 1976, pp. 156–70.

———. Ayala, F. J., Stebbins, G. L., and Valentine, J. W. *Evolution.* San Francisco: W. H. Freeman, 1977.

Dupree, A. H., and Parsons, T. "The Relations Between Biological and Sociocultural Theory." *Zygon* 11, 1976, pp. 1963–66.

Dworkin, G., ed. *Determinism, Free Will and Moral Responsibility.* Englewood Cliffs, N. J.: Prentice-Hall, 1970.

Eberhard, M. J. W. "The Evolution of Social Behavior by Kin Selection." *Quarterly Review of Biology* 50, 1975, pp. 1–33.

Eckland, B. "Darwin Rides Again." *American Journal of Sociology* 82, 1976, pp. 692–97.

Edel, A. *Ethical Judgment: The Use of Science in Ethics.* New York: Macmillan, 1955.

Ehrman, L.; Omenn, G. S., and Caspari, E. *Genetics, Environment and Behavior.* New York: Academic Press, 1972.

———, and Parsons, P. A. *The Genetics of Behavior.* Sunderland, Mass.: Sinauer Associates, 1976.

Ehrlich, P. R., and Feldman, S. S. *The Race Bomb.* New York: Quadrangle, 1977.

Eibl-Eibesfeldt, I. *Love and Hate: The Natural History of Behavior.* New York: Holt, Rinehart & Winston, 1971.

———. *Ethology, the Biology of Behavior.* New York: Holt, Rinehart & Winston, 1975.

Eisenberg, J. F., and Dillon, W. S., eds. *Man and Beast: Comparative Social Behavior.* Washington: Smithsonian Institution Press, 1971.

Ekman, P., ed. *Darwin and Facial Expression.* New York: Academic Press, 1973.

Emerson, A. E. "Termite Nests—A Study of the Phylogeny of Behavior." *Ecological Monographs* 8, 1938, pp. 247–84.

Emlen, J. M. "Natural Selection and Human Behavior." *Journal of Theoretical Biology* 12, 1966, pp. 410–18.

Engelhardt, H. T., and Callahan, D., eds. *Knowledge, Value, and Belief.* Hastings: Institute of Society, Ethics & Life Sciences, 1977.

Erickson, C. J., and Zenone, P. "Courtship Differences in Male Ring Doves: Avoidance of Cuckoldry?" *Science* 192, 1976, pp. 1353–54.

Etkin, W., ed. *Social Behavior and Organization Among Vertebrates.* Chicago: University of Chicago Press, 1964.

Ewer, R. F. *Ethology of Mammals.* New York: Plenum Press, 1969.

Fisher, R. A. *The Genetical Theory of Natural Selection.* (1930). New York: Dover, 1958.

Flew, A. *Evolutionary Ethics.* New York: St. Martin's Press, 1968.

Fox, R., ed. *Biosocial Anthropology.* New York: John Wiley & Sons, 1975.

_____. "Human Ethology." In *Annual Review of Anthropology,* edited by B. J. Siegel; A. R. Beals; and S. A. Tyler. Palo Alto: Annual Reviews, 1976.

Frankena, W. "The Naturalistic Fallacy." *Mind* 38, 1939, pp. 103–14.

Fried, M. H. *The Evolution of Political Society: An Evolutionary View.* New York: Random House, 1967.

Gadgil, M., and Bossert, W. H. "Life History Consequences of Natural Selection." *American Naturalist* 104, 1970, pp. 1–24.

Galton, F. *Inquiries into Human Faculties and Its Development.* London: J. M. Dent & Sons, 1907.

Gauthier, D., ed. *Morality and Rational Self-Interest.* Englewood Cliffs, N.J.: Prentice-Hall, 1970.

Gaylin, W. *Caring.* New York: Alfred A. Knopf, 1976.

Geertz, C. *The Interpretation of Cultures.* New York: Basic Books, 1973.

Geist, V. *Mountain Sheep: A Study in Behavior and Evolution.* Chicago: University of Chicago Press, 1971.

Genetic Engineering Group. "Sociobiology—The Skewed Synthesis." *Science for the People Magazine,* November, 1975, pp. 28–30.

Ghiselin, M. T. *The Economy of Nature and the Evolution of Sex.* Berkeley: University of California Press, 1974.

Gilpin, M. E. *Group Selection in Predator–Prey Communities.* Princeton: Princeton University Press, 1975.

Glass, D. C., ed. *Genetics.* New York: Rockefeller University Press and Russell Sage Foundation, 1968.

Glick, T. F., ed. *The Comparative Reception of Darwinism.* Austin: University of Texas Press, 1974.

Gottesman, I. I. "A Sampler of Human Behavioral Genetics." *Evolutionary Biology* 2, 1968, pp. 276–320.

Gould, J. L. "The Dance—Language Controversy," *The Quarterly Review of Biology* 51, 1976, pp. 211–44.

Gould, S. J. *Ever Since Darwin.* New York: W. W. Norton, 1977.

Graham, L. "Political Ideology and Genetic Theory: Russia and Germany in the 1920's." *Hastings Center Report* 7, 1977, pp. 30–39.

Grant, V. *The Origin of Adaptations.* New York: Columbia University Press, 1963.

Graubard, A. "Sociobiology Squabble." *Working Papers for a New Society.* Summer 1976, pp. 12–17.

Gray, A. *Darwiniana: Essays and Reviews Pertaining to Darwinism.* 1876. Reprinted. Cambridge: Harvard University Press, 1963.

Gregory, M., and Silvers, A., eds. *Sociobiology and Human Nature.* San Francisco: Jossey-Bass, 1978.

Griffin, D. R. *The Question of Animal Awareness.* New York: Rockefeller University Press, 1976.

Gruber, H. E., and Barrett, P. H. *Darwin on Man: A Psychological Study of Scientific Creativity.* New York: E. P. Dutton, 1974.

Haldane, J. B. S. *The Causes of Evolution.* London: Longmans, Green, 1932.

Hamilton, W. D. "The Evolution of Altruistic Behaviour." *American Naturalist* 97, 1963, pp. 354–56.

———. "The Genetical Evolution of Social Behavior, Parts 1 and 2," *Journal of Theoretical Biology* 7, 1964, pp. 1–51.

———. "Altruism and Related Phenomena Mainly in Social Insects," *Annual Review of Ecology and Systematics* 3, 1972, pp. 143–232.

Hardin, G. *The Limits of Altruism.* Bloomington: Indiana University Press, 1977.

Harris, M. *Culture, Man and Nature.* New York: T. Y. Crowell, 1968.

———. *Cannibals and Kings: The Origins of Cultures.* New York: Random House, 1977.

Hartung, J. "On Natural Selection and the Inheritance of Wealth." *Current Anthropology* 17, 1976, pp. 607–22.

Heinroth, O. *"Beitrage zur Biologie, namentlich ethologie und physiologie der Anatiden,"* International Ornithologisches Kongress 5, 1910, pp. 589–702.

Himmelfarb, G. *Darwin and the Darwinian Revolution.* New York: W. W. Norton, 1959.

Hinde, R. A. *Animal Behavior.* New York: McGraw-Hill, 1970.

———. *Biological Bases of Human Social Behavior.* New York: McGraw-Hill, 1974.

Hirsch, J., ed. *Behavior-Genetic Analysis.* New York: McGraw-Hill, 1967.

Hobbes, T., *Leviathan.* Edited by J. Plamenatz. Cleveland: Meridian, 1963.

Hobhouse, L. T. *Mind in Evolution.* 2nd ed. London: MacMillan, 1915.

Hodos, W., and Campbell, C. B. G. *"Scala naturae:* Why There Is No Theory in Comparative Psychology." *Psychological Review* 76, 1969, pp. 337–50.

Hofstadter, R. *Social Darwinism in American Thought.* Rev. ed. Boston: Beacon Press, 1955.

Homans, G. C. *Social Behavior: Its Elementary Forms.* Rev. ed. New York: Harcourt Brace Jovanovich, 1974.

Hrdy, S. B. *The Langurs of Abu.* Cambridge: Harvard University Press, 1977.

Hubbard, R. "Sexism in Science." *Radcliffe Quarterly,* March 1976, pp. 8–11.

Hubbs, C. L. "Concepts of Homology and Analogy." *American Naturalist* 78, 1944, pp. 289–307.

Hudson, W. D., ed. *The Is/Ought Question.* New York: St. Martin's Press, 1969.

Hull, D. *Philosophy of Biological Science.* Englewood Cliffs, N.J.: Prentice-Hall, 1974.

_____. "Altruism in Science: A Sociobiological Explanation of Altruistic Behavior Among Scientists." *Animal Behavior* (in press).

Hume, D. *A Treatise of Human Nature,* edited by L. A. Selby-Bigge. Oxford: Clarendon Press, 1896.

Huxley, J. *The Courtship Habits of the Great Crested Grebe.* (1914). London: Jonathan Cape, 1968.

_____. *Evolution: The Modern Synthesis.* London: Allen & Unwin, 1942.

_____. *Touchstone for Ethics.* New York: Harper's, 1947.

Huxley, J. S., and Huxley, T. H. *Evolution and Ethics.* London: Pilot Press, 1947.

Huxley, T. H. *Collected Essays.* London: MacMillan, 1892.

_____. *Man's Place in Nature,* 1863. Ann Arbor: University of Michigan Press, 1971.

Inden, R. B., and Nicholas, R. W. *Kinship in Bengali Culture.* Chicago: University of Chicago Press, 1977.

Irvine, W. *Apes, Angels and Victorians.* New York: McGraw-Hill, 1955.

Jay, P. C., ed. *Primates.* New York: Holt, Rinehart & Winston, 1968.

Jennings, H. S. *The Biological Basis of Human Nature.* New York: W. W. Norton, 1930.

Jerison, H. J. *Evolution of the Brain and Intelligence.* New York: Academic Press, 1973.

Jolly, A. *The Evolution of Primate Behavior.* New York: Macmillan, 1972.

Kamin, L. *The Science and Politics of I.Q.* New York: Halsted Press, 1974.

Keith, A. *Evolution and Ethics.* New York: Putnam's, 1946.

King, M. C., and Wilson, A. C. "Evolution at Two Levels in Humans and Chimpanzees." *Science* 188, 1975, pp. 107–16.

Klopfer, P.H. "Social Darwinism Lives! (Should it?)." *Yale Journal of Biology and Medicine* 50, 1977, pp. 77–84.

_____, and Hailman, D. P. *An Introduction to Animal Behavior.* Englewood Cliffs, N.J.: Prentice-Hall, 1967.

Kohlberg, L., and Turiel, E. *Research in Moral Development: The Cognitive Developmental Approach.* New York: Holt, Rinehart and Winston, 1971.

Korn, N., and Thompson, F., eds. *Human Evolution.* New York: Holt, Rinehart & Winston, 1967.

Krebs, J., and May, R. M. "Social Insects and the Evolution of Altruism." *Nature* 260, 1976, pp. 9–10.

Kroeber, A. L. *The Nature of Culture.* Chicago: University of Chicago Press, 1952.

Kropotkin, P. *Mutual Aid: A Factor of Evolution.* London: Heinemann, 1902.

Kummer, H. *Social Organization of Hamadryas Baboons.* Chicago: University of Chicago Press, 1968.

_____. *Primate Societies.* Chicago: Aldine-Atherton, 1971.

Lack, D. *The Natural Regulation of Animal Numbers.* Oxford: Clarendon Press, 1954.

———. *Population Studies of Birds.* Oxford: Clarendon Press, 1966.

Lancaster, J. B. *Primate Behavior and the Emergence of Human Culture.* New York: Holt, Rinehart and Winston, 1975.

Laughlin, C. D., and d'Aquili, E. G. *Biogenetic Structuralism.* New York: Columbia University Press, 1974.

Lee, R. B., and DeVore, I., eds. *Man the Hunter.* Chicago: Aldine, 1968.

———. eds. *Kalahari Hunter-Gatherers.* Cambridge: Harvard University Press, 1976.

Lehrman, D. S. "A Critique of Konrad Lorenz' Theory of Instinctive Behavior." *Quarterly Review of Biology* 28, 1953, pp. 337–63.

Levins, R. *Evolution in Changing Environments.* Princeton: Princeton University Press, 1968.

Lewin, R. "The Course of a Controversy." *The New Scientist,* 13, May 1976, pp. 344–45.

Lewontin, R. C. "The Units of Selection." *Annual Review of Ecology and Systematics* 1, 1970, pp. 1–18.

———. *The Genetic Basis of Evolutionary Change.* New York: Columbia University Press, 1974.

Lienhardt, G. *Social Anthropology.* London: Oxford University Press, 1966.

Lin, N., and Michener, C. D. "Evolution of Sociality in Insects." *Quarterly Review of Biology* 47, 1972, pp. 131–59.

Lindzey, G., and Thiessen, D. *Contributions to Behavior–Genetic Analysis: The Mouse as a Prototype.* New York: Appleton, 1970.

Lockard, J. S. McDonald, Z. Z., Clifford, D. A., and Martinez, R. "Panhandling: Sharing of Resources." *Science* 191, 1976, pp. 406–408.

Lockard, R. B. "Reflections on the Fall of Comparative Psychology: Is There a Message for Us All?" *American Psychologist* 26, 1971, pp. 168–179.

Lorenz, K. *On Aggression.* New York: Harcourt Brace Jovanovich, 1966.

———. *Studies in Animal and Human Behavior.* Vols. 1 and 2. Translated by Robert Martin. London: Methuen & Co., 1971.

———. "Analogy as a Source of Knowledge." *Science* 185, 1974, pp. 229–33.

Lovejoy, A. O. *The Great Chain of Being.* New York: Harper and Brothers, 1936.

Lynn, R. "The Sociobiology of Nationalism." *New Society,* July 1, 1976, pp. 11–15.

Maier, N. R., and Schneirla, T. C. *Principles of Animal Psychology.* New York: Dover, 1964.

Malthus, T. R. *An Essay on the Principle of Population.* London: J. Murray, 1817.

Mandelbaum, M. *History, Man, and Reason.* Baltimore: Johns Hopkins University Press, 1971.

Masters, R. D. "Functional Approaches to Analogical Comparison Between Species." *Social Science Information* 12, 1973, pp. 7–28.

Masterton, R. B.; Hodos, W.; and Jerison, H. J., eds. *Evolution, Brain and Behavior in Vertebrates.* Hillsdale, N.J.: Erlbaum, 1976.

May, R. M. "Sociobiology: A New Synthesis and an Old Quarrel." *Nature* 260, 1976, pp. 390–91.

Maynard Smith, J. "Group Selection and Kin Selection." *Nature* 201, 1964, pp. 1145–47.

_____. "The Theory of Games and the Evolution of Animal Conflicts." *Journal of Theoretical Biology* 47, 1974, pp. 209–21.

_____. *The Theory of Evolution.* London: Penguin, 1975.

Mayr, E. *Animal Species and Evolution.* Cambridge: Harvard University Press, 1963.

Mazur, A., and Robertson, L. S. *Biology and Social Behavior.* New York: The Free Press, 1972.

Medawar, P. B., and Medawar, J. S. *The Life Science: Current Ideas of Biology.* New York: Harper & Row, 1977.

Menzel, E. W., Jr., ed. *Precultural Primate Behavior.* Basel: S. Karger, 1973.

Meynell, H. "Ethology and Ethics." *Philosophy* 45, 1970, pp. 290–306.

Michener, C. D. *The Social Behavior of Bees.* Cambridge: Harvard University Press, 1974.

Milo, R. D., ed. *Egoism and Altruism.* Belmont, Calif.: Wadsworth, 1973.

Montagu, M. F. A. *Darwin, Competition and Cooperation.* New York: Henry Schuman, 1952.

_____. *The Biosocial Nataure of Man.* New York: Grove Press, 1956.

_____, ed. *Man and Aggression.* New York: Oxford University Press, 1968.

_____, ed. *The Concept of the Primitive.* New York: The Free Press, 1968.

_____. *The Nature of Human Aggression.* New York: Oxford University Press, 1976.

Moore, G. E. *Principia Ethica.* Cambridge: Cambridge University Press, 1903.

Moorhead, P. S., and Kaplan, M. M., eds. *Mathematical Challenges to the Neo-Darwinian Interpretation of Evolution.* Philadelphia: Wistar Institute Press, 1967.

Morgan, C. L. *An Introduction to Comparative Psychology.* London: Walter Scott, 1894.

_____. *Animal Behaviour.* London: Edward Arnold, 1900.

Morris, D. *The Naked Ape.* New York: McGraw-Hill, 1967.

_____, ed. *Primate Ethology: Essays on Socio-Sexual Behavior of Apes and Monkeys.* Garden City, N.Y.: Doubleday, 1969.

Munson, R., ed. *Man and Nature.* New York: Delta Books, 1971.

Napier, J. R. and Napier, P. H., eds. *Old World Monkeys; Evolution, Systematics and Behavior.* New York: Academic Press, 1970.

Oakley, A. *Sex, Gender, and Society.* New York: Harper & Row, 1973.

Oakley, K. P. *Man the Tool-Maker.* Chicago: University of Chicago Press, 1959.

Ohno, S. "Promethean Evolution as the Biological Basis of Human Freedom and Equality." *Perspectives in Biology and Medicine* 19, 1976, pp. 527–32.

Olsen, R. G. *The Morality of Self-Interest.* New York: Harcourt Brace and World, 1965.

Oster, G. F., and Wilson, E. O. *Caste and Ecology in the Social Insects.* Princeton: Princeton University Press, 1978.

Passmore, J. *The Perfectability of Man.* New York: Charles Scribner's Sons, 1970.

Pennock, J. R. and Chapman, J. W., eds. *Human Nature in Politics.* New York: New York University Press, 1977.

Pfeiffer, J. E. *The Emergence of Society.* New York: McGraw-Hill, 1977.

Piaget, J. *The Moral Judgment of the Child.* New York: The Free Press, 1965.

Pianka, E. R. *Evolutionary Ecology.* New York: Harper & Row, 1974.

Pielou, E. C. *An Introduction to Mathematical Ecology.* New York: Wiley-Interscience, 1969.

Pilbeam, D. *The Ascent of Man.* New York: Macmillan, 1972.

Plog, F., Jolly, C. J., and Bates, D. G. *Anthropology: Decisions, Adaptations and Evolution.* New York: Alfred A. Knopf, 1976.

Power, H. W. "Mountain Bluebirds: Experimental Evidence Against Altruism." *Science* 189, 1975, pp. 142–43.

Pratt, V. "A Biological Approach to Sociological Functionalism." *Inquiry* 18, 1975, pp. 371–89.

Pringle, J. W. S., ed. *Biology and the Human Sciences.* Oxford: Clarendon, 1972.

Pugh, G. E. *The Biological Origin of Human Values.* New York: Basic Books, 1977.

Quatt, D. D., ed. *Primates on Primates.* Minnesota: Burgess, 1972.

Quillian, W. F. *The Moral Theory of Evolutionary Naturalism.* New Haven: Yale University Press, 1945.

Raphael, D. D. "Darwinism and Ethics." In *A Century of Darwin,* edited by S. A. Barnett. London: Heinemann, 1958.

Rensch, B. *Homo Sapiens: From Man to DemiGod.* Translated by C. A. M. Sym. New York: Columbia University Press, 1972.

Reynolds, V. *The Biology of Human Action.* San Francisco: W. H. Freeman, 176.

Roe, A., and Simpson, G. G., eds. *Behavior and Evolution.* New Haven: Yale University Press, 1958.

Rose, H., and Rose, S., eds. *The Radicalization of Science.* New York: Holmes and Meier, 1977.

Roughgarden, J. "Density-dependent Natural Selection." *Ecology* 52, 1971, pp. 453–68.

Rousseau, J. *First and Second Discourses,* edited by R. Masters. New York: St. Martin's, 1964.

Rowell, T. *Social Behavior of Monkeys.* Harmondsworth: Penavin, 1972.

Sahlins, M. *The Use and Abuse of Biology.* Ann Arbor: University of Michigan Press, 1976.

_____. *Culture and Practical Reason.* Chicago: University of Chicago Press, 1976.

_____, and Service, E. R., eds. *Evolution and Culture.* Ann Arbor: University of Michigan Press, 1960.

Schaller, G. B. *The Serengeti Lion: A Study of Predator-Prey Relations.* Chicago: University of Chicago Press, 1972.

Schneirla, T. C. "The Concept of Levels in the Study of Social Phenomena." In *Groups in Harmony and Tension,* edited by M. Sherif and C. Sherif. New York: Harper, 1953.

Scott, J. P. and Fuller, D. L. *Genetics and the Social Behavior of the Dog.* Chicago: University of Chicago Press, 1965.

Selander, R. K. "Behavior and Genetic Variation in Natural Populations." *American Zoologist* 10, 1970, pp. 53–66.

Sellars, W., and Hospers, J., eds. *Readings in Ethical Theory.* New York: Appleton-Century-Crofts, 1952.

Shafton, A. *Conditions of Awareness: Subjective Factors in the Social Adaptations of Man and Other Primates.* Portland: Riverstone Press, 1976.

Simpson, G. G. *The Meaning of Evolution.* New Haven: Yale University Press, 1967.

_____. *Biology and Man.* New York: Harcourt Brace Jovanovich, 1969.

Skinner, B. F. *Science and Human Behavior.* New York: The Free Press, 1965.

Slobodkin, L. "The Strategy of Evolution." *American Scientist* 52, 1974, pp. 342–357.

Somit, A. ed. *Biology and Politics.* The Hague: Mouton, 1976.

Spencer, H. *The Principles of Ethics.* New York: D. Appleton & Co., 1892.

_____. *The Principles of Biology.* Vols. 1 and 2. 2nd ed. London: Williams and Nurgate, 1898.

_____. *The Principles of Sociology.* Vols. 1, 2, and 3. London: D. Appleton & Co., 1910.

Spuhler, J. M., ed. *The Evolution of Man's Capacity for Culture.* Detroit: Wayne State University Press, 1959.

Stebbins, G. L., *Processes of Organic Evolution.* 3rd ed., Englewood Cliffs, N.J.: Prentice-Hall, 1977.

Steneck, N. H., ed. *Science and Society.* Ann Arbor: University of Michigan Press, 1975.

Stephen, L. *The Science of Ethics.* 2nd ed., London: Smith, Elder & Co., 1907.

Stevenson, L., *Seven Theories of Human Nature.* New York: Oxford Univeristy Press, 1974.

Suppe, F., and Asquith, P. D., eds. *PSA 1976, Vol. II: Symposia.* East Lansing: Philosophy of Science Association, 1977.

Symons, D. *Play and Aggression.* New York: Columbia University Press, 1977.

Tax, S., ed. *The Evolution of Man.* Chicago: University of Chicago Press, 1960.

Thorpe, W. H. *Animal Nature and Human Nature.* Garden City, N.Y.: Doubleday, 1974.

Tiger, L. *Men in Groups.* New York: Random House, 1969.

———. *Women in the Kibbutz.* New York: Harcourt Brace Jovanovich, 1975.

———, and Fox, R. *The Imperial Animal.* New York: Holt, Rinehart and Winston, 1971.

Tinbergen, N. *The Study of Instinct.* Oxford: Oxford University Press, 1951.

———. "On Aims and Method of Ethology." *Zeitschrift für Tierpsychologie* 20, 1963, pp. 410–33.

Tiryakian, E. A. "Biosocial Man, *Sic et Non.*" *American Journal of Sociology* 82, 1976, pp. 701–6.

Tobach, F., Adler, H. E., and Adler, L. L., eds. "Comparative Psychology at Issue." *Annals of the New York Academy of Sciences* 223, 1973.

Tobach, E. et al., eds. *The Four Horsemen: Racism, Sexism, Militarism, and Social Darwinism.* New York: Behavioral Publications, 1974.

Trivers, R. L. "The Evolution of Reciprocal Altruism." *Quarterly Review of Biology* 46, 1971, pp. 35–57.

———. "Parent-Offspring Conflict." *American Zoologist* 14, 1974, pp. 249–64.

———, and Willard, D. "Natural Selection of Parental Ability to Vary the Sex Ratio of Offspring." *Science* 179, 1973, p. 90.

———, and Hare, H. "Haplodiploidy and the Evolution of the Social Insects," *Science* 191, 1976, pp. 249–63.

Tuttle, R. H., ed. *Socioecolocy and Psychology of Primates.* The Hague: Mouton, 1975.

Vayda, A. P., ed. *Environment and Cultural Behavior.* New York: Natural History Press, 1969.

Van den Berghe, P. "Bringing Beasts Back In: Toward a Biosocial Theory of Aggression." *American Sociological Review* 39, 1974, pp. 778–88.

———. *Man in Society: A Biosocial View.* New York: Elsevier, 1975.

Van Lawick-Goodall, J. *In the Shadow of Man.* Boston: Houghton Mifflin, 1971.

Von Uexkull, J., "A Stroll Through the World of Animals and Man." In *Instinctive Behavior,* edited by C. Schiller. New York: International, 1957.

Waddington, C. H., ed. *The Ethical Animal,* London: Allen & Unwin, 1960.

———. *Science and Ethics,* London: Allen & Unwin, 1942.

———. ed. *Towards a Theoretical Biology.* 3 vols. Edinburgh: Edinburgh University Press, 1969.

Wallace, A. R. *Darwinism.* London: MacMillan, 1889.

Washburn, S. L., ed. *The Social Life of Early Man.* Chicago: Aldine, 1961.

———, ed. *Classification and Human Evolution.* Chicago: Aldine, 1963.

Watson, A., ed. *Animal Populations in Relation to Their Food Resources.* Oxford: Blackwell, 1970.

White, N. F., ed. *Ethology and Psychiatry*. Toronto: University of Toronto Press, 1974.

Whitman, C. O. *Animal Behavior*. Biological Lectures, Wood's Hole, Summer Session, 1899.

Wickler, W. *The Biology of the Ten Commandments*. New York: Seabury Press, 1972.

_____. "Evolution-oriented Ethology, Kin Selection, and Altruistic Parasites." *Zeitschrift für Tierpsychologie* 42, 1976, pp. 206–14.

Wiener, P. P. *Evolution and the Founders of Pragmatism*. Cambridge: Harvard University Press, 1949.

Wiens, J. A. "On Group Selection and Wynne-Edwards Hypothesis." *American Scientist* 54, 1966, pp. 273–87.

Williams, G. C. *Adaptation and Natural Selection*. Princeton: Princeton University Press, 1966.

_____, ed. *Group Selection*. Chicago: Aldine-Atherton, 1971.

_____. *Sex and Evolution*. Princeton: Princeton University Press, 1975.

Wilson, E. O. *The Insect Societies*. Cambridge: Harvard University Press, 1971.

_____. "Group Selection and Its Significance for Ecology." *bioscience* 23, 1973, pp. 631–38.

_____. *Sociobiology: The New Synthesis*. Cambridge: Harvard University Press, 1975.

_____. "Biology and the Social Sciences," *Daedalus* 106, 1977, pp. 127–40.

Wilson, E. O., and Bossert, W. H. *A Primer of Population Biology*. Sunderland, Mass.: Sinauer Associates, 1971.

Wright, S. "Coefficients of Inbreeding and Relationship." *American Naturalist* 56, 1922, pp. 330–39.

Wynne-Edwards, V. C. "The Control of Population Density Through Social Behavior: A Hypothesis." *Ibis* 101, 1959, pp. 436–41.

_____. *Animal Dispersion in Rerlation to Social Behavior*. Edinburgh: Oliver & Boyd, 1962.

Young, J. Z. *An Introduction to the Study of Man*. Oxford: Oxford University Press, 1971.

Young, R. M. *Mind, Brain and Adaptation in the Nineteenth Century*. London: Oxford University Press, 1970.

_____. "Darwin's Metaphor: Does Nature Select?" *The Monist* 55, 1971, pp. 442–503.

Zirkle, C. *Death of a Science in Russia*. Philadelphia: University of Pennsylvania Press, 1949.

Zuckerman, S. *The Social Life of Monkeys and Apes*. London: Routledge and Kegan Paul, 1932.

Index

1132